A CENTURY OF
PLENTY

A CENTURY OF PLENTY

A story of progress for generations to come

———

By SVEN SMIT

CHRIS BRADLEY

NICK LEUNG

MARC CANAL

With JANET BUSH, SHERLYN CHEN, SUHAYL CHETTIH,
JAN MISCHKE, *and* JEONGMIN SEONG

With thanks to our McKinsey Global Institute colleagues

McKinsey
Global Institute

Published by the McKinsey Global Institute. January 2026.
mckinsey.com/mgi

ISBN 979-8-9939075-0-5 (paperback English)
ISBN 979-8-9939075-1-2 (hardcover English)
ISBN 979-8-9939075-2-9 (ebook English)

CONTENTS

PREFACE

"The size of your dreams must always exceed your current capacity to achieve them. If your dreams do not scare you, they are not big enough."

ELLEN JOHNSON SIRLEAF

—

A CENTURY OF HUMAN INGENUITY and teamwork has created a world that would have been unrecognizable in 1925. One hundred years ago, the world was a leaner place. Lives were shorter, wallets thinner, and horizons narrower. Since then, almost every dimension of our human experience has improved. On average, people now live 40 years longer than they did. From Lagos to London, economic growth has hauled billions of people out of poverty and empowered them to lead rewarding lives. The average Bangladeshi today isn't starving, she's texting.

What have we learned in the past 100 years? This was the question put to us in November 2024 by Sir Ian Davis, former Global Managing Partner of McKinsey & Company. After all, McKinsey was about to celebrate its 100th year. That question prompted us at the McKinsey Global Institute (MGI) to discuss what those lessons were and what they could mean for the future. And so this book was born.

James O. McKinsey, a professor of accounting, founded McKinsey in 1926 in Chicago, a city full of the world's immigrants and strong beliefs in how new, rational scientific methods could improve all areas of life. It was the city of Frank Lloyd Wright's new architecture, the Chicago School of Economics, modern manufacturing, and the first skyscrapers—all at the nexus of booming trade corridors. More rail lines radiated out of the city than anywhere else. It was also the city of Al Capone, Prohibition-era gangsters, and corrupt police.

James McKinsey's big idea was to subject businesses to the same scientific methods used to create the skyscrapers they had begun to occupy. But by today's standards, McKinsey's beginnings were parochial. The opening of its second office in New York City some years later was a big milestone; some considered the cultural differences between the two cities insurmountable, and the distance of rail travel prohibitive. Yet three years ago, current managing partner Bob Sternfels opened our newest office in Quito, Ecuador. That's more than 65 countries. In our own universe, 100 years of progress.

The past century was one of remarkable progress. For firms, yes, but more pertinently for people. In this book, we look back, exploring how it happened, and look forward to show that we can do it again. Many people have written about the future, which is not the easiest undertaking.[1] What makes this book different is that it enumerates an ambitious aspiration and then tests its feasibility, building on what we have learned over the past 100 years.

Can we imagine a century of plenty to be enjoyed by our children and grandchildren?

This book locates our story within the real-world struggle of imperfect but persistent progress, beset by constant challenges and punctuated by frightening crises. We have to run this steeplechase from our real-world starting line and in our real-world state of health. We take this challenge head-on.

Imagine a country that has very high income per capita of, say, $82,000. Life expectancy is 84, up there with Japan. Practically everyone who wants a job has one, and kids spend more than 13 years in education. Ninety percent of people believe they will be looked after if they run into problems. This imaginary place combines thriving, modern, innovative

Three iconic Chicago skyscrapers built in the 1920s.

cities with stunning lakes and mountains. The air is clean, and carbon dioxide (CO_2) emissions per capita are some of the lowest in the world. Sounds wonderful, right?

We have just described Switzerland *today*.

Now imagine that Burundi, the poorest country in the world, according to the World Bank, could have the same in 2100. Progress for all, everywhere. And meanwhile developed countries, like Switzerland, continue to grow to the next frontier. A planet of people who are truly thriving would require a world economy that is about eight times bigger than today's. This is the future of possibilities we explore.

We don't just dream about it. We have done a feasibility study that convinced us that we can generate enough energy to power such a world without choking the planet. That enough food and materials can be harvested from the Earth. And that there will be enough scientific and technological headroom to enable leaps in productivity, despite demographic headwinds.

We hope to bring the facts to show that this future is, in fact, possible and perhaps likely, even if progress is always fraught with challenge and humanity lives on the edge.

Writing in early to mid-2025, for sure things seem tough. Geopolitical rivalries are increasingly intense. War has returned to Europe, and conflicts in some parts of the Middle East continue unresolved. Decades-long vehicles for international cooperation, such as the North Atlantic Treaty Organization (NATO) and the World Trade Organization (WTO), are going through a period of strain and flux. After boom times for the global macroeconomy, turbulence has returned, and growth has shifted down a few gears. Inflation reared its head after lying dormant for 40 years, and productivity growth has been decelerating to an anemic pace since 2008. The specter of climate change remains an existential worry for many, as emissions of CO_2 have kept going up despite trillions of dollars of investment in low-emissions technologies. And in what may be a sign of our shared lack of confidence in the future, along with practical considerations of cost, lifestyle, and culture, birth rates are low and falling rapidly almost everywhere.

And that is just what is in today's news. Potential cataclysms, from nuclear obliteration and enslavement by sentient artificial intelligence (AI), to pandemics and ecosystem collapse, hang over our heads. Books like *Megathreats*, *Permacrisis*, and *The Precipice* capture a doom-laden mood.[2]

We are collectively unnerved. Negative thoughts hold sway. Being positive feels countercultural.[3] We seem to be trapped looking through a microscope, fixating on the very-present issues that surround us. The concern is that a narrative of doom is self-fulfilling. Ultimately, this is a crisis of hope when, paradoxically, we have more reasons for hope than ever before.

Wind the clock back 100 years to 1925, when the mood was far grimmer. The world had emerged battered from the rubble of World War I, but stability had not returned. The Treaty of Versailles hung by a thread. The disaster of the first world war was already seeding the second. Two harbingers appeared in 1925. Benito Mussolini came to power, and Adolf Hitler published *Mein Kampf*. Oswald Spengler argued in *The Decline of the West* that Western nations would become increasingly dominated by "Caesars": strongmen who would seize power amid social and economic chaos. Culture, he said, had exhausted all possibilities and would die. Inequality gnawed at society. In his desolate poem "The Hollow Men," published 100 years ago, the poet T. S. Eliot wrote, "This is the way the world ends / Not with a bang but a whimper."[4]

Yet the world did not end with a bang or a whimper. Quite the opposite.

Taking a long view through a telescope, the past 100 years were a period of unprecedented human progress, even for most of those who today remain poor. There was progress, and there can, and should, be a lot more. We achieved this progress in the face of formidable hurdles. In the short term, the pessimists of a century ago were correct: A giant depression wrecked economies, and World War II unleashed its unspeakable horrors. We certainly do not want to repeat those. But no crisis derailed the machine of progress permanently, and fears that there are limits to growth were dispelled by the force of development. That very fact should give us confidence to dare to be positive about the future.

Human ingenuity and cooperation prevailed. We proved ourselves to be consummate problem solvers. Can we do it again?

In fact, can we do even better?

What makes us cautiously confident is that we have more powerful tools in our workshop than those living in the 1920s had. We have more talented people than ever before. Our brainpower is amplified by the fact that we live in a digital, deeply networked world, increasingly augmented by AI, in which we can generate and share ideas rapidly. Some of the technology we have at our fingertips today astonishes and delights us. To a person in 1925, it would have seemed like magic. We have an array of advantages and resources that give us a promising platform to forge the future we want.

To imagine what progress could be like, first let's measure and understand economic progress and human flourishing over the past 100 years. We do this in Part I, *What on Earth happened?* But we also need to know what powered progress, the "machine" behind it. That's Part II, *How was progress achieved?* In Part III, *Progress at the crossroads*, we explore some of the stresses that may compromise the progress machine in the future and what could be done to get it humming again. Many people have written about the future in general terms, but in Part IV, *The possibility of plenty*, we set a quantified, aspirational bar and test its feasibility. This is where we explore a world of plenty, one in which by 2100 all countries reach the Switzerland of today and beyond. We end Part IV with propositions on how we could think about the next century to increase our collective chances of reaching that plentiful future.

We are not predicting a century of plenty, but we do believe that it is a real possibility. The catch? It is up to us. We need to make smart decisions and approach the rest of this century with verve, invention, and determination, and we must do it together. We can forge a new compact, write a new narrative of progress, and bring it to life.

Chicago, October 2025

PART I

WHAT ON EARTH HAPPENED?

CHAPTER 1

A CENTURY OF PROGRESS

"Humans walked around or rode horses for 999 of the last 1,000 centuries. In this century, we drive cars, fly planes, and land on the Moon."

TIM URBAN

——

In the past century, human prosperity and quality of life flourished as never before.

SOMETHING SIMPLY EXTRAORDINARY happened over the past 100 years. The world we live in today is utterly different from that of our parents or grandparents in the 1920s. The lives of billions of people have been transformed.

Let's take a look at some of the family stories of the authors of this book. We know that we are privileged professionals, but our stories show that two generations ago, our families lived in different circumstances that were not at all unusual at the time. Their trajectories typify the upward mobility and transformation of so many over the past century.

Traditional Dutch windmills and farm.

Our first stop is the Netherlands, one of Northern Europe's thriving economies and home to one of our authors, Sven Smit. In addition to per capita income of about $71,000, the Dutch enjoy universal healthcare, widespread access to high-speed internet, and a robust public transport system, including electric bikes and trams.[5] Sven's work means that he travels far and wide, armed with technology that gives him a world of information at his fingertips.

The lives of previous generations of his family were vastly different. One great-grandfather was the first civil servant in a small town in the north of the country. His job responsibilities included registering births. Many of the children were born to parents digging peat for fuel; they were very poor. On their only day off, they would progress from one "peat pub" to another, turning up at his great-grandfather's desk drunk and often unable to remember their baby's chosen name. Sven's grandfather trained as a land surveyor but lost his job during the Great Depression.

Tourist boat and NEMO Science Museum in Amsterdam.

So dire was unemployment that the government gave him work building a mountain on which to put a fire watchtower. There was no need for that mountain, but it gave him an income. His prospects seemed so poor that the father of his future wife traveled several times from their home in Switzerland to investigate whether the Netherlands was solvent. He gave his consent to the marriage when he saw that Dutch paper money was backed by gold coins.

Sven's other grandfather was an orphan of Jewish descent in Germany. He was being transported to one of the death camps when a bombing raid stopped the train and he managed to get off. He went into hiding and used most of the family's silverware to pay for food. Famine was rife. He married a brilliant woman from a scientific family, and together they ran their village soup kitchen. By war's end, they were in eastern Germany; they fled to western Germany to avoid persecution for their religious beliefs.

Sven's father studied physics and on graduation received a job offer

Vintage engraving of Dundee, Scotland.

from Philips, a future champion of Dutch industry. His father told him not to hesitate. Memories of unemployment and famine were all too vivid for him to advocate looking at other options. He used to mail home his laundry, because that was cheaper than using a launderette! Sven recalls how wonderful it was when his father no longer had to work on Saturday. The family economics were much improved but still tight. In the 1970s, when he was a boy, Sven roller-skated along highways. To conserve oil, nobody was allowed to drive on Sunday. Yes, this was the time of the oil crisis, high inflation, and gyrating house prices. Sven watched the Moon landing, when he was three, on a black-and-white TV. But the family did not have a freezer. He helped his parents pick beans at the farm, wash and wrap them, and take them to the communal freezer. His country has come so far since he was a child.

Now let's head to the other side of the world: Australia. Chris Bradley lives in a harborside suburb of Sydney where he built the family home, but his maternal grandfather, Douglas, grew up in Dundee, Scotland, during the Depression. Life was tough. Douglas lost his brother at age 16

Sydney Harbour.

to pneumonia; the family was too poor to afford medicine.

His maternal grandmother, Zoe, was born to Greek parents living in Alexandria, Egypt, who were too poor to raise her. Luckily, her lawyer uncle had some means and sponsored her education in a French convent, where she mastered five languages. Douglas and Zoe met during World War II when Douglas was stationed in Egypt. Chris's mother was born in Alexandria in 1943 while the war raged. Douglas eventually became headmaster of the British school in Suez and for a time was a prominent member of a thriving, cosmopolitan expatriate community. But the Suez crisis put an end to that, and in 1952, the family migrated to Australia by ship.

The culture shock was huge. Douglas took a job as a schoolteacher in Sydney, and money was tight on a single salary. The toilet was in an outhouse. They got their first family car, an Austin A40, in 1959, when Chris's mother was 16, although Douglas did not learn to drive for many years after that. In fact, Chris's mother said she was never driven anywhere until she had a boyfriend with a car. There was a lot of walking,

A street in old Hong Kong.

buses, and trains. Douglas ended up doing well and had a solid career as a teacher, headmaster, and academic. He died at age 83, survived by his four daughters. Chris's parents were married in 1964 and ended up living in five countries.

Let's now fly north to Hong Kong, where Nick Leung lives and works. He has witnessed China's meteoric rise since the 1970s, lifting some 800 million people out of poverty. Today, Nick lives in a gleaming metropolis of high-rise buildings looking over a "fragrant harbor," so called after the sweet scent of agarwood and sandalwood unloaded at the docks and wafting through the streets. This is a city where the average income is $66,000.[6] Once it stood alone as *the* global city in China; now it is one of several modern cities in the region. Nick navigates a hyperconnected environment with cashless payments, high-speed 5G, and world-class transportation and healthcare, enjoying dim sum brunches with his wife and four daughters.

In the 1920s, however, Nick's grandparents lived in colonial Hong Kong, outpost of an empire and safe haven from turbulence on the

A junk plying Hong Kong's Victoria Harbour.

mainland. The average income was about $3,000, and life expectancy for the Chinese population was probably between 30 and 40 years.[7] It was a very different place from today, not only economically but also socially. The Chinese population was not allowed to live above a certain altitude on the hillside, with "the Peak" reserved for Europeans. Unpaid domestic servants "given" as children to affluent households, in return for food and shelter, were not uncommon.

Trade was the lifeblood of the place, and Nick's grandfather founded a trading company that went on to build a network throughout Southeast Asia and across the world. Eleven of his 12 children lived to adulthood. Six of his seven sons attended universities in Europe and America, and three of them became university professors. Fascinated with the modernity flourishing around him, he was the proud owner of a motorcar in the 1940s and collected color televisions, which he regarded as a kind of magic. He died at the ripe old age of 99 (well above life expectancy) in his Hong Kong high-rise surrounded by his extensive offspring and his many TVs.

Ruins of a village devastated in the Battle of the Ebro during the Spanish Civil War.

Finally, let's return to Europe—to Spain, where Marc Canal's family lives. His paternal grandparents, Josep and Teresa, were born in 1922 and 1939. When Josep was only one, in 1923, there was a coup. Civil war raged from 1936 to 1939. Josep's father was a farmer who was known as the "pigman," and young Josep helped him with the pigs (and cows) in addition to attending school. Before going to school, he woke up early every day and went from house to house delivering milk. His father died of unknown causes when Josep was nine, and starting at age 14, he worked full time on the farm. If he had been born only a year earlier, Josep would have been drafted into *la quinta del biberón,* or the Baby Bottle Levy, which was the conscription of 14- to 18-year-olds in the late part of the civil war. But his life was to take a remarkable turn. He played for his local town football team and went on to play for the first team of Real Madrid. He then had to relocate to Barcelona to do his military service and was hired by Barça. He is one of the few in history to have played for both teams. Unlike footballers of today, he was not rich, but he was able to afford (and brag about) a foreign car: a Citroën Stromberg. Teresa also

Walking the streets of Barcelona toward La Sagrada Familia.

went to school until she was 14 and then worked in a factory making plugs and sockets, where she remained for five years until she married Josep. She became a housewife.

When Josep retired from football in his 30s due to an injury, he became a car salesman. He was good at selling but bad at accounting and management. He and his son Albert, Marc's dad, born in 1958 under the dictatorship of Francisco Franco, managed to keep the company afloat for a while, but Albert's duty to the family meant he never finished his university education and continued working in car dealerships even after the family firm ceased trading. He and his wife, Mariona, had two sons, both of whom have forged interesting careers.

We had fun revisiting our family histories and summarizing them briefly here. But we did so to make a point. These stories show that the century of progress is very close to all of us, in thousands of small ways that matter. That the events that shaped our world, from coups to depressions to wars, also shaped our families. There was good and bad luck. Nevertheless, the general drift was toward a better life. And many of the features of our modern lives that we take for granted, such as cars, indoor plumbing, international travel, and female education, just to name a few, were once firsts in our families. The big story of humanity is a mosaic of little stories.

The prospects of families around the world have been transformed. But let's go beyond anecdotes and personal stories and look at the global statistics to get a full sense of the progress achieved over the past century.

A century of unprecedented growth

All of us care about living better, longer, and happier lives. It would be madness to try to boil that down to a single number. But as sure as night follows day, many aspects of human flourishing, including health, education, happiness, and freedom, correlate positively with GDP per capita. We call it income per person for simplicity.[8] Rising incomes not only track with prosperity but also diminish ills such as childhood mortality, hunger, and deaths from air pollution. Exhibit 1 demonstrates this with 14 measures, but there are many more.[9]

Maybe the Beatles were right when they sang "money can't buy me love," but the facts show that societies that excel at delivering income also excel at the things that drive broad-based human flourishing. Moreover, income is a practical yardstick because it is a simple, comparable, standardized, and widely reported indicator that enables us to compare across countries and time.

In centuries past, incomes were relatively static. In other words, we did not get much better at bettering lives. From 1525 to 1825, incomes hardly grew at all—anywhere (Exhibit 2). A country that achieved 0.4 percent growth per annum passed for very successful. It meant that someone at the end of the century was 50 percent better off than someone at the beginning. Not bad.[10]

That all changed with the Industrial Revolution, which kicked off in Britain. In a potent concatenation of commercial smarts, communal hard graft, and sheer invention—large-scale coal mines, textile spinning machines, steamboats, and steam engines—industry as we know it was created between about 1750 and 1900. With machines came productivity; workers were now able to produce much more, faster, and better. Growth started to take off. Between 1825 and 1925, global incomes grew at 0.8

percent a year.[11] At that rate, we were bettering our lives about two times over a century. Remarkable.

The Industrial Revolution spread from Britain's heartland to other economies in Europe and North America, and to Japan and even as far afield as Australia and New Zealand. The productivity of these first generations of workers augmented by machines distinguished them from people living in parts of the world that remained preindustrial. Economists called this era starting in the early 19th century the Great Divergence. Advanced economies began to pull ahead, while others largely stagnated.[12] India and China did not grow at all.

Change was afoot in some places, but it did not really accelerate until the most recent 100 years. Global growth in income per person beginning in 1925 more than doubled to 1.9 percent a year. From a twofold improvement over a century, we went to sixfold. India and China went from no growth at all to multiplying their incomes by seven and 19 times, respectively. Staggering.[13]

Before we get into how this changed many key aspects of life, ponder this. In the case of the United Kingdom, if incomes had continued to grow over the past century at the same rate as from 1825 to 1925 and not accelerated, today the average British person's standard of living would be that of an average Mexican. Mexico, too, has made enormous strides, but, as Mexicans themselves would acknowledge, they do not yet enjoy the living standards of the typical Brit. Germany would have matched Thailand today. Japan would have the same income per person as India. China and India would barely have improved their living standards, and their incomes today would only have matched Burundi, the poorest country in the world according to the World Bank. It has been said that compounding is the eighth wonder of the world. Tiny percentage points amplify into world-shaping impact given enough time.

Putting that in dollars, over the past 100 years, global income per person soared from about $3,000 in 1925 to more than $20,000 today, measured in purchasing-power parity terms and adjusted for inflation. The average person in 1925 had the living standard of a resident of current-day Rwanda.[14]

Some places did of course experience lower growth rates than others. Since 1950, when wide country-level data coverage commences, East Asia, thanks to the likes of Japan and South Korea, has grown at an impressive

Correlation of progress metrics against income per person

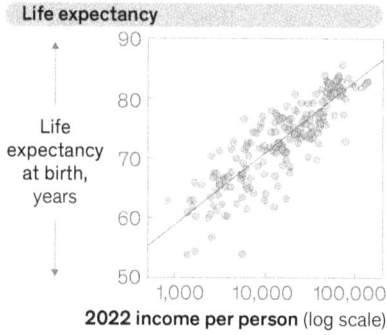

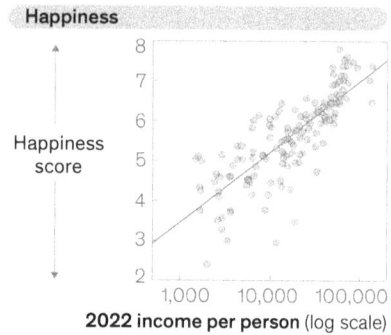

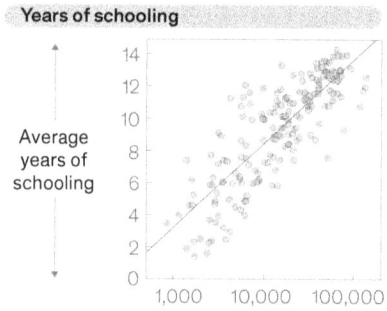

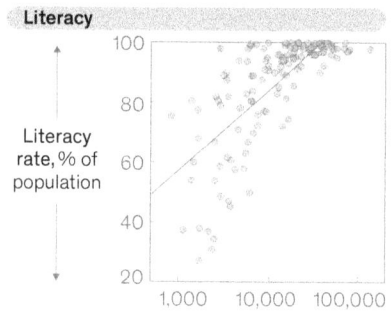

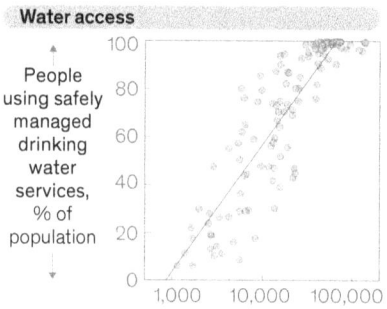

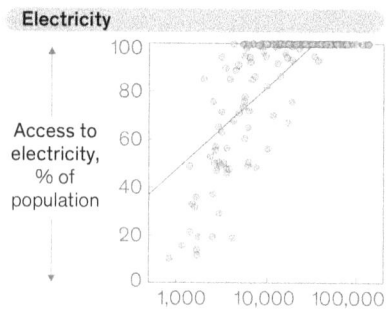

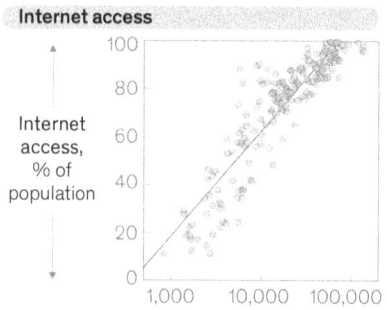

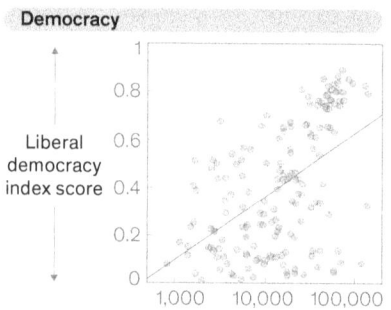

Life expectancy

Life expectancy at birth, years

2022 income per person (log scale)

Happiness

Happiness score

2022 income per person (log scale)

Years of schooling

Average years of schooling

Literacy

Literacy rate, % of population

Water access

People using safely managed drinking water services, % of population

Electricity

Access to electricity, % of population

Internet access

Internet access, % of population

Democracy

Liberal democracy index score

Poverty

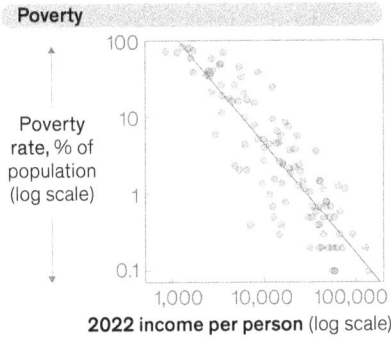

Poverty
rate, % of
population
(log scale)

100
10
1
0.1

2022 income per person (log scale)
1,000   10,000   100,000

Undernourishment

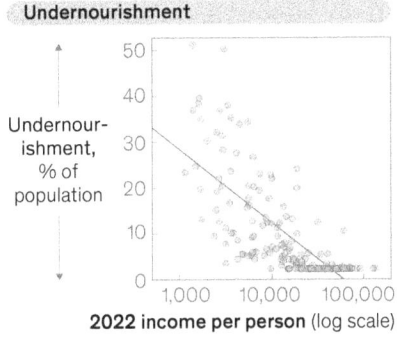

Undernour-
ishment,
% of
population

50
40
30
20
10
0

2022 income per person (log scale)
1,000   10,000   100,000

Maternal mortality

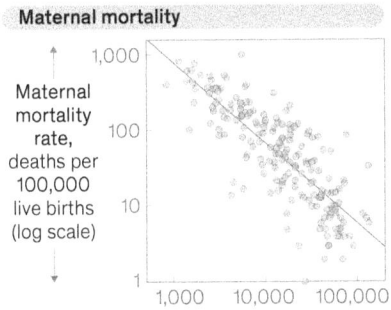

Maternal
mortality
rate,
deaths per
100,000
live births
(log scale)

1,000
100
10
1

1,000   10,000   100,000

Under-5 child mortality

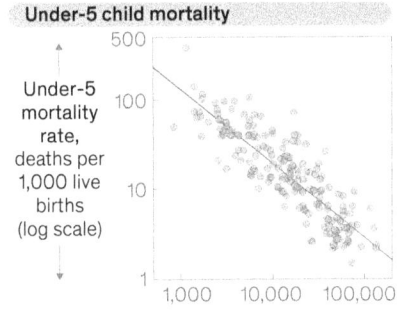

Under-5
mortality
rate,
deaths per
1,000 live
births
(log scale)

500
100
10
1

1,000   10,000   100,000

Deaths from air pollution

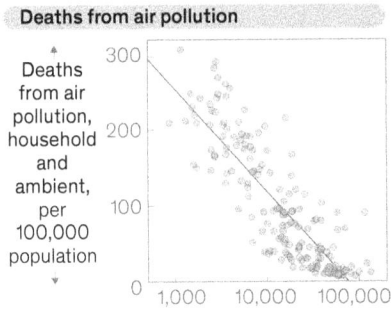

Deaths
from air
pollution,
household
and
ambient,
per
100,000
population

300
200
100
0

1,000   10,000   100,000

Inequality

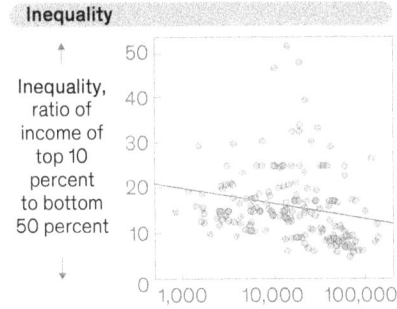

Inequality,
ratio of
income of
top 10
percent
to bottom
50 percent

50
40
30
20
10
0

1,000   10,000   100,000

Note: Income per person is measured using GDP per capita, in constant 2021 international dollars. All data from 2022,
except literacy (2018–23), poverty (2018–23), and deaths from air pollution (2019).
Source: World Bank; *World happiness report 2025*; UN Development Programme, *Human development report 2025*,
processed by Our World in Data; Varieties of Democracy (V-Dem) database, processed by Our World in Data; World
Health Organization; World Inequality Database; McKinsey Global Institute analysis

4.2 percent annually. In Latin America and Sub-Saharan Africa, by contrast, incomes grew at rates below 2 percent. Progress can and indeed should be faster in many other places. And yet even in the poorest places, with the exception of failed states or those in deep conflict, such as the Central African Republic, Syria, or Venezuela, growth in the past century was fast by historical standards.[15]

These numbers represent a triumph of human effort and ingenuity. Obstacles were turned into stepping stones throughout the century. But income per person is just a number, and growth rates mean something only when we see how our lives change as a result.

EXHIBIT 2

Income per person growth over the past 500 years

Compound annual growth rate (CAGR) within each period, %

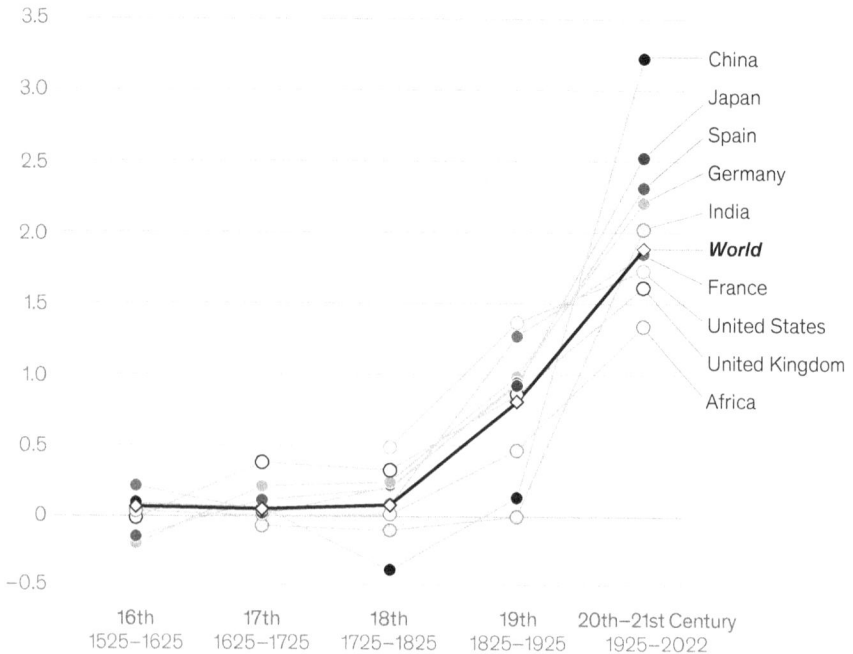

Note: All growth figures calculated based on constant 2011 international dollars. Data not available for India and Japan from 1525 to 1625, and for the United States from 1525 to 1725.
Source: Maddison Project Database 2010 and 2023; McKinsey Global Institute analysis

Improving livelihoods, half of the world empowered

Growth has hauled billions of people out of extreme poverty—arguably the greatest human achievement of modern times. The best estimates say 55 to 60 percent of people were in extreme poverty a century ago, and today that figure is about 7 to 10 percent, depending on which estimate we choose. No matter which way you cut it, 1.3 billion people have left extreme poverty since 1990. That is 130,000 people every day climbing toward increasingly prosperous lives. Poverty fell the most in China and India, but virtually every country experienced it, from Bangladesh to Brazil to Tanzania. There were a few exceptions, often due to political instability or outright war. But even in Sub-Saharan Africa, where most of the world's poorest remain, extreme poverty fell from 57 percent to 37 percent between 1990 and today.[16]

In this section, we rely on work that Swedish physician and geographer Hans Rosling did with his team to show how livelihoods have changed radically in the past 100 years. Rosling not only does the calculations but also vividly defines four levels of income, which we use to show the impressive progress the world has experienced.[17]

According to Rosling, 57 percent of the world's population had daily incomes below $2 in 1925, while today that share is 8 percent (Exhibit 3).[18] What does living below $2 per day, or level 1, mean for real people's lives? Life in extreme poverty is marked by profound deprivation and uncertainty. People often live in cramped makeshift shelters cobbled together from natural materials like mud or scavenged materials like corrugated metal. These dwellings don't have basics like clean water, electricity, or sanitation. People have to walk long distances for water and are at high risk of drawing from contaminated sources that breed disease. Women cannot go to the toilet safely and privately. People cook with dung and wood and are exposed to air pollution, damaging their lungs. They often go hungry. And it is often kids who survive to the age of five who are sent out to forage or beg; they are not at school. Access to healthcare is virtually nonexistent. Minor injuries or illnesses can become life-threatening, while preventable conditions like malaria and diarrhea claim lives. Many people have to travel by foot to reach markets or work, because even the cost of a bus fare is prohibitive. Savings are nonexistent, and work as a subsistence farmer or laborer is grueling. Social isolation compounds the hardship, and the psychological toll of hopelessness and stress is immense.

Crossing the threshold of extreme poverty to level 2, with incomes of $2 to $8 per day, we have 42 percent of the population, up from 30 percent in 1925. At this level, life improves but remains a precarious balancing act with razor-thin margins. People can buy simple medicines, yet one single serious illness could devastate finances. Diets include vegetables or occasionally meat, cooked on gas stoves. Homes, sturdier than those in extreme poverty, use mixed materials and have locks, though space is tight. Mattresses replace floor sleeping, and unreliable electricity powers a bulb or two. Farming and manual labor dominate, but small savings are possible—maybe to buy a bike, useful to cut water-fetching time or provide access to a slightly better-paying job. Extreme weather and unexpected costs threaten to push families back to extreme poverty, keeping life precarious despite modest gains.

Level 3 gets us to $8 to $32. This group includes 2.7 billion people, or 34 percent of the population, up from 12 percent in 1925. Depending on local prices of essentials, households in this band can begin to consume beyond basic necessities, like a scooter for personal transport. Diets diversify, with regular meat, fruits, and varied meals. Homes have solid walls, multiple rooms, and reliable electricity for appliances like fans and refrigerators. Microfinance or savings fund small luxuries, perhaps a short family outing nearby. Work remains long and demanding, and stress persists, but threats like poverty and illness are less immediate. This level marks a leap, though challenges like job insecurity and rising costs linger, requiring careful budgeting.

Earning more than $32 daily at Level 4, the top 1.3 billion have more security and comfort. In 1925, about 1 percent of the global population had this income, while today it is 16 percent. This group is very diverse, including up to billionaires. Closer to $32, access to essentials can vary by country. Nonetheless, many people in this group have jobs that require more than 12 years of education and enable the purchase of cars, eating out at restaurants, and international travel. Homes have hot water and internet, and nearly every home has at least one TV and computer. Nutritious, diverse meals include precooked options. Healthcare is accessible, with insurance and local clinics. Bank accounts, credit, and pensions are common and provide stability. Property is insured, and

EXHIBIT 3

Population distribution across income levels, 1925 and 2025

Breakdown by daily income level, %

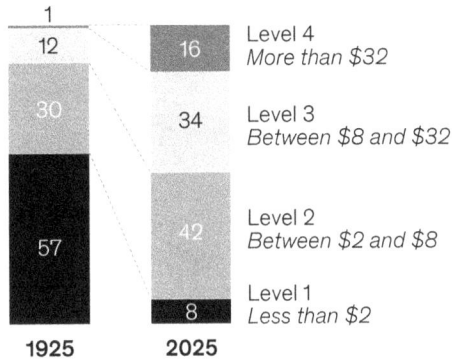

1925	2025	
1		
12	16	Level 4 *More than $32*
30	34	Level 3 *Between $8 and $32*
57	42	Level 2 *Between $2 and $8*
	8	Level 1 *Less than $2*

Source: Gapminder Income Mountains; McKinsey Global Institute analysis

homes are secure. Public transit is better, and personal vehicles are common.

This is all measured at the individual level; these are not country averages. In fact, differences are often more pronounced within than among countries. In Shanghai, you will see skyscrapers and bullet trains, but in rural Gansu, families still rely on patchy electricity and basic clinics. It may not surprise you that the economic distance between Shanghai and Gansu is much larger than between Seoul and Shanghai. It may surprise you, however, as we showed in our report *Pixels of Progress*, that Mapusa, in India, and Porto, in Portugal, have the same income per capita despite Portugal being five times richer than India.[19]

Overall, it is hard to overstate the revolution in livelihoods the world has experienced in the past century. And yet, the world has a long way to go. That's a big reason we devote much of our lives to research and have written this book.

In 2023, we at MGI decided to go beyond existing measures of poverty and focused on a new, complementary metric: the empowerment line.[20] Empowerment is based on consumption, and gauges progress toward a world in which everyone can meet their essential needs and achieve a

View of Porto from Dom Luís I Bridge.

certain level of economic security.

We started with consumption of $12 per day as a global floor, in line with other research.[21] But costs relative to the rest of the economy of essentials like food, housing and energy, safe water access, transportation, healthcare, education, clothing, and communication can be quite different across countries and over time. Additionally, countries have different societal expectations that can affect the costs of meeting basic needs. Think of a country where the average home has six people and compare it with one with much smaller households of three, or where housing must account for snowstorms versus tropical heat. Local conditions matter.

At higher income levels, being economically empowered often means consuming more than $12 per day. Thus, we raised the empowerment line taking into account differences in costs of essentials and societal expectations. This means the empowerment line is $12 for India, Indonesia, and Nigeria, but it can be as high as $47 in the United States.

When people rise above the empowerment line, they start to have some security and the economic breathing room to have agency in the direction

View of Mapusa, Goa, India.

of their lives and realize more of their potential. They have more space to participate in society as they free themselves from the effort to satisfy their most essential needs. They can begin to invest in themselves and have a fuller range of choices about shaping their lives. They still live frugally but can begin to build a modest buffer for weathering emergencies.

In short, while Rosling's levels are best for tracking progress over time, the empowerment line is a more meaningful measure of economic well-being across the world's population at a moment in time. A comprehensive view of progress requires both.

What do we find when we look at economic empowerment? Some 4.7 billion people globally are below the line and three billion are above it. In Sub-Saharan Africa, despite remarkable progress, 90 percent of the population lives below the empowerment line. In China, arguably the biggest development success story in history, the share is about 50 percent, while in advanced economies it ranges between 20 and 30 percent.[22]

The world has made amazing progress. The world needs much more of it.

Better and longer lives

The growth explosion of the past 100 years changed not only livelihoods but also lives, literally prolonging them. We added an astonishing 40 years to the average lifespan. In 1925, a newborn might expect to live to 30 to 40. Today, that figure is 73 years.[23] Centenarians are no longer a source of amazement except to make us wonder how we will fund their long retirements (Table 1).

How did this happen? There were four main culprits holding back life expectancy whose effects have been tamed. Today, 90 percent fewer children die before the age of five. Maternal mortality has been virtually eradicated in advanced economies and has plummeted elsewhere. Mortality rates due to infectious disease have fallen globally by more than 90 percent thanks to vaccines and antibiotics. And deaths from conflict have fallen dramatically. Other medical advances, increased access to healthcare, and a host of other factors contributed, too.[24]

In *Pixels of Progress*, we went beyond country averages and divided the world into more than 40,000 microregions.[25] We set GDP per capita (that is, income per person) and life expectancy thresholds to classify them into "blue zones" (above $8,300 and 72.5 years of life expectancy) and "orange zones" (below $2,400 and 65.5). We found that between 2000 and 2019, the share of the world's population that lived in blue zones rose from 21 to 46 percent, while the proportion for orange zones fell from 19 to 5 percent (Exhibit 4).

Of course, despite rapid progress, gaps remain. Japanese citizens live to 85 on average, enjoying advanced healthcare and nutrition, their lives a testament to progress. Nigerians, by contrast, average 55 years, despite having added nearly ten years since the 1990s. That remarkable gain has allowed Nigeria to narrow the gap, but it is still far from leading life expectancy. The gap in life expectancy between Japan and Bangladesh was almost 25 years in 1990, and today it is ten years. The story of life expectancy, in a nutshell, is one of stunning progress practically everywhere, with poorer countries improving at a faster rate than richer ones, and gaps that remain that should continue to narrow in the future.[26]

Staying alive for a decent span is certainly a prerequisite for a good life but is by no means sufficient. Let's look at broader indicators of progress, too.

Rising prosperity has spread the elixir of education to many more

TABLE 1

Balanced scorecard of progress metrics

Metric	1925[1]	1990	2022/2023
Global average income per person, $	2,900	11,200	20,600
Poverty rate, %	60	44	10
Life expectancy, years	34	64	73
Child mortality rate (under-5), %	32	9	4
Literacy rate, %	32	75	87
Education, average years of schooling	1.8	6.2	9.2
Female labor force participation rate, %	~25[2]	51	49
Maternal mortality per 100,000 births	679[3]	370	212[4]
Gender gap in primary education enrollment, pp	10.3	8.3	2.5
Working hours per year[5]	2,241	1,740	1,664
V-Dem democracy index (pop-weighted)	0.16	0.33	0.29
Average deaths from conflict per year,[6] thousand	650 (1900–1950)	153 (1990s)	148 (2014–2023)

[1]Data points from within 5 years of 1925 based on data availability.
[2]Very little data exists prior to 1960. This is an average of the US, Canada, and Germany in 1921–1925. It has been benchmarked with other sources of data for other similar developed countries at the time, which provide similar results.
[3]Data limited to 10 advanced countries due to data availability. This figure is therefore far lower than the probable actual global average at the time.
[4]This number is a global average. Maternal mortality in advanced countries has been virtually eliminated: the average today in the 10 advanced economies for which there is data in 1920 is 10 deaths per 100,000 births (versus 679 in 1920).
[5]Sample limited to 14 advanced countries across all periods due to data availability and to allow for better comparison across all periods. The current global average is 2,026 hours. While most emerging countries have higher working hours, they have been following a similar trajectory as advanced ones.
[6]Averages over 10-year periods to account for great variance between years.
Source: Riley, 2005; Zijdeman et al., 2015; Gapminder, 2015; UN Inter-agency Group for Child Mortality Estimation, 2025; UNESCO, 1957; UNESCO Institute for Statistics, 2023; Barro and Lee, 2015; Lee and Lee, 2016; ILOSTAT, 2025; World Health Organization, UNICEF, UNFPA, World Bank Group and UNDESA, 2025; UN Population Division, *World population prospects 2024*; WHO Mortality Database, 2025; Gapminder, 2010; Feenstra et al., Penn World Table, 2023; Huberman and Minns, 2005; Jason Lyall, Project Mars, 2020, all processed by Our World in Data; World Bank; Varieties of Democracy (V-Dem) database; Clio Infra; World Health Organization; Maddison Project Database 2023; McKinsey Global Institute analysis

people, opening the door not only to higher incomes and healthier livelihoods but to a more rounded, richer life. In our grandparents' time, illiteracy was common. In 1925, 32 percent of the world's population could read and write; today, 87 percent can. Children, especially girls, spend many more years in school. In the 1920s, less than half of school-age girls were enrolled in primary education; by the 2000s, the figure

Global progress in life expectancy and income per person
2000 vs 2019

■ Life expectancy > 72.5 years and income per person > $8,300   Others/No data
▨ Life expectancy < 65.6 years and income per person < $2,400

2000

19   21

Share of world
population, %

2019

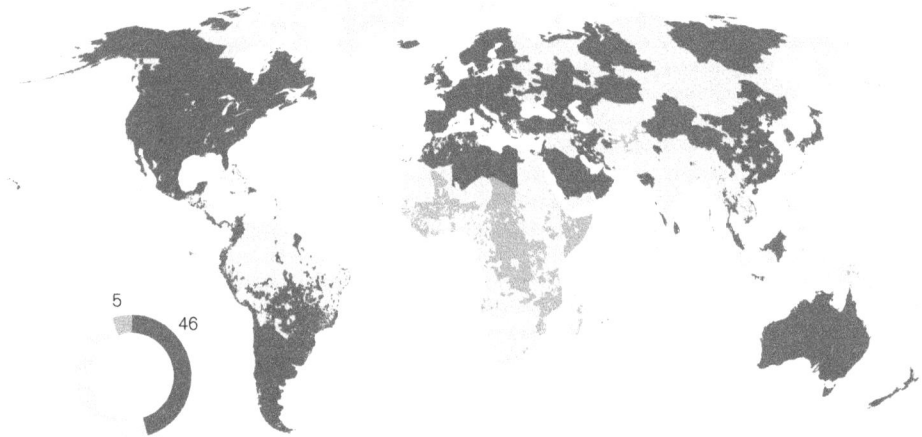

5
    46

Note: The boundaries shown on this map do not imply official endorsement or acceptance by McKinsey & Company.
Source: Pixels of Progress: A granular look at human development around the world, McKinsey Global Institute,
December 2022

was nearly 90 percent, almost the same as for boys. More women attend university than men.[27]

The education of girls and women is just one (important) aspect of broader empowerment of women. A century ago, only about one-quarter of women worked for pay. Many millions more, of course, worked hard in the household, caring for children and the elderly, and keeping the family show on the road for no pay and arguably not enough recognition. Today, 49 percent of women work for pay.[28]

This is not to deny that important differences across countries remain. Even as women's labor force participation rate has risen in most places, it remains stubbornly low in some. In India, a poster child for economic growth, the rate is about 30 percent. Compare this with Iceland, where female labor participation exceeds 70 percent, and women thrive in boardrooms and parliaments. Female work remains a source of potential in many nations racing toward modernity.[29]

The number of hours we work has fallen, thanks to growing productivity. Industrial labor has become more humane, and many people have moved from the farm or the factory to the services and knowledge economy. Even in 1950, in most countries where data exist, people worked more than 2,000 hours every year. Today, it is more common to work about 1,600 a year.[30]

Less work and higher incomes mean more leisure. We travel, go to art galleries, play sports, game and stream, volunteer in our communities, or just read a novel or socialize. There were 4.5 billion airline passengers and 1.5 billion international tourist arrivals in 2019. In 2024, spending on travel and tourism was $10.9 trillion. That's about 10 percent of global GDP. Or just consider that the global consumer wellness market, which includes going to the gym, health supplements, and related activities and products, is estimated to be worth $1.8 trillion.[31]

Freedom has also expanded, even if we still have a long way to go. The liberal democracy index put together by the Swedish think tank V-Dem uses a scale from 0 to 1 that combines information on voting rights, the freedom and fairness of elections, freedoms of association and expression, civil liberties, and executive constraints. Globally, it was 0.16 in 1925 and has inched forward to 0.29 today.[32]

Are we happier? We have already said we believe it is simplistic to say money buys happiness, and yet there is a large body of evidence that higher incomes do indeed come with more happiness—at least to an extent.

Angus Deaton and Daniel Kahneman, who were awarded the Nobel Prize in Economics in different years, demonstrated a clear correlation between income per person and life satisfaction. They found that life satisfaction rises with income, but emotional well-being or day-to-day happiness is subject to diminishing returns beyond a certain income threshold, at about $75,000 in 2010, adjusted for inflation. Other, more recent studies have challenged that view, suggesting that happiness rises continuously with income but that nonmaterial factors like social connections and leisure become increasingly significant in richer societies.[33] Whatever one thinks about this research, at least most will agree that poverty almost surely guarantees a miserable life. GDP may not buy you happiness, but it sure helps.

Progress at the frontier

Taking a planetary perspective, we see an amazing ascent of our human species toward higher levels of development. But the picture is no less astonishing even if we just choose places at the frontier of development. This is important because it shows that we did not just spread progress but fundamentally advanced the edge of our capabilities.

Going back to Rosling's numbers, in 1925 there were virtually no people who earned more than $50 of income per day on the entire planet. Today, almost 800 million people have a daily income of $50 or more. This is close to 10 percent of the world of 2025, which is even more impressive when one realizes that the entire planet had only two billion people in 1925.[34]

The United States was already one of the richest countries in the world by then, with an average per capita income of about $13,000. A century later, that figure is close to $75,000, an eightfold increase. The average American not only earns more but also lives longer: life expectancy has risen from roughly 58 years in the 1920s to more than 79 today. That is impressive, but the United States is far from great on this front. A country like South Korea did not simply approach the frontier but shattered it, from about 33 years in the 1920s to 84 today. It added an astonishing 50 years.[35]

This may come as a surprise, but 100 years ago, even in most advanced economies, more than 10 percent of children died before the age of five. Today, that share is less than 0.5 percent. And a lack of scientific, specifically medical, progress does not differentiate by income. In 1921, Winston and Clementine Churchill lost their two-year-old daughter, Marigold, to septicemia following a throat infection that today would be easily cured with simple antibiotics. In 1924, the 16-year-old son of US President Calvin Coolidge died of blood poisoning following a toe infection caused by a blister from playing tennis. Two of the richest and most powerful men in the world were powerless in the face of a simple infection. Penicillin was invented in 1928, changing everything.[36]

The nature of life has transformed, too. In the 1920s, about one-quarter of the American workforce toiled in agriculture. Today, four-fifths work in services, many in knowledge-based or creative fields that didn't even exist then. The transformation is not just the kind of jobs we do, but how much time we spend doing them. In 1925, Americans worked about 2,300 hours per year, and Germans more than 2,100. Today those figures are fewer than 1,800 for Americans and fewer than 1,400 for Germans.[37]

And even working more than 2,300 hours per year, here are things few or no Americans had access to in 1925: air travel, ballpoint pens, talking movies, credit payments, tampons, oral contraceptives, disposable diapers, refrigerators, vacuum cleaners, washing machines, microwaves, televisions, zippers, health insurance, social security, or insulin, not to mention plastic bags, bottles, and utensils, or vaccines for polio, measles, mumps, rubella, flu, tetanus, or diphtheria. In 1925 America, only about one in five adolescents graduated from high school, and one in five adults owned a car. Less than half of households had indoor plumbing, and only about half had access to electricity—10 percent in rural areas. Women only gained the right to vote in 1920.[38]

We could go on, but the takeaway is clear. The richest countries of 1925 did not stand still. They climbed to new peaks. Their citizens are incomparably richer, healthier, more educated, and overall better off. Frontier progress shows that development is not a zero-sum game. We did not just help others catch up. We built a higher summit altogether.

The balance of progress

Over the past century, human progress has delivered vast improvements in prosperity, health, and opportunity. But no journey of progress comes without questions and complications. While many, many millions have flourished, many others have some way to go to get to a good life. Progress is unfinished business. Indeed, the whole point of this book is to see whether we can plot a viable path toward empowerment and prosperity for all. In a later chapter, we will take a sober look at the broader consequences of this progress, asking not only what we gained but what it may have cost. We will put progress on trial and argue the case of the prosecution.

Is economic growth truly inclusive? Growth has delivered prosperity to many, but it is often characterized as uneven. Prosperity for the few, stagnation for the many. Some people, or even communities, soar, while others struggle. Is that true, though? Can progress lift everyone, or does it leave some, maybe even the majority, behind? We will ask whether economic growth has come with growing inequality, and whether that is an inherent feature.

Can our climate handle continued progress? Abundant energy and materials are the foundation of our prosperity. It is an iron law of history that more economic empowerment takes more energy. However, our energy-powered expansion has increased greenhouse gas emissions and warmed the planet. The future of progress hinges on our ability to power economic progress with low-emissions sources. Has growth come at the climate's expense? We will examine whether growth and climate stewardship are incompatible, or whether progress itself has become the engine of a cleaner, more sustainable world and can continue playing that role.

Are we sacrificing nature for material gain? Beyond carbon, the natural world bears other burdens: air and water pollution, deforestation, habitat loss, and species extinction. We will explore whether industrial progress has degraded the environment and whether that happens inevitably, or if progress can be harnessed to restore and protect it. In fact, we will show that in most cases, economic progress has been the solution to these problems.

Are we any happier now? For sure, poverty creates a lot of misery, and, as we have seen, many studies show that more income creates more empowerment and more life satisfaction. But a common accusation levied against economic progress is that more wealth does not translate into joy. We'll discuss whether we should demur from pursuing economic progress on the grounds that it does not make us happy and confront the apparent paradox of rising prosperity alongside growing concerns over loneliness or depression. Has progress fulfilled its promise of a better, more joyful life?

These are not rhetorical questions. They go to the heart of what progress means and whether, despite its imperfections, it is a force for good. We cover these arguments in Chapter 14, where progress gets put on trial.

❋ ❀ ❋

Over the past century, human progress has delivered vast improvements in prosperity, health, and opportunity. In the next chapter, we observe that progress over the past 100 years didn't come in a smooth, uninterrupted, challenge-free way.

CHAPTER 2

THE WINDING ASCENT

"Civilization is not inherited; it has to be learned and earned by each generation anew."

WILL AND ARIEL DURANT

———

The progress of the past century was not without stumbles.

THE PAST 100 YEARS OF PROGRESS were by no means a straight line heading for prosperity. There were emphatic punctuation marks, stumbles, and times when we lost our grip. These inflection points sometimes seemed to threaten the march upward and at other times created an earthquake to which we had to respond in order to launch ourselves into a new era. World War II was a major, and deadly, shock and inflection point. There was also the inflation burst of the 1970s, the fall of the Berlin Wall, and the COVID-19 pandemic, swiftly followed by Russia's invasion of Ukraine. Sometimes such disruptions came in clusters. Think of the early 1970s, when the first microprocessor was made, the gold standard ended, there was a major shock to oil prices, and Japan overtook Germany in national income.[39] One need only watch 1970s Hollywood films to experience the mood of darkness, rebelliousness, confusion, and sometimes distress in the United States.

Between these punctuation marks were flowing sentences, new eras in which fresh ideas, structures, and technological platforms unfolded. The point is that progress has never been simple or easy or uninterrupted, nor does it happen in the same way over time. We should never think it will be so. We should always be prepared to face challenges, find solutions, and shape our future.

In this chapter, we look at four eras and the disruptions that preceded them.[40] Income per person and other measures of human well-being evolved across these eras (Table 2), which are:

- **Depression and war (1925–44).** This era encompassed the aftermath of one world war and the buildup to the next; a brief period of exuberance that was crushed in the Great Depression.
- **Postwar boom (1944–71).** In this prolonged era, World War II was over and progress took off. Mass manufacturing gave increasingly prosperous households cars and consumer appliances, and confidence meant more babies; these were boom times in the West.
- **Era of contention (1971–89).** The oil shocks ushered in a more difficult period, with recession, stagnation, and the beginning of the end of uncontested Western dominance as economies in the East rose.
- **Era of markets (1989–2019).** As the Soviet Union broke up, a new era of free market capitalism and hyperglobalization ensued. The World Wide Web was born, the first milestone in our journey toward a digitized way of life.

There is, of course, a fifth era. This is the one we are just starting now. Your daily consumption of news will clearly tell you this. But we will dive into that in the next chapter.

TABLE 2

Income per person growth rates by region across four eras
CAGR from start to end of period, %

Region[1]	Depression and war (1925–44)	Postwar boom (1944–71)	Era of contention (1971–89)	Era of markets (1989-2019)
World	1.2	2.4	1.7	2.2
Advanced countries[2]	1.6	2.6	2.6	1.6
China and India	−0.8[3]	1.6[4]	2.2	4.4
Rest of world	1.1	3.0	1.1	2.1

[1]Within regions, the sample of countries measured is stable within periods, but not between periods, because more countries have available data in later periods.
[2]Includes only advanced countries in North America, Western Europe (no former communist countries), and Advanced East Asia and Oceania.
[3]For data availability reasons, this CAGR encompasses the period between 1929 and 1950.
[4]For data availability reasons, this CAGR encompasses the period between 1950 and 1971.
Source: World Bank, *World development indicators;* McKinsey Global Institute analysis

Depression and war (1925–44)

The first of our eras was shaped, and constantly unsettled, by World War I. The peace was fragile and politics fraught. Efforts were made to orchestrate harmony among nations that had been at one another's throats. The 1925 Locarno Treaties aimed to guarantee borders in Europe, and Germany joined the League of Nations a year later. The Kellogg–Briand Pact in 1928 even tried to outlaw war as a means of resolving disputes, but it never had teeth. Autocrats pursued military ambitions. Adolf Hitler became Germany's chancellor, Japan invaded Manchuria, Italy under Benito Mussolini invaded Ethiopia, and Spain descended into civil war. Peacemaking failed.

This was hardly the backdrop to vibrant growth, but the end of war did engender a burst of exuberance. The Roaring Twenties, a time of jazz and *joie de vivre,* was a reaction to what had come before. People wanted to live, they wanted to buy. Manufacturing and innovation enjoyed a mini heyday. Inventors were in fine form. We got television, radar, and commercial aviation. Oil was beginning to take off as a fuel,

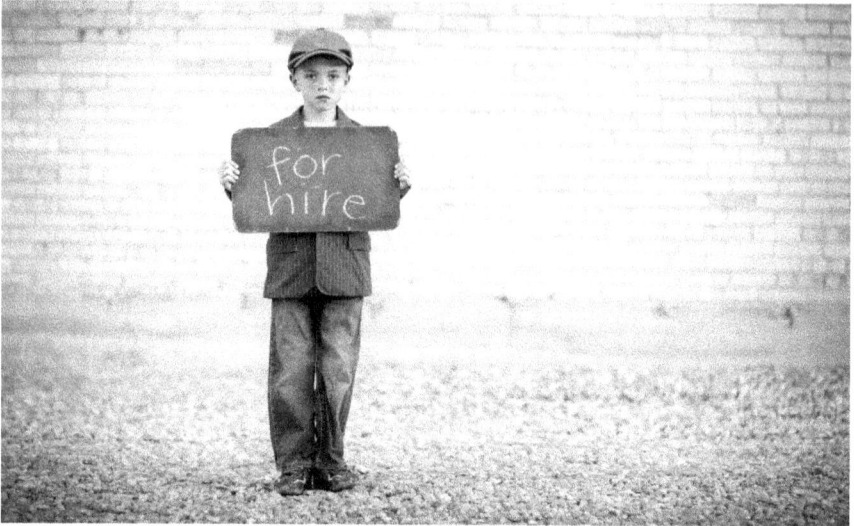

Economic dog days. Impending layoffs. An unemployed boy looking for work.

not least because of large discoveries in Saudi Arabia. Aluminum joined steel as a major material and enabled the production of aircraft. Drilling, refining, and mining techniques improved, helping to support industry and innovation.

Henry Ford's assembly line was the real breakthrough, which was widely adopted in the 1920s and ushered in an age of mass production. Ford is celebrated; less remarked on was the automation of farms, at least in the West, which released so many workers to the factories that were churning out cars and consumer goods. Never before had so many people changed what they did to earn a living, and mass urbanization followed.

The good times were not to last. In 1929, the Great Depression decimated economies, starting with the United States, and continuing with others like Germany, the latter fueling Hitler's rise. In the United States, President Franklin D. Roosevelt's New Deal attempted to combat the consequences of the Depression. The iconic Hoover Dam was a symbol of those efforts. In many ways, the confidence of the 1920s was a fever, as F. Scott Fitzgerald so acutely observed in *The Great Gatsby*. Yes, there was hedonism and materialism, but neither was destined to have any staying power.

Confidence was shattered, and economic recovery faltered. The Smoot-Hawley Tariff Act deepened the Depression, raising import taxes on thousands of goods and triggering a wave of retaliatory tariffs abroad that strangled global trade. Trade had bounced back after the Great War but then dropped by about two-thirds between 1929 and about 1933–34.[41] Financial markets cratered. Private investment dried up. And emerging economies remained constrained by colonial powers, which tightened control over resource-rich regions. They could not even begin to try to emulate the emerging industrial might of Europe and North America.

Then, on September 1, 1939, Nazi Germany invaded Poland. Two days later, the United Kingdom declared war on Germany. Another major event punctuated progress.

Postwar boom (1944–71)

As World War II ended, a new international order rapidly fell into place. The United Nations, World Bank, and International Monetary Fund (IMF) were established, typifying a new kind of multilateral institution designed to underpin aspirations for a multilateral world. In fact, three blocs emerged: the United States, whose currency was chosen as the anchor of the postwar monetary system, leading the West; the Soviet Union in the East; and the rest of the world as it threw off the shackles of colonialism. India declared independence in 1947. There were flashpoints aplenty, from the Cuban Missile Crisis to wars in Korea and Vietnam, all under the newly created specter of mutually assured destruction as nuclear capabilities escalated on both sides. This was the Cold War of spy games and the very real fear of nuclear war. History tells us we came very close to the brink.

But this was also a golden age of engineering, building on innovations made before the war. The electrification of manufacturing enabled the mass production of affordable consumer durables, and consumerism took off big-time. In the West, refrigerators appeared in many a kitchen, and Tupperware became a suburban must-have. Fast, easy transportation became the Western norm. In the United States, there were 2.4 cars for every ten people in 1946; by 1971, that had more than doubled to 5.6.[42] The Ford Mustang, Mattel's Barbie, and Coca-Cola remain powerful global brands today. The technological revolution went far beyond satisfying

Children advertising a refrigerator in the 1960s.

consumption, of course. During these years, the jet engine, modern steelmaking with basic oxygen furnaces, widespread use of aluminum, semiconductors and integrated circuits, lasers, the shipping container, and the television emerged. The pinnacle was the Apollo program, which put men on the Moon.

Confidence built, and the baby boom took off. At its peak, American families were having 3.6 children on average. French families were having close to three in 1950. By 1970, the median age globally was 20. It has never been as low since. Meanwhile, medical advances pushed average life expectancy around the world up into the mid-50s, and child mortality sharply lower.[43]

There was, of course, still considerable scope for progress in a predominantly poor, rural world. In 1971, close to 50 percent of the world still lived in extreme poverty. Most people lived in rural areas; only about 37 percent lived in cities.[44]

This was the age when big oil developed. Huge fields were discovered in the Middle East, we all used much more of the stuff, and it was inexpensive; oil prices were less than $25 a barrel in today's money. The United States was voracious, consuming as much as one-fifth of all the oil in the world. While the black gold was flooding out, there was also a Green Revolution in which agricultural output and productivity increased on the back of a ninefold expansion of ammonia-based fertilizers in the 1950s and 1960s. To the surprise of some, there was more than enough to feed the baby boom generation.[45]

Developed economies achieved surging productivity growth as mechanization and automation spread, and economic growth was robust. Rebuilding from the war boosted activity, debts were paid down, and global trade rebounded. Companies that had largely been local went international. The multinational corporation took off.

But most of the emerging world, except for some initial signs among the "Asian tigers," was stagnant. In this era, the 80 percent living in emerging economies accounted for 54 percent of global growth.[46] For many in these places, this was a bad time for human rights. Mao Zedong's Great Leap Forward, combined with the Cultural Revolution that followed, caused close to 50 million deaths according to some estimates, and hobbled the economy of the world's most populous nation.

The era of contention (1971–89)

A confluence of events conspired to end the boom. The gold standard ended, and the newly assertive OPEC squeezed the supply of oil, triggering an oil shock. The West entered an uncomfortable period of recession and stagflation. What followed was a more contested and less buoyant era. The United States and other Western nations no longer had it all their own way, a point brought home clearly by defeat in Vietnam. The Cold War rumbled on, Japan emerged as an economic powerhouse, and China opened up to the rest of the world as Henry Kissinger and Richard Nixon met Mao. The United States under Ronald Reagan and the United Kingdom led by Margaret Thatcher introduced free-market reforms in a political response to the malaise.

While economics and politics were increasingly contested and messy, technology marched on. Appetite for consumer durables was unabated.

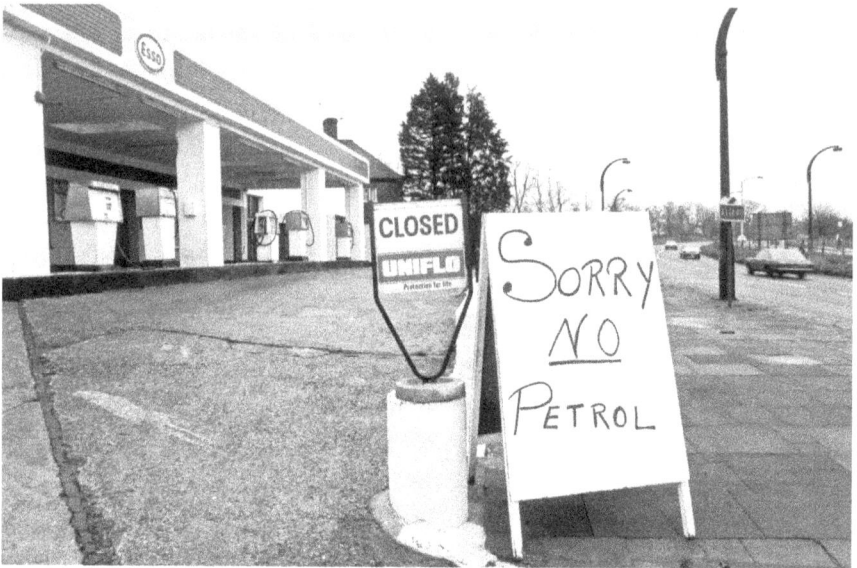

Petrol shortage at a service station.

By the end of this era, the vast majority of US households had a color TV, washing machine and dryer, dishwasher, and electric stove. More pertinently, the foundations of the computer age were laid with the advent of network technology and communication protocols, the widespread use of transistors, and the first commercial production of a microprocessor: the Intel 4004 four-bit central processing unit. In 1971, only about 23 hosts ran the ARPANET, the precursor to the internet. By the end of 1989, it was more than 100,000.[47] The spread of the humble shipping container cut the costs of trade.

Female empowerment coincided with, or contributed to, the end of the baby boom. The contraceptive pill was part of it. More women working was, too. In the United States, the gap between male and female labor force participation rates fell by around 15 percentage points over 20 years. Child mortality continued to fall and life expectancy to rise. The gap between the West and emerging economies grew, and inequality between countries peaked.[48]

As OPEC discovered the will and skill to assert its control over the global oil supply, the world responded by diversifying into nuclear and gas, and boosting energy efficiency. By the end of the era, 10 percent fewer joules were required per dollar of GDP.[49]

Meanwhile, the agricultural revolution continued. We were able to produce enough food for growing populations, despite the Club of Rome report warning of the "limits to growth" in 1972. In Africa and Asia, the daily supply of calories per person increased by 8 and 21 percent, respectively.[50]

Volatility and stagflation reigned, and productivity growth in the Group of Seven leading industrial nations more than halved.[51] The established economic pecking order was beginning to break down. Median wages in the United States went on pause for 20 years; on the other side of the world, East Asia started its long growth journey. Conglomerates, which had become overstretched, overindebted, and overcomplex, had a rethink, many of them selling off business units to streamline and reduce bloat while searching for economies of scale.

Meanwhile, China quietly started a different type of revolution. Starting with the normalization of the US–China relationship with Nixon and Mao's famous meeting, and continuing with the rise of reformer Deng Xiaoping, China unleashed warp-speed growth when it embraced market economics in 1978. Modest at first, reforms like special economic zones and trade liberalization snowballed into decades of double-digit economic growth.

The era of markets (1989–2019)

The punctuation mark that ended the era of contention was the fall of the Berlin Wall in 1989, which symbolized more than anything else the end of the Soviet empire and the victory of market economics and liberal democracy. This is the era in which many of us grew up, the reputed "end of history."[52] The world order had become unipolar.

Market-based economic reform fueled an age of hyperglobalization.[53] Exports of goods and services jumped rapidly from about 19 to 28 percent of global GDP, and China quintupled its share of global exports to far outstrip the tally of the United States and Germany, and become the world's largest manufacturer.

Another earth-shattering event occurred in the year when the Berlin Wall came down. The World Wide Web was born, seeding the digital revolution that is still reshaping all our lives. By 2019, 67 percent of all

Stock trader gesturing in front of price board.

people in the world had a mobile phone, and 54 percent had access to the internet. Just 30 years earlier, those numbers were zero. Even "plain old telephone system" landlines peaked at two for every ten people globally, easily eclipsed by internet protocol (IP) and mobile-based technologies. More recently, disruptive technologies like distributed infrastructure, next-generation computing, applied AI, and virtual reality accelerated in innovation, production, and adoption with large potential to create value in future years. In this era, the continued march of Moore's law ratcheted computational capability exponentially.[54] Today, we have a mind-boggling, scarcely comprehensible amount of data stored: 200 zettabytes. If you think that the average digital book is about five megabytes, every person on the planet has a library of five million such books!

We added even more years to the average lifespan. By 2019, on average we were living more than 73 years. Families continued to shrink, and we saw the first signs of an aging world. For the first time in history, the global median age topped 30 in 2022. And we educated about three-quarters of children at the secondary level, equipping a generation for gainful employment and the digital age. But the most revolutionary change in the way we lived was urbanization, the biggest human migration in history. Over the course of the four eras we have been describing, about four billion more people became urbanites, and they now outnumber those living in the countryside.[55]

By 2019, 56 percent of the global population was urban. As developing economies enjoyed economic expansion, inequality between countries narrowed. But there was growing unease that the fruits of growth were not being equally shared. Africa, particularly Sub-Saharan Africa, experienced slower growth than others despite starting from a poorer baseline. Concern was not confined to emerging economies. For the first time in recent Western history, the assumption that each generation would be better off than their parents' generation faltered.[56]

The fossil-fuel-based energy system kept expanding. Deep-sea drilling, intercontinental pipelines, shale gas, and oil, together with the expansion of liquefied natural gas (LNG), became part of the mix, and we each consumed a great deal more energy. By this time, the average person consumed the equivalent of 580 gallons of gasoline a year.[57] But there was a new feature of the terrain: the increasing awareness of potentially irreversible climate damage. A race to salvage global habitability began, and world leaders struck the Paris Agreement, which laid out a path to reducing the potential damage of fossil fuels to the climate.

People became more prosperous, and demand for food and materials grew explosively. Meat production in China tripled; in Brazil, it quadrupled. Global steel production increased 2.4 times, driven by a 16-fold increase in China's steel production. Cement production quadrupled. By the end of the era, human-made materials weighed more than all the living biomass on Earth.[58]

This was Asia's time. For most of the era, China's economy kept growing by close to 10 percent a year, from an increasingly large base.[59] China and India accounted for about half of global productivity growth. Others like Bangladesh and Vietnam grew fast, too. Central and Eastern Europe caught up with their Western neighbors. It was a time of convergence. And by the end of the era, low- and middle-income countries generated the majority of global growth for the first time. Growth in advanced economies started weakening as the era went on, and productivity growth tapered off. Low inflation and low interest rates encouraged a buildup of debt. By 2020, debt accounted for 256 percent of global GDP. Multinational corporations drove globalization, accounting for roughly two-thirds of global exports. Their presence became especially pronounced in innovation-intensive sectors, such as automotive, electronics, and pharmaceuticals, in which today they account for approximately 80 percent of global trade.[60] Some technology companies were now larger than many economies.

At the end of the era of markets, the world has hit a set of new majorities. The vast majority of people are connected to smartphones and the internet. The majority of economic activity is traded, the majority of people consume at least 30 gigajoules of energy per year, and the majority of people live in cities and work outside agriculture.

We have become so accustomed to the era of markets that we could be excused for thinking that this is the way of the world. But as this short, guided tour of our century of progress has shown, it was really just one special chapter in a diverse book. Things we used to take for granted were temporary artifacts of a world that was temporarily unipolar, at its demographic sweet spot, and with massive headroom for growth in China and India as they entered the global economy.

❃ ❃ ❃

Now we turn our attention to the coming era, which we are already experiencing today. One thing is for certain: For all the bumps in the road and the stumbles on our ascent, we start this era in a radically different place from where we started the most recent one. A globalized, connected, educated, computerized, energized world with new capabilities, but also new challenges. As in past eras, the new one will bring a new set of rules and norms, which, at first, feel confusing and disorienting. But the direction of travel is clear.

CHAPTER 3

ON THE CUSP OF A NEW ERA

"Let me not pray to be sheltered from dangers
but to be fearless in facing them."

RABINDRANATH TAGORE

—

A cluster of disruptive events in recent years has put us on the cusp of a new era. Can we write a new narrative of progress?

THERE IS LITTLE DOUBT that we are entering a new era. In fact, we feel as if we are already living in it. We feel it every day. We are painfully aware of the turbulence of the past few years and are now grappling with the messy new realities that have resulted. As at every past inflection point, several era-defining events have collided in a short time.

Just think of the past few years. A global pandemic, with many governments locking down large parts of their populace and accelerating

Students getting temperature checked before entering school, India.

their indebtedness, and an almost-miraculous vaccine emerging at record speed. The return of war to Europe. Inflation rearing its long-forgotten head with a vengeance. The rapid expansion of geopolitical rivalries, from increased trade disputes to growing military capability. The seemingly sudden explosion of a whole new technology, AI, with large language models, completely upending even the most techno-optimistic forecasts. Energy is once again becoming the focus of politics and geostrategic tensions. Escalation of conflict in the Middle East. The rise of democratic support for anti-establishment politicians.

Five domains that enable us to judge history and eras have been shaken up.[61] Rising globalization and unipolarity are giving way to a multipolar world with trade tensions. The digital revolution looks small in comparison with what is to come in the AI-driven, post-digital world. Demographic tailwinds are slowing or turning into headwinds due to low and plunging birth rates. The energy transition remains key, but geopolitics has resurfaced the need for energy to also be affordable, reliable, and secure. And, finally, debt expansion amid cheap money and low inflation may have engendered a need for an orderly stabilization of the global balance sheet under changing macroeconomic conditions.

Without doubt, a lot is new or unfamiliar. When confronted by an alternative reality, it has become the stuff of popular legend that the crew of the Starship Enterprise observed, "Jim, this is our world, but not as we know it." That is what it is like to live in a new era.

Multipolarity redux

We have become accustomed to an ever-rising tide of globalization. Not just trade in goods, but in services, data exchange, and even the movement of people. The world as it stands today is interconnected and specialized. The Netherlands makes no cars, Australia makes no chips, and the United States makes almost no clothes. But all three countries have lots of each. Our unipolar world was a naturally global one, with shared norms and strong incentives to cooperate.

In the new era, the global order is undergoing a seismic shift, marked by a hard push to make multipolarity real. China was the world's 11th-largest economy in 1990. By 2023, it was the second biggest, and first in purchasing-power parity terms. India climbed from 20th to fifth over the same period. Geopolitical tensions are rising, and realpolitik surging. President Donald Trump used his so-called Liberation Day on April 2, 2025, to announce sweeping trade tariffs aimed at reducing the US trade deficit and boosting domestic manufacturing. The United States and China have strengthened export controls. For example, the United States has been working to curb China's access to semiconductors, a move echoed by allies like the Netherlands and Japan. The US CHIPS Act had driven about $450 billion of private-sector commitments by 2024. America first, China first. The two great powers with increasingly similar playbooks. Nations that regard each other as friends have started trading more with each other. The geopolitical distance of trade has shrunk.[62]

China has invested significantly in its military-industrial complex. Today, it has 370 naval ships, more than the United States has. It has also invested heavily in other value-added manufacturing and now produces, for instance, more electric vehicles (EVs), solar panels, and drones than the United States.[63] Meanwhile, the relationship between old allies in Europe and the United States went through a period of strain when

Trump started his second term and expressed reluctance to continue funding European defense. European leaders responded with some muscularity in building up their own defenses.[64] There is ongoing conflict and instability in parts of the Middle East.

Virtually every election in the past two years has been lost by the incumbent party, Australia and Canada being exceptions. All of this suggests a fragmented yet dynamic world order characterized by competition with a distinct risk of escalation.

Major uncertainties include the landing point for tariffs, their impact, the speed of decoupling, how institutions are reshaped, realignment of blocs, and flexibility of supply chains and production systems. Tariffs, like those proposed in 2025, could disrupt global trade, either balancing economic growth with some degree of self-sufficiency or triggering outright economic downturn. The pace of decoupling between countries and blocs, especially in technology and minerals, may strain supply chains or accelerate regional hubs. Institutional reforms could empower new blocs or paralyze global governance. Production hinges on whether nations like the United States can scale manufacturing to match ambition, potentially easing tensions or entrenching rivalries. These forks could lead to cooperative multipolarity or a fractured, zero-sum world, but historical resilience suggests that adaptability will prevail.

The AI revolution

The constant march of digital technologies, epitomized by Moore's law, became the technological pulse of the most recent era. We are awash in semiconductors. Conservatively, there are several thousand of them per person, connected effortlessly in an increasingly mobile web. Digitization, and its cousin connectivity, have become our norm.

But now we are at the start of a new curve, of humanized (not just digitized) technology. Launched at the end of 2022, by April 2025 ChatGPT had about 800 million weekly active users.[65] Of course, a chatbot is only a tiny part of the AI universe, but for many of us, it was our first surreal experience of talking to a machine that, on the face of it, seemed quite intelligent.

AI is starting to transform work and industries. Computers now "speak" English, and AI is poised to write 90 percent of code. The scale of change is already huge. The cost of achieving a particular level of AI performance is dropping by 50 to 75 percent every year. The cost of a teraflop per second (the ability of a computer to handle one trillion floating-point operations per second) was $315 in 2010, but only $16 in 2022. Algorithms are advancing so much and so fast that effective computing power is doubling every eight months. That's more than tripling in a year.[66] The United States leads on funding and foundation models. China leads on knowledge development and industrial applications, with close to 70 percent of granted AI patents and about 50 percent of all industrial robots installed in 2023. The US–China race may leave Europe and India trailing, underscoring a bipolar tech landscape that drives innovation but risks exclusion.[67]

For the man and woman on the street, a common reaction is that AI will replace them. We agree that AI will automate many tasks. We think that between 15 and 30 percent of current tasks could be automated by 2030. We equally think AI will boost productivity, and, if past technological revolutions are a good guide, increase jobs and lift living standards. Coder vacancies in Silicon Valley have dropped one-third since before the COVID-19 pandemic because AI is doing the coding. At the same time, the productivity of coding has risen. GitHub Copilot has boosted developers' output by 55 percent on certain specific tasks.[68] Lively debate continues about whether AI is reducing employment.[69]

In any case, uncertainties include labor market impacts, the timeline to general intelligence, geopolitics interplay, energy constraints, the AI ecosystem, and chip supply. Labor disruptions could displace millions for a long time or lift all boats, depending on our capacity to adapt quickly. General intelligence can revolutionize economies but also destabilize societies. Geopolitical tensions may fragment AI ecosystems or spur global collaboration. AI uses a great deal of power, and if energy is constrained, this could limit progress, but clean energy sources like solar and nuclear offer hope. Open-source AI could democratize innovation or enable misuse. Bottlenecks in chips or power may hinder scaling, but past technological leaps suggest that solutions will emerge.

Dependency and depopulation?

For most of our lives, the world has lived in a demographic summer. We explore this extensively in the subsequent chapters, but the salient point is that we haven't thought much about demographics and fertility rates because we haven't really had to. We have had steadily more working-age people as a percentage of the population in most places for most of our lives. To the extent we talked about birth rates, it was usually around the (outdated) concern that there were too many people on the planet rather than too few.

However, the demographic winter has been coming for some years, a tide that rises slowly but inexorably. The year 2012 marked the point in human history with "peak births," with about 146 million babies born.[70] Never before had there been more, and there may never be again. The new era we find ourselves in will be an eerily different demographic season. Unlike an actual winter, this demographic winter could be very long.

Two out of three humans live in a country where the fertility rate is below the replacement rate of 2.1. South Korea hit a country record low of 0.7 births per woman in 2024. China's population, due to fertility rates of about 1.0 for decades, and as low as 0.6 in places like Shanghai, has now been declining for three years. Japan's working-age population shrank by about 12 million between 2000 and 2023. Recognizing the challenge, Japan now encourages working until 70. Several European countries, like Germany, Italy, and Spain, have raised or plan to raise the retirement age to 67. Public pension systems are under strain. Budget offices in both the United Kingdom and the United States predict growing deficits coming almost exclusively from demographic factors. But it is not just the usual suspects. India, long worried about population explosion, has been below replacement since 2019, according to the United Nations. Latin America's average fertility rate is 1.8. Brazil will be as "old" as advanced economies in less than 20 years, while its income per person is today about one-third of theirs.[71]

The demographic crunch threatens economic growth and public budgets. Migration, once a release valve, is now a political flashpoint. In the European Union (EU), 41 percent of voters said "irregular" migration was a concern; only war in Ukraine ranked higher. And yet not all trends are negative. Advances in medicine and public health have pushed back

A lone child on a swing in a playground.

the onset of age-related diseases, with therapies targeting senescence and regenerative treatments showing early promise. Countries like Japan and Singapore are investing in "longevity economies," redesigning work and urban infrastructure to support active aging. Technology is enabling flexible, remote, and part-time work that allows older adults to stay engaged longer and holds the potential to raise productivity significantly, as we have discussed. Women and people over 50 have been working more, offsetting the past demographic drag. The picture will indeed grow more complicated, but it is equally true that, so far, countries have been adapting through technology, science, and work.[72]

Uncertainties include the trajectory of fertility, productivity gains from technology that can offset demographic decline, healthy aging, women's labor force participation, migration policy, and the renewal of the social contract. A fertility rebound, driven by economic, cultural, scientific, or policy shifts, is uncertain but possible. AI and automation may ease labor shortages or fall short. Health advances may extend working lives and, more broadly, keep elderly people engaged in society for longer. More women could enter the workforce, particularly in lagging regions, or face persistent barriers. Effective migration policies might ease aging pressures or provoke deeper political backlash. Renewal of the intergenerational social contract will determine whether aging societies stagnate or adapt and thrive.

The energy transition conundrum

For some years now, many leaders in government, civil society, and business have been discussing the goal of achieving net-zero emissions by 2050. This concept and goal arose out of a single sentence in the 2018 report of the Intergovernmental Panel on Climate Change (IPCC): "In model pathways with no or limited overshoot of 1.5°C, global net anthropogenic CO_2 emissions decline by about 45 percent from 2010 levels by 2030, reaching *net zero* around 2050." Net zero by 2050 became mainstream, and a rallying cry, in less than ten years.[73]

Yet even as more and more governments and businesses signed up to the goal of net zero, the fossil-fuel-powered energy system steamed forward relentlessly. Positive supply shocks abounded, perhaps most notably in the shale oil fields of the United States, where the biggest single addition to the world's energy supply was made in just two decades. Combined with relatively unfettered globalization and improvements in energy transportation, energy was a constraint almost nowhere. This fed a relaxed attitude toward energy supply, and perhaps the emblem of this was Germany's reliance on Russian gas. The feeling of energy abundance likely contributed to governments leaning into aggressive carbon reduction promises, partly enshrined in the Paris Agreement.

The Russia–Ukraine war triggered an energy shock that reminded the world of an uncomfortable truth: Energy needs to be clean, but it must also be reliable, affordable, and competitive, a combination that defines the new conundrum. In 2024, global investment in renewables reached $680 billion, including a record $500 billion in solar alone. Yet investment in fossil fuels also rebounded, with oil and gas majors pouring capital into new exploration and LNG terminals. The United States formally exited the Paris Agreement in early 2025. China has overtaken the EU as the world's largest oil importer. Carbon emissions, while falling in many countries and maybe soon plateauing in China, are still rising globally.[74]

The pace of technological change is impressive but uneven. Growth in the use of solar power has been fast. So, too, has energy storage. In 2023 alone, the global energy storage market almost tripled. But against what will be needed in a more fully electrified system that relies more heavily on intermittent renewables, storage remains limited. Nuclear energy is showing signs of a renaissance. More than 60 reactors were under construction globally as of February 2025, with new small modular reactors gaining regulatory traction. Japan is reopening reactors that were shut down after the 2011 Fukushima accident. EV sales are growing, increasing to more than 18 million units globally in 2024. They now account for more than 20 percent of all new car sales, with China leading. But some companies are quietly backpedaling on net-zero and broader environmental, social, and governance commitments, citing cost and complexity. Hydrogen remains largely grounded. Meanwhile, electricity demand is surging from unexpected sources like data centers, driven by AI workloads.[75]

Uncertainties include progress on adaptation, AI-driven energy demand and the geopolitical impact on energy security, nuclear feasibility, battery economics, the reliability of intermittent systems, and grid infrastructure bottlenecks. Adaptation may proceed rapidly or remain underfunded and fragmented. AI could strain power systems or encourage accelerated innovation. Nuclear may become a baseload staple or remain niche. Intermittent-heavy grids may stabilize with storage and demand response or expose reliability gaps. Energy security shifts could foster cooperation or intensify rivalries. Battery breakthroughs might scale clean flexibility or stall on materials. Grid expansion and modernization will be either the backbone of the transition or its choke point. Historical energy transitions suggest that solutions, rather than problems or shortcomings, prevail. They can do so again.

Macroeconomic turning points

The prepandemic decades baked in regularities about the world economy. One was cheap money, with the greenback as an uber currency. Another was consistent high growth in some large economies, notably China, providing a global supply and demand boost, supported by solid productivity growth. And, related to the points above, the assumption that globalization would only increase or stay high. This all combined to create a bout of high global growth and low inflation at the same time. Global balance sheets responded by swelling profusely, with net wealth growing from 4.5 times GDP in 2000 to 6.1 times in 2021, propelled by higher and higher asset prices. Debt ballooned, too: Public debt grew from 66 to 99 percent of global GDP over the same period, corporate debt from 71 to 93 percent, and household debt from 68 to 82 percent.[76]

The past few years have shredded these macroeconomic norms.

After years of being dormant, inflation reared its head once more, the result of huge lifeboat spending by governments during the pandemic and the energy price shock triggered by Russia's invasion of Ukraine. Inflation has since cooled from its 2022 highs in most countries, with core inflation back near central bank targets in the eurozone and parts of Asia. But the outlook remains volatile. In the United States, the pre-2025 disinflationary trend has slowed, with new price pressures resulting from trade and fiscal policy. The inflation spike may not have been anywhere as severe as bouts of hyperinflation in the past, but psychologically it came as a shock because nobody had thought much about it for so many years.[77]

The era of cheap money ended. Whether it will return and where is hotly debated. Could we be in a new normal of higher structural rates driven by debt loads, energy and defense investment needs, and global labor shortages? Or will we go back to the low-rate regime of the decades before COVID-19?

This all coincided with another change: the end of an era of extremely high Chinese growth. One of the world's most reliable growth engines has, not surprisingly, slowed down. Europe's growth is anemic, too. Conversely, India's economy is still growing at more than 5 percent a year. US growth, too, came back robustly from the pandemic on the back of solid investment and a renaissance in productivity. The world's growth picture is mixed. Real global growth has been hovering around 3 percent, but there are risks that it could slow. Fractured geopolitics and the potential for that to disrupt trade sounds an uncertain note, as do big shifts in US policy, from tariffs to a new tax and spending bill.[78]

The global balance sheet remains frothy. High and growing debt burdens risk fiscal trouble. Governments face a difficult balancing act of funding their priorities, from necessary infrastructure to clean energy to new defense commitments, while not expanding deficits. Higher productivity growth is the way out, as it would reduce the deficit and debt burden relative to economic activity while automatically raising government revenues.[79]

Uncertainties include the sustainability of mostly government and some private debt, the risk of balance sheet and asset price corrections, the dollar's global role and the volatility of exchange rates, the inflationary consequences of debt, deficits, and policy decisions, and of course the possibility of an AI-driven productivity revolution resolving many of these uncertainties. Debt burdens may become self-limiting and spark gradual austerity or trigger a fiscal reckoning. Balance sheet adjustments could be orderly or destabilizing. The dollar could retain dominance or face challenges from alternative systems. Trade disruptions may embed structural inflation or equilibrate through new alignments. Whether policy, technology, and coordination rise to the challenge will shape the next macro chapter.

❄ ❄ ❄

The early days of a new era can be unnerving. For all of us authors, and we suspect most of our readers, our lives have played out on a relatively consistent landscape. But our known rulebooks no longer apply. We might be experts at the wrong game and novices at the new one. The challenge of all inflection points is to rethink, recalibrate, and make the right choices.

The tremors of recent times may seem to have come on suddenly, but as in other times of transition, they reflect a longer buildup of tensions, which we now need to resolve in the new era. Our goal should be to establish a new narrative of progress at this time of disequilibrium. For that, we need to understand the mechanics of the progress machine that propelled humanity forward over the past century. That is the aspiration of Part II.

PART II

HOW WAS PROGRESS ACHIEVED?

CHAPTER 4

THE MACHINE OF PROGRESS

"One man's magic is another man's engineering."

ROBERT A. HEINLEIN

———

Humans advanced in the face of many hurdles. For this to continue, we need to know how the progress machine worked.

THE IMPRESSIVE ADVANCES of the past 100 years may seem like a magic trick. Or maybe we were just lucky. Neither is true. A dollop of good fortune is always welcome, but when we look at what propelled progress, we find there were mechanics behind the magic. The Wizard of Oz offered a compelling illusion for the denizens of the Emerald City, but behind the curtain was an ordinary person pulling mechanical levers. Not a wizard but a proficient engineer.

If we are to replicate or even exceed the progress of the past century to raise every person to empowerment and beyond, we need to understand the levers that were being pulled. The progress machine has eight interlocking parts that work together in an elegant jigsaw to create forward momentum. When all parts of the machine are whirring away, it offers maximum power, at peak efficiency with minimal waste. And that has an impact on all of us in the form of economic growth and all the benefits thereof, delivered through the drivetrain of productivity growth.

In 1950, the average worker in a sample of 24 European and Latin American countries with consistent data produced the equivalent of $19,000 a year. Today, the average worker produces $85,000 a year, working 400 fewer hours or ten fewer weeks per year. That figure, output per worker, is how economists measure productivity. From 1997 to today, median economy productivity jumped six times. The reason is not that today's workers work harder. How are individuals able to produce so much more output than in the past and yet work fewer hours? The answer is that people have a higher level of skills, more and better machinery, more technological helpmates, more energy, and more coworkers to bounce ideas off. They have more inputs and technological know-how from around the world and likely work in larger firms with better managerial practices, surrounded by effective institutions.

Let us explore each of these elements in turn.

Workers are the first part of the machine. Over the past century, fertility patterns delivered a demographic dividend, farmers became industry and service workers, and the female workforce surged. The world's population quadrupled from about two billion people in 1925 to more than eight billion today, and the evolution of fertility rates meant that an increasing proportion were of working age. Thanks to increased agricultural productivity, we managed not only to feed them but to enable billions to leave their farms for new jobs in industry and services. And a new wave of women moved out of the home and into the workplace. Overall, employment in the industrial and service economies grew at more than double the pace at which the population grew.[1]

Second, **skills**. We became more educated and more skilled and therefore better equipped to earn a good wage and finance a good life. As we have seen, a century ago, only one-third of people in the world were able to read. By 2022, that share was nearly 90 percent. In the 1920s, children spent an average of two years at school; now it is nine. Even advanced economies experienced a huge increase in the development of what economists call human capital. In comparison with 100 years ago, eight times more Americans now earn a tertiary qualification. A century ago, most people got by with manual skills, whether on the farm or in the factory; today the median worker is a service-sector worker. The evolution of the modern corporation as a creator, storehouse, and propagator of know-how means that a great deal of human capital improvement actually comes from working.[2]

Third, we increased the amount of **investment**. The number one reason humans became more productive is that they had more tools and infrastructure at their disposal. Think about all the things that enhance the performance of a Dutch farmer: yes, tractors, but now also automated hydroponic systems, AI-driven climate control, robotics for planting and harvesting, greenhouses with enhanced CO_2 levels, and Internet of Things sensors for real-time soil and crop monitoring, among others. Compare that with the same farmer in 1925. She worked with basic tools like hoes and manual irrigation, with limited or no mechanization, basic seed varieties, and minimal or no access to fertilizers. The amount of capital per worker has grown ninefold over the past century, and in the past 25 years, this has been the source of 70 to 80 percent of productivity growth. The amazing thing about capital equipment is the way it embodies the knowledge of civilization in physical form.

Advancement is not only about *more* tools. It is also about *better* tools and new ideas. Over the past 100 years, **invention** yielded a multitude of scientific discoveries and technologies that solved many of humanity's most pressing problems and improved lives for all. Alexander Fleming's discovery of penicillin in 1928 marked the beginning of the antibiotic era; it arrived too late to save Churchill's and Coolidge's children, but since then it is estimated to have saved more than 500 million lives. Cars and planes revolutionized how we get around. We created industrial robots, microprocessors, and satellites. Today, can you imagine a world without the internet and your smartphone? In a few years, you may not be able to imagine a world without your AI agents, either. The "mad scientist" working away in his garden shed was part of it, of course, but we created an entire ecosystem of innovation, from science to development to commercialization, funded by states and profit-seeking firms and with the benefit of a cumulative and globalized system of knowledge.[3]

All machines need raw ingredients, and the fifth part of the machine was **energy**. We discovered, mobilized, and consumed far more energy than ever before. In fact, ten times as much today as we did in 1925. Consider electricity, just one of the numerous ways in which we use energy. In the 1920s, about 20 percent of the world's people had electricity. Today, that figure is 92 percent. In the vast majority of populated areas, light is available at the flick of a switch. And many homes, poor and rich, have a TV and perhaps a washing machine. Of course, it wasn't only energy that fired our world. The most basic fuel we need as humans is food, and we produced more than enough of it to feed the growing number of people on Earth. And it is Earth's riches in the form of metals and minerals that built our cities and factories.

Cities punch enormously above their weight in the economic contribution they make. We urbanized. In the early 20th century, about 80 percent of the world's people lived in the countryside, but today nearly 60 percent of us are urbanites, and that share could be 80 percent by 2100, a mirror image of the past. When people, infrastructure, and capital are concentrated and networked in cities, ideas collide and opportunities ignite. Cities supercharge the efforts of people and businesses. Urban centers that take up less than 1 percent of Earth's entire surface generated half of all economic growth in the past couple of decades.

Seventh, **trade** brought about shared prosperity. The world has become an intricate, interconnected web of products, services, financial capital, people, and ideas flowing from one corner of the globe to another. Trade is hardly new, with evidence of beads made from seashells having been traded as early as 80,000 BC.[4] But in the past century, it exploded. Global exports of goods and services as a share of GDP have tripled from 10 to 30 percent over the past century. This rise was by no means linear: The ratio halved during World War II before rebounding in the decades that followed.

The eighth and final part of the machine was **markets**, which enabled us to cooperate at scale. The unsung hero, within which most cooperation happens, is the firm. It is businesses pursuing profit, growth, and survival in a competitive landscape that power the machine. Firms interact in the often-maligned market. The market mechanism is the invisible hand driving the progress machine forward, the collective result of millions of individual decisions by buyers, sellers, and investors. Forward momentum is solid when the market works relatively freely. Firms, in turn, intersect with institutions responsible for formal and informal rules, legal systems, and international agreements. Together, firms and institutions are the organizing units in which people worked, honed their skills, invested, invented, energized, urbanized, and connected through trade and more.

* * *

Over the past century, these eight parts of the machine interlocked to produce the considerable power that propelled remarkable human progress. In the rest of Part II, we explore each of them.

.

CHAPTER 5

WORKERS: FROM FARM TO FUTURE

"It was not by gold or by silver, but by labour, that all the wealth of the world was originally purchased."

ADAM SMITH

———

The world now has four times as many people, but nine times as many nonfarm workers, as a century ago.

SHERLYN CHEN, ONE OF THE COAUTHORS of this book, comes from Singapore, well known these days for being one of the richest countries in the world. It is a center of innovation and technology, an advanced manufacturing powerhouse, and a global financial hub.[5] The fortunes of Sherlyn's family, like those of many others, have been transformed by the game-changing role that people and their skills played in the progress of the past 100 years.

Her grandparents were born in the 1920s in Fujian, a southern province of China. They worked on farms with their parents from an early age. When they were teenagers, they migrated with their families to Singapore in search of a better life. There, Sherlyn's maternal grandfather worked as a dockhand, unloading sacks of rice and sugar from boats that docked along the Singapore River and reloading them with rubber and pineapples. Her maternal grandmother steamed tapioca cakes to sell to students and mended school uniforms for the neighbors' kids, a stalwart of the informal economy like many women in those days.

A generation later, Sherlyn's mother was one of eight children—her father was one of six—part of the postwar baby boom. Unlike the previous generation, all 14 children in the two families survived to adulthood. As women in the workforce were becoming much more commonplace in the '60s, Sherlyn's mother entered formal employment, assembling board games in a factory before shifting to the shipping industry, a linchpin of Singapore's export-driven growth. When she gave birth to Sherlyn, her third child, she quit her job to become a homemaker.

In the present day, the vast majority of Sherlyn's Singaporean peers, men and women alike, work in services, ranging from finance to healthcare to professional services. Most women continue to work after having children, although they bear far fewer than their grandparents did. Sherlyn has two children (a son and a daughter), one more child than the average Singaporean in 2024. Farming seems a distant memory, with less than 0.1 percent of the labor force in this urban city-state engaged in agriculture.[6]

While some details of this narrative are unique to Singapore given its status as a tiny city-state at the crossroads of global trade, the general contours are common to most developed economies. The population boomed after the war (although growth has slowed more recently), people increasingly work in industry or services rather than on farms, and women and men alike participate in the economy in myriad occupations.

Over the course of 100 years, the world's population quadrupled from two billion to eight billion, as did the global labor force, which grew from 900 million to 3.5 billion. More importantly, the number of nonfarm workers, the number of people working toward objectives beyond just keeping the rest of the population fed, surged nine times, from 300 million to 2.7 billion. In other words, the number of workers in the industrial

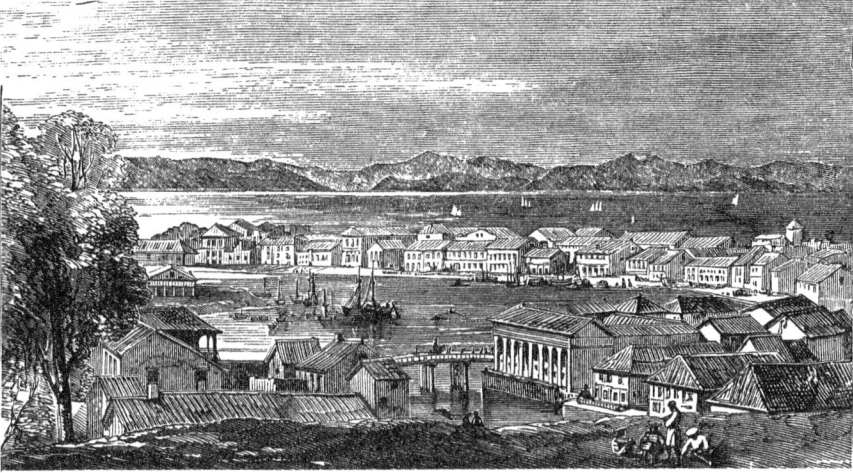

Engraved illustration of Singapore.

Shipping containers and container cranes at Keppel Harbour, Singapore.

economy grew at more than double the rate of the population.[7]

Where did all these new workers come from? In three words: fertility, farms, and females. Fertility patterns that gave rise to a demographic dividend in the form of a larger share of working-age individuals accounted for about 30 percent of the growth in nonfarm workers. The greatest economic migration, the movement off farms, was the biggest driver, accounting for 45 percent. The remaining 25 percent came from a different revolution: a huge influx of women into the workforce as societies' views on women learning and working shifted.[8]

Fertility patterns delivered a demographic dividend

For much of the past century, families grew and the world's population growth rate accelerated. The global population quadrupled, from two billion people in 1925 to more than eight billion today. To put this into perspective, from 1825 to 1925, the number of people living on the planet roughly doubled from one billion to two billion. And how did we get to that milestone of the first billion? It took humanity some 300,000 years, from the very dawn of Homo sapiens to 1800.[9]

What accounts for this acceleration in population growth? Three indicators give us a large part of the answer: declines in infant and maternal mortality rates, and a very substantial increase in life expectancy (see Part I for statistics). These big wins reflect a revolution in healthcare, technology, and agriculture, through vaccines, antibiotics, clean water, sanitation, high-yield crops, and modern farming techniques. As fertility rates remained high globally through to about 1970, this converged into unusual levels of population growth, a trend we come back to because today, fertility rates are the lowest they have been in history.[10]

Medical breakthroughs transformed human survival, dramatically reducing deaths and enabling population growth. Penicillin launched the era of antibiotics. By the 1950s, global vaccination campaigns starting with smallpox and expanding to polio, measles, and diphtheria cut childhood mortality by 90 percent in many regions. The smallpox vaccine alone eradicated a disease that killed 300 million in the 20th century. Maternal mortality plummeted as antiseptic techniques, improved surgical practices, and prenatal care became widespread; in advanced economies, maternal deaths dropped from 700 per 100,000 live births in 1925 to fewer than ten by 2025. Clean water and sanitation, driven by infrastructure investments, curbed waterborne diseases like cholera, saving millions, particularly in urbanizing areas. Medical imaging, from X-rays to MRIs, and advancements like insulin for diabetes and cardiovascular treatments further extended lives. These healthcare revolutions created a larger, healthier population, setting the stage for economic progress.[11]

This larger population could have faced starvation, as Thomas Malthus warned in 1798. He argued that population growth would outpace food production, leading to inevitable famines. In 1968, Paul Ehrlich's *The Population Bomb* echoed this assertion, claiming, "The battle to feed all of humanity is over. In the 1970s hundreds of millions of people will starve to death in spite of any crash programs embarked upon now." These predictions proved wrong. Between 1961 and 2020, while the global population increased 2.5 times, food production surged 3.7 times, through advances we explore in chapter 9.[12]

Thanks to better medicine and more food, fewer people died young. Birth rates were consistently high, at least until the latter part of the 20th century, when family planning and broadening access to education began to lower fertility rates. In 1925, families had between four and eight children. For many families, having more children was an emotional and economic form of insurance. Since its peak at 5.3 live births per woman in 1963, the global fertility rate has steadily declined to the current average of 2.3 per woman. That figure is very close to the replacement rate of 2.1: the number of children needed to replace their parents. In fact, today, two-thirds of us live in countries where the total fertility rate is below replacement. The average family size is now 3.5 people, meaning that most families have just one or two children, if they have any at all.[13]

This pattern of a period of high fertility rates followed by a decline to lower levels has resulted in a once-in-a-lifetime boost to income per person, through what is known as a demographic dividend. As the many children of the postwar generation entered the workforce and then had fewer children, the proportion of the working-age population supporting a smaller share of dependents both young and old increased. There are no free lunches in economics, but this may be the closest thing to one.

Due to variations in fertility and mortality trends across the world, we have observed this demographic dividend effect playing out in three distinct waves (Exhibit 5). The first wave, including advanced economies and China, grew steadily through 2010, when it peaked. These economies have now been in the demographic drag zone for about 15 years. The second wave, with the other emerging economies except Sub-Saharan Africa, is still gathering momentum and will peak soon, in the 2030s. Sub-Saharan Africa's working-age population, the third wave, will peak well into the second half of the century.[14]

EXHIBIT 5

Population aged 15–64 years
Share of total population, %

First wave	Second wave	Third wave
• Advanced Asia	• Emerging Asia	• Sub-Saharan Africa
• Central and Eastern Europe	• India	
• Greater China	• Latin America and the Caribbean	
• North America	• Middle East and North Africa	
• Western Europe		

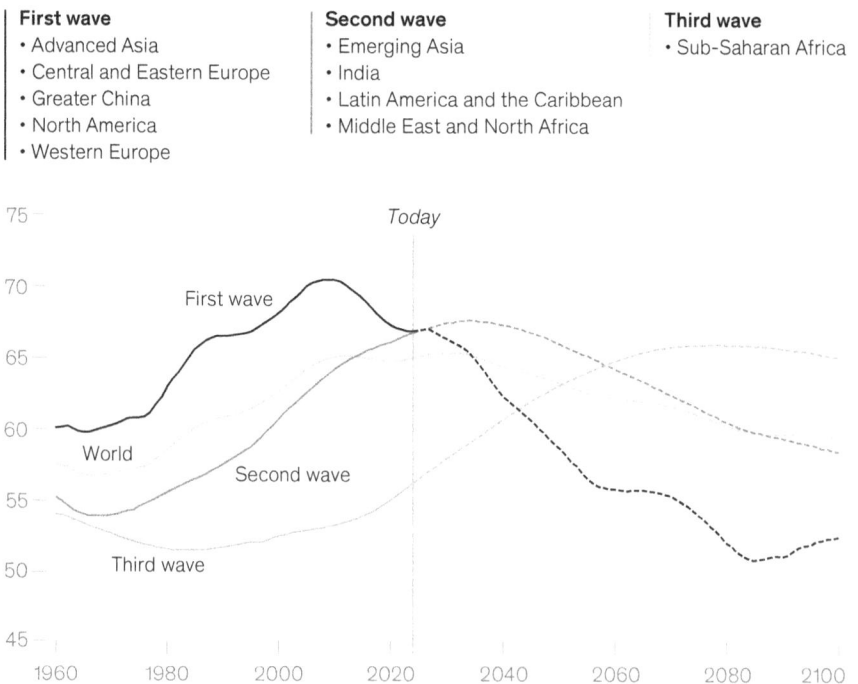

Source: UN Population Division, *World population prospects 2024*; McKinsey Global Institute analysis

Farmers became industry and service workers

As remarkable as the demographic dividend was, simply growing populations—even working-age populations—would not lead to a material improvement in income per person. Each worker had to become much more productive. The shift from agricultural to nonagricultural work is one of the most significant economic transformations in history. In 1925, the vast majority of people in the world lived in rural areas, and most of them worked in agriculture. Back then, 60 to 70 percent of all employment was in agriculture, with significant variations among early industrializing economies such as the United Kingdom, the United States, and Germany.[15] The rest of the world was still largely preoccupied with feeding their populations, with the vast majority of jobs in farming. By 2023, this ratio had flipped; only 26 percent of the global labor force remains in agriculture. Only about 1 to 2 percent of workers in the United Kingdom, United States, and Germany remain on farms, with other workers having long migrated to manufacturing, construction, transport, mining, and service industries, among others.[16]

The makeup of entire economies utterly changed (Exhibit 6). There were many interrelated reasons for this. The fact that the migration began in earnest during the Industrial Revolution in Europe and North America suggests that the promise of higher-paid work in the new factories was a powerful magnet drawing people away from the land. Of course, those factories tended to be in cities: The migration off the farm was not only out of agriculture but also from the countryside to cities. Economists call this a "pull" factor.

In the United States, for example, people were attracted to cities like Chicago, Detroit, and New York to find work in the automobile, steel, and textiles industries. Millions of former farm workers and their families relocated, and between 1925 and today, the share of urban population rose from about 50 to 80 percent.[17]

Of course, nations still needed to be fed, but that is where what economists call a "push" factor comes in. The Industrial Revolution affected farms, too, in the form of tractors, combine harvesters, and chemical fertilizers. As farms grew more productive, they no longer required the many hands once needed for heavy agricultural labor, liberating people to pursue new opportunities in the cities.[18]

EXHIBIT 6

Share of total employment by sector in the United States
Distribution, %

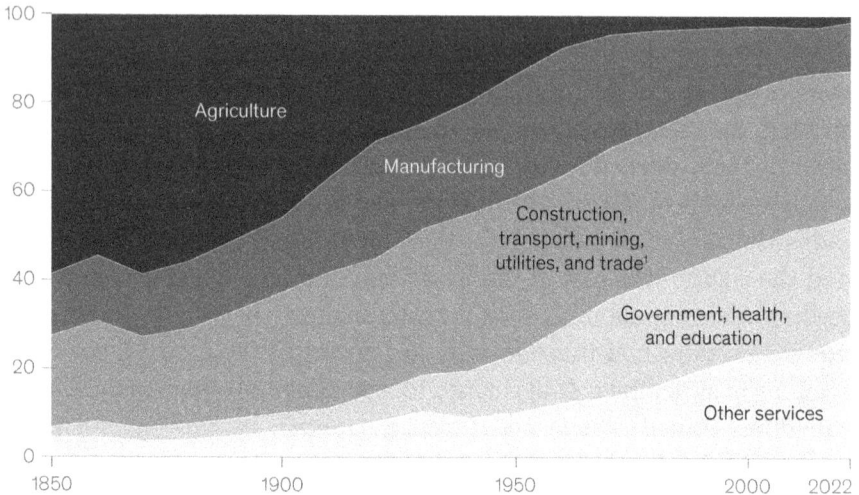

This category includes: construction, transportation, mining, utilities, trade (retail and wholesale), business and repair services, telecommunications, and professional services.
Source: Integrated Public Use Microdata Series USA, 2017; US Bureau of Labor Statistics, "Employment"; McKinsey Global Institute analysis

Mechanization meant that farms became fewer and bigger. In the United States, there were nearly seven million farms in 1925. By 2024, there were fewer than two million, and on average they were triple the size of the ones in 1925. And they produced a great deal more with many fewer workers. The output of US farms tripled between the end of World War II and today even as they depopulated.[19]

Higher agricultural productivity not only liberated workers to pursue other jobs; it also boosted their wages, which generated new consumption needs—new goods and services—that they could now afford, driving the creation of their own jobs. Simply put, jobs in the production of home appliances and manicures were not plentiful when citizens' incomes were not high enough to purchase home appliances and manicures. Even today, in a country like India that is still in the middle of this transition, the productivity of a farm worker is about one-quarter that of a nonfarm worker. Industrialization sets off a powerful virtuous cycle of higher-productivity jobs, in turn driving demand for more of them. India's productivity more than quadrupled between 1990 and 2022, and a lot of that came from people moving off farms.[20]

Nowhere has this farm-to-factory migration been larger or more transformative than in China. It alone contributed almost 600 million more people to the global workforce over the past century, of which 450 million were nonfarm workers. A lot of this occurred in the second half of the century, propelled by rapid population growth, urbanization, and industrialization. In just 45 years since 1980, some 400 million people moved to live and work in cities like Shenzhen and Shanghai, whose industries had a voracious appetite for people in factories and construction sites. It paid much better than the farm. In the 1990s, a job in an urban factory paid as much as three times more than being an agricultural worker even as agricultural wages also increased with productivity gains.[21] China's entry into the global industrial base resulted in a massive positive supply shock, with the effects rippling throughout the world. As it provided huge volumes of relatively low-cost labor manufacturing all sorts of goods, global prices for products such as electronics fell by 45 to 90 percent between 1997 and 2010, while labor markets as far-flung as the United States and Bangladesh faced competition, and sometimes disruption.[22]

This part of the progress machine has some life in it yet. In Sub-Saharan Africa, nearly 50 percent of the workforce remains in agriculture, but the great migration to cities and to industry and service jobs is well underway. In Nigeria, for instance, agricultural employment dropped from 70 percent in 1960 to 34 percent in 2023. In India, nearly half of all workers still toil on thousands of small, inefficient farms. This share is expected to plunge from 46 percent in 2022 to 29 percent in 2050, and those people will be going into jobs where they can be much more productive.[23]

Female participation added to the workforce

The third part of this story is about women. When we mentioned the working-age population above, we referred to the number of people that we generally accept *can* work given their age. But how many *do* in fact work is what really matters, and many more women did. Women's labor force participation doubled globally, from about 25 percent a century ago to about 49 percent today. It is worth noting that over the same period, men's labor force participation fell, in large part due to more years spent in schooling and the phasing out of child labor in most parts of the world, as well as more years spent in retirement (see Exhibit 7 for the US trend).[24]

In the 1920s, society tended to expect women to stay at home and run their households. Indeed, married women were often barred from working in some professions, including, in many school districts in the United Kingdom and the United States, teaching. In advanced economies, by the 1930s and 1940s, more women worked outside the home, especially when men going to fight in World War II left gaps that women filled. They not only kept the home fires burning but kept factories and farming alive. Think Rosie the Riveter and the Land Girls. Although

EXHIBIT 7

United States labor force participation by sex
Share of male and female populations aged 16+, %

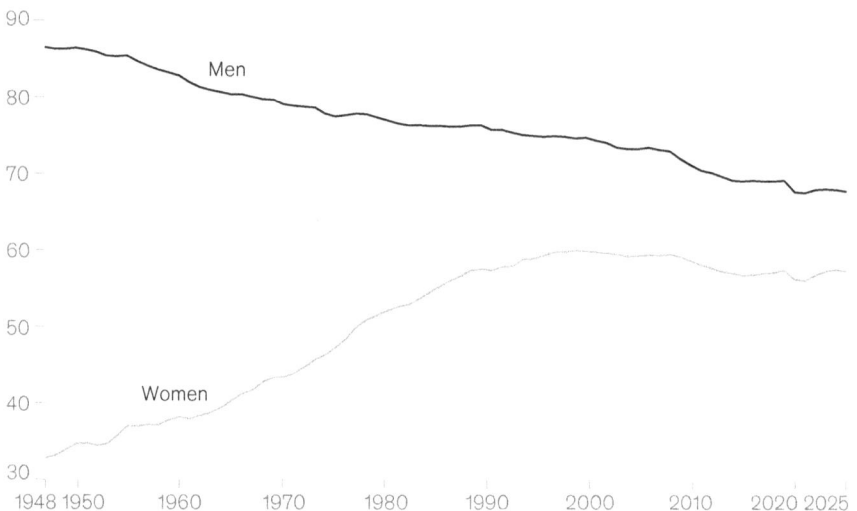

Source: US Bureau of Labor Statistics, Labor Force Statistics from the Current Population Survey; 2025 data based on Jan–June 2025 average rate; McKinsey Global Institute analysis

many of these women were supplanted when men came back from war, in the 1950s and 1960s, their participation grew steadily. Peak growth in women working was in the 1970s and 1980s, when feminists pushed for workplace equality; contraception became more widely available, enabling women to control the number of children they had and when; women's access to education spread; and the stigma of married women and mothers working waned. Technological change was key. The advent of electricity, indoor plumbing, and household appliances gave women more time to work for pay.[25]

This wave of working women added trillions of dollars to global GDP and boosted income per person in most countries. Gradually over time, women's wages have narrowed the gap with those of men and are near parity in developed economies. But there is still vast potential for more women to work for pay and for their pay to improve. The rate of women's participation in the labor force is 53 percent among OECD members—reasonably close, but still far from men's at 69 percent. Madagascar had the highest female participation in the world at about 83 percent in 2024, reflecting economic necessity in a low-income economy where agriculture dominates more than gender-inclusive policies. But in India, as we have seen in Part I, only about 30 percent of women participate in the labor force, largely reflecting cultural norms. This is a massive source of untapped potential, and therefore a great opportunity for countries to keep growing their labor forces.[26]

Japan shows both the power and the limits of this structural dividend. Between 2000 and 2023, its working-age population fell by about 12 million, but its labor force did not shrink, instead edging up from 68 million to 69 million. The difference came from women. Prime-age female participation surged from 67 to 83 percent in that period. In recent years, older workers have become the main source of growth. The number of Japanese aged 65 and over in the labor force has more than doubled since 2000. But with female participation near its ceiling and demographic aging accelerating, the cushion that has so far sustained Japan's workforce is wearing thin. Unless productivity rises or new sources of labor are found, the labor force will eventually bend to demographic drag.[27]

✲ ✲ ✲

Many more workers, and in particular nonfarm workers, have delivered more growth and rising prosperity for all. Conducive fertility and mortality rates laid the foundation by growing populations, people moved off the farm and became more productive, and women augmented this effect when they came out of the home and into the market. Sheer numbers alone were enough to propel the progress machine, but their impact was all the more powerful because all these people became more educated and more skilled. This is what we discuss next.

CHAPTER 6

SKILLS: MOBILIZING MINDS

"An investment in knowledge pays the best interest."

BENJAMIN FRANKLIN

———

People have gone from using brawn-power to brainpower in huge skills ecosystems.

GOING HAND IN GLOVE with the social and economic transformations detailed in the previous chapter was an evolution in what we term "human capital": the knowledge, skills, abilities, and attributes individuals have that contribute to their productivity and economic value creation. In simple terms, the type of work they can do and how effectively they do it. To illustrate this, we return to the story of Sherlyn's family.

Having started life in rural poverty in Fujian, China, none of her grandparents could read or write. After moving to Singapore, her maternal grandfather's options were limited, and the nature of his work was entirely manual, relying on his physical strength to move heavy goods. Similarly, her maternal grandmother's work relied on her domestic cooking skills and manual dexterity in sewing.

A generation later, Sherlyn's mother went to school, a beneficiary of the postindependence reforms by the Singapore government that made universal primary education a national priority. To absorb the postwar baby boom and raise literacy, the government was building dozens of new schools annually, and primary school enrollment skyrocketed from about 50 percent in the early 1950s to more than 90 percent by the late 1960s.[28] Sherlyn's mother was one of the lucky ones who went on to obtain a secondary education. Only about one in three of her cohort did so, and indeed her elder siblings did not have that opportunity.

After secondary school, she had to work to help support the family. Armed with the superpower of literacy and a broader academic foundation, she was able to work in manufacturing, starting on the factory floor producing games like Monopoly and Cluedo, and over time working up to managerial roles. Later on, she moved to a sales and marketing role in the shipping industry, selling container storage and freight cargo space. After completing a bookkeeping course, she was able to manage the accounts for the business, drawing up ledgers—with pen and paper!

By Sherlyn's time, English was well established as the primary medium of instruction in schools alongside a bilingual policy to ensure that the multicultural population kept in touch with its roots. Primary and secondary education had become top-notch by global standards, preparing Sherlyn and her siblings to attend leading universities in Singapore, the United Kingdom, and the United States. They all entered the knowledge economy upon graduation as researchers or consultants.

By the time Sherlyn's children were born, in 2019 and 2021, the average Singaporean adult had 13 years of education, and more than one-third held a university degree. Two of Singapore's six universities rank in the global top 20, and secondary students consistently top the Programme for International Student Assessment (PISA) scores. At the same time, Singapore has focused on lifelong learning and the continuous raising of skills through formal programs for adults, such as SkillsFuture.[29]

In a mere three generations, Singapore's income per person soared from $5,000 to $128,000, second only to Luxembourg's when adjusted

Woman in a library, Singapore.

for purchasing-power parity. While a confluence of factors delivered this progress, Singapore's consistent investment in the development of its only natural resource—people—has paid off. Its success is a testament to the power of mass education and the development of a highly skilled workforce employed in the most productive sectors. Today, it is primarily a service-oriented economy, with 86 percent of the workforce employed in the services sector.[30]

Work has evolved dramatically since 1925 and has shifted the demand for skills from agricultural and manual to cognitive and creative, the type of skills that serve the knowledge economy. The first driver of this shift was education, from basic literacy and numeracy to more advanced skills. These enabled people to do more complex and, crucially, more productive jobs. Firms, too, had an unsung role. About half of the value of human capital came from on-the-job learning as firms consolidated knowledge and became the places where individuals could collaborate and build on the collective.[31]

Economies changed, skills adapted

Economies change, and we change with them. Over the past 100 years, many parts of the world have followed a similar economic development trajectory. At each transition, machines took over certain tasks, such as plowing, weaving, and number-crunching, and people shifted toward tasks that required oversight, judgment, and coordination. The skills required at each stage of this journey could not be more different.

Globally, the median worker in 1925 worked on the farm; today the median worker is engaged in services, with the world only recently having reached the 50 percent threshold. In the United States, where the agricultural share of work had already declined, the median worker of 1925 was engaged in manual labor outside agriculture. Today, though, the largest share of workers is knowledge workers performing nonroutine cognitive work. This type of work requires abstract thinking, problem-solving, and communication skills on the back of extensive education and training. Knowledge-related work has more than doubled, while manual

EXHIBIT 8

Change in nature of labor between 1920 and 2024
Breakdown of labor in the US by type, %

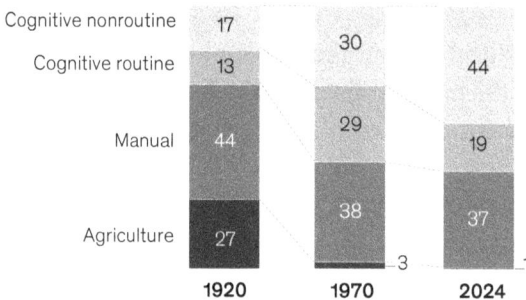

Note: Cognitive nonroutine workers include managers, officials, and proprietors; professional, technical, and kindred workers; and sales workers. Cognitive routine workers include service workers (excluding private household workers) and clerical and kindred workers. Manual workers include craftsmen, foremen, and kindred workers; operatives and kindred workers; laborers, except farm and mine; and private household workers. Agricultural workers include farmers and farm managers, farm laborers, and foremen.
Source: US Census Bureau, *Historical statistics of the United States, colonial times to 1970*, 1975, and 2024 Current Population Survey; McKinsey Global Institute analysis

work, including agriculture, halved (Exhibit 8).[32]

The agricultural workers of 100 years ago toiled on the farm, aided by varying degrees of mechanization depending on the country. A smaller share of manual workers were in building construction. As the number of factory jobs increased, work remained essentially manual but required a different set of skills and ways of working. Having the literacy to understand instruction manuals and more precise hand-eye coordination to operate machinery safely became more important.

A larger transformation in skills happened as economies shifted toward services and knowledge. Manual skills faded as a requirement. Creative, interpersonal, technological, and managerial skills came to the fore. Collaboration has long been a mainstay of human activity, whether on the farm or the factory floor, but service workers arguably interact with a wider range of people in a more formalized, often corporate setting. This requires a different kind of savvy. So-called soft skills.

As the digital age dawned, everyone needed to learn and adapt to new technologies. Farmers use mobile apps for real-time data on weather and soil health. Servers use tablets to take restaurant orders. A warehouse worker may well use customer relationship management software. And with the rise of generative AI, cohorts of doctors, lawyers, and software engineers are learning to incorporate these new tools into their workflows to enhance their capabilities. Beyond technology, the "brain economy," an economic paradigm that recognizes cognitive, emotional, and social capabilities as critical for growth, is gaining preeminence.[33]

Workers will need to keep evolving as the economy changes. Many people will need to upgrade their skill sets. Overall, by 2030, up to 605 million workers, including construction laborers, food servers, and pharmacy technicians, may need to pivot to new roles or reskill substantially to stay employable. In China alone, as many as 220 million workers, or about 30 percent of the workforce, may need to change occupations.[34]

And they need to change fast. Digitization and automation are estimated to have slashed the half-life of skills to a mere five years, down from ten to 15 years previously. This means that skills learned today will be only half as valuable in a mere five years or less.[35]

Human capital is the bedrock of wealth and prosperity. This kind of capital accounts for about two-thirds of any individual's total wealth. We accumulate this capital at school, and increasingly in the university of life and work, given the rapid pace of the evolution of work. It is a lifelong investment in our capabilities, and over the past 100 years, that investment has grown. The return on that investment has risen, too, as each wave of technology has introduced new ladders for people to climb.[36]

Education was the foundation

Few forces have reshaped human opportunity over the past century as profoundly as education, expanding the range of vocations open to us. Once the preserve of elites, schooling has become a global engine of individual potential, social mobility, and economic and scientific progress. From crowded city classrooms to remote village schools, learning opened doors that had been locked for centuries. The transformation of education has touched every region of the world. It goes beyond today's emerging economies: In 1920, literacy rates stood at 73 percent in Italy and 56 percent in Spain. Today, both countries have achieved universal literacy. But that was just the beginning. As economies evolved, skills like critical thinking, problem-solving, and adaptability became as vital as knowing how to read and write. That's why, since 2012, the OECD's standardized PISA assessment for schoolchildren has gone beyond testing reading, math, and science to include measures of students' ability to solve unfamiliar problems and think flexibly—skills closely tied to workplace success.[37]

Investing in education equips people with the knowledge and abilities they need to boost their personal productivity, increase their earnings, and progress. As more people were able to go to school, a world of opportunity opened up, and billions were able to escape poverty by working. The link between education and economic growth is well proven. Indeed, some economists attribute recent slowdowns in growth to the fact that the "low-hanging fruit" of mass schooling in advanced economies has already been picked.[38]

At the heart of the education revolution of the past 100 years was an expansion of access that turned schooling from a privilege into an accessible good. Governments poured resources into schools and teachers, boosting spending dramatically. In 1915, Norway and the United Kingdom, to take two examples, allocated just 1.4 percent and 1.1

percent of GDP, respectively, to education. By 2023, that had risen to 4 percent and almost 5 percent. And some lower-income economies even matched advanced ones. Rwanda has been spending the same share of GDP as the United Kingdom. Demand for schooling increased to match this supply as farmers became more productive, freeing up their children to be educated. Overall, the time children around the world spent at school on average quadrupled from less than two years in 1925 to nearly nine today. In Germany, people on average spend 14 years at school; in Africa, six.[39]

And the education bonanza was not confined to school. Tertiary education expanded enormously, too. In Spain, for example, almost nobody went to university in 1925; today, more than half of young adults enroll, and more women than men.[40]

Advanced knowledge has been democratized, and, over time, the impact on people and economies from expanded access was amplified by improvements in teaching techniques, quality management systems, and global knowledge sharing. Countries reformed teaching methods and accountability systems, often guided by international benchmarks and learning from one another. At the same time, knowledge transfer and technology helped spread effective solutions. Kenya's Tusome program reached every primary school with structured support textbooks, lesson plans, and teacher coaching, while tools like solar-powered tablets and radio lessons bridged gaps in remote or underresourced classrooms in Sierra Leone and Malawi.[41]

Progress is far from complete. While advanced economies made extraordinary progress in education over the past century, recent returns on education may be diminishing. Increased funding has failed to improve outcomes. Indeed, PISA scores have been stagnating or falling. According to the OECD, between 2018 and 2022, advanced economies experienced a record 15-point drop in math scores, and reading scores declined by ten points. Science scores were flat. Emerging economies have made huge strides, but in many places, there is a long way to go. One billion children remain in "learning poverty," most of them in poorer countries, unable to read a simple sentence even by the end of elementary school. There is still work to do to ensure that the quality of education continues to improve and that nobody is left behind.[42]

Firms were skills factories

Formal education systems are a part of our lifelong journey to build our capabilities. The other half of what we learn, and the value we create for society, comes from working—from experience.

Across a typical working life, skills developed and used on the job contribute about half of an individual's total human capital, according to our research, *Human capital at work: The value of experience.* In countries like Germany, the United Kingdom, and the United States, that share is about 40 percent. In places where people spend fewer years in school, such as India, it rises to 58 percent. Sometimes, this experience has more impact than education in boosting incomes. In the United States, 28 percent of high school graduates earn more than the median associate degree holder, and 37 percent of associate degree holders outearn the median bachelor's graduate over a lifetime. Schooling matters, but it doesn't always predict who will go furthest.[43]

Companies not only produce goods and services but are platforms for human development. Formally, this happens through training programs. Across the OECD, 40 percent of adults participate in job-related learning each year. In the United States alone, companies spend more than $100 billion annually on training, which is roughly 1 percent of labor costs. Public–private partnerships can be a particularly effective mechanism for developing human capital; Germany's dual apprenticeship system that combines classroom instruction with firm-based training is a well-known example.[44]

But the real magic often lies beyond formal training programs. Firms are vast repositories of technical and organizational know-how, accumulated over decades through processes, patents, data systems, and shared expertise. The interactions of workers with these knowledge systems, through daily collaboration, problem-solving, and immersion in specialized workflows, lead to the greatest improvement in human capital. The role that firms play in augmenting human capital is less through provision of structured training and more through providing a low-friction environment for knowledge to be pooled, built upon, and shared across dense networks.

As consultants who often interact with many large companies, we are often amazed at how this collective knowledge works. In a major modern retailer, bank, or telecommunications company, no one person truly understands how the entire company works. But the shelves are stocked, the loans are written, and the calls connect, day in and day out. With each person bringing their skills, following their routines, and responding to their local situations, the collective whole comes together. These are amazing nexuses of shared skills and cooperation, somehow a melded hive mind that can produce incredible complexity.

The challenge ahead is clear. As work changes, and especially as the pace of change accelerates, we need to make sure every worker can keep learning and keep up. Sherlyn's grandparents worked with their hands. None could read or write. Today, Sherlyn's tools are digital dashboards and AI models. Her children will need to master technologies that haven't even been invented yet. The task is to prepare them—and everyone else—for that future.

❀ ❀ ❀

More people, more of whom are educated and learning the skills they need to thrive in the workforce—and in life—contribute to the march of progress. This is the effect of boosting human capital. But workers and every other aspect of economic activity need the support of another form of capital: investment. That's the part of the progress machine we turn to next.

CHAPTER 7

INVESTMENT: BUILDING CAPITAL

"One generation plants the trees.
Another enjoys the shade."

CHINESE PROVERB

—

We gave the average worker nine times more capital—from infrastructure to technology—to boost productivity.

ANOTHER COAUTHOR, JAN MISCHKE, is originally from Germany. In 1925, his grandparents Maria and Hubert were teachers in higher education. Before he died in World War II, Hubert's main tool was chalk. As was common in those times, when Maria married him, she became a housewife: Her tools were in the kitchen. It was a dreadful time for their country. Germany's infrastructure and economy were decimated by the war. Many roads were now unpaved and railways damaged. Indeed, Jan's grandparents' house

Women in a marketplace in old Nuremberg.

was bombed, and Maria rebuilt it largely with her own hands. Productivity was low, testament to a dearth of capital.[45] But after 1945, with help from Marshall Plan aid, Germany started investing heavily. This laid the foundations of its postwar economic miracle, its *Wirtschaftswunder*.

Over the past 100 years, Germany's capital stock per hour worked has surged 12-fold. In plain words, the average German worker today has 12 times more buildings, roads, machines, and software at his or her disposal than a 1925 counterpart.[46] German cities were rebuilt and are now gleaming, modern, and safe. Workers have been supercharged. In 1925, an automotive worker in the Daimler factory in Stuttgart bolted car parts to a Mercedes frame by hand, his output meager. By 2025, his descendant might program robots to do the manual work for her in Mercedes-Benz's Sindelfingen plant. The total real, or nonfinancial, capital stock in Germany in 2024 reached a staggering €16 trillion (without the value of land), and the most productive parts (infrastructure, equipment, and intangibles) accounted for as much as €4.3 trillion, or more than €90,000 per worker.[47]

Jogging in Berlin's government district.

There is more to capital than just physical stuff. Jan's grandfather used his knowledge and brainpower to educate the next generation. His mother became a doctor. Today, we call this type of capital "intangible," and in our modern economy the power of the brain rather than muscle is increasingly the arbiter of success and failure. Jan's grandfather had a blackboard and a bookshelf in his classroom; today, Jan has access to an array of tools and a global communications network that can reach an audience perhaps one million times larger than his grandpa could reach. His mother would have had only her stethoscope to monitor vital signs. Today, his brother operates a $10 million cardiac catheter lab that helps extend the lives of many patients. The work that Jan and his brother do is enormously augmented by the capital investment that Germany, and German firms, have made.

Globally, investment has also increased rapidly. On average, compared with 100 years ago, the amount of capital available per worker has jumped ninefold in countries for which we have long-term data.[48] The correlation between income per person and capital per worker is as close to perfect as

EXHIBIT 9

Income per person and capital stock per hour worked

1925 ○——● 2015

Income per person, $

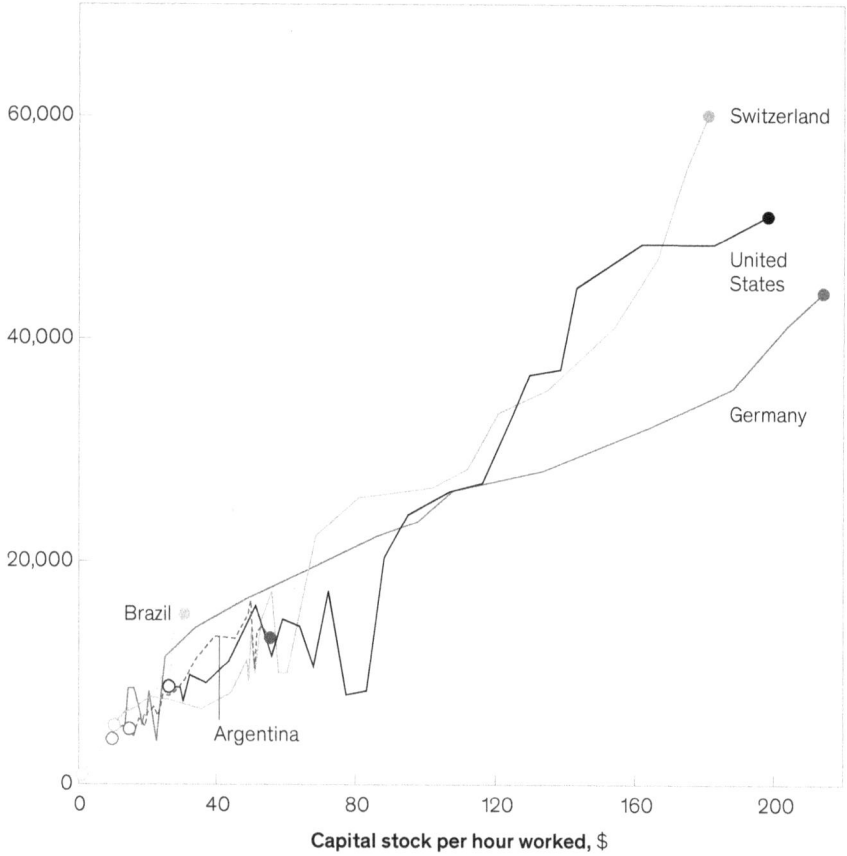

Note: Income per person in constant 2011 international dollars; capital stock per hour worked in constant 2010 international dollars.
Source: Income data from Maddison Project Database 2023; capital intensity data from Bergeaud, Cette, and Lecat, 2016, processed by Our World in Data; McKinsey Global Institute analysis

a correlation can get (Exhibit 9).

That said, some countries have surged ahead while others lag. High-income countries like Germany, Switzerland, and the United States are capital rich, averaging about $180 to $220 in capital stock per hour worked. Conversely, Argentina began on a par with Germany but grew its capital only threefold over the past century. It now lags far behind, at about $50 per hour worked, limiting its workers' productivity.

Capital grows by investing, and when we use capital in our jobs, we get more done and become more prosperous. Germans do not produce more goods and services per hour worked than Argentines because they "work harder." They may or may not. The main difference is that Germans' work is more effective because more capital is available to them.

Investing in infrastructure, equipment, and intangibles drives productivity. Emerging economies can achieve catch-up growth by investing in existing technologies. Financial markets mobilize and channel resources to where investments can generate productivity and returns. And finally, firms organize the people and the money that make the investments and are the storehouses of almost all the physical capital. In fact, capital intensity is one of the main reasons for the existence of very large firms.

Capital investment supercharged workers

In chapters 5 and 6, we described how more labor and smarter labor have propelled economic growth. But labor alone isn't enough. We supercharge ourselves with capital.

With more tools at our disposal, we can do more, better, and faster. Indeed, capital investment fueled 70 to 80 percent of productivity gains over the past 25 years in both advanced and emerging economies.[49] Economists often emphasize innovation, and that matters, of course. It is what first created the machines, engines, robots, and AI that make us so much more productive (see the next chapter for more). But all ideas need to emerge from the brain and get deployed into the real world, and that is what capital investment does. Capital embeds knowledge and technology. The two go hand in hand.

Let's examine this through the automotive industry, born in Stuttgart in the 19th century. It shifted to the United States with the likes of Ford by 1925 and is now dominated by China, which produces three times as many vehicles as the United States, especially dominating EV production.[50]

Capital investment played a large role in this, with infrastructure, equipment, and intangibles each flowing through to productivity in their own ways.

First, infrastructure connects. In 1925, a logistics clerk in Detroit scribbled orders for car parts in a ledger and relied on telegrams to contact foreign suppliers. Cargo shipping and handling relied on hundreds of dock workers and basic cranes. The infrastructure supporting the US automotive industry was sketchy, and supply chains rudimentary and often unreliable. Today, Chinese car makers use real-time digital tracking to leverage advanced communications infrastructure and the Internet of Things. Lead times have been slashed from months to days. Port infrastructure in Shanghai and Shenzhen now encompasses automated cranes, robotic cargo handlers, and AI-driven logistics, which enable them to handle hundreds of times more tonnage than in 1925.[51]

Second, equipment automates. Before 1913, factory workers built cars in a static position, requiring dozens of people and more than 12 hours per car. But then Ford introduced the moving assembly line, including investments in factory expansion, conveyor systems, and the power generation to move them. That reduced the time it took to produce one Model T to only 93 minutes. Fast-forward to 2025, and highly automated production lines churn out a new car every 40 seconds. China's BYD produced 4.3 million vehicles in its 30 factories in 2024.[52]

Third, intangibles amplify. In 1925, a Ford employee sketched Model T blueprints with pencils, his prototypes taking 12 weeks to develop with costly errors. In 2025, engineers use computer-aided design software and digital twins, or virtual models capable of simulating car performance. It is possible to test aerodynamics and other features, saving millions per model and halving development time.

Investment in intangibles is growing in importance. Over the past quarter century, the share of intangibles in total investment rose by about 30 percent in the United States and Europe. Firms that invest more in intangibles grow more and, it appears, have higher productivity. Why? A key reason is that they can scale quickly at almost no cost. Some argue that Britain's most famous innovation is not the radar or hovercrafts but the Harry Potter books, which offer both scale and synergies that create enormous value. The manuscript is written, millions of books are printed, the movies are made, and software creates animated versions. Value proliferates.[53]

Similar transformations appear across industries. Consider Taiwan's semiconductor manufacturing giant TSMC. Its workers are some of the most capitalized in the world, with $2.5 million per worker worth of cutting-edge extreme ultraviolet lithography machines, process control software, and extensive R&D for production technology. This makes its workers far more productive; TSMC generates about $1.4 million in revenue annually per employee.[54] This is a stunning example of human achievement and requires many investors to pool their resources to make it happen.

Emerging economies invested to catch up

Investment is crucial for all economies, but especially vital for emerging ones. They do not need to push the innovation frontier themselves; instead, they catch up by investing in technologies developed elsewhere.

Advanced economies from Germany to Switzerland to the United States need to keep pushing the boundaries of innovation to avoid stagnation, say by creating smarter robots for manufacturing. Countries not yet at the cutting edge can grow faster by investing in technologies they do not possess yet. Capital embeds the knowledge of the world in a tangible form accessible by millions. Purchasing capital does not just mean acquiring steel and concrete; it means acquiring the lessons of humankind packaged and delivered into a tool.

This is the main reason poorer economies are expected to—and often do—grow faster than richer ones. Many former emerging economies, such as Japan and South Korea, have successfully closed the gap. Others have been catching up at different speeds.

Some economies, including Bangladesh, China, India, Vietnam, and much of Central Europe, have been in the fast lane of productivity growth over the past quarter century (Exhibit 10). Investment was what put them into the fast lane. These economies channeled an astounding 20 to 40 percent of their GDP into capital investment that they used to build the

Productivity growth per employee and productivity level by region
Rolling five-year CAGR, 1997–2022, %

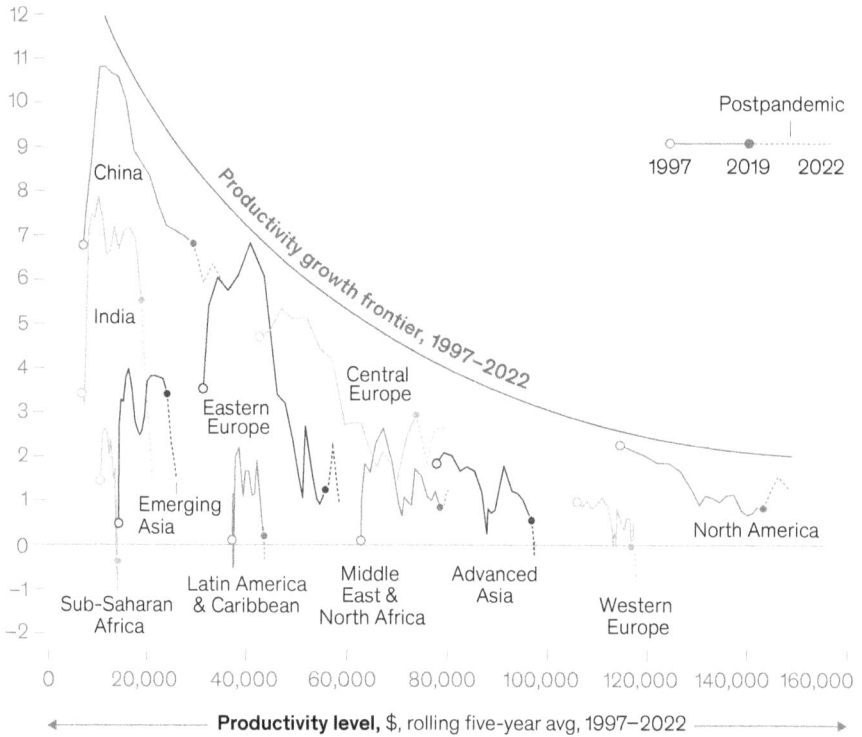

Note: N=242; weighted averages for 11 regions in 21 rolling five-year periods.
Source: The Conference Board's Total Economy Database, "Output, labor, and labor productivity"; McKinsey Global Institute analysis

cities and infrastructure that underpin successful urbanization, higher productivity in service sectors, and globally connected manufacturing. This is highly visible in China, which has been adding as much as 112,000 kilometers of road and 5,700 kilometers of new railway track every year, and one to two new coal plants every week. In 2018 and 2019 alone, China produced nearly as much cement (4.4 billion metric tons, henceforth tonnes) as the United States during the entire 20th century.[55]

In contrast, regions like Latin America and Sub-Saharan Africa have been stuck in the slow lane due to low investment and have witnessed their productivity growth slip further behind that of advanced economies. Only by investing more can they hope to switch lanes.[56]

Financial markets were the arteries of investment

Investment is critical, but how do we find the resources needed to make it? Financial markets, of course. Many people may dismiss banks and stock and bond markets as far too complicated and technical to devote any attention to them, or maybe downright boring. But financial markets turn our savings into the investments that build our collective future. Banks, stock markets, and debt markets are the arteries through which capital investment flows. All of these instruments rely on trust. Without confidence in promises repaid, investments cannot flow. Ultimately, it is about the most important belief of all: belief in the future.

Let's put this in terms of what we call the global balance sheet—a colossal ledger of all assets and liabilities in the world. By end of 2024, the world had $600 trillion or more than five times global GDP in assets, from machinery and equipment to infrastructure and intangibles to—two-thirds of the total—property and the land it has been built on. Against those were $580 trillion in financial liabilities, such as equity, bonds, and loans. Meanwhile, the financial sector was $530 trillion in size. That means for every dollar of financial liabilities, the financial sector, on average, intermediated 90 cents.[57] Economic growth and growth in finance are deeply intertwined (Exhibit 11).

It was largely in the era of markets, since 1989, that financial systems expanded and deepened enormously. Indeed, we named that era to reflect this. Since 2000, the global balance sheet has tripled, far outpacing real GDP growth. Expansion has introduced risks, too, including rising debt and asset-price inflation, which we discuss later in this book.[58]

Yet finance remains crucial. In 1925, banking was only for the elite, but today 76 percent of adults worldwide, and 94 percent in OECD economies, have bank accounts. Banks lent $49 trillion to households and $60 trillion to firms and institutions in 2023 alone, enabling larger investments and matching money—deposits to loans—efficiently to its best use.[59] Through credit creation, defined as the recycling of savings into loans into more savings and more loans, they amplify the economy's money supply.

Real GDP and total liabilities of nonfinancial corporations and households

Value in real local currency, 1950–2024, index (2024 = 100)

○ Each circle = economy's value for 1 year between 1950 and 2024

Real GDP

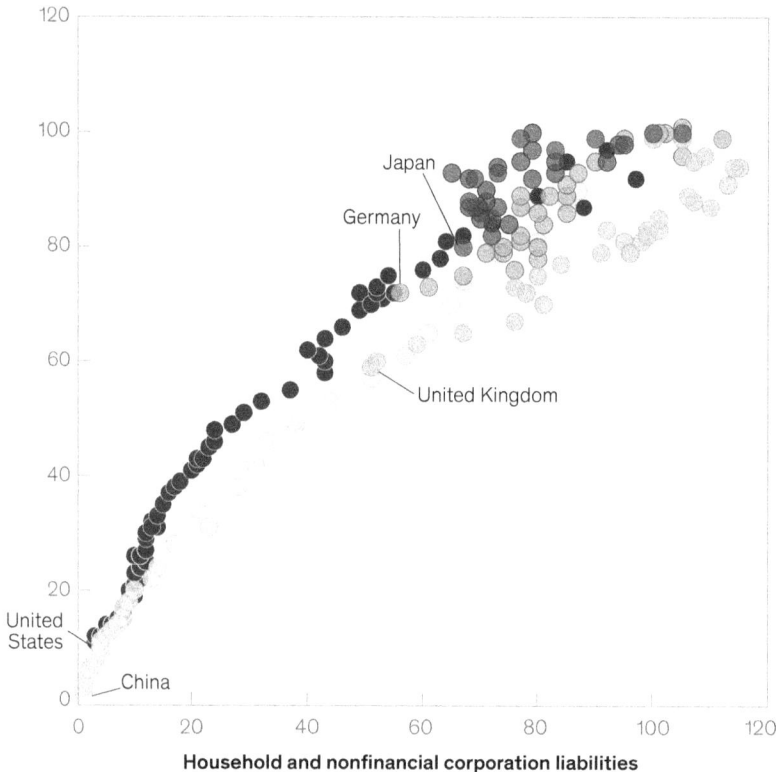

Household and nonfinancial corporation liabilities

Note: Due to data limitations, different time periods are covered for each country. US: 1950–2024; China: 1978–2024; Japan: 1994–2024; the United Kingdom: 1995–2024; and Germany: 1996–2024.
Source: US Federal Reserve; OECD; CASS; PBC; NBS; World Bank; McKinsey Global Institute analysis

Unfortunately, many savings remain idle, especially in developing economies. Take Indonesia as an example. Its savings rate is high, at 38 percent of GDP in 2023, but much of this remains trapped outside formal financial systems, in local cash economies and family businesses. Indonesia's financial assets-to-GDP ratio is just 72 percent, compared with Brazil's 194 percent, limiting productive investment through a broad and deep financial system.[60]

Stock markets, like the New York Stock Exchange, list equity that firms issue for multiple purposes, such as expansion into new countries or developing new products. Disney, for instance, sold stock to bankroll its construction of Disneyland. We often see these markets as abstract leviathans, but in reality they represent human cooperation at a massive scale. Today, 62 percent of Americans own shares, compared with just 10 percent in the 1920s. Globally, stock market value reached $124 trillion by 2025, between 75 and 150 times more than in 1925. This includes about 13,700 companies listed in China and 2,700 in India worth about $22 trillion combined.[61]

And then there are the bond markets. Essentially, they lend governments and companies money that they promise to pay back later with some interest. It is a giant system of IOUs that gives governments and firms the funds they need to build schools, hospitals, roads, factories, and the next big tech breakthrough. Bond markets today are jaw-droppingly huge, worth an estimated $140 trillion in 2023 and surpassing global GDP.[62]

Finance not only supplies the funds to make investment but spreads the risks that come with it. Every single financial investor can now choose from a plethora of financial products that allocate funds in a diversified way across many asset classes, companies, and countries. And real economy investors can make bold bets, confident that if there is a failure, financial supporters will not suffer unduly. Back in 1925, much of this was done inside company conglomerates, much less efficiently.

Insurance markets play a silent but essential role in investment by sharing risk. Imagine building a factory, shipping goods across oceans, or laying down a fiber-optic network. Each requires confidence that if disaster strikes, losses won't be fatal. Insurance shifts these risks from individuals and businesses to diversified pools that absorb shocks. By reducing the financial impact of fire, theft, flood, or lawsuits, insurance frees individuals and businesses alike to take calculated risks. This isn't merely psychological comfort. It materially enables investment. Without insurance, many high-capital projects would become too risky, and credit would dry up. Reinsurers extend this protection further, spreading large risks across continents. When disasters strike California or Japan, it's quite possible that part of the loss is absorbed by a reinsurance firm in Zurich.

Banks, stock markets, and debt markets are far from dry and boring. They channel the lifeblood of our modern world, one loan, share, or IOU at a time.

Firms scaled the investment

Who made all the investments that drove productivity and income growth over the decades? The answer, for the vast majority, is firms. Globally, more than half of all investment is done by corporations, with about a quarter each by government and residential investment. In the United States, firms account for 80 percent of nonresidential investment, and the ratio is marginally higher in Europe. In China, the state plays a much bigger role, with the public–private sector split about 50-50.[63]

For firms to make these investments, they need the right institutional environment and the incentives—that is, the chance to reap returns. As our research shows, US-listed corporations invested $400 billion more than European ones in 2022, and their returns on invested capital were four percentage points higher. One ingredient for this formula is size. US firms grow much larger. Large US public firms have twice the average market capitalization of their European counterparts and, sector by sector, 60 percent higher revenue.[64] Big investments require big firms.

A disproportionate share of investment, particularly the most transformative, is concentrated in large firms. Globally, about two-thirds of R&D investment is concentrated in just 250 companies, 36 and 18 percent of which were American and Japanese, respectively, in 2018. This translates into higher productivity in large firms. In advanced economies, micro-, small and medium-size enterprises are only 60 percent as productive as large firms, while in emerging economies, they are only 29 percent as productive.[65]

It is therefore not surprising that firms have grown larger over time. Research shows a positive correlation between the size of a firm and its productivity growth and profits, which in turn enable the business to become even larger.[66] Corporate behemoths like Walmart and Amazon employ 1.5 million to 2.0 million people, equivalent to the entire population of Houston or Hamburg.

It may run counter to intuition how concentrated productivity growth has, in fact, come from relatively few large firms that invest in bold strategic moves. In our report *The power of one: How standout firms grow national productivity*, we found that fewer than 100 standout firms out of a sample of more than 8,300 large firms in Germany, the United Kingdom, and the United States fueled two-thirds of productivity growth. Just a few dozen more of the highest-contributing firms could double national productivity growth. US retail has about 2.5 million firms, and just six of them contributed more than half of the entire sector's productivity growth. This is remarkable.[67]

The other critical characteristic of firms, as opposed to government institutions, is that they typically operate in a fundamentally competitive and contestable environment. Survival is earned every day, not granted top-down. They grow and shrink, enter and exit in a constant tumult. And in fact, the higher level of dynamism in the US economy explains almost half of its current outperformance versus Europe. In America, good firms grow faster, poor ones shrink more quickly, and people move toward higher-productivity firms more rapidly.[68]

◈ ◈ ◈

For millennia, a strong backbone enabled human evolution—scaffolding for every step, every lift, every swing of an arm. But increasingly, capital investment, in people, businesses, and infrastructure, became the spine that props up human effort. More tools mean greater productivity. That is, if you like, the mechanics. Then there are human ingenuity, imagination, and invention. That is the part of the machine that we turn to next.

CHAPTER 8

INVENTION: IDEAS THAT MATTER

*"Any sufficiently advanced technology is
indistinguishable from magic."*

ARTHUR C. CLARKE

—

Astonishing scientific and technological innovation has
transformed lives and economies.

JANET BUSH, A COAUTHOR AND EDITOR of this book, had a long career in
British journalism before joining McKinsey. Her grandfather Eric came
from a Jewish family who had emigrated from Germany before World
War I. He worked for a wholesale jewelry firm in North London, spending
a lifetime on the road armed with a trunkful of leather jewelry boxes.
There were no electronic ordering systems, no websites for customers to
browse. Business was done face-to-face. Only the size and range of the

Typesetting the old way.

salesman's car changed over the years when Eric's two sons joined the business. Her other grandfather, Thomas, was a clerk in London's famous Smithfield meat market, entering orders and prices into a huge book using a fountain pen. His wife, Minnie, a proper East Ender, did other people's washing by hand to help make ends meet. By 1939, about 1.5 million electric ovens were in British homes, but vacuum cleaners and washing machines were unaffordable for most people. Thomas and Minnie had no TV, only a radio. They didn't have a car and occasionally traveled by electric tram or bus. Electricity was becoming more common for public transportation, but many working-class homes still had to make do with gas lighting and cooking. It was rare to have a telephone at home; most people used public phone boxes.

That iconic red phone box still performed a vital service in the 1980s, when Janet trained as a journalist. Early in her career, she covered an epic meeting of OPEC at London's Intercontinental Hotel. Hundreds of journalists had converged to report on the meeting, which was vital for setting the oil price. No news was emerging from the talks. Sheikh

A vlogger armed with modern technology.

Yamani, Saudi Arabia's influential oil minister, had not been seen and had said nothing. A photographer tipped Janet off that Yamani was staying at his flat in a swanky part of London. So she went there one early morning and caught the sheikh as he was leaving. Quote in notebook, she ran frantically to the nearest telephone box and dictated her story to a stenographer in the office. That quote moved the currency and oil markets, but such a cumbersome way of working would seem laughable to journalists today.

In the space of just a couple of decades, technology changed everything. In the early 1980s, the first personal computers arrived in Britain. Janet started her career on a manual typewriter. Newspapers were laid out on hot metal. Tiny metal letters were arranged in the right order in lines or "slugs" on a large stone. Rupert Murdoch ended the hot-metal era, taking *The Times* and his other newspapers digital in 1986 with early software designed for layout. Newspapers around the world followed. That was just the start of a digital revolution. In 1984, Britain had launched JANET (the Joint Academic Network), which connected universities and research institutions. JANET later became the main gateway through which the internet reached UK academia. In 1989, British scientist Tim Berners-Lee proposed the World Wide Web. Shortly thereafter, the first UK internet service providers emerged, offering dial-up access to businesses. By the mid-1990s, the internet became affordable for ordinary people. The BBC launched an online presence in 1994. Around 2010, online news overtook print. Today, journalists use cloud-based tools and AI. Everyone works on a smartphone. High-resolution cameras and drones provide images. Data tools have become commonplace.

This story is about how technology transformed just one industry and one career. This transformation wasn't limited to journalism, of course. It has reshaped our lives profoundly. Gas lamps gave way to smart LEDs, steam locomotives to high-speed maglev trains, encyclopedias to internet search and now large language models that answer any question you can think to throw at them. Agriculture adopted high-yield varieties and precision irrigation to feed the world. Medical innovations like antibiotics and organ transplants doubled lifespans, while mRNA vaccines rolled out at warp speed during the COVID-19 pandemic saved millions of lives. Even seemingly mundane technologies—think container shipping or barcodes—revolutionized trade, enabling big-box retail and complex logistics.[69] And, of course, the technological frontier keeps moving. We are only now entering the new age of AI.

Technological innovation not only created new goods and services but dramatically reduced their cost over time, thereby making them accessible to billions. In 1927, a three-minute transatlantic call cost about $1,400; today billions converse globally nearly free thanks to fiber optics, undersea cables, and satellite networks. The cost of computer random access memory storage fell from over $20,000 per megabyte in 1980 to fractions of a cent today. Computing power costs declined from $10,000 per gigaflop in the 1990s to mere cents now. TVs costing $40,000 in 1997 now sell for about $200 thanks to manufacturing efficiency and other process improvements.[70]

By contrast, costs of labor-intensive services or items less affected by innovation have often increased or stayed stable. The price of haircuts has doubled since 2000, and the cost of a newly built single-family house has increased 12-fold since 1970 due to regulation, labor and material costs. Crude oil prices, despite advancements in extraction methods, rose sixfold since 1970.[71]

Innovation is the ultimate force behind long-term economic progress. We can invest in producing more, scale existing knowledge, and trade with new markets, but without creative destruction to spur *new* technologies, products and processes, growth stagnates.

Jumps onto new innovation platforms are commonly known as "industrial revolutions." The economic history of the past couple of centuries is a succession of episodes pushing the frontier of our technological possibilities: steam engines in the late 18th and early 19th centuries, electricity from about 1870 to 1914, and computing in the late 20th century. It is common to speak about the current era as the fourth industrial revolution, with digital technology and AI at the center.

These are all impressive innovations, often referred to as general-purpose technologies. But they of course interact with many others, amplifying one another. Innovation emerges from recombining existing ideas. Some thinkers call this "ideas having sex."[72] The list of innovations that have sprung from human brains is unfathomable, and we have made our best attempt to capture some of the most important ones since the 1920s in Table 3.

TABLE 3

Most significant inventions, 1920–2020

Invention	Importance	Year invented	Decade adopted
Insulin isolation	Life-saving diabetes treatment	1921	1920s
Frozen food (flash freezing)	Enabled long-term food storage	1924	1930s
Radio altimeter	Aircraft landing precision	1924	1940s
Liquid-fuel rocket	Foundation of space exploration	1926	1950s
Power steering	Automotive safety and ease	1926	1950s
Sound in film	Transformed cinema industry	1927	1930s

Most significant inventions, 1920–2020 (continued)

Invention	Importance	Year invented	Decade adopted
Television	Revolutionized video communication	1927	1950s
Quartz clock	Precision timekeeping	1927	1960s
Geiger counter	Radiation detection tool	1928	1930s
Penicillin (discovered)	Antibiotic revolution	1928	1940s
Defibrillator	Sudden cardiac arrest treatment	1930	1950s
Electron microscope	Ultra-high magnification	1931	1940s
Neutron discovery	Basis for nuclear fission	1932	1940s
FM radio	Clear, static-free broadcasting	1933	1940s
Radar	Long-range object detection	1935	1940s
Nylon	First synthetic fiber	1935	1940s
Helicopter	Vertical takeoff flight	1936	1940s
Jet engine	Enabled faster aviation	1937	1940s
Teflon	Easier cooking and cleaning	1938	1940s
Photocopier (Xerography)	Document duplication	1938	1950s
Nuclear power reactor	Civil nuclear energy	1942	1950s
Aqualung (scuba gear)	Enabled underwater exploration	1943	1950s
Kidney dialysis	Simulation of organ function	1943	1960s
Electronic digital computer (ENIAC)	Birth of modern computing	1945	1950s
Microwave oven	Fast food preparation	1945	1970s
Disposable diaper	Revolution in infant care	1946	1950s
Point-contact transistor	Enabled revolution in electronics	1947	1950s
Photodiode (light sensor)	Foundation of modern electronic sensors	1948	1960s
Holography	3D imaging technology	1948	1960s
Compiler	Software development interoperability	1949	1970s
Commercial jet airliner	Mass international travel	1952	1950s
Barcode	Automated retail and logistics	1952	1970s
DNA structure discovery	Genetics and biotechnology revolution	1953	1950s
Industrial robots	Industrial automation	1954	1960s

Most significant inventions, 1920–2020 (continued)

Invention	Importance	Year invented	Decade adopted
Organ transplant	Medical care revolution	1954	1960s
Photovoltaic solar cell	Solar power generation	1954	1970s
Intermodal shipping container	Shipping and trade revolution	1956	1960s
First human-made satellite	Start of space age	1957	1950s
Integrated circuit (chip)	Faster and cheaper computing	1958	1960s
Credit card (magnetic)	Financial transaction revolution	1958	1970s
Oral contraceptive (first release)	Birth control revolution	1960	1960s
Green Revolution seeds	Agricultural productivity surge	1960	1970s
Light-emitting diode (LED)	Efficient lighting and display tech	1962	1970s
Liquefied natural gas (LNG) plant	Energy transport revolution	1964	1970s
Data packet switching	Foundation of digital networking	1965	1990s
Heart transplant	Surgical milestone in cardiology	1967	1960s
Automated teller machine (ATM)	Revolutionized banking access	1967	1970s
Saturn V rocket and lunar module	Breakthrough in space exploration	1968	1960s
Concorde (supersonic jet)	Advanced air travel	1969	1970s
ARPANET	Precursor to the modern internet	1969	1990s
Microprocessor	Faster and cheaper computing	1971	1980s
Lithium-ion battery	Efficient energy storage for electronics and automobiles	1972	1990s
Genetic engineering (recombinant DNA)	Engineering of living organisms	1973	1980s
Magnetic resonance imaging (MRI)	Diagnostic medical imaging	1973	1980s
Cellular phone (first call)	Mobile telecom foundation	1973	1990s
Smart card (credit card, SIM, identity cards, etc)	Secure digital identity card	1974	1990s
DNA sequencing (Sanger)	Revolution in biotech and forensics	1977	1980s

Most significant inventions, 1920–2020 (continued)

Invention	Importance	Year invented	Decade adopted
Personal computer	Mass market home computing	1977	1980s
Digital camera	Explosion in photography	1978	1990s
Mobile GPS	Precision navigation	1978	1990s
Graphical user interface (Xerox Star)	Foundation of user-friendly computing	1981	1980s
Laptop computer (portable PC)	Mobile computing	1981	1990s
Reusable space shuttle	Cheaper and frequent space exploration	1981	2000s
Polymerase chain reaction (PCR)	DNA replication revolution	1983	1990s
3D printing	Revolution in manufacturing	1983	2000s
DNA fingerprinting	Forensic science breakthrough	1984	1990s
Flash memory	Portable digital storage	1984	1990s
Prozac (fluoxetine)	Major antidepressant drug	1987	1990s
Laser eye surgery (PRK/LASIK base)	Vision correction tech	1988	2000s
World Wide Web	Internet as an information platform	1989	1990s
Web standards (HTML)	Usable and consistent websites	1991	1990s
Scramjet	Hypersonic jet engine	1991	N/A
Search engine	Limitless data retrieval	1993	1990s
MP3 audio compression	Enabled digital music era	1993	2000s
Smartphone	Transformed personal computing	1993	2000s
Bluetooth	Short-range wireless communication	1994	2000s
Java programming language	Web application revolution	1995	2000s
Streaming media	Seamless entertainment distribution	1995	2000s
Social media	Foundation of digital social networking	1997	2000s
Wi-Fi standard	Wireless internet access	1997	2000s
First camera phone	Telecommunications shift from text and voice to images	2000	2000s

Most significant inventions, 1920–2020 (continued)

Invention	Importance	Year invented	Decade adopted
Wikipedia	Collaborative knowledge model	2001	2000s
Human Genome Project (completion)	Revolution in genetics	2003	2000s
P2P video conferencing	Remote work revolution	2003	2010s
Graphene	Supermaterial discovery	2004	2010s
M-PESA mobile money	Fintech revolution for the unbanked	2007	2000s
Gig economy platforms (Uber, Airbnb, etc)	New labor model	2007	2010s
Blockchain technology	Decentralized finance innovation	2008	2010s
Large Hadron Collider	Revolution in particle physics	2008	2010s
Self-supervised learning for natural language processing	Low-data AI training innovation	2008	2010s
CRISPR-Cas9 (gene editing)	Precision genome engineering	2012	2010s
Lab-grown meat	Alternative protein revolution	2013	N/A
mRNA vaccine platforms	Rapid vaccine development	2013	2020s
Deep learning facial recognition	Widespread automated facial recognition	2014	2010s
Gravitational wave detection	Confirmation of theory of general relativity	2015	2010s
Reusable orbital rockets (SpaceX)	Space cost reduction	2017	2020s
CAR-T cell immunotherapy	Personalized cancer treatment	2017	2020s
Large language models	Natural language AI	2018	2020s
Protein-folding modeling (AlphaFold)	Solved protein-folding problem	2018	2020s
Quantum supremacy	Exponential increase in computing power	2019	N/A

Arthur C. Clarke said that any sufficiently advanced technology is indistinguishable from magic, and it is. Yet behind that "magic" lies collaboration among thousands of researchers, businesses, and institutions. In this chapter, we look at the Apollo program and many other examples to illustrate this. The Apollo program alone involved 400,000 collaborators to put humanity on the Moon.[73]

Science was the bedrock

Basic science—the pursuit of fundamental knowledge about the universe—is the foundation for technological breakthroughs. The Apollo program would never have taken off without it. Isaac Newton's laws of motion and universal gravitation were essential to calculating orbits, trajectories, and the dynamics of spacecraft. Rocket propulsion relied on thermodynamics to design engines that efficiently converted chemical energy into thrust. Knowledge of heat transfer, aerodynamics, electromagnetism, and materials and computer science was crucial to the Saturn V rocket's success.

Much of this basic research was underwritten by governments. Public grants sustained universities and institutes, the United States' National Institutes of Health funded breakthroughs in medicine, and defense agencies poured billions into early computing and semiconductors. But corporate labs drove a great deal of innovation and progress in the 20th century, too. In the 1950s, Bell Laboratories' semiconductor research underpinned Apollo's computing systems. Let's explore how the industrial research lab came to be.[74]

Thomas Edison invented the light bulb, now symbolizing invention itself. Yet that everyday life-changing item was just one of Edison's many inventions; he has more than 1,000 patents to his name. But his greatest contribution has arguably been underplayed. He pioneered the industrial research lab with the development of Menlo Park in New Jersey in 1876, bringing together teams of engineers, chemists, and machinists to work together on multiple projects simultaneously. He systematized innovation, transforming it from the occasional breakthrough of a brilliant individual to an efficient process in his "invention factory."[75]

This laid down the template for the corporate R&D labs of the 20th century, probably the most celebrated of which was Bell Laboratories.

Founded in 1925 by AT&T and Western Electric, over the past 100 years it has won at least nine Nobel Prizes. Out of that lab came the transistor, lasers, the UNIX operating system, and the Telstar satellite.[76] Flash memory emerged from Toshiba's lab and the first practical LEDs from Texas Instruments. BioNTech and Moderna did not invent mRNA vaccines but brought the first mRNA vaccines to market in 2020. DuPont brought us nylon and Teflon; IBM innovated enormously in computing; and Xerox developed the graphical user interface. Today, much innovation happens in corporate labs at ASML, TSMC, BYD, Novo Nordisk, Meta, and OpenAI.

Some philosophers have tried to distinguish between science, which is generation of knowledge, and technology, or what we could call engineering. Some have even tried to determine which one matters most.[77] This is not our business, but what is undisputable is that even if we could place a blurry line between them, we would see that they interact in multiple ways, reinforcing each other. Sometimes engineers draw inspiration from a prior scientific discovery to develop a solution, and at other times the pursuit of a solution leads to a scientific discovery. Scientific principles also help understand and codify engineering breakthroughs, making them replicable and more likely to be improved upon in a systematic way.

Technological and thus economic progress cannot be explained without scientific progress.

Firms and institutions made it real

Firms often translate potential into progress. Without them, many of the past century's breakthroughs could have stalled in the lab or remained academic curiosities. Firms make innovation productive by integrating research from universities and labs with operations, investing, and ensuring that the products and services created out of that innovation are brought to market on a large scale. NASA may have catalyzed the Apollo mission, but firms made it happen: Grumman Aerospace built the lunar module, Boeing built all other major parts of the Saturn V rocket, and IBM provided guidance computers.[78]

As we have said, the main locomotive of productivity growth is a small subset of standout firms. These standout firms generate bursts of productivity by scaling innovation, shifting portfolios and business models, and reallocating capital to the most productive uses. They are the firms that commercialize innovation, turning scientific potential into widespread impact. Take BioNTech and Pfizer. Before COVID-19, they had a small-scale research partnership, and mRNA vaccines remained only a futuristic concept. When the crisis hit, they moved decisively, combining BioNTech's innovation with Pfizer's industrial capabilities and scale to deliver billions of vaccine doses within two years.[79]

Public funding often seeds early-stage research, accepting long-term risk in areas that the market won't. Just the top five agencies in the United States committed more than $170 billion in R&D funding in 2023. The Apollo program cost about $300 billion in today's dollars and represented 2 percent of the US economy, demonstrating that large-scale investment can hugely accelerate innovation timelines.[80]

Private capital plays a critical role in taking ideas further. Venture capital and philanthropic foundations fund early translation; firms fund R&D and commercialization. Today, global private R&D spending exceeds $1.1 trillion—more than 20 times what it was in 1960. In 2024 alone, six major global companies invested $500 billion into R&D and capital expenditures, almost twice the spending of the Apollo program, and they did it in a single year compared with 13 for Apollo.[81] This ecosystem of public and private funding creates a pipeline through which ideas move from hypothesis to product to impact.[82] These investments have made possible the most transformative innovations of the past century. They will be just as critical for those still ahead.

Technology amplified people

One reason people are suspicious of technology is, they argue, that it replaces humans. This is a centuries-old concern, from the Luddites in the early 19th century—textile workers who smashed mechanized looms—to today's worries about AI. Yet automation hasn't destroyed overall employment; global employment is at historic highs.

The way we work has changed dramatically, but not by eliminating jobs wholesale. Manufacturing robots and ATMs automated manual or repetitive tasks, freeing workers up for harder-to-automate and increasingly higher-value roles such as financial advising and relationship building. As IKEA's AI chatbot took on addressing customer queries, many of its human call-center staff became interior design advisers instead.[83] Global employment grew from 2.2 billion in 1991 to more than 3.5 billion today even as automation expanded across sectors. Labor-saving technologies have had no negative effect on overall employment, and job markets in technologically advanced locations are generally more resilient in downturns.[84] This growth in employment reflects technology's role in enhancing productivity, enabling workers to produce more value in less time.

As productivity rises, so do wages, which in turn boosts demand for goods and services, often spawning entirely new industries. A century ago, dog hairdressing skills were not valued or even thought of; today, rising incomes have created demand for pet grooming and other industries that would have been unthinkable a mere two or three decades ago. One author is pretty sure his dog has a bigger hair-care budget than he does. The rise of digital platforms has birthed roles like app developers and social media managers, jobs that simply didn't exist in the pre-internet era. Technology-driven productivity growth creates economic opportunities, expanding the labor market in unforeseen ways.

This transformation, however, is not painless. Creative destruction includes destruction, rendering some skills obsolete and disrupting livelihoods. The decline of typewriters made typist pools redundant, and the shift to digital photography decimated jobs in film processing. These transitions can be challenging, requiring workers to retrain or relocate. Yet history shows that resisting technological progress to preserve outdated jobs stifles growth and keeps societies poorer. The solution lies in embracing adaptation—investing in skills development, refining processes, and fostering a culture that races with machines, not against them. By equipping workers with digital literacy and problem-solving abilities, societies can harness technology to unlock new opportunities, ensuring that the benefits of innovation, including higher productivity, better wages, and novel industries, continue to drive prosperity for all.

❀ ❀ ❀

We worked more, acquired more skills, invested in factories and equipment, and invented new technologies. Behind all of this was another ingredient, the raw materials that make the world go round: energy, metals and minerals, and, perhaps most fundamentally, food. We became energized to a level never before seen.

CHAPTER 9

ENERGY: POWERING PROGRESS

"After the electric light goes into general use, none but the extravagant will burn candles."

THOMAS EDISON

—

Energy and resources make the world go round.

KENZA BOUHAJ, WHO WORKED with us on this book, is Moroccan. Her grandparents grew up in the late 1920s in rural areas in the Middle Atlas Mountains when Morocco was still under French colonial rule. Kenza fondly remembers her grandpa telling her stories of life in the village. Life moved with the sun. He used to say, "The day ends when the light disappears." They mostly ate grains and vegetables; meat was a luxury

A historic fortified village on the old caravan route from the Sahara to Marrakesh.

Moroccan village house with solar panels.

for festivals. With no refrigerators, they dried fruit and preserved lemons. Almost all their neighbors farmed, although one or two mined lead and zinc in the mountains.

Morocco began to change after it gained its independence from France in 1956. Like many families, Kenza's grandparents made their way to the cities, where her parents were born and raised. Large cities had constant electricity even at that time. The family liked listening to football, Umm Kulthum's songs, and the king's speeches on the radio. While they still cooked with butane gas and did the family washing by hand, Kenza's family bought a television, with the two main news channels running only a few hours of programming a day. By contrast, life in the countryside looked vastly different. Many villages did not have access to electricity until 1996, when the country launched its rural electrification program. Electric wires were strung above olive trees, lighting the streets.

Meanwhile, Morocco was beginning to emerge as a mining powerhouse. Huge phosphate deposits had been found in 1920, but mining was managed by the French colonial authorities, and Moroccans saw little financial benefit. That changed with independence, and phosphate production soared.

Fast-forward to 2025, and a lot in Kenza's life has changed; she lives in New York now. Her homeland has changed dramatically. Income per person has surged from about $1,200 in 1913 to about $8,900 today. That is an eightfold increase.[85]

Today, Morocco is a much more modern and diversified economy, and a minerals and metals leader. It holds 70 percent of the world's phosphate reserves and is rapidly emerging as a global player in EV battery supply chains. Africa's first battery gigafactory is under construction with initial capacity of 20 gigawatt hours. Tens of thousands of tonnes of lead and zinc are now mined from the Atlas Mountains and exported for alloys and batteries. Preserved lemons, dried fruit, and couscous are still beloved, but now Moroccans eat much more fresh fruit and vegetables grown in thousands of greenhouses; of course, they also buy many processed and packaged products from other parts of the world in their local supermarkets.[86]

By 2021, every household had electricity, and 200,000 remote rural households used solar power. Morocco does not have much in the way of oil and gas reserves, but it has a great deal of sunshine. Noor Ouarzazate is the world's largest concentrated solar power plant. The country also has significant wind farms and major hydropower plants, and renewables produced 26 percent of the nation's electricity in 2024.[87] Families now have solar water heaters, LED bulbs, and apps that track electricity use.

Energy touches every aspect of our lives. It lights and heats where we live and where we work. It gets us from A to B. Air conditioning makes scorching days comfortable, and electric lighting makes life possible at night. And energy powers the tools and machinery that allow us to work more productively than we could ever have managed with just our bare hands. With it, we can run tractors, industrial machinery, and home appliances. Energy has driven industrialization.

Total global energy consumption has grown tenfold over the past century. The average person now consumes energy equivalent to 1,800 kilograms of crude oil a year. This is also equivalent to the labor of 115 people working full time for a whole year—and the richest economies consume double or triple that.[88] Energy consumption and economic progress go hand in hand; there are no rich countries with low energy consumption (Exhibit 12).

We also extract eight times more metals and minerals from the earth than we did 100 years ago.[89] They have provided the nuts and bolts of our industrial world. And from the brown soil have come bountiful crops to feed us all. Agricultural production has quadrupled since the 1960s, and today we produce more than enough food to feed everyone on Earth. The tragedy, of course, is that while we produce enough, many people worldwide still go hungry.[90] And similarly, much of the world lives on a very limited supply of energy. We can do more, but remarkable progress has been made on expanding people's access to resources. Let's look at how that happened, starting with energy.

A vast and diverse energy system powered life

Today's energy system is humungous. The world has well over 60,000 power plants, delivering electricity to more than seven billion people. There are more than 1.3 billion passenger vehicles on the road. The majority of them are powered by internal combustion engines (ICE) that run on fossil fuels, but battery-propelled vehicles are coming up

Energy use relative to income per person
2024 data

Gigajoules per person (log scale)

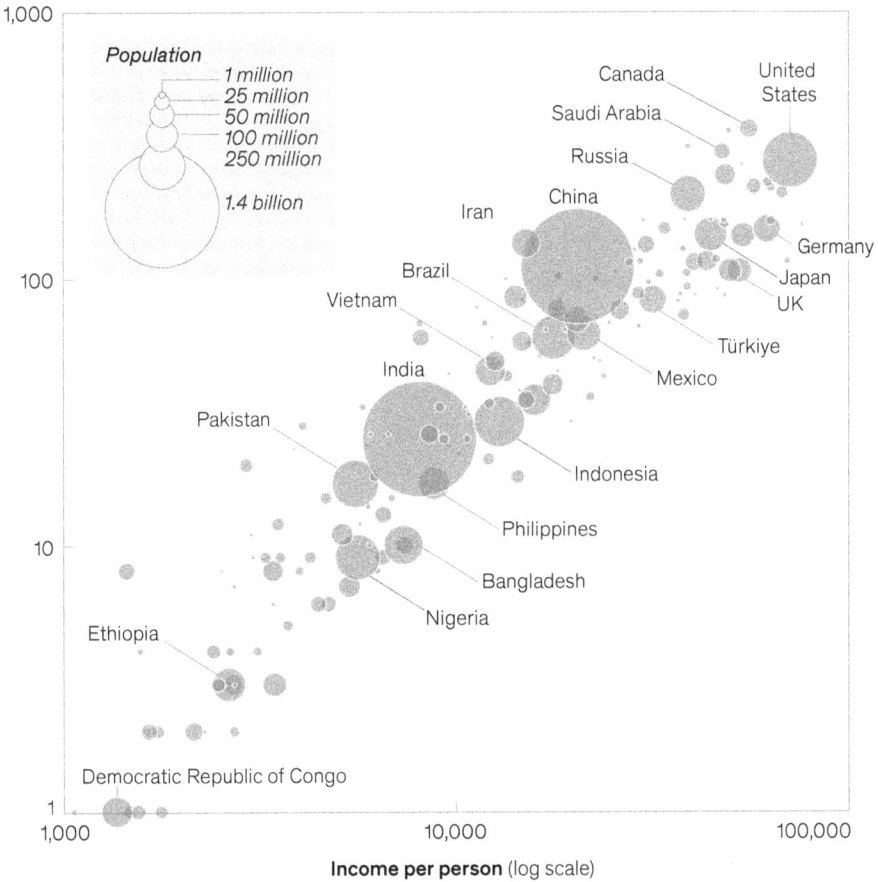

Income per person (log scale)

Note: For readability, excludes 9 countries with income per person >$70,000, 1 country with income per person <$1,000, and 4 countries with >400 gigajoules per capita. Labels shown only for countries with >75 million people (except Canada, Saudi Arabia and the United Kingdom). Income per person expressed in constant 2021 international dollars. Bubble sizes represent the population of each country and grow by area, not radius. 2023 figures used for income per person and population sizes.
Source: World Bank; US Energy Information Administration, 2025; Energy Institute, *Statistical review of world energy*, 2025; UN Population Division, *World population prospects 2024*; McKinsey Global Institute analysis

fast. Energy fuels every industry, making the products we use every day and powering the production of about seven billion tonnes of industrial materials every year. The length of the global oil and gas pipeline network is about two million kilometers, equivalent to traveling from the Earth to the Moon and back twice.[91]

Today's energy system is high-performing. This may come as a surprise because we often hear about the energy system only in terms of its impact on global warming. And indeed, the energy system is responsible for more than 85 percent of global CO_2 emissions, because it continues to be based mostly on fossil fuels.[92]

But before coming to terms with its externalities, we must recognize that the fossil-fuel-based energy system has useful properties that have revolutionized life, from the Industrial Revolution to today. Fossil fuels can be moved relatively easily to where they are needed because they are energy dense and easily transportable. Just one average tanker carrying LNG can power more than 40,000 homes in the United States for an entire year. The system can ramp energy supply up or down quickly to match demand. Open cycle gas turbine power plants can move from full shutdown to generating power at full capacity in less than ten minutes. And fossil fuels are what we call "chemically flexible." They can be used as an input for many materials we use to build our world and to provide the high-temperature heat needed to make them. Natural gas, for instance, is used to make fertilizers, plastics, and steel.[93]

Over time, we have become better at using energy, too. Today we are at about 50 percent efficiency when converting energy inputs like fuel into useful energy services such as moving a car or heating a home. That's up from roughly 20 percent in the 1800s.[94] Sweeping technological innovation has enabled us to extract far more energy per unit of fuel than previously. An internal combustion engine is more efficient than a steam engine. A combined cycle gas turbine is far more efficient than a gas turbine. And battery-powered EV engines are more efficient than any of these, though many EVs still receive power through electricity systems that involve higher thermal energy losses upstream of the battery (Exhibit 13).[95]

As we squeeze more energy out of what we have, costs have fallen, leading to even more energy use. A transatlantic journey from Britain to the United States that once took seven days and cost $3,000 by ocean liner now takes seven hours by plane for just $800.[96] Even when we pay a similar amount or more per unit of energy, the share of spending on energy in many economies has fallen. In the United States, while the nominal costs of energy commodities like coal, oil, and natural gas have increased several times over since 1980, the country spends about half as much as a share of GDP, 6.4 percent down from 13.0 percent.[97]

Not only has the system grown, but its mix has changed. In the 1920s, as much as 90 percent of energy consumed around the world came from coal and biomass, including wood, charcoal, and dung. There were some dams and a few sources of oil and natural gas, but they were small. Oil contributed about 10 percent of global energy and fueled mass production of cars and shipping; Mexico, Russia, and the United States were early

EXHIBIT 13

Maximum efficiencies of engines and turbines
%

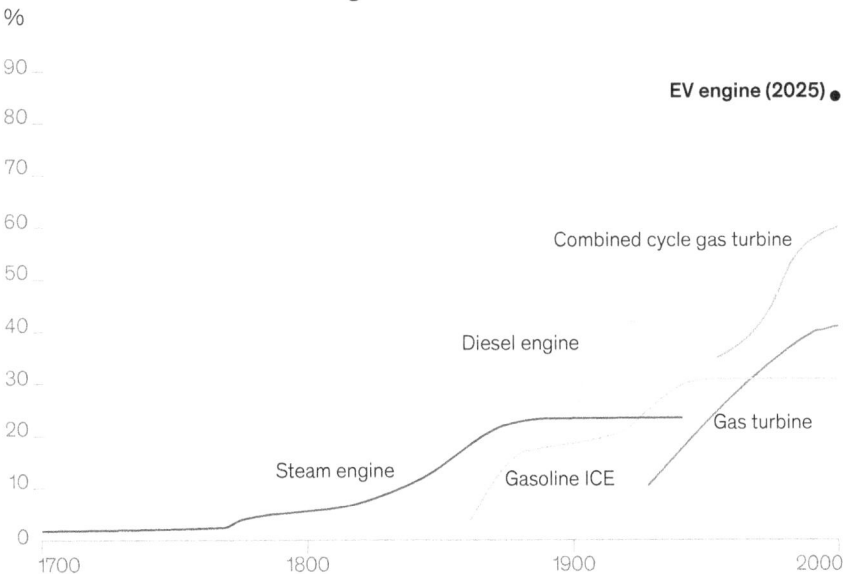

Note: Efficiency values for fossil-fuel vehicles represent the ratio of fuel burned to useful mechanical work performed; values for electric vehicles (EVs) represent battery-to-wheel efficiency. For engines, efficiency represents the amount of final energy that is converted into useful energy (forward motion); for turbines, efficiency represents the amount of primary energy converted into final energy in the form of electricity.
Source: Smil, *Energy and Civilization*, MIT Press, 2018; Yang et al., "Energy efficiency of lithium-ion batteries," *Energy*, 2025; McKinsey Global Institute analysis

producers. With huge discoveries and the development of oil fields, especially in the Middle East, oil overtook coal as the leading energy source in the 1960s. By 1970, oil accounted for 40 percent of the mix, coal 30 percent, and gas 20 percent. And now, increasingly, low-emissions energy sources are emerging, including renewables like solar and wind that are feeding into the power system alongside biofuels and nuclear. Despite their rapid growth recently, low-carbon energy represents a relatively small fraction, less than 20 percent of the total (Exhibit 14).

Notably, diversification historically has *added* new energy sources globally, rather than replacing those already used. Today, we consume significantly more coal and biomass than in 1925, although their contribution to the mix has fallen from more than 90 percent to about 30 percent, simply because we collectively use much more primary energy.

Demand for energy is voracious. And the reality is that many people in the world still do not have enough of it, even as more energy sources have been added to the mix. While in much of the world, energy is taken for granted, in other places, easy access to energy is still a daily struggle. Sixty percent of the global population, some five billion people, live with less than the global average of 77 gigajoules per year, roughly the level in Thailand and only half of what Germans use. That is about the equivalent of what a Toyota Highlander midsize SUV consumes annually. In 2022, 760 million people mostly living in Sub-Saharan Africa and South Asia had no access to electricity at all. The energy they used was primarily fuels they could find themselves, like wood.[98]

This vast, high-performing, increasingly efficient and diverse energy system has been a powerful part of the progress machine. When more energy is available, economies grow and incomes rise. South Korea's 22-fold rise in income per person since 1965 parallels a 26-fold increase in energy use. This is hardly a coincidence. Contrast that with Egypt, which increased income per person by only seven times and energy use by three times. Clearly, more growth goes hand in hand with more energy.[99]

The overall story of the past 100 years of energy use is one of remarkable human advancement. From dimly lit homes to electrified cities, from subsistence living to thriving economies, access to energy has consistently marked the difference between stagnation and growth. Though uneven, the arc of history is clear: Where energy flows, progress follows.

Global primary energy consumption by source
Thousand TWh

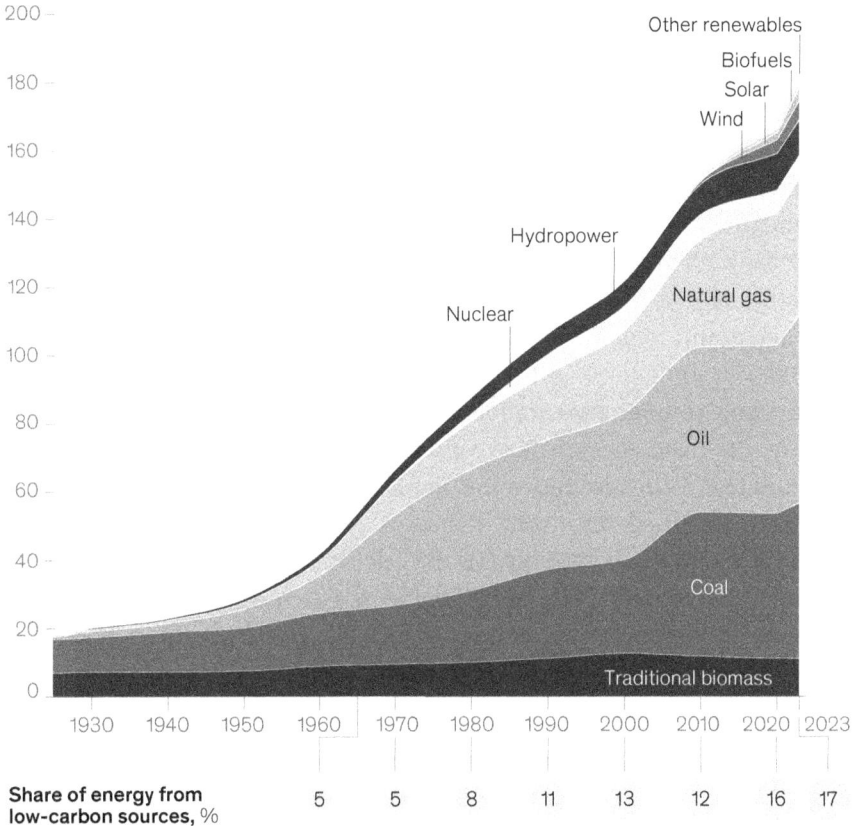

| Share of energy from low-carbon sources, % | 5 | 5 | 8 | 11 | 13 | 12 | 16 | 17 |

Note: Energy consumption and share of low-carbon assets are measured using substitution method, to reflect the share of low-carbon sources in overall energy mix. For more on accounting methods for primary energy, see Ritchie and Rosado, "What's the difference between direct and substituted primary energy?" Our World in Data, 2021.
Source: Energy Institute, *Statistical review of world energy*, 2025; Smil, *Energy Transitions*, Praeger, 2017, processed by Our World in Data; McKinsey Global Institute analysis

Minerals and metals forged the physical world

Drilling for oil and natural gas was not the only factor that helped us grow; digging for metals, minerals, and even apparently mundane materials like sand, has built our modern world. The downtowns of cities all over the world are filled with skyscrapers. They have become an urban cliché. There are 60,000 or so large dams and millions of smaller ones. And more than 60 million kilometers of roads crisscross the Earth.[100] Think of how much steel, concrete, glass, aluminum, and bitumen that has taken. In comparison with 1950, production of steel has increased tenfold. Mining for sand and limestone has more than tripled in the past 20 years.[101]

The $4 trillion metals and mining industry is largely engaged in the extraction of just five materials: iron ore for steel, thermal coal, copper, gold, and aluminum. Mining may not be a glamorous industry, or maybe it is. What is undeniable is that it is the backbone of the global economy. If you want to judge how important mined resources are, just consider that they are the second-most-valuable category in world trade, after automobiles.[102] Or take the smartphone, a pocket-size testament to the centrality of mined resources. It has lithium and cobalt in its battery, tantalum in its capacitor, gold in its wiring and connectors, tin in its soldered components, rare earth elements (such as neodymium) in its speaker and vibration unit, copper in its wire, aluminum in its body and frame, and silicon in its chip and screen.

Technology has driven the expansion and efficiency of this resource backbone. Time and time again, skeptics have been concerned that we will run out of some key minerals. This was one of the core messages of the 1972 *Limits to Growth* report. But as demand for minerals has risen, we have been able to deploy more science and technology toward finding new sources and have consistently increased new deposits identified even faster than we have managed to extract them from the ground. Take copper, a material that humanity has been extracting since prehistoric times. From 1950 to 2025, the world produced almost 800 million tonnes of copper. During that period, however, almost 900 million tonnes of new copper reserves were identified. This is partly attributable to new discoveries, like Argentina's Filo del Sol deposit. But it is also due to technological developments that enabled us to improve how we extract, refine, and distribute the metal, bringing previously uneconomical deposits "into the money." Russia's Udokan deposit is one example; its millions of tonnes of copper were discovered in 1949 but became economically viable and started production only in 2024.[103]

In short, ever-evolving technology and know-how have allowed us to find and extract the materials we need to build and manufacture elements of our increasingly prosperous world. And the importance of mining shows no signs of waning. Demand for rare earth elements and minerals, many of which are vital for the transition to low-emissions energy, is intense. The extraction of lithium surged 30-fold between 1995 and 2023.[104] In Part IV, we will explore whether we can continue to find and extract these critical materials in the future.

Agricultural productivity made food for all possible

Our planet supplies not only cold, unyielding minerals, but the nourishment we need to live. Food grown from the earth. A hundred years ago, most of the world's food was still grown by hand. Farmers sowed seeds, tilled soil, and harvested crops using draft animals and hand-forged tools. Agriculture had progressed, but yields remained low and harvests so dependent on weather that survival still hinged on the whims of nature in many parts of the world. Yet, as we have seen, between 1925 and 2025, food production grew faster than the number of humans. That was made possible by waves of agricultural innovation. Today, the Food and Agriculture Organization of the United Nations estimates that the world produces 1.5 times as much food as is actually needed to nourish the global population.[105]

The story of agricultural progress over the past century is one of humanity's most impressive and consequential ones, from muscle to machine, intuition to data, and scarcity to the real prospect of abundance. The first great leap came with mechanization. Starting in the early 20th century, the introduction of tractors, combine harvesters, mechanical planters, and irrigation pumps drastically reduced the burden of manual labor and made farming far more efficient. What once took days of backbreaking human (and animal) effort could now be done in hours with machines, freeing up labor and enabling larger-scale production.

Then, between the 1940s and 1970s, came the Green Revolution, a seismic shift in global agriculture, driven by science and the urgent need to reduce hunger in the world's fast-growing population. Norman Borlaug, often called the "father of the Green Revolution" and one of the unsung heroes of the 20th century, developed and championed high-yield, disease-resistant wheat varieties in Mexico in the 1940s and helped scale them across South Asia in the 1960s. Improved seeds were only part of the equation. Their success hinged on a powerful combination of complementary innovations: synthetic fertilizers, chemical pesticides, and irrigation infrastructure. Governments and international institutions helped, too, delivering credit, subsidies, and technical training to farmers across Asia and Latin America. Today, an estimated half of the world's population is supported by food grown with nitrogen fertilizer derived from gas, using the Haber-Bosch process.[106]

The payoff was extraordinary: Cereal yields nearly doubled, rising from 1.4 tonnes per hectare in the early 1960s to 2.7 tonnes by the early 1990s. Over just three decades, world agricultural production doubled. These rapid gains helped stave off a looming food crisis in Asia and laid the groundwork for the economic rise of China, Southeast Asia, and South Asia. In the United States, one farmer fed 18 people in 1940; by 1985, that number had soared to 115. In developing countries, undernourishment fell sharply, from about 35 percent in 1970 to 13 percent by 2015.[107] In much of the world, food production not only kept pace with rapid population growth but outstripped it, transforming survival into the possibility of thriving for many millions.

As agriculture has become more productive, it has also become more intelligent. Selective breeding resulted in faster-growing chickens, higher-yielding cows, and pest-resistant plants. In recent decades, genetic engineering and gene-editing tools like CRISPR have added precision to this tool kit, allowing for targeted changes that improve drought tolerance, nutritional content, and resistance to disease. Precision agriculture, aided by satellites, sensors, and GPS data, helps farmers monitor soil conditions, weather patterns, and crop health in real time.[108] Instead of blanketing entire fields with water or fertilizer, they can target specific zones, saving resources and reducing environmental damage. These technologies are becoming essential as land and water become scarcer. The future of food is not just high yield. It is high efficiency and climate adaptive.

Alongside changes in how food is grown, there has been a radical transformation in what we eat. A century ago, diets were largely plant-based and localized; today, they are richer in calories, animal protein, and processed ingredients. Since 1961, the amount of food available for each person in the world has gone from about 2,200 calories a day to nearly 3,000 in 2022. In fact, in some ways, we produce too much food. Nearly a billion meals daily are wasted. And overnutrition and diet-related diseases have surged.[109] Many countries have not only solved the food-scarcity problem but are oversupplying food.

As in much of our story, food progress is unfinished business. Hunger persists in some places, and in some others, diets do not have all the variety needed. For example, they often lack protein. And the enormous scale-up in production came with environmental costs like deforestation and biodiversity loss. We will discuss these in detail later in the book, when we reckon with the side effects of economic progress to date (Part III) and look toward the future (Part IV).

＊ ＊ ＊

Earth has afforded us enormous bounty: energy, metals and minerals, and food. Over the past century, they have become more abundant, and people have thrived. Another vital form of energy comes from being able to interact with other people at close quarters. This is the magic of living in cities, once described as the greatest of human inventions. In the next chapter, we look at how urbanization powered the progress machine.

CHAPTER 10

CITIES: BETTER TOGETHER

"Cities concentrate opportunities;
it's not just an accumulation of houses."

ALEJANDRO ARAVENA

—

In cities, people are more than the sum of their parts.

OUR COLLEAGUE MARIIA MOLODYK who worked on this book is Ukrainian. A century ago, her country was predominantly agricultural, with mile after mile of wheat, sunflowers, and sugar beets. It was known as the breadbasket of the Soviet Union, and agriculture accounted for 80 percent of all employment. Mariia's four grandparents were raised in small villages by single mothers who had lost their husbands in World War II. Their early lives were shaped by the trauma of wartime and the long, grinding years of postwar reconstruction. Their resourceful mothers taught them to farm and forage, giving strict instructions to the children about which tree bark was safe to eat when food was scarce.

A woman in the countryside, Ukraine.

In 1939, about 30 percent of Ukrainians lived in cities, but the massive destruction of World War II left few cities of any size. Mariia's grandmother still remembers her first wide-eyed visit to the port city of Mariupol, which was the size of Geneva in those days. Its vibrant market stalls and colorful clothes seeded a desire for a metropolitan life. Realizing that dream took time.

Ukraine's industry suffered severe damage in World War II, with 80 percent of its industrial base destroyed. Much was rebuilt after the war, and industry expanded. Cities started growing, and people flocked to them to work in the new factories. From an urban population of just 18 percent in 1925, by the early 1950s 30 percent of Ukrainians once again lived in cities. That share would have been higher if many rural families had not been tethered to collective farms—*kolkhozy*—limiting their ability to move. But some did. One of Mariia's great-grandfathers, departing for the front during the war, left his wife, Nina, with a clear wish: "Ensure Victor gets an education." That meant moving to Kharkiv, a city of one million by the late 1950s. Nina stayed in the village, laboring with her daughters on the kolkhoz so that Victor could be spared for school. They

Kharkiv on a winter afternoon.

saved a piglet each year to celebrate his return in the summer. His letters, which his sisters strained to read, brought news of city life, and he always arrived with stories—and treats—like the legendary "Miner's Cake," a dense chocolate dessert from Donbas.

Victor was just the first. Mariia's other grandparents subsequently left their villages to pursue degrees in engineering, part of the vast wave of rural youth who powered Ukraine's industrial boom. They then settled in the Donbas, building lives in a major industrial city where Mariia's parents were born. Determined that their daughter would not be posted to remote rural areas after finishing university, Mariia's grandparents steered her mother away from a teaching degree, which could lead to rural job placements, and toward mechanical engineering, seen as a surer ticket to urban work.

By the time Mariia was born, in 1992 in Luhansk, a city roughly the size of Zurich, the Soviet Union had collapsed. Factories shuttered, and the economic system unraveled. In search of new opportunities, her parents moved to Kyiv, a metropolis of three million where better jobs and education awaited. In 2015, Mariia graduated from the leading university in Kyiv and was accepted by Cambridge University, which opened the door to a career in London's knowledge economy and life in a city of ten million people.

The arc of Mariia's family story is one that has been followed by many millions of families. As we have seen, the migration from rural to urban places is one of the most tangible changes over the past century. In 1925, about eight of every ten of us lived in rural areas. One hundred years later, that has flipped. Now six of every ten people live in a city, a shift that has driven unprecedented economic progress. In advanced economies, it is more like eight or nine (Exhibit 15). For most of us, our natural habitat is no longer the cow shed but the coffee shop. This has utterly changed the life prospects of people around the world.

Cities are the hubs where all the elements of the progress machine come together most densely and most explosively. It is where people, knowledge, capital, technology, and energy clump together and multiply their power.

EXHIBIT 15

Urban population
Share of total population, 1920 vs 2023

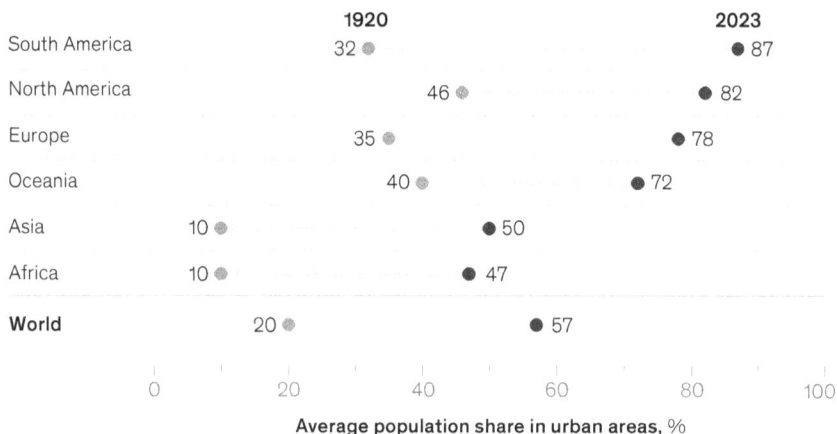

	1920	2023
South America	32	87
North America	46	82
Europe	35	78
Oceania	40	72
Asia	10	50
Africa	10	47
World	20	57

Average population share in urban areas, %

Source: HYDE (History Database of the Global Environment) 3.3, 2023, processed by Our World in Data; McKinsey Global Institute analysis

Humanity embarked on the greatest migration

The shift from rural, bucolic lives to urban dynamism wasn't just about numbers. It was a transformation of how we live, work, and dream. Megacities—urban giants with populations exceeding ten million— epitomize this change. Only New York and Tokyo met that threshold in 1950. Today, 35 others, including Delhi, Shanghai, São Paulo, and Lagos, have joined the ranks, each a sprawling testament to human ambition. These megacities didn't just grow; they concentrated economic activity and increased in importance. Shanghai, already a leading Asian treaty port in the 1920s, claimed the crown as the world's busiest port in 2010, as its population swelled more than ten times to about 25 million. Farmland in the Pudong district transformed into an urban core, marked by skyscrapers shooting skyward like a forest of steel giants. Lagos grew from a modest colonial port surrounded by fishing villages into one of Africa's economic powerhouses.[110]

Megacities are the most visible manifestation of what has essentially been a global redistribution of where and how people live. The share of the world's population living in towns and cities nearly doubled between 1950 and 2025. In that same period, the share of people living in megacities grew eightfold, while the share of people living in large cities of between one million and ten million inhabitants tripled to 18 percent of total population (Exhibit 16).

Today, the median person has several million neighbors rather than about 30,000 within a 20-kilometer radius—a 150-fold increase in social density compared with 100 years ago. Cities didn't just grow upward. They pressed outward and even emerged from nothing, drawing more of humanity into dense networks.[111] The result is a world in which cities are no longer a rarity but a defining feature of the human experience for most.

Why do people flock to cities, even when romantic notions of pastoral life tug at our hearts? The countryside may promise tranquility, but cities deliver something that is perhaps less primal and more practical: job opportunities. In cities, industries cluster, offering work from factory floors to corporate boardrooms. A young woman leaving a rural village in India for Delhi might find a job in a call center or a textile factory, roles that simply don't exist back home. In 2020, for instance, urban areas in India accounted for 60 percent of the country's GDP despite occupying

EXHIBIT 16

Distribution of total global population by city size
Share of total population, 1950 vs 2025, %

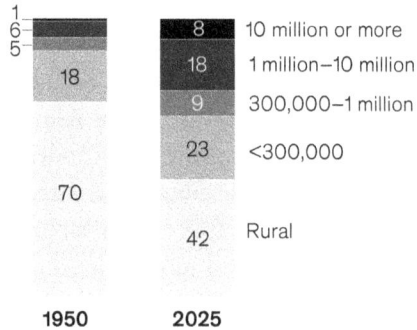

		10 million or more
1	8	
6	18	1 million–10 million
5		
18	9	300,000–1 million
	23	<300,000
70		
	42	Rural
1950	**2025**	

Note: The graph draws on United Nations data, using historical figures from 1950 and projected estimates for 2025.
Source: UN Population Division, *World population prospects 2024* and *World urbanization prospects 2018;* McKinsey Global Institute analysis

just 3 percent of its land. And this shift from rural agriculture to city jobs has improved the lives and livelihoods of millions. Urbanization boosts productivity, which translates into higher standards of living. China's urban boom from 1980 to today was a key factor in lifting some 800 million people out of poverty. In 2025, the urban disposable income per person for Chinese workers was more than twice the rural figure.[112]

But it's not just about paychecks. Cities are playgrounds of possibility. They offer theaters, restaurants, museums, shops, and music venues that rural areas can't match. In New York, a night out might mean catching a comedy show or stumbling into a jazz club in Harlem. In Tokyo, it's the electric buzz of Shibuya's nightlife. With the market scale provided by cities, businesses can invest in developing niche, upmarket options, catering to just a small subset of the population. Cities also weave dense social networks. A coder in Bangalore might meet a startup founder at a café, sparking a collaboration that changes their lives. Professional, romantic, and creative connections are the invisible threads that pull people to urban centers.

Of course, cities have their flaws. Congestion chokes streets, housing costs soar, and inequality can feel stark. In 2025, the average Londoner has to cough up between 45 and 50 percent of income for rent.[113] Yet cities remain magnets, because they are where dreams find traction. The rural idyll may soothe the soul, but the city fuels the fire of ambition.

Cities were economic multipliers

Cities don't just collect people. They amplify their potential. Economists attribute this phenomenon to "agglomeration economies," the idea that proximity breeds productivity. When people and businesses are packed tightly together, something extraordinary happens: The whole becomes greater than the sum of its parts.[114]

One key ingredient is the supply chain's closeness. In cities, firms are near their suppliers, customers, and competitors, slashing costs and speeding up innovation. Proximity means faster delivery of materials, lower transportation expenses, and the ability to adapt quickly to market demands. Face-to-face interactions with suppliers build trust and streamline coordination, allowing businesses to troubleshoot issues or tweak designs in real time. Take Bangalore in the early 2000s. Known as India's Silicon Valley, the city became a hub for software development because tech firms, from Infosys to Wipro, were surrounded by a dense network of hardware vendors, data centers, and skilled programmers. This enabled rapid software prototyping, testing, and deployment, resulting in Bangalore exporting $64 billion in IT services in 2023. The city's compact ecosystem allowed firms to pivot swiftly, collaborate seamlessly, and outmaneuver competitors in less connected regions.[115]

Another advantage is economies of scale. Cities make infrastructure and services vastly more efficient. The dense concentration of people and businesses allows for shared infrastructure that reduces costs per person. A single power line or water main in a city like Tokyo can serve thousands of households far more cheaply than extending utilities across sprawling rural areas. To serve roughly the same population of 5.5 million, Scotland has some 50,000 kilometers of water pipes, compared with Singapore's 6,000 kilometers.[116] Public transportation systems, like London's Underground, move millions daily at a fraction of the cost of individual car travel. Hospitals, schools, and even restaurants and cultural institutions like museums and theaters have enough critical mass to make their existence sustainable. A nice side effect is that, maybe counterintuitively, density also benefits the environment: Compact urban living cuts down on car use, smaller apartments conserve energy, and reduced land use preserves natural habitats. Suburbs generally *look* greener, but they are often browner.

Thanks to these effects, cities have become ever-more-powerful engines of economic growth. It is astonishing how hugely the urban world punches above its weight. Between 2000 and 2019, the fastest-growing cities accounted for half of the world's GDP growth, while covering less than 1 percent of the world's landmass (Exhibit 17). By 2023, cities generated about 80 percent of global GDP, with the 1,000 largest accounting for 60 percent of global GDP from only 30 percent of the world's population.[117]

It all boils down to higher productivity. Urban workers are, according to some studies, 20 to 30 percent more productive than their rural counterparts, and this is reflected in the urban-rural wage gap. In more

EXHIBIT 17

Urban centers that account for 50 percent of GDP growth
2000–19

Source: *Pixels of Progress: A granular look at human development around the world*, McKinsey Global Institute, December 2022

extreme cases, capital cities like Bangkok and Mexico City have levels of income per person four to six times higher than their countries' rural regions.[118] Cities don't just work. They multiply what we can achieve.

Ideas and investment collided and formed ecosystems

Cities ignite innovation when ideas, investment, and specialized talent come together. Time and again, we have seen new industries emerge from the confluence of these factors. The more of these there are, the more powerful the effect. Face-to-face interactions supercharge innovation. In 2019, 85 percent of patents globally came from innovation hot spots, all of them urban areas, and 69 percent came from just the top 30 of these.[119]

Cities are intellectual cauldrons for the exchange of ideas. When people bump into each other at workplaces, conferences, and coffee shops, ideas spark and spread. Silicon Valley has thrived on this. In the 1970s, engineers at Xerox's Palo Alto Research Center would grab drinks at Walker's Wagon Wheel, swapping insights that shaped the personal computer revolution. That kind of intentional or serendipitous interaction is less likely in a small town. A potent concoction of this kind of talent and investment coming together has transformed the Valley into the multitrillion-dollar tech hub it is today.

Plenty of other examples abound across the globe. Take Bollywood in Mumbai. In the early 20th century, India's film industry was a scattered affair. But Mumbai's density, along with its network of actors, directors, financiers, and theaters, turned it into a cinematic powerhouse. By the 2000s, Bollywood was producing more than 1,000 films a year, captivating billions and exporting Indian culture worldwide.[120]

Or let's swing back to Stuttgart, which we mentioned in chapter 7. It was here that Karl Benz created the first gasoline-powered car in 1886, and Daimler and Maybach industrialized production the following year. From those beginnings, the city has become the preeminent hub of German car making. Other manufacturers, including Porsche, set up headquarters in the city. Costs are kept competitive by leveraging the same supplier base. The companies feed off a burgeoning network of parts suppliers, including Bosch, also founded in Stuttgart and now the world's largest auto supplier. Many of them are in or near the city, minimizing logistical costs. Stuttgart's automotive and machine construction industries employ nearly 200,000 people.[121]

A great deal of research and development is centered on the city, too. The region invests more than €9 billion a year in automotive R&D. That's half of the city's home state of Baden-Württemberg's industrial R&D.[122] Research institutions share resources, while local universities and technical colleges train thousands of students a year in the skills the industry needs. Interaction with others creates new thinking, and firms have adopted lightweight materials and fuel cells developed by the German Aerospace Center's Stuttgart institute. The city itself plays its part, providing excellent infrastructure and a large airport. Stuttgart is not just a city but a tightly woven ecosystem.

This clustering of industries drives specialization. Cities become hubs for specific industries because talent and resources converge. New York's Wall Street isn't just a street. It's a magnet for finance, drawing bankers, traders, and analysts who draw from one another's expertise. Los Angeles is home to a high concentration of entertainment. Silicon Valley has the tech, Washington the institutions, and Boston the medical science. Of course, it cannot be a coincidence. The gravitational force of cities is hard to resist.

Shenzhen became the world's electronics manufacturing capital thanks to its deep supply chain networks. Its Huaqiangbei district, an area of less than three square kilometers, hosts 110,000 businesses. Synergies abound from the concentration of related companies in the same location. And for us as consumers, electronics have become cheaper because manufacturers consolidate operations where costs are lowest and where expertise is most established.[123]

These are no accidents. Cities provide the stage where ideas meet money and talent meets opportunity. The result is a cascade of innovation. New companies, new industries, new ways of living. From the skyscrapers of Shanghai to the studios of Los Angeles, urbanization has been the spark that lit the 20th century and continues to drive the 21st.

＊ ＊ ＊

Living in a city is a very special form of connection, but we interact with one another in a huge web spanning the globe. Trade crisscrosses the world. So do we, as students, as businesspeople, as vacationers. And ideas whiz across borders, too, enriching all of us. We have, as the phrase goes, become global citizens. Never have we been more connected to one another, and that, too, has powered progress. Let's look at how.

CHAPTER 11

TRADE: SHARED PROSPERITY

"A day will come when there will be no battlefields,
but markets opening to commerce
and minds opening to ideas."

VICTOR HUGO

———

The world is three times more connected than it was 100 years ago, creating choice and opportunities for people everywhere.

IN THREE GENERATIONS, the way of life for the family of another of our coauthors, Jeongmin Seong, changed beyond recognition as they seized

Illustration of old house in Bukchon village, Seoul.

the opportunities afforded by South Korea's embrace of open markets and free trade.

Jeongmin's grandparents were farmers in a remote village in Chungcheong-do. Like many rural areas across Asia, their village was a tight-knit community where people sharing the same surname had lived together for generations. Born in the 1920s under Japanese colonial rule, his grandparents' life was tough. They farmed everything from rice to fruits, and even tobacco, living a life of near self-sufficiency. The outside world felt distant; most needs were met within the village. This was typical for Korean families in those days: Close to 80 percent of them worked on the land, on average, for less than $2 a day.[124] During peak seasons, neighbors supported one another through *Poomasi*, a traditional practice rooted in community solidarity of rotating labor. It was a small, self-contained world shaped by the land, the seasons, and shared effort.

They were traditional people, but that didn't stop them from making bold choices. In the late 1950s, as Korea began to rebuild after the war and urbanization took hold, the family sent Jeongmin's father to Daejeon, the

Overlooking the Han River and the Gangnam night lights in Seoul, South Korea.

nearest city to their village. They were betting on education as the pathway to a good future. There, Jeongmin's father studied business and started his own furniture company just as the economy started booming. By the 1980s and 1990s, global trade was reshaping the nation. This lowered the cost of raw materials, expanded access to technology, and fueled the rise of a new middle class. The furniture business rode that wave. South Korea today is an advanced economy, with workers on average earning more than $60 a day, often working for large firms in manufacturing or technology. By 2025, South Korea had become the world's sixth-largest exporter and seventh-largest importer, a true trading titan.[125]

South Korea's growing global ties didn't just fuel the economy. They reshaped daily life. Jeongmin grew up listening to New Kids on the Block on a Walkman made in Japan and grabbed meals at McDonald's, the ultimate youth hangout of the time. He was shaped by a whole raft of new global opportunities. His first overseas trip was sponsored by a Korean *chaebol* (conglomerate) eager to nurture global talent. University exchange programs sprang up. Korea set up its young people to operate on a global stage by prioritizing the teaching of English, which is mandatory from the third grade through high school. Nearly half of children under six attend *hagwons*—private academies or "cram schools"—that often include English education. Exposure to the wider world raised the bar for Jeongmin's generation. He studied in the United States and built a career in China, seizing opportunities in his country's two most important trading partners.[126]

If Jeongmin is global, his daughter is even more so. She was born in South Korea, raised in China, and studies in Japan. She is multilingual and moves across cultures with ease. South Koreans are avid travelers and made a record 29 million outbound trips in 2024. That's a lot out of a population of about 52 million. Their own culture is known around the world. K-pop fills stadiums on every continent, and Korean films have won Oscars. *Squid Game* is the most-watched Netflix series of all time.[127]

From a grandfather in a self-sufficient village to a daughter navigating the world, Jeongmin's family story reflects how global connection doesn't just shape nations but rewrites the trajectory of individual lives across generations. South Korea's journey from poverty to prosperity, and from isolation to global leadership, is known as the Miracle on the Han River.

We have never been more connected. The web of global interactions through trade of goods and services, and through flows of capital, data, and people, is much larger than it used to be. Trade has been a hardworking spider spinning that web. Exports as a share of GDP have tripled from 100 years ago to about 30 percent, picking up from the post–World War II low of 5 percent (Exhibit 18). Certainly, interruptions, disputes, wars, pandemics, and recessions have periodically slowed the momentum of global trade, but it has always marched on.[128]

Trade has been good for growth. The WTO posits that when openness to trade rises by one percentage point of GDP, income per person increases by 0.2 percent. It is very unlikely that the dramatic decline in extreme poverty over the past century would have been possible if economies had remained isolated instead of opening up to doing business around the world. For firms, free-flowing trade boosts productivity by allocating resources efficiently and strengthening competition. It also benefits them through more rapid global diffusion of technology and know-how, access to a wider range of quality inputs, and even larger markets for greater economies of scale. For individuals, it creates jobs by opening

EXHIBIT 18

Trade intensity
Sum of global goods and services exports as a proportion of GDP, 1925–2024, %

Depression and war	Postwar boom	Era of contention	Era of markets

— Goods

--- Services[1]

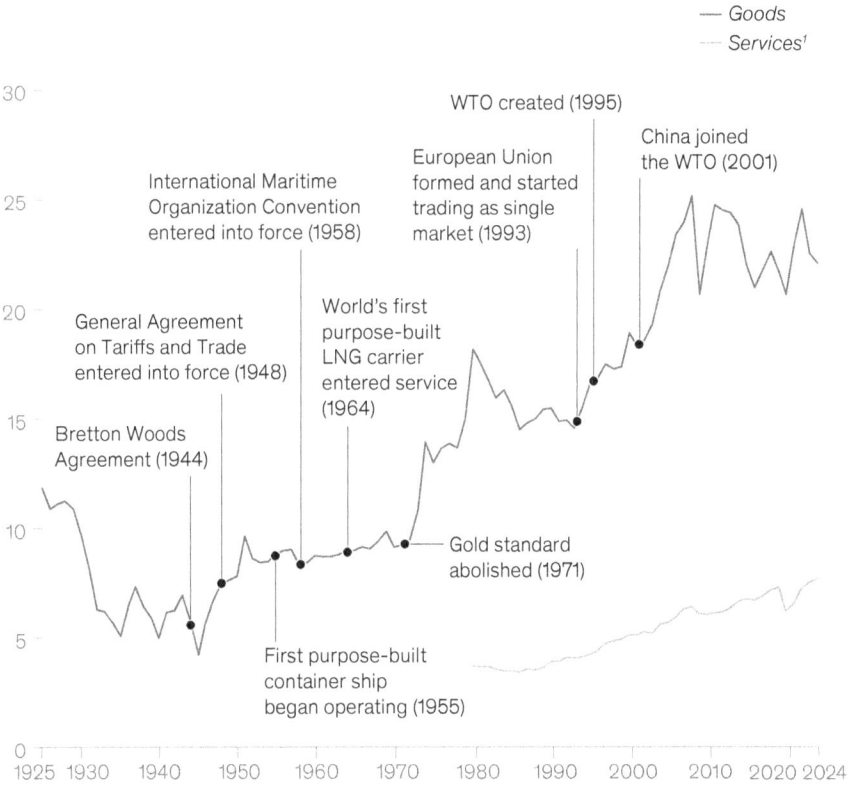

WTO created (1995)

European Union formed and started trading as single market (1993)

China joined the WTO (2001)

International Maritime Organization Convention entered into force (1958)

General Agreement on Tariffs and Trade entered into force (1948)

World's first purpose-built LNG carrier entered service (1964)

Bretton Woods Agreement (1944)

Gold standard abolished (1971)

First purpose-built container ship began operating (1955)

1925 1930 1940 1950 1960 1970 1980 1990 2000 2010 2020 2024

[1]No trade data available for services before 1980.
Source: Fouquin and Hugot, *Two centuries of bilateral trade and gravity data: 1827–2014*, CEPII, 2016 (1925–70); World Bank (1970–2024); McKinsey Global Institute analysis

up new markets and creating demand for a broader range of skills and professions, while for consumers, trade helps to increase quality, lower prices, and offer more and better choices.[129]

These manifold benefits of a connected world did not happen overnight. Several forces were at work. Let's look at them.

Innovation crushed the cost of distance

Shipping goods used to be prohibitively expensive, but innovation has helped to cut transportation costs by 50 to 60 percent relative to value since the 1960s, fueling exponential trade growth. We moved seven trillion tonne-kilometers in 1965, and 78 trillion by 2020. The volume of trade today is 43 times higher than in 1950.[130]

When people hear the word "innovation," they often think of digital technologies, AI, or medical advances. However, one of the most transformative developments of the past century was the humble container, pioneered by American entrepreneur Malcolm McLean. The simple box enabled a broader set of complementary innovations that reshaped the entire transportation and logistics chain.[131] In some ways, the container is the operating system of global trade.

Before containerization, shipping goods across oceans was a chaotic and labor-intensive process that could take days or even weeks at each port. Cargo arrived as barrels, crates, sacks, and loose items, each needing manual handling by large teams of dockworkers. The introduction of standardized steel containers, which could be efficiently stacked on ships like LEGO bricks, streamlined this process by enabling faster loading and unloading by cranes, reducing the turnaround time for vessels to mere hours and allowing for greater voyage frequency.

Standardized containers also enabled much larger ships to operate. Early container ships in the 1960s carried between 500 and 800 20-foot-equivalent units (TEUs); the largest today have a capacity of 24,000 TEUs, or 40 times as much. This in turn spurred the construction of larger, more efficient ports. Ports expanded to accommodate larger ships, investing in specialized berths, bigger cranes, and sophisticated storage and handling systems. Additionally, intermodal transportation, made possible by standardized dimensions across all forms of transport, seamlessly linked shipping with rail and truck transport, eliminating the need to unpack goods at ports. This dramatically shortened delivery times, increased the reliability and predictability of deliveries, and allowed for deeper integration of global supply chains. Together, these complementary changes allowed for massive economies of scale and significantly boosted productivity, paving the way for an explosion in trade volume. Today, approximately two-thirds of maritime trade is containerized.[132]

New ways of moving energy around emerged, too. By condensing gas to one-600th of its original volume, LNG could be shipped globally on dedicated tankers without prohibitively expensive pipelines. Asia especially benefited, importing more than 60 percent of global LNG by 2023. Here, too, innovation in ship design played a part in ever-increasing economies of scale; modern LNG carriers carry ten times as much as their 1960 counterparts, and oil tankers seven times as many barrels' worth.[133]

Moving goods by air has also changed enormously since the 1950s. The introduction of large cargo planes, advanced logistics systems, and hub-and-spoke networks helped to cut the cost of air shipping tenfold.[134]

Beyond intensified connection through trade, people became far more mobile, too. Just two generations ago, a trip from Seoul to Jeju Island was a major undertaking, involving a train or car journey and then an overnight ferry. It was expensive, slow, and far from comfortable. Today, that same trip takes just over an hour by air, and it has become the busiest flight route in the world, with hundreds of flights per day.[135] Technological advances including more efficient engines, lighter materials, and larger planes alongside the proliferation of low-cost carriers have made air travel widely accessible.

Liberalization set the engine free; institutions kept it running

A century ago, if you wanted to buy an item from another country, you would encounter steep trade tariffs, complicated paperwork, or even outright bans. Such concerns have faded over time. Globally, the average tariff dropped from more than 20 percent in the 1940s to less than 3 percent in 2024. Average US tariffs have remained below 5 percent for the past 30 years.[136] Although the situation became dynamic in early 2025 when US President Donald Trump began a flurry of tariff announcements, some 60 percent of world trade had been tariff-free for some years, and an additional 20 percent was subject to tariffs of less than 5 percent.

The effect of this, when combined with huge reductions in transportation costs, has been to knit the world closer together. Unlike our grandparents, we no longer rely on whatever food or energy or tools are produced close to our village or town. The entire world is our marketplace. All of this has given consumers and businesses a proliferation of choice. Breakfast in the 1920s was likely cereal and some bread if you were in the West. Now the first meal of the day could include coffee from Colombia, oranges from Spain, granola with Greek yogurt, an avocado from Mexico, or smoked salmon from Norway—all from the local supermarket. And prices have fallen, too. A study of 43 members of the WTO found that 59 percent of them experienced a decrease in relative consumer prices after joining.[137]

Trade is not only about physical objects that we can touch and eat. We are increasingly trading things that are intangible, like services, software, intellectual property, and data. These intangible flows are fast becoming the new engines of connection and competitiveness. Today, we shop, pay, learn, socialize, consult, and connect online and often globally. It doesn't matter where we are physically. Most of us have experienced customer service via foreign call center. Digital services trade was worth almost $5 trillion in 2024, outpacing some goods sectors and growing at about 8 percent annually since 2005.[138] The COVID-19 pandemic accelerated its growth, as firms like Netflix and Zoom leveraged global networks to compete, and growth has remained robust since. And data flows have been growing even more swiftly, at 32 percent per year over the past five years, leading to a tripling of bandwidth demand over the same period and highlighting the fact that ideas travel faster than cargo.[139]

The impact of an open world, of course, runs far deeper than being able to buy exotic fruit or the latest gadget from far-flung places or streaming the latest K-drama on said gadget. Our connections to one another simply make our lives better. We learn from different cultures and become invested in others. History tells us that when nations trade with one another, their incentive to conflict logically diminishes, and indeed interstate conflicts have dwindled as international trade has climbed.[140]

Underpinning this explosion in trade is a web of international agreements and coordination, from the General Agreement on Tariffs and Trade, put in place in 1948, to its replacement by the WTO in 1995, and a proliferation of up to 600 regional trade agreements since. Recently, continental-size agreements such as the African Continental Free Trade Area and the Regional Comprehensive Economic Partnership in Asia have been signed, following in the footsteps of Mercosur in South

America, which predates the WTO. And what these agreements cover has deepened. In the past, they tended to focus on tariffs, but increasingly they have covered services and intellectual property, too.[141]

Beyond trade agreements, there were maritime laws, defense alliances, and other multilateral institutions designed to keep the peace. NATO ensures safe passage for merchant ships. The IMF promotes trade, by not only helping to provide economic and exchange-rate stability but also more explicitly enabling trade through loans predicated on trade liberalization. The World Bank finances projects like ports, railways, and roads that support the logistics of conducting trade. There is no doubting the role that these institutions have played in fostering global trade. Yet even so, they have not been above criticism. Leveled at them, for instance, is the charge that their policies have given disproportionate bargaining power to developed nations. Another critique is that their existence and approach have potentially eroded the autonomy of domestic policy.[142] Overall, however, it cannot be denied that strong multilateral institutions and a rules-based order helped to unleash trade.

Specialization turned global trade into a win-win

Specialization is another spell in the magic of our interconnected world, boosting quality by tapping into the best expertise and innovation. This is the core idea in the theory of comparative advantage articulated by 19th-century economist David Ricardo.[143] He explained that countries benefit from specializing in goods they can produce most efficiently and importing the rest. This boosts global output and lowers costs. Think Bangladesh sewing clothes, Brazil producing coffee, Germany engineering cars, or Japan manufacturing televisions.

This level of specialization is not new. What has emerged over the past century, though, is the "unbundling" of supply chains, by breaking products down into their components and subcomponents. Each link in the value chain is now hyperspecialized, enabling players to develop deep expertise in very specific parts, then scale up to serve the global market. For an everyday example, take a tour through your wardrobe. You might notice the letters "YKK" on some zippers. This Japanese company specializes not in clothes nor bags, but just a very small part thereof, and it makes some ten billion of them every year. YKK zippers make their way all around the world, ending up on fast-fashion jeans, luxury handbags, car seat covers, suitcases—and even on the spacesuits worn by Neil Armstrong and Buzz Aldrin on the Moon.[144]

The benefits of specialization being pushed to this extent were threefold: Companies could enjoy global economies of scale in subcomponents, task-level specialization dramatically improved productivity (as Adam Smith presciently illustrated with the pin), and countries that could not produce an entire product competitively were still able to gain a foothold in a niche in the value chain. Oftentimes, these served as an entry point into global markets via a relatively low-skill stage. Over time, countries were able to develop know-how and move up the value chain. Consider Samsung, which is today a global leader in high-value semiconductor manufacturing and smartphones, producing advanced chips and devices critical to global technology. It had humbler beginnings when it first entered global markets in the 1960s, getting its start assembling low-skill electronics like basic black-and-white TVs.[145]

The flip side of supply chain unbundling and creating opportunities for many more hyperspecialized producers is, of course, a much higher degree of complexity for the companies at the end of the value chain. Multinational corporations have constructed intricate global value chains that serve as the backbone of international trade by orchestrating the production, distribution, and sale of goods and services across borders. By the 2020s, some 70 percent of global goods trade was in intermediate goods, requiring sophisticated coordination on the part of the final producer. Multinational corporations, with their international reach, act as agents of global economic integration. Enabled by advances in information and communications technology, they coordinate and source components from producers worldwide in pursuit of efficiency, higher quality, and lower cost.[146]

What does this look like in practice? In his essay *I, Pencil*, economist Leonard Read used the example of a humble writing implement to illustrate the remarkable coordination of the market.[147] A pencil is made up of a surprising number of materials, sourced from different places: the wood from the United States; the graphite from Sri Lanka; the exterior paint from any country with a chemical industry; zinc and copper, perhaps from China or Chile, in the brass band holding the eraser in place; and the eraser made from rubber, which might come from Indonesia or Germany. If even a humble pencil manufacturer requires this degree of coordination, imagine firms that produce complex electronics or sophisticated aircraft.

Another unintended effect of specialization is greater interdependency between economies. Most of us buy our energy from other places. Asia–Pacific, including China, imports more than 35 percent of the energy resources it needs, and Europe more than 60 percent. The Middle East and North Africa, the world's largest net exporter region of energy resources, depends on other regions to provide more than 60 percent of the food crops its people consume (Exhibit 19). Most of the technology we use comes from outside our borders, too. For instance, China alone accounts for three-quarters of the world's production of personal computers and

EXHIBIT 19

Net imports or exports as share of domestic consumption
2023 or most recent available, %

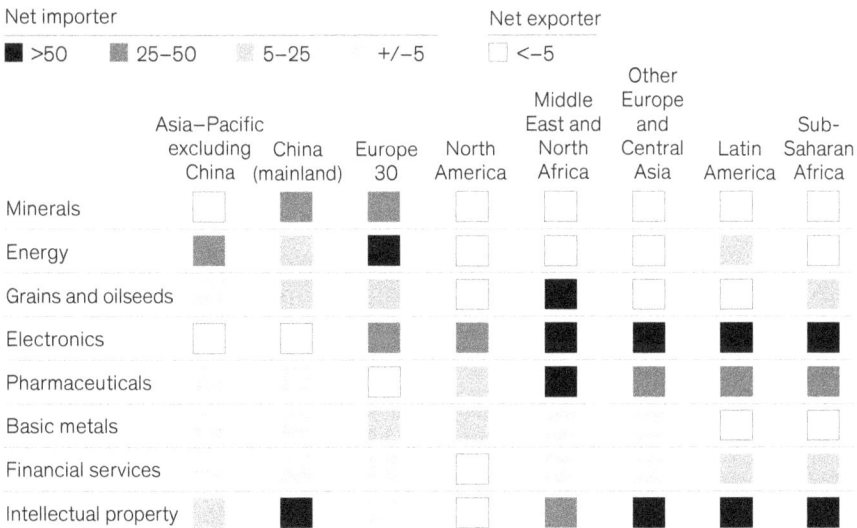

Net importer ───────────────── Net exporter

■ >50   ▨ 25–50   ░ 5–25   +/−5   □ <−5

	Asia–Pacific excluding China	China (mainland)	Europe 30	North America	Middle East and North Africa	Other Europe and Central Asia	Latin America	Sub-Saharan Africa
Minerals	□	▨	▨	□	□	□	□	□
Energy	▨	░	■	□	□	□	░	□
Grains and oilseeds		░	░	□	■	□	□	░
Electronics	□	□	▨	▨	■	■	■	■
Pharmaceuticals				□	■	▨	▨	▨
Basic metals			░				□	□
Financial services				□			░	░
Intellectual property	░	■		□	▨	■	■	■

Note: Intellectual property net import share of domestic consumption is calculated as net imports as a share of total trade. Data for Sub-Saharan Africa based on a limited sample (5 countries) for manufactured goods and services. Source: S&P Global; WTO–OECD Balanced Trade in Services; FAOSTAT; IEA World Energy Balances; McKinsey Global Institute analysis two-thirds of mobile phones.[148]

This intricate web of specialization and interdependence, while a boon for efficiency and innovation, also introduces vulnerabilities in an increasingly geopolitically tense world. As economies rely on far-flung partners for critical inputs, like rare earth minerals from China or semiconductors from Taiwan, supply disruptions from conflicts, tariffs, or other trade barriers can ripple globally, inflating costs and stalling growth. We've already seen echoes of this with the tariff hikes initiated in the late 2010s and escalating in 2025. We have observed a recent reconfiguration of trade toward more geopolitically aligned partners, and our research indicates that a scenario in which global trade fractures could reduce long-run global GDP by 1.5 percent. Other analysis has estimated the impact at up to 7 percent of GDP.[149] That said, the counterpoint of this dependency is that such global connections keep the world interacting across geopolitical fault lines, and this acts as a binding thread, weaving cooperation where geopolitics alone might fail.

We do note that even during the biggest recent shock in any of our experiences—the COVID-19 pandemic—world trade increased to record levels. It proved remarkably resilient. One reason we felt a lot of pressure was a demand boom (anyone for a Peloton?) rather than supply gaps. Either way, this underscores the need for diversified supply chains and resilient alliances to safeguard the gains of our connected era.

※ ※ ※

The seven parts of the progress machine that we have described offer a relatively comprehensive explanation of what has transformed lives over the past century. There is an eighth part: a guiding hand, a supervisor, if you like, a coordinator. The funny thing about this supervisor, though, is that it is, as Adam Smith says, practically invisible. In the next chapter, we look at how firms, markets, and institutions have worked together to create coherence and integration for a world economy and society made up of billions of people and trillions of individual decisions.

CHAPTER 12

MARKETS: SCALING COOPERATION

"No human mind can comprehend all the knowledge
which guides the actions of society."

FRIEDRICH HAYEK

—

Sustained by institutions and markets, firms coordinate workers, knowledge, and capital, powering innovation and growth.

THE FAMILY OF OUR COLLEAGUE Elinor Martinez, another contributor to this book, is the very definition of America's melting pot, with grandparents

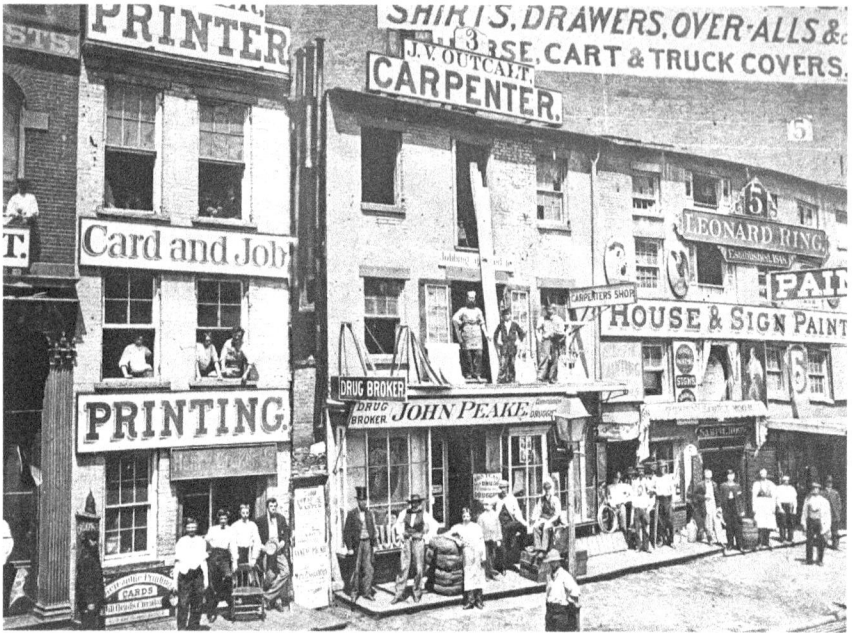

Old-school commerce in downtown Manhattan.

Modern multinationals clustered in lower Manhattan.

from Irish, Pennsylvania Dutch (Amish), Native American, and Spanish heritage. They each took very different paths, but one element stands out: the importance of firms to the opportunities they seized to make their way, and how those firms have themselves changed over the past three generations.

Having worked as a telegram boy while growing up, Elinor's maternal grandfather, William, studied architecture in Pennsylvania before going on to work for the Radio Corporation of America. He then became president of the HH Brown Shoe Company. Incidentally, HH Brown was later taken over by celebrated US investor Warren Buffett's Berkshire Hathaway group. Buffett likes strong brands that are durable and attract repeat demand. With HH Brown, the shoe fit. From small beginnings, it became part of a conglomerate with the Buffett investment, an arc that typifies the evolution of companies from small to large. Elinor's mother, one of William's six children, became an astronomer for NASA, working on the Hubble Space Telescope project in Baltimore near Johns Hopkins University.

Elinor's paternal grandfather, Eugene, was raised in New Mexico. Along with his brother, he worked in the fields to make the family's ends meet. He later moved to Colorado to study, supporting himself by working in a carpet repair shop. It was at university that he met Elaine, who was studying music. They moved to Washington state where Eugene became a school principal, raising three children. Often the only Hispanic family in town, they battled against racism. Elinor's father worked extremely hard to put himself through college, graduating with a PhD in physics from Johns Hopkins University, where he met his wife, the astronomer. He then went on to work for IBM and subsequently at the MIT Lincoln Laboratory as a software architect. Business was pivotal to this family's upward trajectory, from small beginnings in a carpet repair shop to a position in one of the largest tech companies in the world.

Machines are not, at least not yet, autonomous. They are designed by engineers, run by operators, and repaired by mechanics. They incorporate an element of oversight and system design and coordination. It is no different with our machine of progress. Firms are the stars of the show. They are the primary economic actors, coordinating workers into collectively innovating, investing, and delivering much more than anyone could alone, and making products and services easily accessible to customers. Their evolution, from informal, small, local enterprises to global giants orchestrating complex value chains, reflects the interplay of innovation, competition, and cooperation that drives prosperity. Our rising incomes are tightly linked to the increasing sophistication and scale of firms.

Firms do not exist in isolation. They are in a constant tussle of transactions with employees, capital providers, suppliers, and, of course, customers. Markets act as supercomputers, coordinating progress through price signals and profit incentives, spontaneously allocating resources, spawning new firms and technologies, and forcing incumbents to adapt or disappear.

Institutions provide the backbone to the system, creating the playing field, boundaries, and codes on which markets can operate—and stepping in directly where market mechanisms are prone to failure. Most often these institutions are formalized in governments backed by the power of state, but all sorts of other coordinating institutions like professional bodies existed before those top-down forms.

These three elements—firms, markets, and institutions—work together and organize the way people work, learn, invest, innovate, energize, and connect.

Firms as superhuman agents

In chapter 11, we saw that an object as simple as a pencil depends on highly complex global value chains, with components from around the world. But that is not the end of the story. You can easily travel to the countries that pencil parts are sourced from. Can you make a pencil?

Harvesting cedar trees for wood involves loggers, sawmills, and transportation networks. The graphite core demands miners extracting raw graphite, chemists refining it into a precise mixture, and factories pressing it into rods. The yellow paint, made from pigments, binders, and solvents, requires chemical plants and quality control labs. The metal ferrule and eraser involve mining tin, smelting, and rubber production, each step relying on distinct expertise. Machinery to shape, assemble, and package requires engineering capabilities, while global supply chains coordinate delivery. We could literally write a whole book on how a pencil is made.

Firms are the superhuman agents that bring together dispersed human capabilities. Firms align the incentives of employees toward a common goal, around shared assets, creating organized systems of decision-making that allow teams or individual employees to specialize without having to understand every part of the process they're a part of. Walmart's $648 billion revenue in 2024 represents not just commercial success but a feat of extraordinary coordination: two million employees operating tens of thousands of stores globally, served by an integrated digital and physical logistics infrastructure.[150]

Crucially, firms possess the legal rights and responsibilities typically associated with individuals, such as owning buildings or machines, entering contracts, and assuming debts. This legal status makes them more than a network of contracts between individuals. They are collective minds and bodies able to think and act strategically as agents in the economy. This also means they need to follow certain rules, just as people need to be governed by laws.

Firms are economic powerhouses that drive productivity growth. As we have noted, just a handful of firms—100 of approximately 8,300 studied by MGI—are the main engines of productivity growth, accounting for nearly two-thirds of overall productivity advances. These firms are usually big; they average 65,000 employees. Far from all large companies are standouts, but large firms are on average more productive than their smaller counterparts.[151] This is not only because large firms have more capacity to innovate and invest but also because small, highly productive firms grow over time, becoming large.

As we will see, the small number of firms that drive productivity are not always the same—there are stars in the show, but the roster is always evolving.

Without large productive firms, progress remains subdued. Indonesia illustrates what happens when they are underrepresented. Almost 80 percent of employees work in mostly informal companies with fewer than 50 employees and low productivity. To become an empowered, high-income country, its development path will likely require doubling the share of employees in firms with more than 50 employees from a quarter to half of the workforce. This process would contribute to a tripling of capital per worker, delivering the productivity growth needed to reach high income within 20 years.[152]

Firms operated the machine of progress

Firms are the beating heart of the progress machine. They drive and combine the power of the seven other parts of the machine—workers, skills, investment, invention, energy, cities, and trade.

Firms are the air traffic control towers of capital, accounting for about three-quarters of non-dwelling global investment in 2024.[153] The largest firms generally are the biggest investors. Investment translates into innovation: Roughly 60 percent of all global R&D spending originates in the private sector, and in some places, like Japan and South Korea, it is closer to 80 percent.[154] More importantly, go back to the list of inventions of the past 100 years in chapter 8. Many of them, from transistors to oral contraception to nylon, were invented by firms, and those that were not were often improved upon, scaled, and commercialized by them.

Firms have also become the world's employer of choice. Our salaries, and thus our livelihoods, depend on them. The larger they get, the better the jobs they generally provide. Large firms typically pay 25 to 50 percent more than their smaller counterparts. We have also seen how firms have become the world's premier skills factories. Work experience accounts for about half of lifetime earnings. In other words, skills acquired within firms are as important as or more important than formal education for people's life chances and earning power.[155]

Finally, firms weave the global economy together. Airbus sources parts, components, systems, and services from 26,000 suppliers spanning all continents.[156] The top 1 percent of firms alone is responsible for half of export volumes. These "export superstars" leverage scale and efficiency, lowering costs and connecting markets. But they don't just trade between them; they optimize global value chains and share technology and best practices within them. Internal cross-border flows of capital and knowledge within multinationals, which transfer R&D, skills, and management practices, are key, and are one of the most powerful development levers for emerging economies. Apple is a prime example. It helped train 28 million workers in China, spurring a budding tech ecosystem, and was one of the leading firms that accounted for more than 60 percent of global foreign direct investment.[157]

The rise and rise of large firms

From the postwar dominance of ExxonMobil, General Motors, Siemens, and Shell Oil in the 1950s and 1960s to today's tech-centric giants like Alphabet, ASML, Samsung, Tencent, and TSMC, the corporate world has been transformed. Where companies once wielded power through steel, oil, and industrial machinery, today they shape our lives through invisible networks—of code, chips, and logistics. These are no longer just businesses; they are the architects of how we shop, work, communicate, and even think.

Take the United States as a case in point. In the 1950s, General Motors was the embodiment of American industrial might. It didn't just make cars—it orchestrated a vast supply chain of steel, glass, labor, and capital, all culminating in gleaming sedans that symbolized middle-class aspirations. By the 1990s, the script had shifted. IBM moved beyond the clunky boxes of mainframes into the abstract world of services and consulting, while Walmart quietly revolutionized how goods moved from factories to store shelves, thanks to relentless efficiency in distribution and data-driven inventory control. Today, the titans are firms like Amazon, Apple, and Microsoft, whose core products often aren't tangible at all. Instead, they build digital ecosystems, cloud infrastructure, and artificial intelligence.

In fact, in the 1960s eight of ten top US firms by revenue were industrial giants. Today, only one of the top ten is industrial, and half of them did not even exist in 1960 (Exhibit 20).

They're not just different; they are also bigger. Even adjusting for inflation, the total revenue of the top ten US firms is seven times as large today as it was in 1960.

It is not only a few megafirms that are getting bigger. In 1955, the revenue of US Fortune 500 companies was equivalent to nearly 40 percent of US GDP. Now it is close to two-thirds. Large firms represent one-third and one-fifth of employment in advanced and emerging economies, respectively, and those shares are increasing. As economies grow in scale and complexity, it seems an iron law that the share of activity concentrated in large firms, and the size of these large firms, keep going up. The rise of very large firms is both an indication of our progress and a driver of it.[158]

Market capitalization, which reflects where markets see new and

EXHIBIT 20

Top US companies by revenue over time
All values in 2024 $ billion

1960		1995		2024	
General Motors	135	General Motors	341	Walmart	681
Standard Oil, NJ	94	Ford Motor	283	Amazon	638
AT&T	86	ExxonMobil	222	Apple	391
Ford Motor	57	Walmart	195	Berkshire Hathaway	371
General Electric	45	IBM	148	CVS Health	371
Sears	44	General Electric	144	McKesson	359
US Steel	39	Chrysler	110	Alphabet	350
Socony Mobil	39	Philip Morris	109	United Health Group	346
Gulf Oil	34	Sears	71	ExxonMobil	341
Chrysler	32	Procter & Gamble	69	Cencora	294
Total	**605**	**Total**	**1,692**	**Total**	**4,142**

Source: McKinsey Value Intelligence; *New York Times*; Federal Reserve Bank of Minneapolis; McKinsey Global Institute analysis

future economic value creation, shows an even starker change (Exhibit 21). Compared with 1995, a mere 30 years ago, only two of the top ten firms remain there today: Microsoft and Walmart. The average market capitalization, adjusted for inflation, has increased by a factor of 13.[159]

When we recently looked in detail at 3,000 global firms between 2005 and 2023, the data told a clear story. A small group of industries—what we call "arenas"—punched far above their weight. We found 12 of them, including cloud services, consumer electronics, and semiconductors. Although they accounted for only a tenth of total corporate revenue, they

Top US companies by market capitalization over time

All values in 2024 $ billion

1960		1995		2024	
AT&T	236	General Electric	248	Apple	3,785
IBM	163	ExxonMobil	206	NVIDIA	3,289
General Motors	125	Coca-Cola	192	Microsoft	3,134
DuPont	93	Merck & Co.	166	Alphabet	2,324
Standard Oil, NJ	90	General Motors	161	Amazon	2,307
Ford Motor	75	Philip Morris	155	Meta	1,478
General Electric	71	Procter & Gamble	117	Tesla	1,296
Texaco	52	Johnson & Johnson	114	Broadcom	1,087
US Steel	46	Microsoft	107	Berkshire Hathaway	978
Eastman Kodak	45	Walmart	105	Walmart	726
Total	**995**	**Total**	**1,572**	**Total**	**20,403**

Note: Figures may not sum to totals, due to rounding.
Source: McKinsey Value Intelligence; New York Times; Federal Reserve Bank of Minneapolis; McKinsey Global Institute analysis

generated nearly half of all market value growth. What set them apart wasn't just what they sold but how they operated. These firms invested more in innovation, moved faster, reached more global customers, and created higher economic returns than their peers. They were part of all-or-nothing races for reach and capability, propelling huge investment.[160]

The arenas of the future also show how firms transform more and more aspects of our lives. Robotics, AI, and cloud change how we work. E-commerce streamlines how we shop, and video streaming and video games shape our leisure time. Biopharma—for example, new obesity drugs—improves our health and quality of life, electric and shared autonomous vehicles reshape how we move, and modular construction transforms how we build. Each arena weaves innovation into the fabric of daily existence.

A global web of markets enabled cooperation

Firms don't just dream up progress in a vacuum. They thrive in markets, where ideas, goods, and ambitions collide.

Markets act like global matchmakers, linking people, resources, and needs across vast distances and time. They use price signals to process information, guiding millions of separate decisions into a coherent and efficient system, helping firms source goods, labor, and capital. When more people grab a burger in Seoul or Cape Town, global beef prices tick up, ranchers in Texas or Argentina raise more cattle, and a farmer in Brazil upgrades her tractor to grow more soy for feed. Market feedback loops enable distributed, spontaneous, uncoordinated cooperation on a vast scale.

Markets are also where new ideas take flight. When at their best, markets keep firms on their toes thanks to creative destruction. Go back to the fiercely competitive arenas, marked by rapid technological breakthroughs, escalatory investments, and large (very often global) markets. They are incubators of economic vitality, and they ensure that market leaders innovate continuously or risk displacement. Tesla's multibillion-dollar investments in EVs and battery technology revolutionized transportation, overtaking traditional automotive giants like General Motors. Department store chain Sears has dwindled to a shadow of its former self as Amazon redefined shopping. Walmart became an "omnichannel" retailer. Today almost 20 percent of Walmart's revenue comes from its online channel.[161]

Uber today is a leading player and has revolutionized the transportation market by *becoming* the transportation market. It created new ways of matching demand and supply through dynamic pricing and by connecting passengers and drivers algorithmically. It also created transparency into the journey for passengers, simplified payments, and reinforced trust through ratings systems and driver authentication. Its very innovation was to make markets more liquid and perfect. However, having been a disruptor ten years ago, Uber is now adapting as well, due to the entrance of companies like Waymo, which leads the pack in autonomous driving. In San Francisco, Waymo is reportedly already number two, and in fact the two companies now partner in a number of markets. Tesla is also entering some markets. The cycle of innovation and change continues.[162]

Markets are not just about products and services. Financial markets allocate funds to their most productive uses, from mortgages to risky enterprises, based on risk and return profiles. They also play the critical role of placing a value on the future. Labor markets allocate people. Jobs appear, disappear, and change. Just like firms, jobs are often replaced by new, more productive (and better-paid) ones. Our research shows that reallocation of employment from less productive to more productive firms added a full percentage point to US productivity growth in 2011–19.[163] And firms operate at the nexus of financial, product, and labor markets, balancing many competing interests.

What works at the firm level works at the country level. Market-oriented reforms around the world show just how powerful markets can be. There has not been a successful path to prosperity without them. Despite heavy state supervision, market reforms in China helped lift 800 million people out of poverty. India followed suit roughly a decade later. This growth happened because the market allowed the most effective solutions to come to the fore. China first became the world's factory of simple products, rapidly became increasingly sophisticated, and today competes with the United States for global technological supremacy. Some of the world's largest and more successful global firms were created there. Alibaba's e-commerce platform and its embrace of marketplace dynamics allowed it to outmaneuver traditional retailers, grow to more than $130 billion in revenue by 2024, and bring ever more choice to a rising Chinese middle class.[164]

But markets can and do fail. One common failure is the inability of markets to account for so-called externalities. For example, firms often emit pollutants in the course of production, and their costs are borne not by them alone, but by society as a whole. Similarly, the 2008 financial crisis exposed how information asymmetries and moral hazard in opaque financial markets can trigger systemic collapse. Many markets fail to provide sufficient incentives for some goods and services to emerge, such as vaccines during early development stages, or basic infrastructure in remote rural areas, because the returns are too diffuse or uncertain.

Monopolies can undermine fair competition, stifling innovation and growth. Contestable markets are necessary to ensure that incumbent firms get disrupted by new ones.

In many cases, market players self-regulate to establish trust because it is in their long-term best interest to do so. A good example is the Generally Accepted Accounting Principles. GAAP is a private initiative, which started as a response by private actors after the 1929 market crash to reestablish trust in financial markets and between firms.[165] Companies use their brands, too: Consumers know that a McDonald's burger is the same in Tokyo or Toronto. Reputation is a powerful market mechanism.

But these are far from sufficient. A thoughtful institutional setup that creates the right incentives is just as crucial.

Institutions provided a framework for cooperation

Nobel Prize–winning economists Daron Acemoglu, James Robinson, and Simon Johnson attribute differences in economic development to one thing: institutions.[166] Institutions form the bedrock of growth, ensuring trust among societies, firms, and governments. While we typically amalgamate institutions and government, they are much more than the state. They are all the "rules of the game" that govern an economy.

At a high level, we can differentiate between inclusive and extractive institutions. Today, the poorest nations suffer from extractive institutions and illiberal regimes, where powerful insiders route resources to themselves and their allies. Conversely, countries like Sweden and Japan support the growth of firms by providing predictable legal environments, safe from expropriation or state capture. Sweden has one of the most vibrant tech startup ecosystems in the world, with giants like Spotify and nascent AI challengers like Lovable. Crucially, Sweden's government and powerful incumbents do not attempt to capitalize on these upstarts with windfall taxes, intervention, or hostile takeovers. This encourages future entrepreneurs to take risks and innovate. This might seem elemental, but extractive institutions hinder economic growth and discourage investment, because entrepreneurs' successes risk being poached by powerful insiders.

Traditionally, many institutions are grouped together under the umbrella term "the rule of law." In an economic sense, the rule of law is more than maintaining public order and prosecuting pickpockets (though those are important, too). It sets limits on the power of government. It upholds the rights of individuals and firms. It ensures that contracts are enforceable in a court of law. It creates legal constructs that protect intangibles, like intellectual property.

Inclusive institutions don't just protect firms and consumers from the government; they protect society against firms becoming monopolies or causing harms like pollution. Regulation requires a tricky balance: It needs to encourage competition and reduce externalities without stifling innovation. Carbon emissions pricing in the EU has helped reduce emissions drastically in affected sectors.[167] The breakup of monopolies like Standard Oil enabled new competitors to innovate, driving sustained economic growth. Today, there is an active debate about the power that tech giants have amassed. Such tension, evident in US antitrust battles and EU privacy laws, ensures that governance adapts to the scale of superhuman firms.

And yet, an institutional focus on competition is more effective still. It is competition that constantly disrupts leaders and forces them to adapt. Historically, making international voice calls relied on a handful of telecom operators. But the emergence of internet-based communication tools transformed the market, offering faster, more flexible, and virtually cost-free alternatives. Similarly, generative AI is changing the dynamics of the search and advertising businesses.

Beyond setting the rules of the game, public institutions provide critical public goods and services such as infrastructure and defense, as well as other goods and services, like education, that markets and firms alone do not supply adequately. Many of these underpin markets. Labor markets in most developed economies depend on a steady supply of educated and skilled young people, most of whom owe their education to some form of public funding. Highway systems are the veins of our countries and cities. Publicly funded research, such as early investments by the Defense Advanced Research Projects Agency, seeded foundational technologies in networking and computing that, for example, gave us the internet.

There is no determined right size for effective governance. Different models exist and succeed: Switzerland and Scandinavian countries both enjoy tremendous standards of living despite vastly different forms of government. The Danish government is bigger than most, but it has an explicit policy of nonintervention in labor markets, leaving negotiations to employers and unions. The result is high wages despite no minimum wage, and income security despite flexibility thanks to private unemployment insurance. Switzerland has a small state but spends significantly on education, giving Swiss teachers the third-highest salaries in the OECD and Switzerland two public universities in the global top 40.[168]

The state's dual nature as both problem solver and problem creator continues to fuel political debate. Whether people view government more as the former or the latter largely determines their placement on the political spectrum. The universal left-right push and pull is ultimately what ensures the stability of institutions: It creates a balance between the two views that ensures that government is called to act when intervention is required—and ensures pushback when government oversteps.

The final powerful force that drives economic success is social capital, the trust and cooperation that naturally emerge when people share a space, interact, or trade with one another. When we participate in regular market interactions, our instincts are subtly rewired toward trust, making us kinder and more cooperative with strangers. Uber, again, serves as a great example. On the face of it, getting into a stranger's car at 3 a.m. is far from rational. Yet repeated positive interactions with Uber give us confidence to step in and perhaps strike up a conversation with the driver. This invisible bond, built from countless interactions, becomes the quiet engine powering exchange and dynamism, fueling lasting economic prosperity.[169]

Ultimately, the dynamic interactions among firms, markets, and institutions continue to drive economic evolution, powering prosperity through enhanced cooperation, continuous innovation, and robust governance. History shows that good institutions are a necessary condition of progress. If they are absent, we feel it. History also shows that one of their most important roles is to effectively unleash the power of markets and firms.

⁂

The eight parts of the progress machine have changed the world. Working together, they have delivered on growth, on prosperity, and on a transformation in the quality of people's lives. But no machine, no matter how well calibrated, runs forever without tweaking, retooling, refurbishing. And the progress machine that we have described is, indeed, showing signs of stuttering. Can this machine deliver plenty in the next century? Additionally, the machine was not perfect; it produced some exhaust and some side effects. Inequality, climate change, maybe even unhappiness. Was all this progress actually worth it? In Part III, we delve into these two questions.

PART III

PROGRESS AT THE CROSSROADS

CHAPTER 13

CAN THE PROGRESS MACHINE KEEP HUMMING?

"One never notices what has been done; one can only see what remains to be done."

MARIE CURIE

—

The progress machine may be losing power, and it needs upgrading to take us into the next century.

POWERFUL AS THE PROGRESS MACHINE has been over the past century, some might argue that it is not fit for purpose, that it creates too much dirty exhaust, or that it doesn't have enough power to propel every human forward. That's not new. The progress machine has never been perfect or frictionless. It has always rubbed up against the challenges of the times. And it has never been static. The machine is a dynamic, adaptive system that is constantly renewing itself—with our help.

We have talked about 100 years of eras interrupted with inflection points. The world is at one of those inflection points now. It is at these times of uncertainty and mounting strains that we have done our best work as engineers of progress. Think of the sweeping economic and institutional changes of 1946, the energy and macroeconomic realignment of the 1970s, and the political and international trade earthquake of 1989.

What challenges should we be contemplating now? Going into enormous detail would require another book, but let's at least briefly take stock of what might be the major items filed as "most important" on our jobs sheet. We highlight six.

The way we tackle these challenges could have profound effects on the character of the new era into which we are entering.

Demographic decline or lifelong vitality

The doomsayers warned of overpopulation, but a more pressing and legitimate concern now looms: depopulation. The demographic dividend that powered growth in much of the past century has ended in most countries. This part of the progress machine is not just less powerful but is potentially a drag on the entire engine. Our challenge now is to offset this demographic drag by nudging fertility rates upward, extending healthy working lives, and adapting economies to aging populations. We explored this in depth in our 2025 report *Dependency and depopulation: Confronting the consequences of a new demographic reality.*[1]

Family sizes are shrinking as fertility has declined in 90 percent of the world's countries. Two-thirds of humanity lives in places with fertility below the replacement rate of 2.1. In South Korea, the fertility rate is a mere 0.7. To put that in perspective, 100 grandparents would have only 13 grandchildren on current trends. By 2100, the country's population could drop by more than 60 percent.

Fewer births and more older people mean fewer workers, and that means less economic growth. The impact could be stark. Over the next 25 years, income per person could decline by $10,000 in Western Europe and $6,000 in China. Strain on public budgets is mounting, and the risk of a generational divide is growing, with younger people facing higher

Grandmother spending time with her grandchild, South Korea.

taxes, higher housing costs, and slower growth as they shoulder rising pension burdens.

And the demographic winter is arriving sooner than expected in emerging economies. While the working-age share of the population has already peaked in advanced economies and China, the rest of the world (except Sub-Saharan Africa) will follow in the next one to two generations. Even Sub-Saharan Africa, the last region with high fertility rates, will see its working-age share peak by the 2080s before it also starts to decline. Most emerging economies will soon be just as "youthless" as the developed world.

To counter this, we need a multipronged upgrade to the progress machine.

One lever we can pull is lengthening working lives. Advances in personalized preventative medicine can add vibrant years, enabling people to remain active into their 70s, just as many Japanese already do.[2] It makes sense, at a minimum, to enable and encourage people to keep working through their 50s and 60s. These are years in which labor participation falls rapidly, often due to built-in legal incentives, health limitations, and a labor market not geared to attract and integrate older workers. Already, up to 25 percent of older adults who are not working say that they would like to do so, so providing the right conditions would go a long way toward improving labor participation amongst seniors.[3]

We may well witness the end of the rigid three-stage life pattern of education-work-retirement as it gives way to a more dynamic model that reflects longer, healthier lives.[4] That may mean a different type of career. Those in physically demanding jobs need viable pathways into less strenuous work as they age. Older people will need to keep pace with the lightning speed of technological change. And recruiters need to rethink. Can you remember when you last saw a job ad featuring a 50-year-old? Companies could also foster collaboration between generations, pairing tech-savvy young workers with seasoned veterans to combine their strengths.

Another lever is continuing to open doors to women working for pay. In many countries, more women have entered the workforce, but in some others, cultural and policy barriers are still a bar. Removing those barriers and supporting participation with the right policies could add millions more women to the workforce, powering growth.

One more way to strengthen the demographic part of the progress machine is to lift productivity radically, decoupling incomes from hours worked, for instance, through more automation. Robotics in particular can shoulder some of the burden in aging societies, from manufacturing to eldercare, filling critical gaps where human labor is scarce. A productivity boost will be important in advanced economies, but arguably even more so in low-productivity regions with rapidly falling birth rates, like most of Latin America. Some of the countries in that region will soon be as "old" as today's advanced economies, but with productivity and income levels less than half as high.[5]

A final lever is changing demographics itself. Restoring fertility rates to a level closer to 2.1 would take profound shifts: from hope and community to empowerment through family-friendly policies and other economic measures. People who feel supported and optimistic about the future are more likely to want to have children. In fact, many people already want more children than they have. The barriers they encounter range from unaffordable housing and childcare to biological obstacles like infertility. Extending women's reproductive lives could be a breakthrough, similar to how new home appliances and antibiotics drove the mid-20th-century baby boom.[6] Economic growth, empowerment, and science—and optimism—could help bend the curve on fertility.

Any upgraded machine will also need to be recalibrated for the future state of public finances. Even if fertility rises, it takes decades for a newborn to enter the labor force, contribute to economic growth, and pay taxes, and for the drag to become a dividend again. While we improve on health, work, and productivity, we also need to rethink pension and healthcare systems to avoid overburdening a shrinking cohort of young workers. We need to rewire the social contract for a new demographic reality.

Weak investment or building the future

Investment is at the heart of the productivity equation, and we're falling short. In much of the world, we simply aren't investing the way we used to: in housing, in infrastructure like roads and grids, in technology such as machinery and robotics, and in intangibles like R&D and software. The drive to build has weakened, and progress has slowed.

We had an extraordinary confluence of events in the fiat money era that allowed mass financialization and capital deepening at very low real interest rates. As a result, productivity growth was robust. In the past 50 years, one-quarter of the world's population lived in countries growing at more than 5 percent. Today, it is less than 3 percent.[7]

As we showed in *Investing in productivity growth,* since the 2008 financial crisis, productivity growth has slowed almost everywhere, largely due to weak investment. In Germany, Japan, the United Kingdom, and the United States, a marked decline in the growth of capital per worker accounts for half the productivity slowdown since 2008. Net investment fell from about 7 percent of GDP to less than 3 percent in these economies. The trend points in the same direction in many emerging markets, with some in Sub-Saharan Africa and Latin America experiencing decades of stagnant investment. Instead of narrowing productivity gaps with advanced economies, some are falling further behind.[8]

And the issue is not only that investment is weak, but also where some of the funding that was available has gone. Financial capital has flowed disproportionately into inflating asset prices, leading to outsize growth of

Truck parked next to potholes on a city street, Illinois, United States.

the global balance sheet and a rising burden of debt.[9] From 2000 to 2021, the global balance sheet quadrupled, far outpacing GDP growth. Debt soared, as did asset prices, for both real assets like property and financial ones like equity. Productivity failed to keep pace. Over the past 25 years, for every $1 in net new investment into the economy, the world added $2 in net new debt and grew household wealth by almost $4.

Since 2000, less than a third of new wealth has been capital formation that drives productivity growth. Another third is price increases in line with general inflation, protecting owners against wealth erosion as prices rise. The last third is asset price appreciation above and beyond that.

Healthy balance sheets are anchored in productive investment. But when the balance sheet outpaces the economy, risks mount.[10] Paper wealth can prop up demand. Until it doesn't. Debt can be sustainable when interest rates are low. Until they rise.

When balance sheets unwind through asset price corrections and deleveraging, the damage can be severe. We witnessed that in Japan in the 1990s, the United States after 2008, and Greece in the 2010s. Global debt now sits at 2.6 times GDP. That's up 50 percentage points since 2000. Some pockets are extreme: Japan's government debt and China's corporate debt stand at unprecedented levels of 2.3 and 1.8 times GDP, respectively.[11]

The solution? Revamp productive investment. Grow the economy. Invent and build the future!

But we seem to have lost the will to build. Infrastructure is aging and undermaintained. In the United States, growth in electricity transmission lines, for instance, hasn't kept pace with population growth, let alone met the needs of electrification. Housing shortages are a problem in many places. In Spain, 2.4 million new households have formed since 2008, against only 1.5 million housing starts. Young, smart, productive workers can't afford to move to the places where their collective minds thrive. Without investment, cities risk losing their edge as growth engines.[12]

This isn't inevitable. Our failure to invest and build is largely the result of policy inertia, regulatory bottlenecks, and a mindset of scarcity. But we can change that. Restoring our capacity to build requires a cultural and policy shift toward prioritizing growth and prosperity.[13] A positive-sum mindset in which building benefits all through lower costs and expanded opportunities can move us past zero-sum debates and toward a politics of plenty. For instance, permitting processes that delay projects for years could be streamlined to cut costs and fast-track infrastructure for both housing and clean energy. Houston, with minimal zoning and flexible land-use rules, permitted more housing units in 2023 than San Francisco, New York, and Boston combined, and the price of homes has risen by far less than in these cities as a result.[14]

By channeling capital into high-impact areas, governments and firms can unleash productivity and economic growth while improving the health of the global balance sheet. Emerging markets can also close productivity gaps by prioritizing infrastructure, skills, and technology, such as digitization. This requires strong institutions and deeper financial systems. In India, digital public infrastructure added $31.8 billion to national income (0.9 percent) in 2022 by streamlining service delivery, expanding access to financial services, and cutting transaction costs across sectors.[15]

Imagining a prosperous future is a start. Building it is what counts.

Innovation stagnation or a new dawn from AI

It may seem surprising to readers that we are presenting this dichotomy given that newfangled inventions seem to crop up weekly. Indeed, according to many figures, innovation seems alive and well. In 2023, more than 3.5 million patents were filed, up nearly 2 percent from a year earlier.[16] In recent decades, the internet and the digital world have bloomed. More recently, from AI to biotech to renewable energy, we seem to break new ground constantly.

But some researchers say that the low-hanging fruit may have been picked and ideas are getting harder to find. We have roughly kept pace with invention, but by throwing more and more resources into it. For example, computing performance of chips has kept improving, but now takes 18 times more researchers to achieve the same improvement it did in 1971.[17] Others argue that the more recent innovations have not been as transformative as the ones we enjoyed earlier in the 20th century, which would explain more sluggish productivity growth since the 1970s. Electricity completely changed the way we live. But does the internet, for example, pull off the same trick? Maybe AI and next-gen robotics can?[18]

Alongside concerns about dwindling innovation are worries about AI and what that might mean for jobs, or even more existential anxieties. Some harbor fears about AI becoming smarter than humans and going rogue. Science fiction is replete with such cautionary tales, from Skynet in *The Terminator* to *Westworld*. Certainly, guardrails need to be put in place as AI is developed further to safeguard humanity and balance innovation with safety.

But our purpose here is not to be too speculative. Instead, we see the potential for AI to be the next technology that humanity can harness to revolutionize productivity growth and, with it, living standards. It can also help solve some research and innovation challenges by transforming the research process itself. We elaborate on the mechanisms, as well as potential impacts on the future of work, in Part IV.

There are huge opportunities beyond AI, too. Current breakthroughs include biology-based innovation such as gene editing and obesity drugs that have burst onto the scene in a big way; energy and mobility-related leaps forward, like the continued improvement and deployment at scale of nuclear power and EVs; or the next physical frontiers, like modular construction and the next era of robotics. We experience constant progress, whether on the new best large language model, the world's first personalized CRISPR therapy given to a baby with genetic disease, a novel material that calcifies carbon as it sets, or bamboo that has been manipulated to be stronger than steel.[19]

We challenge the notion that our recent innovations have not been transformative and that coming ones do not have large potential to be truly transformative and raise living standards fast. Slow productivity growth has been a function of low investment and the fact that new ideas and technologies take time to affect the economy at large. Skills, business processes and cultures, and other intangibles need to transform alongside technology to reap the full rewards that technology can offer.[20]

The world is now much wealthier and better educated than it was a century ago. The innovator base has gone global; millions more creative minds are hard at work solving the toughest challenges of today. Combined with the power of new technology, the innovation machine has a unique chance to be upgraded once again.

Energy and climate conundrum or scaling technologies

Energy is critical to economic empowerment and growth, but it is also the source of carbon emissions and other environmental harms. Some say, "Just end fossil fuels." But while we need to transition away from them, stopping them today would mean stopping the world as we know it. In 2023, fossil fuels accounted for just over 80 percent of the energy we produce, and low-emissions sources for most of the rest. In the case of electricity generation, we are further along. Clean sources now generate about 40 percent and fossil fuels about 60 percent of electricity.[21]

Energy generation needs to be clean, but it also needs to be abundant, affordable, and reliable. The challenge is exacerbated by the rise of AI and its accompanying demands for energy; some large players have begun to source their own power plants for the purpose of running their energy-thirsty data centers.[22] As it is, we don't have the energy we need to power prosperity and therefore are faced with the dual goal of growing the energy supply while transforming it to reduce its emissions.

There is momentum on many, but not all, fronts, as we analyzed in our report *The hard stuff: Navigating the physical realities of the energy transition*. About 90 percent of all battery EV sales and almost 60 percent of existing solar and wind power capacity was added in the past five years.[23] But overall, the energy transition is in its early stages. Deployment of low-emissions technologies is currently at only about 10 percent of the levels required for countries to meet their stated climate commitments, and it has largely happened in comparatively easy use cases. While some areas like solar generation have grown rapidly, others have not. For low-emissions hydrogen, for example, less than 1 percent of required deployment has been achieved thus far.[24]

We identified 25 physical challenges we need to tackle. These are barriers to switching from high- to low-emissions assets and processes, and include imperatives as diverse as growing storage capacity through batteries, unearthing critical minerals, and investing at scale on heat pumps. Within these 25, the "demanding dozen" are particularly hard. These occur when there are gaps in technological performance, large interdependencies exist, or their transformation is just beginning, and include loading up electric trucks or furnacing low-emissions steel. Eliminating between 40 and 60 percent of the energy system's emissions depends on addressing the hardest challenges.[25]

We can, and must, continue pushing on. We need to accelerate our investment in low-emissions technologies that are technically feasible and in the money, from solar to nuclear, while innovating furiously. Deployment on a sufficient scale is still not happening as fast as needed in order to have the energy we need while reducing emissions.[26]

We need nothing less than a reinvention of our energy system to meet the dual imperative of making it large and affordable enough to serve everyone and therefore deliver prosperity, and clean enough to limit global warming. We return to how we think we can pull this off in Part IV. But for now, it suffices to say that we have a major challenge on our hands: More innovation, investment, and deployment are needed.

A fracturing world or redesigned collaboration

Free-flowing global trade has been a powerful part of the progress engine, but the system is becoming more fragile as geopolitical rivalry exerts a more pervasive influence. Well-established forums for global cooperation may have lost traction, or at the very least are going through a period of reckoning and change. The number of new global trade restrictions each year has increased substantially, from about 670 in 2017 to about 3,500 in 2024.[27] Fragmentation that weakens the part of the machine that powers valuable global connections looms, especially given the flurry of trade-related shocks in 2025.

As we have studied in multiple reports including *Geopolitics and the geometry of global trade,* the prospect of disrupted supply chains and trade disputes could have a damaging effect on every region of the world. Each of them relies on trade with others for more than one-quarter of at least one important type of good. And there is a further risk if global connections unravel. About 40 percent of trade is "concentrated," which we define as when importing economies rely on just a few supplying economies. For 10 percent of global goods, such as laptops, rare earths, and soybeans, trade is reliant on three or fewer exporters.[28]

Concentration is rife in goods regarded as strategically important. China accounts for 90 percent of the processing of rare earths. China and India dominate the active pharmaceutical ingredient market. Taiwan produces more than 60 percent of the world's semiconductors and more than 90 percent of the most advanced ones.[29] If exports from Taiwan were disrupted or shut off, the global technology industry would grind to a halt. Businesses and entire economies are significantly exposed to the risk of a precious few suppliers raising their prices or otherwise changing their terms.

Governments and businesses have become more sensitive to the risks attached to relying on imports of goods deemed to be vital for national interest. Moves to protect their interests against potential disruption in the sourcing of important products have started to reconfigure trade. The average geopolitical distance of trade declined by about 7 percent between 2017 and 2024, a period when trade tensions between China and the United States were ever present and during which Russia invaded Ukraine, returning to levels last seen in 2007 (Exhibit 22). China, Germany, and the United States have all experienced sharp reductions on this measure.[30]

Still, there is a silver lining to this close interdependency. Decoupling is hard, and there is considerable incentive to shore up global cooperation. Rearranging trade from one supplying economy to another seamlessly

EXHIBIT 22

Geopolitical distance of trade

Index (0–10 scale, greatest distance = 10)

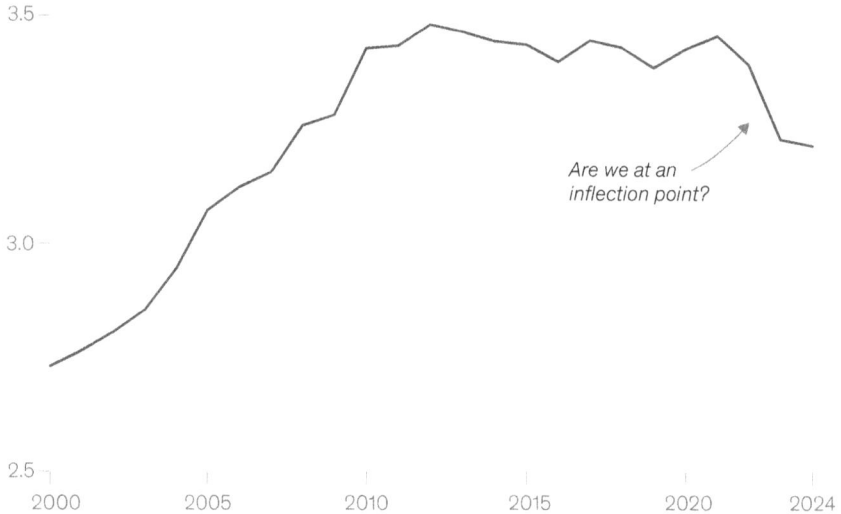

Are we at an
inflection point?

Note: Geopolitical distance is defined as the difference between countries' positions on a spectrum ranging from 0 to 10
of geopolitical positions based on their UN General Assembly votes between 2005 and 2022.
Source: Voeten, 2017; UN Digital Library; McKinsey Global Institute analysis

is far from easy. If the United States tried to stop importing Christmas decorations from China, it would need five times more than the amount the rest of the world currently exports to fill the gap, for example.[31]

The economic benefits of trade and pragmatism continue to hold sway. Our analysis shows that Asia, for instance, engages in significant intraregional trade even where countries hold diverse political stances. Countries know that there is a danger in not playing the big game of globalization. At least 10 percent of global GDP is dependent on cross-border flows of various kinds. Some estimates put that figure as high as 40 percent in an extreme scenario.[32]

In the face of global connections fraying, we would do well to direct our efforts into shoring up international cooperation. In a world in which trade rules, or at least the ones we are accustomed to, are being questioned, some semblance of cohesion at the global institutional and political level seems necessary.

We have a tough job on our hands in this regard. In 2024, McKinsey and the World Economic Forum published a new Global Cooperation Barometer, which takes the pulse of five pillars of global cooperation: trade and capital flows, innovation and technology, climate and natural capital, health and wellness, and peace and security. This inaugural barometer indicated that global cooperation has stalled after being on a positive trend for much of the past ten years.[33] Some countries are questioning the sustainability of today's trade "imbalances," pointing to persistent deficits and surpluses from specialization, risks of high dependency on a few partners for critical inputs, and distortions from currency valuations.

Can we turn this around? We have done so before. From the abyss of World War II, we put together an entire system of global cooperation. And while the global picture may appear more fractured, pockets of enthusiastic cooperation exist. Regional trade agreements, including the Regional Comprehensive Economic Partnership, the Comprehensive and Progressive Agreement for Trans-Pacific Partnership, and the African Continental Free Trade Area, are on the rise. In the case of global institutions, there is a true incentive to address criticisms leveled against organizations such as the WTO, one being that its dispute system is failing.[34] A redesigned model of collaboration could extend beyond trade to shaping critical global agendas such as setting technology standards, advancing climate goals, preventing future pandemics, ensuring financial stability, and resolving cross-border conflicts. The precise form this cooperation will take—whether it echoes the past or breaks new ground—remains uncertain. What is clear, however, is that the absence of cooperation would be the most troubling outcome.

Of course, businesses can weigh in and put the pressure on. Two-thirds of global trade is channeled through multinational corporations, meaning they have a great deal of skin in the game.[35] They need a more predictable and collaborative framework and could use their economic clout to act as "corporate diplomats" to try to revive cooperation and preserve highly valuable global trade and supply chains.

Fraying social compact or reignited culture of growth

Beneath these structural challenges lies a deeper erosion: the fraying of the social compact that binds societies together in pursuit of shared progress. Trust in governments, businesses, media, and markets is low, particularly in advanced economies. This fuels pessimism that threatens to stall the very progress engine we've celebrated. In the United States, for instance, a 2023 Pew Research survey found that 65 percent of adults believe the world is getting worse, up from 41 percent in 2017.[36] This gloom is even more pronounced among youth, with polls revealing a generational divide. Recent research has found that young Americans are more likely to see the world as zero-sum than their older counterparts.[37]

This pessimism manifests in striking attitudes toward foundational elements of society. Pew Research also found in 2024 that only 22 percent of Americans trusted the federal government to do the right thing "just about always" or "most of the time," among the lowest readings in 60 years. In Germany, trust in the government fell to 35 percent in 2025, far below the 59 percent in 2021. High energy costs and a loss of faith in the government's competence were blamed.[38]

People seem to trust businesses more than governments and the media but to carry a general sense of grievance, particularly targeted at the wealthy. In the 2025 Edelman Trust Barometer Survey, an unprecedented 69 percent of respondents said they worry that government officials, business leaders, and journalists deliberately mislead them; that's up 11 points since 2021.[39]

This is consistent with a more broadly pessimistic global mood: only 36 percent of people worldwide say they believe the next generation will be better off. But country-level differences are striking. In China and India, for example, about two-thirds of respondents say the next generation will be better off, and in African countries including Nigeria or Kenya, half do. Meanwhile, in all advanced economies, the share is below 25 percent, and as low as 9 percent in France.[40]

This bleak worldview could be influencing life choices, even whether to have children. According to one US survey, affordability is a primary issue, but 38 percent of respondents cited concerns about the state of the world as a major reason for not becoming parents, and 26 percent concerns about the environment.[41] If pessimism abounds, it may affect the very existence of future generations.

This erosion of trust, of belief in progress itself, is one of the core reasons we have written this book. In our own small way, the qualified (and quantified) optimism of this book hopes to counter a slide into pessimism and inertia. We do need to upgrade the progress machine. But if the next century is to be one of abundance, it will also require a cultural shift, a narrative reset, a renewed "culture of growth."[42]

If we fix the parts of the machine that have lost power or that are no longer fit for purpose, progress is possible. The past century's miracles weren't inevitable; they stemmed from bold visions and collective will. Embracing a growth mindset today gets us closer to tomorrow's era of plenty.

※ ※ ※

Even the best-designed and -operated machine suffers from wear and tear. There is a need to examine the progress machine from surface to innards to work out whether its parts are working as well as they could, and must, to power another century of progress. We have done this before, ironing out glitches, making the machine better, and prospering. We adapted to the circumstances.

At moments of historical transition, shared narratives become the scaffolding for renewal. This is one of those moments. This won't come from consensus on every issue; disagreement is healthy and necessary. But it will come from a renewed commitment to common purpose, rooted in first principles: that prosperity is possible, that innovation matters, and that investing in the future is both a moral and a practical imperative.

Before looking into the future, into the possibility of a next century of plenty, let us weigh the benefits and side effects of the remarkable progress of the past 100 years.

CHAPTER 14

THE BALANCE OF PROGRESS

"Our problems are man-made;
therefore, they can be solved by man."

JOHN F. KENNEDY

——

Do the side effects of growth outweigh the benefits?

WE HAVE PAINTED AN AMAZING PICTURE of economic growth and human progress and described the machine behind it. We have also discussed some of the challenges the machine faces today. But we have not really questioned progress itself.

To be sure, many good things happened: higher incomes, longer and better lives, less disease, more education, more freedom, more people (and women in particular) empowered. But there were also inequality, climate change, and environmental damage, weren't there?

No progress is ever without side effects. Let's offer a rounded assessment. A serious reckoning. Even with its flaws and imperfections, can we describe the progress of the past 100 years as on balance "good"?

Was it worth it? In this chapter, we put progress in the dock and charge it with some of the most common accusations it faces. Call this set of arguments "the prosecution." We then assess these arguments and offer facts on the case.

The main charges we see are that economic progress has been unequal and left many people behind; that our climate can't handle it; that progress causes too much deterioration in the natural environment; and that in any case it doesn't really make us happier. Let the trial begin!

Is economic growth inclusive?

The first item on the prosecution's charge sheet is a potent one: that despite the many wonders of progress, economic growth has left many people behind. The prosecution argues that prosperity may have increased in aggregate, but the lives and livelihoods of many have stagnated or fallen behind. Many people struggle to afford basic necessities like housing, healthcare, and education. Sometimes their wages may grow, but they are left worse off because the cost of living increases by even more.

The result is growing inequality. Even if economic growth can theoretically lift all boats, it has disproportionately favored the affluent, the prosecution argues. Economic disparities can foster social division and reduce economic and social progress.

What makes matters worse, the argument continues, is that the very sources of aggregate progress—creative destruction of markets, automation, and globalization—can leave people behind and increase inequality.[43] A potent mix of global access to cheap labor and goods as well as the rise of automation has displaced workers and hollowed out communities. Free markets, highly successful companies, international trade, and technological innovation have all been potent drivers of progress, but they have side effects. While consumers enjoy greater variety, from German cars to Mexican avocados to American and Chinese tech platforms, many workers can't keep up with fast progress, and they fall behind. Some further assert that progress is exploitative: Corporations reap the profits while workers endure unstable, low-paying jobs.

In short, economic progress, the argument goes, has not been inclusive.

Let us start by evaluating whether only some people have benefited from economic progress while others have not. We first focus on absolute gains before turning to inequality and finally the effects of creative destruction in markets, automation, and globalization.

We saw in Part I that most of humanity, across all income levels, has experienced stunning progress since 1925. Very few people would want to turn back the clock 100 years. But it is often argued, for example in the United States, that the typical worker has not made any progress for several decades, since the 1970s or 1980s.[44] The reality is that the real wage of the median US worker grew by about 40 percent between 1980 and 2023 and, today, is the highest ever recorded.[45] The same is true if we look below the median: Since 1980, the incomes of the poorest 20 percent in the United States have grown by 53 percent, and by 99 percent after taxes and transfers. And we can go beyond the United States. In France, incomes of the bottom 10 percent grew by 34 percent. In China, the figure is 63 percent (pretax).[46]

Progress lifted all, or almost all, boats.

This does not mean, however, that we should be complacent. We can do better. While wages have grown, the pace of progress has slowed down compared with the period after World War II due to lower productivity growth and median wages lagging behind productivity.[47]

Despite remarkable progress, 20 to 30 percent of people in advanced economies remain below the empowerment line. In the United States and many European countries, the link between rising incomes and empowerment is less clear than in lower-income regions, because the prices of education, healthcare, energy, housing, and food have often risen faster than inflation.[48] These are basic necessities and represent a larger share of the consumption of people with lower incomes.

The question is how to accelerate progress and empower increasing numbers of people. It requires more and better job opportunities and more, better, and more affordable education, health, transportation, energy, and housing, all of which can benefit from economic growth and a mindset of plenty.

Now let's turn to inequality. We explore its evolution between countries and within them over the past century (Exhibit 23).[49]

Inequality between countries has been falling for the past 55 years. In fact, if the world were a single nation, inequality would be at its lowest level in 100 years.

Global income inequality (pretax), between-country and within-country
Ratio of top 10% to bottom 50% by income

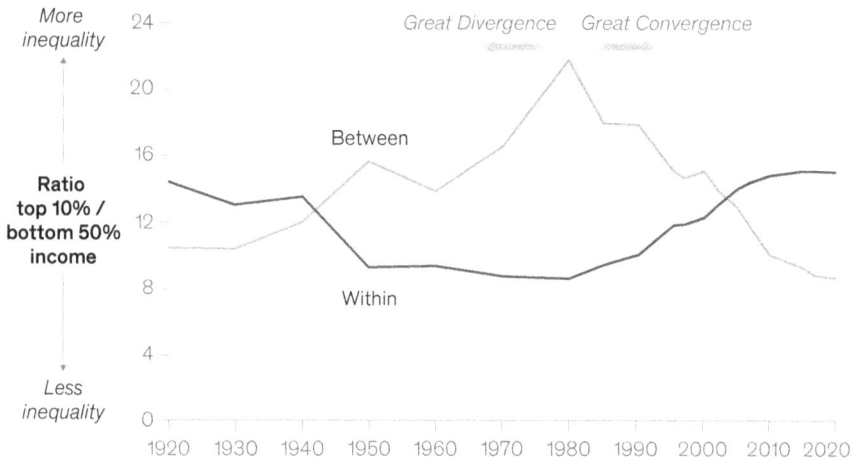

Note: Between-country inequality, as measured by the ratio T10/B50 between the average incomes of the top 10% and the bottom 50%, rose between 1920 and 1980 and has strongly declined since then. Within-country inequality, as measured also by the ratio T10/B50 between the average incomes of the top 10% and the bottom 50%, declined between 1920 and 1980 and has risen since 1980.
Source: Chancel and Piketty, 2021; McKinsey Global Institute analysis

The trend has been in the shape of an inverted U. In the first half of the 20th century, inequality between nations soared in what economists have called the Great Divergence.[50] The industrialized nations of Western Europe, North America, and later parts of Asia industrialized, advanced technologically, and invested the fruits of rising wealth in education. They pulled ahead of the rest of the world, which remained largely agrarian, often colonized, and closed off.

Inequality between countries peaked around 1980, and the Great Convergence began. Many emerging economies grew faster than their advanced counterparts, benefiting from their own industrialization, the liberalization of trade, and technology transfer via the multinationals who broadened their footprints to benefit from the new growth hot spots. Inequality between countries fell sharply. China was a large feature of the story but was far from alone. Countries like Bangladesh, India, and

Vietnam also harnessed the complementary forces of technology-driven industrialization and globalization. If one values every human life equally, this is a story of *falling* inequality.

How about inequality within countries? Here the prosecution appears to have a stronger case, although it is a nuanced one.

Day to day, people are more likely to evaluate how we are doing in comparison with our near neighbors rather than people who live on the other side of the world. Local inequalities, such as the ability to afford a house, can be deeply felt. Here, the story is almost the exact opposite of inequality between countries—a U instead of an inverted U. Essentially, inequality within countries fell during World War II and remained low until the 1980s. But then it started to rise and continued to do so into the mid-2010s. In the United States, the Gini coefficient after taxes and transfers rose from 0.31 to 0.39 between 1980 and 2023.[51] In Europe, the picture was mixed. Several countries did not experience growing inequality, while others saw much more moderate increases than the United States. In Spain and France, for example, inequality did not rise at all, while the Gini index for both Germany and the United Kingdom rose from 0.26 to 0.31. Perhaps surprisingly, inequality has been flat or falling across every one of these countries, including in the United States, since the early 2010s.

Growing global within-country inequality has not only been driven by some advanced economies. Inequality has been rising in China, India, and many other emerging economies. This is a common story, a phenomenon known as the "Kuznets curve." When countries start to develop, inequality usually rises and then falls. Some areas urbanize and prosper first, pulling ahead and increasing inequality, but then more citizens join the ranks of the prosperous, and inequality declines. China's Gini coefficient rose sharply from 1980 to 2010 and has been falling ever since.[52]

Is there a growth-equality trade-off? No. At least not necessarily. In fact, less prosperous countries generally have higher inequality than more prosperous ones. Economies have flourished while inequality moved up and down.

The main driver of inequality is not economic progress per se, nor the exploitation of the many by the few, but well-understood differences across the sectors and companies in which people work, the skills they possess, the technologies they use, and the markets they can access.

Korail slum and modern Gulshan area in Dhaka, Bangladesh.

Workers in tech sectors earn higher wages than workers in construction. Larger multinationals, on average, pay higher salaries than small and medium-size firms. This is simply because the tech sector and large multinationals are more productive than their counterparts.

So rather than halting progress or stopping economically successful people, companies, and sectors, the better approach is to increase opportunities and incomes for those that lag behind, improving everyone's lot.

Economic growth can be a force *for* inclusion and lower inequality in at least two ways. First, it creates resources to invest in the physical and human capital (infrastructure, skills, and health, among others) needed for everyone to prosper. Second, wealthier economies can afford larger welfare states and redistribute income.

This is reflected in the data. Social spending has grown faster than national income over the past century, and it is much larger in advanced economies than in emerging economies. Consider Australia, where the Productivity Commission has conducted comprehensive studies.

Australia's Gini coefficient is about 0.45 before taxes and transfers. That's the middle of the pack. But it dives to about 0.30 when measuring disposable income after progressive tax and welfare systems have done their work. And if one counts in-kind services provided by governments and communities, the coefficient falls again to just above 0.22. In other words, inequality is cut in half through strong societal cooperation. Across the OECD, social spending as a share of GDP has risen from about one-tenth in the 1950s to about one-quarter today.[53]

Imagine that without economic growth. Redistributing a fixed pie, let alone a shrinking one, is politically difficult and economically ruinous. A growing pie allows for redistribution while everyone makes gains.

Finally, let's turn our attention to the charge that a combination of the creative destruction of markets, automation, and globalization causes an intolerable burden on those left on the wrong side of change. Is it true?

It is certainly true that when new technologies emerge, they can be disruptive and make some skills—historically, physical and repetitive ones—less valuable and technological, social, or creative ones more valuable. As a result, some people benefit more than others. International trade, while improving aggregate welfare, can also have a concentrated negative impact on the livelihoods of those who compete with international producers. But overall, we have experienced wave upon wave of disruption to find ourselves, over the long term, with fairly consistent low unemployment, growing wages, and broad-based economic growth.[54]

That said, some of these disruptions are harder to tackle than others. Some communities have indeed been heavily affected by a combination of globalization and technology.[55] Flint, Michigan, was once the thriving hub of the US automotive manufacturing industry. At its peak, General Motors employed more than 80,000 people in the city. But from the 1970s onward, global competition from European and Japanese manufacturers exporting to the United States, and later setting up factories there, prompted GM to outsource production to other countries. In Flint, Detroit, and indeed across Michigan, auto jobs dropped by 65 to 70 percent between the late 1970s and about 2010. And as auto industry jobs went, so did people. Between 1960 and 2010, Flint's population dropped by nearly half and Detroit's by nearly 60 percent. This exodus of jobs and people left local economies hollowed out. Today, Flint is no longer the symbol of unchecked collapse it once was. While scars of deindustrialization remain, the city has stabilized and is cautiously rebuilding, attracting new investments, balancing budgets, and working to restore trust. But 50 years is, indeed, a long time.[56]

Flint is not alone. Many other areas, like Tiruppur in the Indian state of Tamil Nadu and Germany's Ruhr Valley, have faced economic decline for long periods.

The world economy is dynamic. No one can be assured of staying competitive forever. Change can disrupt livelihoods, and this must be dealt with properly. Using the fruits of growth to support and create opportunities for those left behind is critical—and surely better than stopping progress. Adapting and thriving often requires place-based policies, investments to transform entire towns, retraining workers into new roles and sectors, and safety nets to protect people while they adjust.

We have already shown how, over time, most people have experienced growing prosperity. Many communities have, too, successfully reinvented themselves. Pittsburgh, Pennsylvania, was a steel town but today is a highly diversified local economy on the back of robotics, medical research, and excellent universities. Bilbao's turnaround from the implosion of its shipbuilding, steel production, and heavy industry in the face of global competition even spawned the term the "Bilbao effect." Today the northern Spanish city is a cultural and tourism hub, famous for its Frank Gehry–designed Guggenheim Museum and 12 Michelin-starred restaurants. It has also been ranked as a top European city for foreign investment.[57]

Now let's go back to the United States. It has been suggested that globalization, more specifically the North American Free Trade Agreement (NAFTA) and China's rise, came at the expense of the American worker. We have already discussed how median and bottom wages have increased since 1980. Yet it is true that workers, particularly men, seemed to lose ground during a troubling stretch from the mid-1970s to the mid-1990s. But this did not coincide with NAFTA or the explosion in China trade (Exhibit 24). Rather, it was a time of persistent inflation, oil shocks, and productivity doldrums. The median US worker remains significantly better off than the median worker in almost any other major economy.[58]

Stepping back, we have seen inequality ebb and flow alongside progress, and many more people have become empowered. Progress, where it was present, lifted most—almost all—boats over the long run, including those

Abandoned factory in Detroit.

at the bottom of the distribution. But there have been times of disruption. Continuing to spread progress through better skills, technologies, infrastructure, organizational practices, and safety nets, where needed, is what will improve lives for the largest number. Economic growth also produces the resources that can be spent, and often have been spent, in a way that benefits most people and helps limit or reduce inequality.

A common theme is discernible in all the evidence we have presented. Economic progress does not have to be zero-sum: No one needs to lose out for some to benefit; everyone can prosper at once. We lack imagination when we think of progress only as a competition of different groups for the same static basket. We can do much better: A growing tree shares its fruits more broadly.

Evolution in hourly earnings
Real hourly earnings in $, index (1980 = 100)

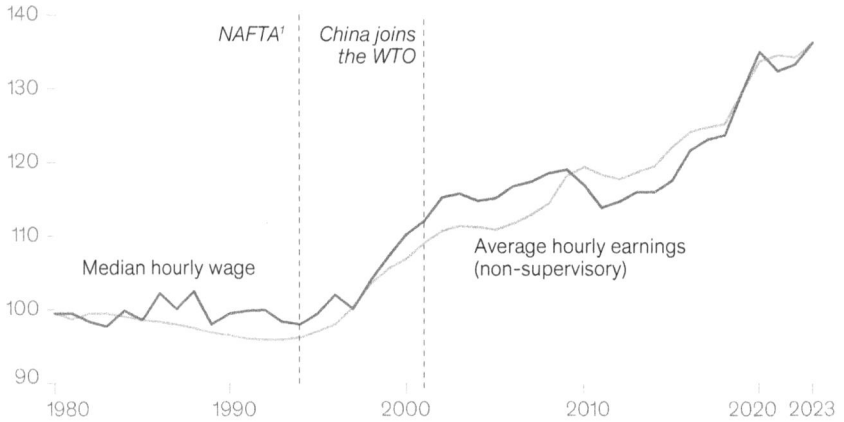

NAFTA[1]   China joins
            the WTO

Median hourly wage

Average hourly earnings
(non-supervisory)

140
130
120
110
100
90

1980   1990   2000   2010   2020 2023

[1]NAFTA came into effect in January 1994.
Source: US Bureau of Labor Statistics data, processed by the Economic Innovation Group; McKinsey Global Institute analysis

Evolution in earnings by sex
Median real hourly wage, $

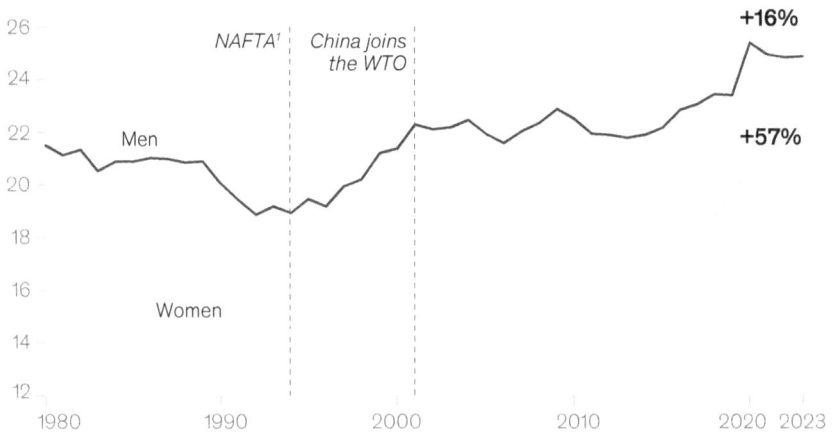

NAFTA[1]   China joins
            the WTO

Men

+16%

Women

+57%

26
24
22
20
18
16
14
12

1980   1990   2000   2010   2020 2023

[1]NAFTA came into effect in January 1994.
Source: US Bureau of Labor Statistics data, processed by the Economic Innovation Group; McKinsey Global Institute analysis

Does progress come at the climate's expense?

Rising greenhouse gas emissions show that economic prosperity can come with environmental costs. The prosecution's case argues that the relentless pursuit of economic growth has warmed the planet, threatening the foundations of future prosperity. The case is bolstered by the unequal distribution of economic gains compared with the globally shared climate harms that come with it. It concludes that there are limits to growth if the world is to stay livable.

Growth has come with rising emissions and rising temperatures, according to the IPCC, on whose analysis we rely. But it has also brought progress and poverty reduction that few would want undone. As we argued in chapter 9, central to the economic boom of the past 100 years was a dramatic increase in access to energy courtesy of abundant and affordable fossil fuels. Today, global energy consumption is roughly ten times higher than in 1925, powering industries, homes, and transportation networks that underpin modern life.

There is simply no way to grow an economy without growing energy. Let us repeat: Energy makes the world go around.

The energy revolution has indeed driven rising greenhouse gas emissions, particularly CO_2. In 1925, global greenhouse gas emissions in CO_2-equivalent (CO_2e) tonnes from fossil fuels and industry were about five billion tonnes per year. By 2024, this figure had surged to about 57 billion tonnes.[59] Some of the change was due to population growth, but growing energy consumption per person played a big role, too. Cumulative emissions have warmed the planet by approximately 1.2°C above preindustrial levels, with cascading effects on climate systems.[60]

Wealthier nations, which historically consumed the lion's share of fossil fuels, have contributed disproportionately to emissions. The United States and Europe are home to less than 15 percent of the world's population but have accounted for close to half of historical CO_2 emissions since 1850.[61] Meanwhile, poorer nations in Africa and parts of Asia, which contributed little to the problem of emissions, could face the worst consequences in the form of droughts, flood, and food insecurity, all of which could exacerbate existing inequalities.

But we must balance the externality of carbon emissions against the positive effects of abundant energy and materials; they have been, and remain, related.

Take the case of China. Between 1990 and 2023, it was responsible for almost a quarter of total global greenhouse gas emissions and about 60 percent of incremental emissions. But in the past four decades, it also accounted for 75 percent of the world's poverty reduction. China's economic rise was inexorably linked to its rising energy use. Income per person multiplied by 14 between 1990 and 2023, and energy consumption per capita by five. If we could go back in time and stop the emissions from happening, we would also stop their progress and condemn 800 million people to remaining in poverty in China alone, and many more globally.[62]

The IPCC states that humans play the dominant role in the observed recent increase in the frequency or intensity of hot extremes and the decrease in the frequency or intensity of cold extremes. It has also presented evidence of human-induced effects on extreme precipitation. In some regions, primarily southwestern South America, climate change has probably contributed to an increase in meteorological droughts, while in northern Europe it may have contributed to their decline.[63]

Warming may, in the future, intensify those hazards, according to the IPCC. It could also increase displacement, reduce productivity, damage economies, and put hundreds of millions at risk, particularly in coastal and low-income areas. The risks increase progressively with temperature, becoming much more severe beyond 2°C of warming, sometimes because of potentially irreversible tipping points.

Having said that, it is also worth noting that the IPCC itself has shifted emphasis away from worst-case emissions scenarios like RCP8.5, which were once treated as baselines but are now considered to not be aligned with current policy trends. Under RCP8.5, for example, temperatures were expected to rise beyond 4°C above preindustrial levels by the end of the century. Most research, including from the IPCC, now deems scenarios such as SSP2-4.5, with temperatures rising between 2.1°C and 3.5°C, and a best estimate of 2.7°C, more aligned with current policy. This still involves significant risks, but they are more manageable through innovation and investment.[64]

Climate change is real, and the prosecution's argument must be taken seriously. Some might quibble that temperature changes over the past several millennia have at times been more dramatic than what we are now experiencing, that vegetation greenness (measured by the Leaf Area

Index) over most land areas has been increasing since the 1980s due to carbon fertilization effects and growing seasons in mid to high latitudes, or even that more people have died from excessive cold than heat.[65] But these could be the subjects of another book—or many of them. The argument we are addressing is whether the environmental impacts of growth negate its benefits, standing in opposition to progress itself.

Could further progress in fact be the answer? Economic progress is, indeed, our best way to *mitigate* rising temperatures and *adapt* to climate hazards.

Let's start with mitigation, namely our capacity to reduce emissions to limit how much temperatures rise. Economic growth can foster innovation in low-emissions technologies as well as generate the resources to deploy them at scale.

In fact, we do not need to speculate; this is already happening. The idea that economic growth and climate progress are inherently at odds is being challenged. Many developed nations have decoupled economic growth from emissions, thanks to increasing energy efficiency and the adoption of clean energy. A shift toward service-based economies also helps—another feature of richer economies. Since 1990, Germany has boosted its national income by more than 50 percent while slashing CO_2 emissions by 30 percent, adjusting for trade, that is, incorporating "offshored emissions." The United Kingdom has seen total emissions fall to levels not seen since the 1850s, despite doubling economic output since 1985. In the United States, emissions have declined since 2005 while the economy grew, perhaps ironically because of a boom in gas that accelerated coal replacement.[66]

Emerging economies are also showing progress. China, the world's largest emitter, accounted for about 30 percent of global CO_2 emissions in 2024. Yet, since 2010, it has halved the carbon intensity of its economy, driven by a massive expansion of renewable energy. Hydro, solar, and wind power now account for 30 percent of China's electricity mix, with installed solar capacity nearing 600 gigawatts. That's close to one-third of the world's solar capacity. China is also commissioning new nuclear reactors rapidly. While coal still dominates, its share of electricity generation dropped from 77 percent in 2010 to 61 percent in 2023. Some signs indicate that China's total emissions may have peaked in the early 2020s due to clean use of energy rather than a reduction in power demand, although only time will confirm this.[67]

As usual, technology is our biggest weapon. Solar and wind costs have plummeted by 88 and 74 percent, respectively, in just 15 years, making them some of the cheapest point sources of new electricity in many regions. Nuclear energy remains a reliable and underutilized low-carbon option, with countries like France deriving about 70 percent of their electricity from it.[68] Emerging technologies, such as carbon capture, utilization, and storage (CCUS), low-emissions hydrogen, and new battery chemistries, hold promise for decarbonizing hard-to-abate sectors like heavy industry and aviation. If adoption accelerates, these innovations could significantly curb emissions. All of these are what we call progress and are enabled by economic growth.

The second leg is adaptation, that is, our capacity to manage the risks and impacts of climate change. The proven path to reducing climate vulnerability in poor countries is to make them rich. Wealth comes with in-built climate adaptation, because the things we buy with extra wealth like concrete foundations, air conditioners, quality infrastructure, and capable emergency services are fundamentally weatherproofing. Wealthier societies, enabled by growth, can invest in adaptation, turning potential catastrophes into manageable crises. One might argue that the entire path of human development is escaping our vulnerability to the elements.

Continued progress is not a gamble. It is our best source of resilience.

The data bear this out. Despite the rising frequency of climate-driven events, related casualties have fallen dramatically. A century ago, floods, hurricanes, and droughts claimed millions of lives annually, often with little warning. Global deaths from natural disasters have plummeted from more than 500,000 per year in the 1920s to fewer than 40,000 annually by the 2020s with four times more people. Bangladesh has reduced cyclone-related deaths by a factor of more than 100, from hundreds of thousands in the 1970s to thousands or fewer today, thanks to better forecasting and evacuation plans. Also, note that in the past three decades, about half of deaths from natural disasters were from earthquakes and tsunamis. These sometimes get mixed up with climate-related disasters, but they have nothing to do with temperature fluctuations.[69]

We need mitigation and adaptation, both of which can, and have, benefited from economic progress. And yet the extent of investment in each of them is a source of intense debate. Some argue that alarmism is worse for humanity than actual climate change.[70] Singapore, for instance, has developed rapidly into one of the world's most prosperous societies despite being a hot, low-lying island, prone to rising sea levels and flooding, with limited freshwater resources.

In this framing, the argument is that the threat is lower and investing significantly in mitigation results in higher overall costs—mitigation, adaptation, and damages—than spending less on mitigation, adapting to the impacts that occur, and accepting some level of residual risk. We do note that US cities in warm and weather-prone places are growing, although they are also starting to face rising insurance costs.[71] When people vote with their feet, it is not clear that climate risk is top of mind, but cheap housing and access to air-conditioning probably is.

Others argue that the optimal balance involves more mitigation. If damages could be large, either adapting to reduce them significantly or accepting the residual risk would be costly, so reducing greenhouse gas emissions now could improve future welfare substantially.[72]

Where does the panoply of evidence leave our jury? This one is tough, and it is no wonder that the topic of climate change has become politically hot. The different viewpoints are ultimately driven by uncertainty surrounding two key factors: the extent of risks we expect a changing climate to bring, and how much it will cost to mitigate those harms in comparison with adapting to them. Differing views on how these factors project into the future will lead us to choose a different balance between mitigation, adaptation, and accepting risks today.

In the short term, while high-emissions energy sources still power economic growth in many parts of the world, there may be trade-offs, and emphasis on different values can lead reasonable people to different conclusions.[73] Differences might include the value of a known benefit today versus an unknown future risk, the faith in government coordination to reengineer complex systems, and the belief in future technological progress. The largest downsides and risks lie in the future and therefore rely on forecasting scenarios. We need to look toward the future and make the best risk-adjusted moves with a long time horizon, without perfect information.

If you believe that adaptation to changing climate will remain a reliable, viable, and affordable approach to dealing with further rises in temperature, you prioritize growth and lifting people out of poverty.

Even more so if you believe that technological and economic progress will make both mitigation and adaptation easier in the future, as in the past. If, however, you emphasize risks of future tipping points and runaway climate, focus on noneconomic costs of adaptation like migration, or have less faith in future advances in technology, you may accept lower growth in some places for mitigation today.

While the trajectory ahead requires much action on both mitigation and adaptation, *so far* an energy-rich humanity is far ahead compared with a century ago: better off, and much less affected by climate. As to the future, we develop the argument more later in this book, but—spoiler alert—our argument is that progress is good for both adaptation (resilience) and mitigation (investment and technology) if steered in the right way. Conversely, withholding progress (perhaps in the name of climate) is probably bad for adaptation and can even stand in the way of creating the resources and innovation needed for mitigation.

Are we sacrificing nature for progress?

Many of our environmental debates center on carbon emissions and climate change. But there is more to nature: Pollution, deforestation, and loss of biodiversity are other environmental challenges that matter.

Let's start with the prosecution's contention that industrialization has polluted our air, water, and soil. There is truth to this. Since 1925, the rise of factories, vehicles, and chemical-intensive agriculture has spiked pollutants like sulfur dioxide, nitrogen oxides, and plastics, among others. In the 1970s, cities like Los Angeles choked under smog so thick it obscured skylines. Rivers like the Cuyahoga in Ohio caught fire from oil and chemical slicks. Globally, air pollution still claims eight million lives a year. To give just one instance, Delhi's air quality index often hits hazardous levels, forcing school closures and surges in hospitalizations.[74]

But air pollution's peak is behind us. Sulfur dioxide emissions, a key driver of acid rain, have halved since 1980. Nitrogen oxides peaked in the 2000s and have declined by almost 20 percent. All local air pollutants except ammonia, which is mostly used for agriculture, have passed their peak.[75]

These figures are global and promising. More importantly, wealthier economies have improved much faster. Yet again, economic progress may have contributed to the problem, but it is also the solution. The United Kingdom's sulfur dioxide emissions have fallen from more than six million tonnes a year in the 1970s to virtually zero today; those of the United States, from 30 million to two million. In 1952, London suffered its infamous Great Smog, which killed thousands of people. But air quality has improved by 70 to 95 percent since the 1970s with low-emissions zones and electric buses.[76]

The prosecution might argue that these wealthy countries have registered improvements simply because they exported their pollution to other places by offshoring their industry. Not the case. Germany remains a considerable industrial power, and it has achieved similar improvements in air quality. In China, which is still in the throes of industrialization, sulfur dioxide emissions have dropped by three-quarters in the past 15 years, and nitrogen oxides by one-third. Pollution in Beijing, once tagged with the unfortunate sobriquet "airpocalypse," fell by 55 percent between 2013 and 2020.[77]

Ocean plastics are another form of pollution that is often debated. Production of plastics is still growing. In the 1970s, global production was about 50 million tonnes; now it is about 460 million tonnes. We have all seen clips of marine animals tethered to plastic waste and crabs making homes in fragments of plastic. But only about 0.5 percent of it ends up in the ocean. The reason: waste mismanagement. In wealthier economies, most plastic is recycled, incinerated or landfilled, so it does not end up in the ocean. Ocean plastics come not from the countries that use more of the materials but from those that do not have the resources to devote to waste management—in other words, countries that lack economic progress.[78]

The next accusation is deforestation, which is mostly driven by agriculture. Since 1900, the world has lost approximately one billion hectares of forest, an area roughly the size of Canada. This has disrupted ecosystems and released stored carbon. About 17 percent of the Amazon, the planet's largest rainforest, has been cut down over the past 50 years. Two-thirds of this was due to cattle ranching, and most of the remaining one-third to soy production. In Africa, cocoa farming in countries like Côte d'Ivoire has cleared millions of hectares of forest, transforming carbon sinks into sources of emissions and compromising biodiversity.[79]

Deforestation is a fact. But there has been some improvement. Global deforestation peaked in the 1980s at 16 million hectares a year and is now

Crab making a home in a discarded bottle cap.

about 10 million hectares. Even in the Amazon, deforestation peaked in the early 2000s and has improved since then. Some regions are turning the tide, particularly but not only wealthier ones. Forests covered 26 percent of France's land in 1990; today the share is 31 percent. In China, forests grew even faster, from 16 to 23 percent. Even India, Thailand, and Vietnam have been reforesting.[80]

Overall, we see that where there is economic progress, the threat to forests lessens or reverses. In fact, when countries start developing, they cut down more forest for energy, building, and food. But as they grow wealthier, forests recover as countries use alternative sources of energy and their increasingly mechanized agriculture becomes more productive, using less and less land to produce food.[81] A more developed world has better technologies to increase crop yields, satellites to track deforestation, alternatives for energy and building materials, and better institutions to enforce the right policies.

One rather desolating by-product of deforestation is a loss of biodiversity, another item on the prosecution's rap sheet for progress.

Since 1925, human activity has pushed up to 7 percent of species to extinction, with three-quarters of at-risk species threatened by agriculture and deforestation. In Madagascar, 70 to 85 percent of original forests are gone, endangering unique species like the aye-aye and indri lemur.[82] Coral reefs, vital for 25 percent of marine life, have declined by 50 percent since the 1950s due to warming oceans and pollution. Australia's Great Barrier Reef has suffered mass bleaching events. Even so, the Australian Institute of Marine Science Long-Term Monitoring Program reported record-high coral cover in the Great Barrier Reef in 2022.[83] Other iconic species such as lions are threatened by poaching, habitat loss and fragmentation, and human-wildlife conflict.[84]

And yet, there is hope. Conservation efforts have real momentum. Nearly 200 countries adopted the Kunming–Montreal Global Biodiversity Framework in 2022. The EU adopted a Nature Restoration Law in 2024 to reinforce conservation efforts that have already resulted in many European wild mammal populations flourishing again. While lion populations are declining, conservation is successful in "intensively managed areas" of southern Africa—small, usually fenced reserves with high funding, strong law enforcement, and active interventions.[85] Some governments have turned to conservation as a tool for economic development. Costa Rica is a prime example. Once ravaged by deforestation, it now protects 25 percent of its land, cloud forest and rainforest are growing again, and ecotourism generates 6 percent of its national income. Around the world, protected areas now cover 17 percent of terrestrial ecosystems. Money is beginning to flow into conservation. Some estimates put biodiversity-related public and private finance at about $200 billion a year. That's still not enough—estimates reckon that more than $700 billion is needed.[86] But it is a start. A more prosperous world not only puts more weight toward the preservation of biodiversity but has better management capabilities and more resources to invest in it.

In sum, challenges linger, but there is good news, too. In fact, there is a common thread: Even if the early stages of development can be messier, economic progress is generally not the cause of but the solution to most of these challenges. There is a convincing case that more prosperous countries will devote resources to reversing environmental damage and preserving the natural world in the future.

Does progress make us happier?

The final criticism we want to evaluate is a more philosophical one. The prosecution argues that the pursuit of wealth has failed to deliver happiness, asserting that true contentment lies in strong relationships and community bonds, purpose and meaning, activity and engagement, autonomy and agency, personal progress and mastery, and physical and mental well-being, none of which money can easily buy.

Incomes may have soared, the prosecution contends, but this prosperity has coincided with rising rates of depression, anxiety, and loneliness. In wealthy nations like the United States, depression rates nearly doubled in ten years, with 13 percent of adults reporting a diagnosis in 2023, up from 7 percent in 2013. A 2023 survey found 52 percent of Canadians feel lonely at least weekly. Consumerism, fueled by growth, fosters materialism; people chase status through possessions, only to feel empty. Social media, enabled by technological progress, amplifies comparison and isolation, with studies linking heavy use to increases in stress, anxiety, self-harm, and suicidal thoughts. The prosecution's case argues that progress has prioritized measurable outputs over human well-being, creating societies richer in goods but poorer in connection and meaning. Witness, for example, the doubling of "deaths of despair"—suicides and deaths related to drugs and alcohol—in the United States over the past 50 years.[87]

Once again, some of this is true, but assessing it requires nuance. We discussed in chapter 1 the strong positive correlation between incomes and self-reported life satisfaction. The things we do for life satisfaction also create higher incomes and vice versa, from striving for personal progress to building healthcare systems. GDP measures goods and services that societies produce and consume. That includes TVs, cars and fridges, and live concerts, but also housing, infrastructure, healthcare, education services, and cultural activities. Wealth increases access to quality healthcare and housing. Education empowers individuals. Infrastructure connects people.

Some aspects of modern lifestyles may indeed be making us more depressed or lonely, but these need not be consequences of economic progress. In fact, depression rates are often higher among poorer people due to financial stress or health issues, among others.[88] Strong relationships and community bonds are extremely important, and they are certainly possible without economic progress. But this is a very different statement from saying they are incompatible with it. Economic growth expands our potential and ability to choose. It is up to us to decide how to use it. Humans will not always make the "right" choices, and they may take some time to adjust to technological or cultural shocks. But it is difficult, even paternalistic, to argue that restricting people's possibilities by making them poorer is the way to make *them* happy.

Economic growth also makes people less likely to feel that life is a zero-sum game. When the economy expands, everyone's slice of the pie can grow at once, as we have argued before. Without growth, Joe's gain is necessarily Joanne's loss. As a result, growth can make societies more inclined toward openness, tolerance, and democracy.[89]

And yet democracy and freedom do not happen automatically. Over the past century, the Liberal Democracy Index showed improvement globally, from 0.16 in 1925 to 0.29 today. It peaked at 0.38 during the 2000s and has retreated since about 2010.[90] It remains the case that economic progress does not automatically translate into liberty.

We suspect that critics often conflate the obviously true statement that economic progress isn't the sole driver of happiness, maybe not even the main one, with the false claim that it makes people unhappy. While modern challenges can strain mental health, these are not inevitable outcomes of prosperity but rather issues we can address through mindful choices. At the end of the day, progress is about the expansion of agency: the ability of individuals to make real choices about education, work, family, and their participation in society. Seen through this lens, prosperity and happiness are linked not only because money buys comfort but because it can buy freedom—the chance to live with dignity, purpose, and opportunity.[91] Economic progress done right empowers us to pursue meaningful lives, fostering societies that are not only wealthier but also freer, more dynamic, and more cohesive.

※ ※ ※

Economic growth is not without hazards. The issues and tensions that we have highlighted are real and serious. We need to address them. But they do not negate the tremendous progress that humanity has made over the past century and should not derail our efforts to continue bettering people's lives. More importantly, it is often where there was little economic progress that such issues were most pressing, and growth itself remains the most powerful tool to address them.

Now we look ahead to the rest of this century and ask ourselves: Can we raise every human being to empowerment and beyond? Can we progress even faster than we have in the past century? And on to Part IV.

PART IV

THE POSSIBILITY OF PLENTY

CHAPTER 15

THE AMBITION OF PLENTY

"We do not need magic to change the world.
We carry all the power we need inside ourselves already:
We have the power to imagine better."

J. K. ROWLING

———

We imagine a bountiful world in 2100 in which everybody thrives.

WE BEGAN PART I BY LOOKING back to 1925, the world of our grandparents, a time of coal fires, handwritten ledgers, and uncertain futures. Now we look ahead to 2100. It may feel distant, but it is very close. Many of our children will still be around, and their kids will be well into their life journeys.

The past 100 years confounded expectations. What human beings achieved should be celebrated, even though our journey of progress has

View of Interlaken, Switzerland.

been uneven and remains unfinished. The question before us is simple but profound: Can we deliver a bountiful world to our children and their children in 2100?

To answer this question, we invite you to join us as we conduct a thought experiment over the next few chapters. First, to define in granular terms the bar for plenty: What is the threshold of human progress we should aim to clear? Then to rigorously test that possibility of plenty against each of the obvious necessary conditions required: energy, materials, food, climate, and innovation. This is not a prediction. Rather, it is a test and, perhaps, a hope.

Our arguably surprising starting point in this experiment, as we said at the start of this book, is Switzerland.

We imagine a future in which even those born in the poorest countries— say, Afghanistan, Burundi, or Somalia—enjoy at least the living standards of today's Switzerland. In 2100, the world economy measured as GDP is 8.5 times as large as it is today. We don't mean only Switzerland-level incomes but also the access that the Swiss have to healthcare, education,

Women collecting clean water, Samburu, Kenya.

safety, and opportunities for getting on in life. In our imagined 2100, today's Switzerland marks the floor, and every country reaches or exceeds that level of development.

Why Switzerland? Not because we think every country should emulate Swiss culture or institutions, much as we think they are great. Countries will have their own distinct paths to prosperity. Rather because Switzerland represents a rare and powerful blend of many aspects of prosperity, stability, equity, and natural beauty. It shows what's possible when a society combines economic dynamism with social cohesion. Today, Switzerland ranks among the wealthiest nations in the world, with annual income per person of $82,000.

Lazy stereotyping used to focus on watches and chocolate, and Switzerland still makes excellent versions of both. But its economy is very different today, a rich blend of financial services, pharmaceuticals, high-tech engineering and machinery, and luxury goods and services. This is a country that is home to only 0.1 percent of the world's population but to many world-leading firms. UBS, the Swiss bank and financial services firm, is one of the largest wealth managers in the world. Novartis and Roche are leaders in global pharmaceuticals. Nestlé is a household name in food and beverages. Zurich is home to one of the world's best engineering universities, and Switzerland consistently ranks first in global innovation rankings.[1]

Switzerland's biggest success is that it has used its prosperity to enhance the lives of its citizens. Opportunity abounds. Unemployment is low; 80 percent of Swiss adults aged 15 to 64 are employed. With the possible exception of the bankers on Bahnhofstrasse, they work regular hours. On average, Swiss people spend 13 years in education, including in vocational training. Ninety percent of them say they have someone to rely on in times of need. The Swiss are well looked after when life throws curveballs at them. The country can afford a robust social safety net. Swiss democracy, heavily reliant on referenda, helps people to feel involved in the destiny of their nation. Nearly 90 percent say they feel safe walking alone at night. Some say Switzerland has nine million policemen and -women, because every Swiss citizen polices the others. And during the COVID-19 pandemic, the country emerged with strong health, social, and economic outcomes while many peer countries were stuck with debt and division.[2]

Switzerland is also clean, with good air quality, monitored water, and low CO_2 emissions per person.[3] And it is beautiful, with vibrant cities and a stunning landscape of lakes and mountains, managing to achieve the benefits of modernity while retaining a stunning natural heritage and cultural charm.

We do not mean to imply that Switzerland is heaven on earth or is free of challenges. In their infinite critical predisposition, many readers may now be mentally listing its flaws, and we bet Swiss readers will be the first, knowing their realities better than anyone else. And yet a world in which the poorest countries catch up with today's Switzerland and the rest of the world pushes even higher seems a worthy aspiration.[4]

This world of plenty in 2100 is not a prediction. It is a hypothetical, ambitious, and desirable future, but just one among an infinite number of possible futures. If the poorest countries today fall short and reach, say, Malaysian living standards instead of Swiss ones, it would still be a vastly better world and well worth striving for.

Ambition is justified, because the change is not unprecedented. We have shown that, over the past 100 years, life expectancy soared, literacy spread, extreme poverty plunged, and technologies once reserved for the elite became ubiquitous. Many nations that once lagged behind are now global leaders in renewable energy, digital services, or manufacturing.

It is also a thought experiment, a test case. And as a test case, it needs to be specific. Do we have enough energy to power this world? Enough metals and minerals? Enough food? Can we achieve plenty within planetary boundaries? And will science and innovation deliver? These are the questions we try to answer in the next few chapters. If we can show that this specific, ambitious, quantifiable future is possible, it means many other great futures are possible, too.

What once seemed miraculous proved to be possible. What seems miraculous today may well be reality in 2100.

Every human empowered

We have discussed the concept of empowerment, the point at which people not only escape poverty but can reliably meet basic needs, save for the future, and exercise agency. Today, despite rapid progress, 4.7 billion people—about 60 percent of the global population—still live below the empowerment line. Higher incomes and more affordable access to essentials like housing, food, education, and healthcare can lift everybody above it. This is the defining challenge of the century, and we want to imagine a bountiful 2100 where we not only reach it but could even go well beyond it.

Our ambition is certainly not just a macroeconomic target. It is about everyone harvesting the fruits of progress.

First, the proven elements of prosperity that already exist in Switzerland and other frontier economies will have spread everywhere. The poorest people in the world today will get their first water pumps, solar panels, and motorbikes. Over time, as their countries catch up and they become more empowered, they will enjoy more of what most residents of higher-income countries have today. Universal access to nutritious food, top-notch education and healthcare, great housing, clean air, reliable public transportation, high-productivity jobs, and strong safety nets will be the baseline. When someone loses a job, there is a fair chance to retrain. When illness strikes, everyone receives care without falling into destitution. What was once an outlier—high employment, long lives, a confident middle class—could by 2100 be the norm in Lagos, Lahore, and La Paz as much as in Lausanne.

Second, the development frontier of today will have been pushed even further out by novel technologies that continue to build lives and livelihoods. Where previous generations marveled at antibiotics and smartphones, future generations take for granted a suite of tools that were once unimaginable. Smart infrastructure will connect everyone as ideas, technology, and energy spread. With greater prosperity will come wider access to affordable, high-quality healthcare and personalized medicine. Biomedical innovation will mean more people live to a ripe old age. Centenarians could be a common sight—100 years old is a huge milestone these days; in 2100, it may well be that lifespans extend to 120 years and beyond. And our elderly could prolong their working lives, if they wish, by constantly updating their skills in a world in which employers recognize their value and give them flexible options that suit their age. Or, alternatively, that may not be needed in a world in which new technologies have made us hyper-productive. With the confidence that comes from prosperity, fertility rates could well edge back up to replacement level. Children are included in a century of plenty, not as drags on our ability to progress but as one of life's great purposes and joys. Artificial intelligence tutors could guide every child at their own pace, tailoring high-quality education to individuals.

As low-emissions technologies spread around the world, affordable, abundant, clean energy will power homes and industries everywhere. And prosperity will give us, vulnerable today to climate and other hazards, more resources to adapt. Many of the tools needed are already being developed, including new types of infrastructure and farming systems that are more resilient in the face of extreme weather events. Air-conditioning, which is hardly affordable for many families, will be a staple. Every country will benefit from the increasing efficiency of electric devices.

Third and finally, underpinning this progress are institutions and cultures that have evolved, everywhere, to unlock this full potential. Technologies and best practices alone do not guarantee empowerment. The difference comes when markets reward innovation and governments guarantee fairness. Legal systems uphold rights, welfare states ensure that no one falls behind, and cultures value shared progress. Progress is not just material but civic: trust rebuilt between people and institutions, hope returned to politics, and the narrative of growth as a positive-sum game becoming widely accepted.

This is a generation liberated from scarcity and emboldened by opportunity. It is not science fiction. It is simply following the historical curves of human development forward.

Running the numbers on plenty

Back to numbers. We know that incomes are not everything, but as we explained in chapter 1, they are a simple and useful yardstick to compare countries and are highly correlated with most things we value. So we focus on that metric. Let's set up a century of plenty. In our hypothetical 2100, we imagine a world in which Burundi, currently the poorest country in the world according to the World Bank, increases its real income per person by 6.1 percent a year until 2100 to match that of Switzerland today. That's $82,000.[5] Switzerland and other similarly prosperous economies do not stagnate. They grow by 1.5 percent per year, which is about the average for advanced economies over the past 50 years. This puts Swiss 2100 incomes at a whopping $257,000. Every country in between maintains its ordering relative to Burundi and Switzerland. In this thought experiment, relative convergence is achieved, and inequality between countries shrinks. Burundi ends up one-third as wealthy as Switzerland, compared with a mere 1 percent today. China grows from about one-quarter to half as rich (Exhibit 25).

Globally, income per person would need to grow at an average of 2.6 percent per year. This is above historical growth rates but not insurmountably higher. Global incomes have increased by about 2 percent since 1960, and by 2.3 percent over the past 25 years (Table 4). Dividing the world into four income groups shows that the largest acceleration is required at the bottom. Note that we also show China in a separate row, given its high growth rate. The most advanced economies, the top group, need to reinvigorate growth at the frontier, while the middle two groups require a very similar pace of growth to what was achieved in the past quarter century.

Accelerating income growth is not easy, but growth rates required are perfectly achievable and far from unprecedented. Plenty of countries

EXHIBIT 25

Income per person future growth trajectories and rates by country
2023–2100

● ≥ Switzerland in 2023   ● < Switzerland in 2023

Future country growth trajectories

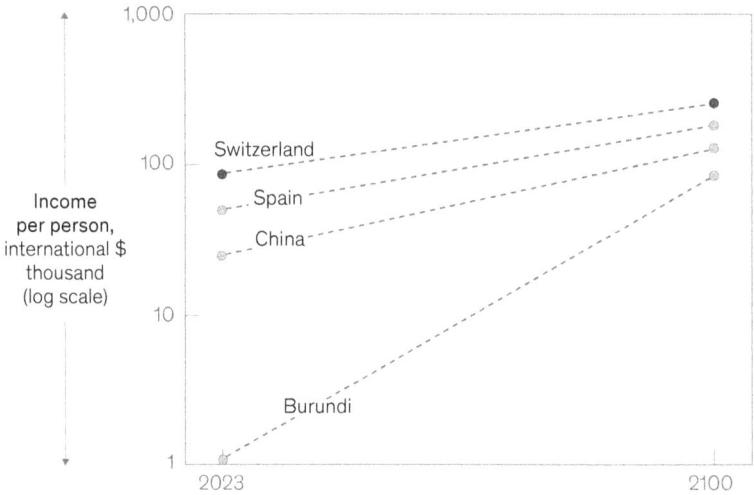

Future country growth rates

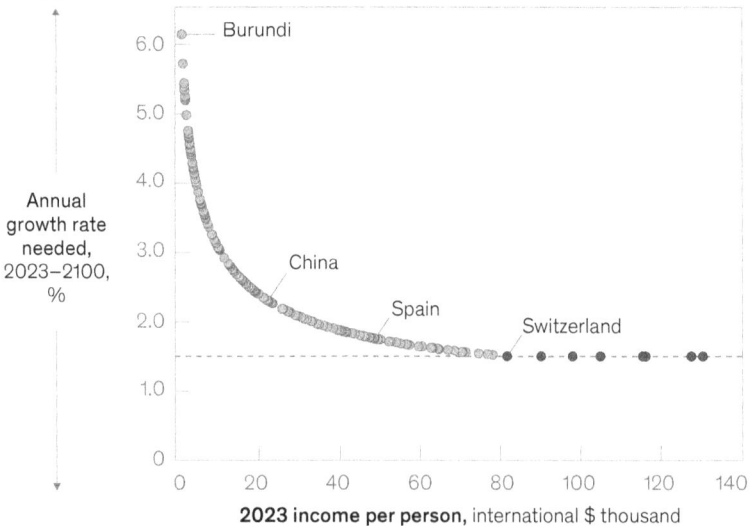

Note: For the century of plenty, we modeled all country growth trajectories, but the exhibit shows only 4 countries to illustrate the convergent effect. Income per person is measured using GDP per capita, in constant 2021 international dollars.
Source: World Bank, *World development indicators;* McKinsey Global Institute analysis

TABLE 4

Income per person growth rates, historical and needed, by income group

Country groups by income levels[1]	Population, 2023, billion	Average income per person, 2023, international $ thousand[2]	Annual growth, %[2]		
			1960–2023	1997–2023	2023–2100
All	8.0	26.8	2.0	2.3	2.6
Top	1.1	64.9	1.9	1.1	1.7
Second	2.4	27.4	2.0	2.4	2.2
Third	2.9	11.6	1.5	2.8	3.0
Bottom	1.5	3.4	2.8	3.2	4.4
China[3]	*1.4*	*22.1*	*6.4*	*7.7*	*2.3*

[1]Membership of the groups varies slightly between columns. For the current and forward-looking metrics, membership is determined by income rankings in 2023. For the backward-looking metrics, membership depends on income rankings in 1960 and 1997.
[2]All averages are simple averages of the countries in the income group, not weighted by population. This is to more accurately reflect the historical performance of an average country without skewing by figures for countries with large populations. This can then serve as a benchmark for future requirements for an average country in a given income group.
[3]China was in the bottom income group in both 1960 and 1997, but has since moved into the second income group. It is shown separately here but is also included in the second and fourth income groups' averages where relevant.
Source: United Nations; World Bank, *World development indicators;* McKinsey Global Institute analysis

have achieved the income growth rates that a century of plenty requires, even in the bottom income group. And today we have more tools, more knowledge, and more resources than ever before.

The decades immediately ahead pose somewhat more of a challenge. Falling fertility rates mean fewer workers in many economies, and globally, we need about 0.3 percentage point of growth just to make up for that effect. Some places, like China, Italy, Spain, South Korea, and parts of Latin America, need more than that. Many countries historically benefited from growing employment, particularly advanced ones. Over the past quarter century, Western Europe gained 0.4 percentage point of growth from increasing employment, especially among women. But that was a one-off. As growth in the labor force slows and in some places even reverses, future gains will depend increasingly on productivity. With fewer workers, every worker will need to contribute more to sustain rising living standards.

We discuss the necessary productivity acceleration, examples of countries that have done it in the past, and the knowledge and tools available in chapter 20.

Different challenges for different starting points

One way of looking at a century of plenty is that the fastest boats (the top group of countries) can, and would, benefit from going faster, but the bulk of the transformation comes from getting all boats sailing closer to their potential.

That is not to say that advanced economies, those in the top group, can't accelerate, too. They can. But they have a *frontier challenge*. In our century of plenty, they would need to accelerate income growth to 1.7 percent a year on average. To achieve that, they need to revamp investment and boost technological innovation to increase the rate of productivity growth and keep older people happily productive for more of their lives.

The current batch of middle-income countries, roughly the second and third income groups, have *political and investment challenges*. On average, their economies need to grow by 2.2 and 3.0 percent a year, respectively, roughly their average pace of the past 25 years and a bit faster than the past 50. Some countries have already achieved these growth rates. For instance, Poland and South Korea grew at 4.2 and 3.7 percent a year over the past 30 years.[6] Others will need to accelerate.

Middle-income countries need to avoid the so-called middle-income trap by mobilizing investment and building institutions that can operate effectively, continually adapt, and serve broad public interests. The critical question is whether they can channel resources to their most productive uses.

In our report *The enterprising archipelago: Propelling Indonesia's productivity*, we studied what it would take for Indonesia, a country of 280 million people just at the edge of the middle-income level at $3,900 annual income per person, to join the ranks of high-income countries. It is ultimately about making the transition from a large informal economy, where 80 percent of employment is in microenterprises, into a well-capitalized economy. This would require the formation of 200,000 medium-size and 40,000 large companies, and the surrounding entrepreneurial, human, and institutional capital to enable it.[7]

History offers stark contrasts. Some nations with tremendous potential, such as Argentina and Venezuela, have stumbled through mismanagement. Contrast them with Spain, which shares many traits and had an extremely turbulent past. By midcentury it had modernized its institutions, built state capacity, and embraced the market economy. This may surprise you. In 1950, Spain's income per person was less than half that of Argentina and Venezuela. Today, it is twice that of Argentina and nearly eight times that of Venezuela.[8]

Finally, the least developed countries have a *development challenge*. They would need to increase their incomes by 4.4 percent a year, and in some cases by up to 6.0 percent, to catch up with a country like Switzerland today. As we have said before, even if these countries were to fall short of those growth rates by one or two percentage points, they would still become vastly better off. The problem is that some countries, such as Burundi, Haiti, and Zimbabwe, have not grown at all in the past 25 years, and others, like Jamaica, Côte d'Ivoire, and Papua New Guinea, have managed anemic growth of only about 1 percent. The growth trajectory for the least developed countries is challenging. Countries including China, Cambodia, and Rwanda posted annual income growth rates of 7.7 percent, 5.9 percent, and 5.0 percent, respectively, over the past quarter century. In other words, this target may sound ambitious, but it is far from unheard of.

Some countries will need to grapple with a "cold start" problem in which human, institutional, physical, entrepreneurial, and financial capital are all underdeveloped at the same time. These deficits reinforce one another, creating a coordination trap that holds economies back. For such countries, the challenge is not just whether a single sector or policy can deliver growth but whether an entire system can be lifted at once. All forms of capital need to deepen in parallel. Educational outcomes have to improve and skills develop to match what the market needs. Institutions must be strengthened to lower risk, increase trust, and provide the right incentives. More and better infrastructure needs to be built to connect people to markets. More entrepreneurs, and a system that unleashes them, are vital to turn local talent into high-growth ventures. Domestic savings need to be channeled to where they can be deployed most usefully. The upside is enormous. Once the flywheel begins to turn, each piece accelerates the next.

Except for the richest economies, none of this requires a massive shift in the technical limit, or the proven productivity frontier that the best developers have carved. But we do need to ensure that no one is stuck in the slow lane of productivity growth.[9]

The question of fertility rates

We have discussed income per person at length, but we have not discussed people. How many humans may there be in a bountiful 2100? Is demography destiny? Could fertility rates, today well below 2.1 in many countries, reverse course and crawl back toward the replacement rate? Can we reach "plenty" if populations keep declining at the current pace?

In our century of plenty, we posit that fertility rates will gradually converge toward the replacement level of 2.1 children per woman across countries, guaranteeing long-term stability in populations and preventing rapid depopulation that would otherwise ensue in countries such as China, Italy, and South Korea.[10] In fact, if this were not to happen, the population of the world, after peaking in the 2080s, would decline in every subsequent generation. Some countries in our first wave (advanced economies plus China) are already beginning to see their total populations decline, while their workforces have been shrinking since around 2010. We explored the implications of this rapid depopulation, including overly burdened public budgets and labor shortages, in chapter 13.[11]

We acknowledge that the slide in fertility rates does appear endemic, universal, and long term. Fertility rates are falling fast virtually everywhere, and so far, government programs have had very limited or no success in turning the tide.[12]

Having children is undoubtedly a personal choice subject to very specific personal circumstances, and we cannot predict with any accuracy whether this return to fertility will occur. Crucially, our plentiful 2100, with high incomes, broad-based progress, and empowerment for everyone, does *not* hinge on fertility rates rising. It is possible with lower fertility rates, although that would mean greater dependence of the elderly on a smaller working population and more stretched public budgets. The productivity challenge would be greater in this case. Alternatively, with higher fertility and more people overall, we would need more of everything—energy, resources, and so on.

In this way, as fertility rates slowly return to 2.1, we envisage a world of plenty for 11.7 billion people by 2100. It is worth noting that while we believe plenty can be reached with or without a return to replacement-level fertility rates by 2100, in the even longer term, low fertility rates are a foundational challenge. By definition, if humanity does not maintain at least replacement-level fertility rates, populations will decline and eventually disappear.

Our three-part argument is simple. First, we find it hard to define as plentiful a future in which the populations of some countries collapse exponentially, with economic and social consequences that are hard to predict.[13] We believe a world with an exponentially declining population could be less happy, but more importantly, it will be less capable, less dynamic, and less innovative. Second, a future in which every person is empowered may make this return to replacement more probable. A highly functioning society could be the kind of place in which people feel confident enough about their circumstances and the future to want to have children. Third, this makes our thought experiment complete. If we can show there are no physical limits to progress for almost 12 billion individuals, there will surely be no limits for fewer people.

In countries with high fertility today, we model a gradual decline toward replacement levels as access to health, education, and opportunity grows, especially for women. This is in line with the UN's medium variant. In countries where fertility has fallen well below replacement, we assume a gradual rebound. Not every country gets to 2.1 by the end of the century, but in all of them, fertility is on a rising trajectory. Given its low fertility rate of 1.0, China's population would halve by 2100 if current trends were to continue.[14] This is not a picture of abundance! In our world of plenty, fertility rates gradually rise to 1.8 by 2100, in line with the UN's high scenario. That would still leave China with a smaller population than today, but with a much less dramatic decline; this pattern would apply to countries like South Korea and Italy, too. In short, we are not imagining huge population growth, merely avoiding fast population collapse.

Is this unthinkable? Historically, we have seen fertility drop as countries grow richer, but maybe it doesn't always have to be that way. The bump in fertility rates that drove the postwar baby boom was accompanied by widening home ownership, economic optimism, and improved domestic automation. Maybe we can create those conditions again. In fact, research shows that people who feel financially secure, supported by good policies, and hopeful about the future are more likely to have children.[15] Our century of plenty could get us there. Scientific advances in reproductive health and fertility science could enable people to have children later in life, and therefore more children overall, if they wish to. At the very least, we would want a world in which everyone who wanted children can have them.

The possibility of a century of plenty

Based on the growth of income per person and fertility rates in a century of plenty, the world economy would grow 8.5 times between today and 2100 (Exhibit 26). While this may seem like an enormous number, if we simply extrapolated historical growth rates from 1960 for the next 75 years, it would jump 5.5 times. In other words, achieving a century of plenty is not orders of magnitude larger than simple momentum, but this shows that small annual differences in growth rates compound over time into a sizable gap. Of the projected total growth in our plentiful world, 22 percent comes from advanced economies, 18 percent from the second group, 33 percent from the third, and 27 percent from the lowest-income countries.[16]

The big question, which we explore in the next chapters, is whether this is technically possible within the laws of physics, within Earth's resource capacity, and within historical precedent. We have already said this is not a prediction. The smartest person on the planet in 1925 would not have predicted the world in which we live in 2025, and we would be seriously overreaching if we were to make specific forecasts about 2100.

It may well be the case that by 2100, we will no longer forge steel in dirty blast furnaces but will use hydrogen and will make steel alloys using quantum computing and synthetic biology. Advanced plasma arc furnaces powered by nuclear fusion could recycle scrap with near 100 percent efficiency. Indeed, we may have replaced steel altogether with graphene composites, high-entropy alloys, or ceramic composites inspired by, say,

Population and income per person change by region
2023–2100

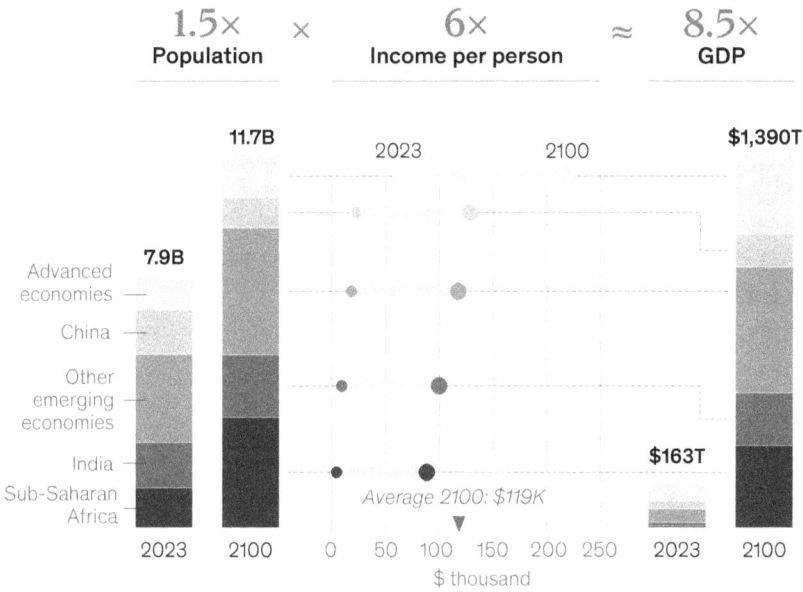

$$1.5\times \quad \times \quad 6\times \quad \approx \quad 8.5\times$$

Population   Income per person   GDP

11.7B   2023   2100 $1,390T

7.9B

Advanced economies —

China —

Other emerging economies —

India —

Sub-Saharan Africa —

$163T

Average 2100: $119K

2023   2100   0   50   100   150   200   250   2023   2100

$ thousand

Note: Income per person is measured using GDP per capita, in constant 2021 international dollars.
Source: UN Population Division, *World population prospects 2024*; World Bank, *World development indicators*;
McKinsey Global Institute analysis

mother of pearl.

Instead of making predictions, here is our thought experiment. We take our century of plenty and test the material implications of it to see whether it is possible. We are optimistic about the forward trajectory of science and technological innovation, but we put large leaps aside. They would just be a bonus. For instance, nuclear fusion could meet much of our energy needs one day, but we test whether current existing and proven technologies like nuclear fission, solar, and wind can power a world of plenty by 2100, and we explore the building requirements it will take.

There is one nonnegotiable on any path to a century of plenty. We have to be here, we have to survive. We know that we could face existential threats. Four stand out: AI going rogue, a more dangerous pandemic than COVID-19, nuclear conflict, and runaway climate change.[17] This is not our area of expertise, and we leave it to others to explore these threats in detail. Our pursuit of plenty could be a double-edged sword. On the one hand, plenty can generate its own perils. More advanced technologies (AI or otherwise) could bring greater destructive potential, while more interconnected economies could mean faster global spread of disease. At the same time, we are more likely to be able to deal with existential risks with economic resources than without them. It is up to us how we use these resources.

Potential disasters aside, there are, we posit, five necessary conditions for a bountiful century, and we ask a key question about each:

- Can we produce enough clean energy to power prosperity for everyone in the world?
- Does our planet have enough material resources, like metals and minerals, to sustain growth everywhere?
- Can we produce enough protein-rich food to feed 12 billion people while preserving biodiversity?
- Can we do all of this without increasing CO_2 emissions or even while reducing them?
- Can scientific and technological innovation deliver the productivity growth we need to achieve a century of plenty?

We answer yes to all of them, even under conservative assumptions about innovation. We don't attempt to prove that a bountiful world in 2100 is likely—just that it is *possible*. We are optimists at heart, so we reckon that the odds are pretty good if we act decisively and make the right calls, as we have done so many times in the past.

※ ※ ※

Our century of plenty will no doubt be "precisely wrong," but only by going through this exercise can we understand whether we can put the pieces together that make another bountiful century realistic. In the next chapters, we test whether the math adds up, starting with energy.

CHAPTER 16

THE ENERGY TO MAKE THE WORLD GO ROUND

*"The Stone Age came to an end not for a lack of stones,
and the Oil Age will end, but not for a lack of oil."*

AHMED ZAKI YAMANI

———

Prosperity requires a bigger and cleaner energy system and
overcoming the physical challenges to building it.

NO ECONOMY HAS EVER THRIVED without increasing its energy use, and
that's unlikely to change in the decades ahead. We already have a gigantic
energy system that has served many millions of people well, but it is not
large enough to power prosperity for all. And demands on the system are
growing, not least from AI, robotics, and other technologies that are going

to drive growth over the next century.

If every country becomes prosperous, as we posit in our scenario, how much energy will we need, what new energy infrastructure would need to be in place, and how would our physical world need to change? That's what we explore in this chapter.[18] We test the physical limits of the system. We do not look at many other important limitations or risks. Politics may underdeliver, and geopolitical tensions may block progress. These are real challenges, but they are human challenges. The roadblocks we see are not physical but social, and we hope that we can figure out how to remove them.

The key point we make is that we can overcome the physical challenges in building the energy system we need to power prosperity for all.

Let's look at some big numbers. In our scenario, the world economy is 8.5 times larger than today. Demand for energy could be double or triple what it is today. Most supply would come from electricity. From 20 percent of the mix today, electricity could account for 70 to 80 percent. That would raise demand for electricity by up to 12 times. To make that electricity clean, low-emissions generation would need to expand 30 times.[19]

We think that this is possible, but only with a fundamentally different energy system. Just as today's infrastructure bears little resemblance to that of the 1950s, we must build something new. We need to refresh our thinking.

We will demonstrate that we can meet our needs largely with nuclear, solar, and wind power, backed by storage, some natural gas paired with CCUS, and other energy sources like hydro and geothermal.[20] In our scenario, fossil fuels are a much smaller part of the energy mix, but more of them may be used as inputs for petrochemicals and fertilizers. In other words, we largely stop *burning* most fossil fuels, the main activity that causes emissions, but continue to *embed* them in a growing number of products we consume (more on this later).

We don't presume to know exactly what the energy mix will be in 2100, not least because new technologies will surely emerge. But we propose a bold view of what's possible when humanity dares to build, powered by technologies that are commercially available today.

We need two to three times more energy

Much debate today concerns how to replace fossil fuels with renewable energy. But the task goes well beyond replacement to scaling and reinventing the entire system. To power a prosperous world, we will need two to three times the energy we have today. The real debate should be about how to double or triple the output of the energy system, and how to do it with low emissions. If we look back at the energy system in 1925, it was tiny compared with today's. And by 2100, we think it will have to be much larger.

As we like to do, let's start with the numbers. In 2025, the world will consume about 175,000 terawatt hours of energy. If that were all gasoline, it would be enough to fill the tanks of 26 billion cars.

With an economy 8.5 times larger, if we produce the same GDP for every unit of energy, we would need 8.5 times the amount of energy. But history has shown that we have consistently produced more with each unit of energy we use. Today, each dollar of GDP corresponds to one kilowatt hour of energy: an "energy intensity of GDP" of 1.0.[21] If that energy intensity remains exactly the same, in 2100 we would be consuming 1.4 million terawatt hours, or enough gasoline to fill 220 billion cars. But energy intensity has been falling. In 1970, the same amount of real GDP took 2.3 times more energy to produce than today.

The energy intensity of GDP has been falling steadily in two ways. First, we made existing technologies more efficient. As noted in chapter 9, the gas turbine advanced from 15 percent efficiency in 1940 to 40 percent by 2000. We also developed entirely new technologies that delivered leaps in efficiency. The steam engine, for example, converted only about 20 percent of the heat it consumed into forward motion. A diesel engine, by contrast, can convert about 45 percent, while an electric power train can convert up to 90 percent.[22]

Second, we now generate more GDP per unit of energy consumed. As economies advance, they tend to move more into services, whose energy intensity can be up to 20 times lower than that of industrial sectors. Take digital services as an example. The amount of energy that data centers use is certainly growing rapidly, but these centers produce far more output per unit of energy than industrial sectors like manufacturing. Aluminum, for instance, consumes about 15 megawatt hours of electricity per tonne

Server room, the Netherlands.

of production. The same amount of energy in Google's data centers can generate roughly $150,000 of advertising revenue, which is about 60 times the value of the tonne of aluminum.[23]

As AI becomes a more prominent feature of our lives and economies, will the same be true? Will AI deliver more value per unit of energy consumed? AI is power hungry and already starting to face power constraints. We forecast that in the United States, data center energy consumption grows by more than 20 percent per year from 2025 to 2030, while US power generation has grown at less than 1 percent per year in the past decade. This is pushing the US grid to the limit and making the need to increase electricity supply front-page news.[24] And as AI use expands throughout the world, other regions will feel similar power crunches.

Could AI be big enough to totally change the relationship between GDP and energy? Maybe. But all that new energy will also create new GDP. We also note that while computing power is growing rapidly, it benefits from awesome rates of efficiency improvement: A modern AI chip uses 99 percent less energy for the same task than a 2008 chip. Naturally there are a lot of variables here, which is why in our calculations we add an

EXHIBIT 27

Historical trend of energy intensity and historical growth in primary energy with 2100 range of scenarios

Energy intensity of GDP, TWh per billion international $

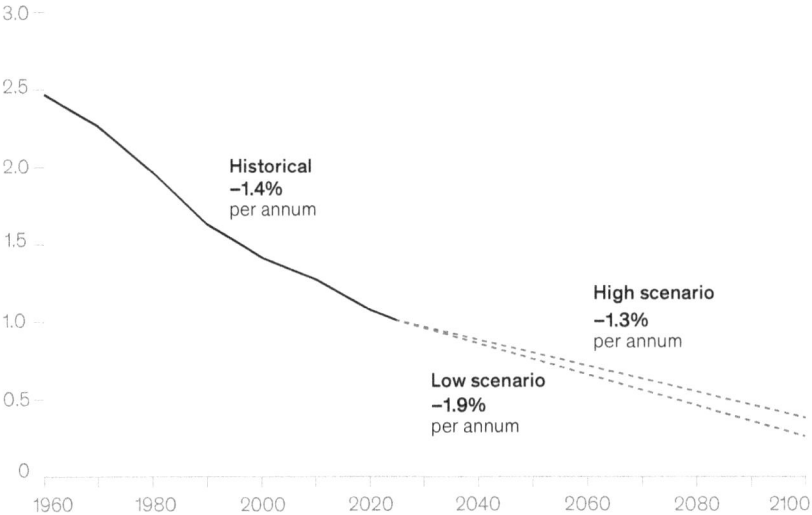

Primary and electrified energy, thousand TWh

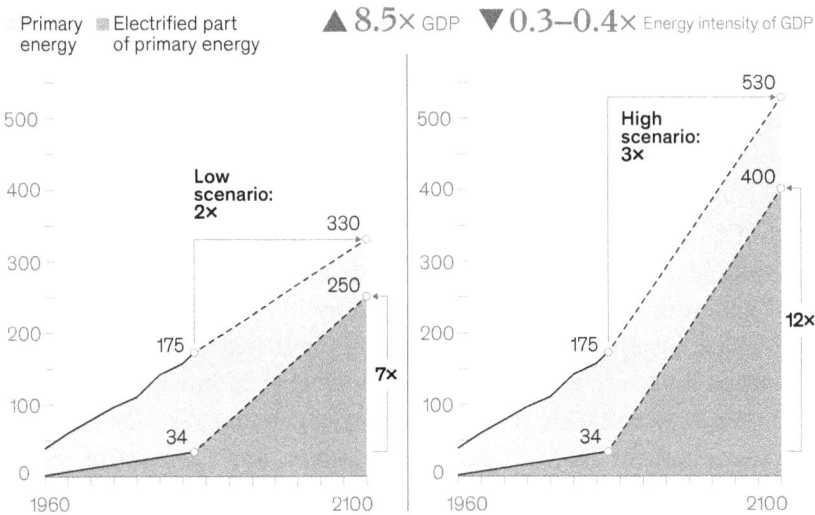

Source: World Bank; Paolo Malanima, *WEC world energy consumption, a database 1820–2020*, 2022; McKinsey Global energy perspective 2025; McKinsey Global Institute analysis

additional 20 percent range for energy intensity.[25]

Factoring in both the efficiency of the energy system and the amount of GDP produced for every unit of energy, we believe that energy intensity of GDP can decline by between 1.3 percent and 1.9 percent a year over the next 75 years (Exhibit 27). Since 1960, energy intensity has improved 1.4 percent per year as we have learned to squeeze more value from each joule, and we see this continuing. In fact, electrification may even improve it.

If we improve at a slightly slower rate than the historical trend on energy intensity, at 1.3 percent per year, that would triple energy demand to about 530,000 terawatt hours per year. However, if we improve faster, at 1.9 percent per year, we would need double the energy, or 330,000 terawatt hours. Either way, constantly improving how much we get out of the energy we use means that we do *not* need 8.5 times more energy to match an economy that is 8.5 times larger, a punishing ask. But we do need to expand our energy system profoundly, not just replacing the current sources but making the whole thing two to three times larger. Where on this range we end up depends on how much we electrify.

The magic of electrification

The future world of energy we envision is electrified, delivering a major efficiency gain. This is a true transformation from today, when electricity accounts for only 20 percent of all the energy we use. Electricity plays a meaningful role in industry and buildings but contributes relatively little to transportation (Exhibit 28).[26]

In a century of plenty, as we have said, electricity would supply 70 to 80 percent of all the energy we use. That would mean increasing electricity production seven- to 12-fold. That would require a much larger grid. Beyond generating and supplying the electricity, how we use it would need to change radically, too. You can't simply deliver electricity to any car. It needs a battery to receive it and an electric motor to turn it into motion. We need to tackle tricky technological challenges. Electricity is already excellent for lighting, powering motors, and performing many stationary tasks. It is less suitable for generating very high-temperature heat, storing energy, and being transported efficiently over long distances. Fossil fuels currently do all of these things better than electricity.

Share of electricity in total final energy consumption
Total final energy consumption by sector, 2025, %

◾ Electrified energy ◾ Non-electrified energy

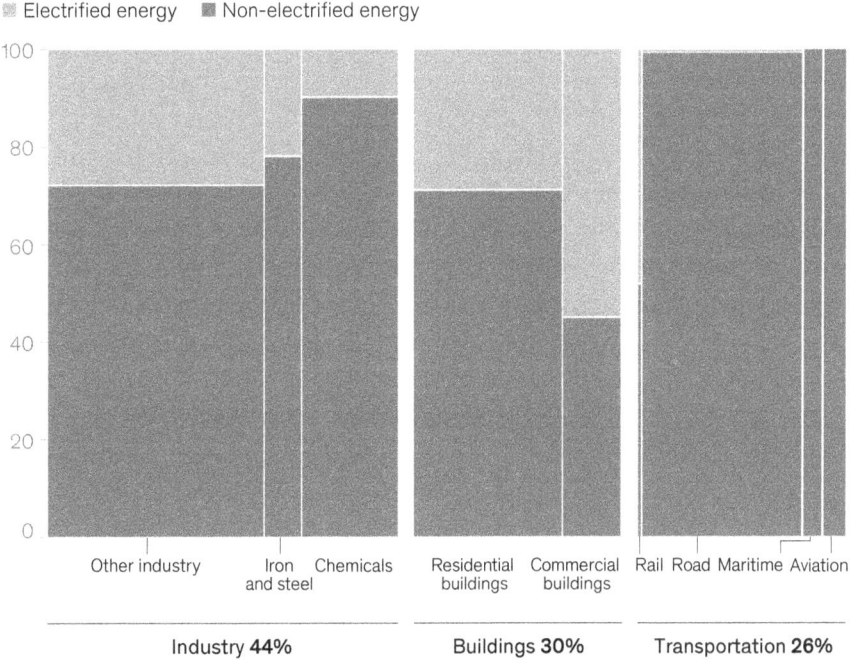

Other industry Iron Chemicals	Residential Commercial	Rail Road Maritime Aviation
and steel	buildings buildings	
Industry **44%**	Buildings **30%**	Transportation **26%**

Source: *McKinsey Global energy perspective 2025*

Let's look at the way different sectors would need to adapt. As we have said, electricity is not hugely prominent in transportation, which accounts for about 26 percent of all the energy we consume.[27] The energy we use to move ourselves around still largely comes from fossil fuels. Vehicles that run on gas can travel long distances using small tanks that can easily be refilled at millions of gas stations. Electricity is indeed coming to our vehicles. Batteries have improved enough to give EVs hundreds of kilometers of range, and the vehicles now compete well on efficiency, performance, and cost. But they are still not nearly as convenient or versatile as vehicles that run on fossil fuel. By 2100, however, most transportation could be electric. This would deliver a massive efficiency boost. ICE vehicles lose much of their energy through combustion and friction. A battery-powered passenger vehicle could be 70 percent more energy-efficient than an ICE vehicle, even accounting for manufacturing the vehicle and building the charging infrastructure.[28]

Now let's look at the heating and cooling of buildings. That's an additional 30 percent of the energy we use. Today, cooling uses electricity and is pretty efficient, but heating still relies largely on burning gas. There is an electric alternative: the heat pump, which moves heat in or out of buildings rather than creating it through combustion. Replacing gas furnaces in billions of homes and offices is a huge undertaking, but one well worth doing, because heat pumps can be more than twice as efficient as gas heating systems. Even if powered by a natural-gas-fired power plant, a heat pump uses about 40 percent less gas to generate the same amount of heat as burning that same gas in a home boiler.[29]

We now turn to one of the biggest challenges: electrifying industry. That's 44 percent of the energy we use. It is all about temperature. Many

Steel rolls, United States.

industries use low to medium temperatures, which can be provided efficiently using industrial heat pumps, waste-heat recovery, and heat from nuclear or geothermal sources. But the "big four" industries that underpin modern civilization—the manufacture of ammonia, cement, plastics, and steel—need extremely high-temperature heat, and so far there has not been an alternative to fossil fuels, which are supremely good at generating it. We are looking into it. We are exploring new electricity-based technologies, like electric arc furnaces for steel, rotodynamic heaters for cement, and electro-cracking for plastics. None of these are yet viable on the scale needed, and in any case would need massive retrofitting of industrial plants. This is both costly and complicated. In our 2100 energy scenario, we assume that 50 to 60 percent of heavy industry is electrified. Even this would be a huge transformation.[30]

The incentive to push ahead and overcome difficulties to create a majority electric energy system is huge. Not only is electricity clean in comparison with fossil fuels, but it could dramatically improve efficiency. Today, we convert less than half of the energy produced into useful stuff or useful processes. A more electrified system that increases that to 75 or 90 percent is a very rich prize. Winning it will require a truly monumental transformation. It will be hard, but it can be done.

Three times energy, 30 times clean electricity

If we have to double or triple energy, that is 1.0 to 1.5 percent annual growth in the energy system to 2100. That is slower than the 1.8 percent annual growth achieved since 2000. That seems doable.[31]

Electricity would need to grow much faster, though, at about 3.3 percent a year, compared with 2.8 percent a year since 2000. An acceleration but not a dramatic one. China has already been far faster than that, expanding its electricity system by 8.7 percent annually in recent years. China has been rapidly electrifying end uses as well, doubling electricity's share of final energy from less than 15 percent in 2000 to about 30 percent by 2024, surpassing the United States and Europe, with rates closer to 20 percent.[32] In 2023, China's electricity system had 1.8 million kilometers of transmission and distribution lines, enough to wrap Earth along the equator 45 times.[33] Now, our scenario is not assuming every country builds at the rate of China. Far from it. China has expanded electricity generation tenfold in the past 25 years, and 25-fold over the past 40. To achieve a century of plenty, we would need seven to 12 times in 75 years.[34]

What kind of energy system would we build? There are many possible paths, but we looked at one plausible mix in order to gauge whether we can succeed.

So, let's get into it. In our scenario, 40 percent of energy comes from solar and wind and another 40 percent from nuclear—all of them low-emissions sources. Ten percent would come from natural gas and the rest from hydro, geothermal, and biofuels. They would also have a neutral carbon footprint, assuming that natural gas is paired with carbon capture or removal, or created through waste.[35]

Of course, this is just one possible mix for the energy system of the future. In reality, we are witnessing a race between myriad energy technologies, from carbon capture to nuclear fusion. One key lap in that race is between battery storage and nuclear power generation for the technology to most effectively supply firm baseload power. The electric grid needs stable backup power to function, and that can be provided by renewables paired with batteries, or by sources like nuclear that produce predictable quantities of energy. We don't yet know which technology will provide the best performance for a given cost: batteries, nuclear energy, or even a new technology. Here we explore a scenario with 40 percent renewables and battery storage and 40 percent nuclear power, but their shares will depend on how fast costs decline for each.

Having 80 percent of energy come from nuclear and renewables may seem ambitious. But we don't think it's impossible to increase the amount of energy coming from low-carbon sources by about 20 to 30 times. Let's look again at China. It has not only spectacularly ramped up electricity generation but also increased generation from nuclear, solar, and wind tenfold over the past ten years. Again, we should acknowledge that China has been exceptional when it comes to making electricity, but its trajectory makes a 30-fold increase in 75 years look reasonable.

China and other countries that are in their rapid development phase are not the only economies transforming their energy profiles. Just look at the United States and its shale revolution. Two decades ago, shale barely registered, but now shale contributes more to US energy production than conventional oil and gas combined (Exhibit 29).[36] In 2023, US shale production exceeded Saudi Arabia's total oil output. Meanwhile, between 2003 and 2023, coal's share in the US energy mix dropped from 24 percent to less than 9 percent.[37] This helped the United States cut emissions faster, measured in absolute terms, than any other developed country.

Both China and the United States have surprised on the upside. This gives us confidence that it's possible to greatly expand the energy system to power a century of plenty, increasing overall energy two to three times, electricity seven to 12 times, and clean energy 20 to 30 times.

Growth rates of new energy sources

Global energy supply (exajoules), indexed to years after passing 2 exajoules of global supply

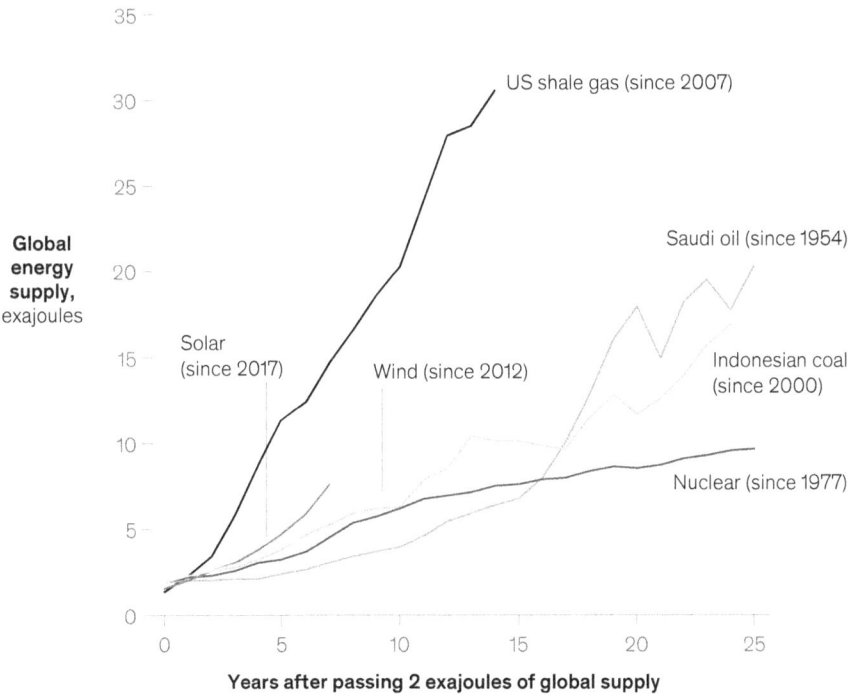

Global energy supply, exajoules

US shale gas (since 2007)

Saudi oil (since 1954)

Solar (since 2017)

Wind (since 2012)

Indonesian coal (since 2000)

Nuclear (since 1977)

Years after passing 2 exajoules of global supply

Source: US Energy Information Administration; Energy Institute, *Statistical review of world energy*, 2025; McKinsey Global Institute analysis

Harnessing solar and wind

Solar and wind energy could provide a large share of the energy we need. They have manifold advantages: they're abundant, rapidly accessible where they are generated, and coming down in price. And in the case of solar, the proportion of sunlight that can be converted to electricity is improving rapidly.[38]

There is no doubt that getting solar and wind to 40 percent of total energy would be a considerable undertaking. We would need 66,000 gigawatts of solar panels and wind turbines in 2100, up from about 3,350 gigawatts today. That is about a 20-fold increase. Every year, we would need to add about 1,000 gigawatts of solar and 400 gigawatts of wind.[39]

We are not far from that pace today. In 2024, we added 600 gigawatts of solar energy, or 60 percent of our annual target. The world added more solar capacity in 2022 and 2023 than the entire amount cumulatively installed before. Wind installations are averaging about 100 gigawatts a year, one-quarter of what we would need. The IEA suggests that this could grow to about 190 gigawatts annually by 2030 in its main scenario and to 340 gigawatts in its net-zero scenario, close to what our suggested energy scenario requires. Maybe not that ambitious after all.[40]

There are two "ifs," though, and they have been big ones so far. The first is if we can handle intermittent generation from solar and wind. The second is if we can move electricity from the many, often dispersed places where it is generated to where it is consumed. In short, solar and wind have to be useful and dispatchable. That means much more storage of all kinds and a larger, more connected, grid.

Let's start with the first "if": intermittency and storage, first for managing variability within the day and then for managing variability over weeks or months.

Managing variability during the day seems within reach in our 2100 energy scenario. First, a broadly electrified world gives us opportunities to manage demand more flexibly to match variability in supply. AI can play a role in automating the management of an increasingly complex grid. Incentives could be put in place to smooth out demand, shifting any loads that are not time sensitive. People could be encouraged to charge their EVs during periods of peak afternoon sunshine and energy-intensive industry to run processes in off-peak hours. Connected buildings could automatically shift when they consume energy, generating heat when lots of energy is being produced and using that heat when less energy is available. EVs can actually feed energy back into the grid when they are not using it themselves. When there are several billion EVs around, that could make a huge contribution. Oakland, California, is already piloting a school bus–to-grid project with about one gigawatt of battery capacity. Virtual power plants can also give us flexibility. These plants connect batteries, EVs, heat pumps, and more into a single "virtual asset" that can both consume energy and supply it back to the grid. South Australia is developing the world's largest virtual power plant, which connects thousands of solar panels and Tesla home batteries into a flexible system that smooths out demand and eases pressure on the grid.[41]

Automated demand management can go a long way but is not a total solution. We would also need to manage variability of supply through more energy storage. We estimate that generating 40 percent of global energy demand using intermittent renewables would require intraday and inter-day (within the same day or from one day to another) storage capacity of about 90 to 140 terawatt hours. That is equivalent to an average of five hours of electricity demand. To visualize this, it would be the energy stored in about 1.0 billion to 1.5 billion EV batteries weighing a total of 500 billion to 800 billion kilograms.[42]

Some of this storage could be provided by energy users, such as EVs, buildings, and other assets hooked up to a smart grid. But utilities would also need to add storage at the grid level to balance the overall system. They have several options, including batteries, mechanical storage like pumped hydro, and thermal storage.

Battery storage is already commercial and growing fast. Grid battery capacity increased by more than 50 percent globally in 2024. US installations are expected to double in 2025. Global manufacturing capacity for lithium-ion batteries reached three terawatt hours in 2024 and could more than triple by 2030. Battery prices have fallen by 90 percent in ten years.[43] And new chemistries like sodium-ion and vanadium redox could provide additional storage options.

Now let's look at mechanical storage. Pumped hydro plants already store more than nine terawatt hours of energy globally. That is nearly one-tenth of what we could need in our energy scenario.[44] Other mechanical solutions, such as compressed air energy storage and flywheels, are also being tested.

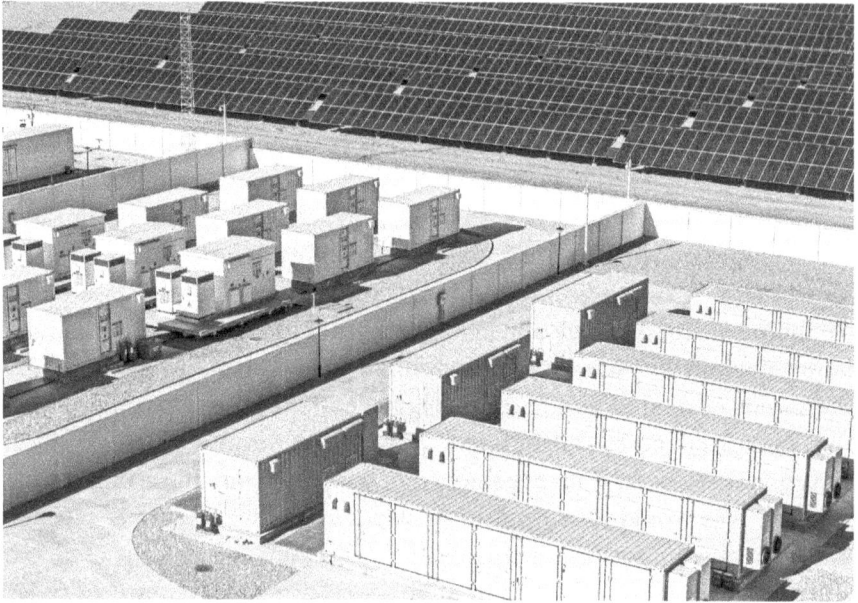

Energy storage power station, China.

And then there is thermal energy storage. Our system would generate a lot of heat, and we are already exploring good ways to store it in concrete, molten salts, rocks, and water. In June 2025, the world's biggest sand battery became operational, delivering one megawatt of thermal power and storing up to 100 megawatt hours. It is a modest start, but a promising one as the technology matures.[45]

Smart management combined with these storage technologies will probably be sufficient for daily fluctuations. But extended periods without wind or sun, known as *Dunkelflaute* (dark lull), pose a tougher challenge. In February 2025, North Sea wind farms produced just 15 percent of expected output over ten days due to low wind and overcast skies.

Battery, mechanical, and thermal storage could provide some multiday backup. In the Netherlands, a 500-megawatt compressed-air storage project will pump energy into underground caverns during periods of low demand and release it to turbines when needed. This mechanical storage system will be paired with high-capacity batteries, enabling both short-term and multiday storage.[46]

Still, this may not be enough for longer seasonal gaps, like summer to winter. But there are options. Natural gas power plants that are not needed for most of the year can ramp up during a *Dunkelflaute*. Hydrogen, a chemical storage option, can also be burned for power generation, albeit with large energy losses.[47] Stronger grid interconnections between regions can also help with not only short-term but also long-term variability. Strong sunlight in Chile's Atacama desert, for example, could offset a windless and cloudy week in coastal Peru.

Now to the second "if." Solar panels and wind turbines are placed where the sun shines and the wind blows, but not always close to people who use the power. The power needs to get from source to consumer. The answer is a much larger and more connected grid. In our work on the physical aspects of the energy transition, we estimated that the grid would need to double in size by 2050. That is a big ask given that over the past decade, grids have grown by just 2 percent per year, from just over 60 million to just under 80 million kilometers.[48]

And our 2100 energy scenario calls for much more than doubling. The system would have to transport up to 12 times more electricity, and that may require even greater capacity. With wind and solar dispersed and intermittent, the grid must be large enough to cope with peaks in demand, say on a cold night when heat pumps are running at full power.

This is a large challenge, although the difficult parts are political and social rather than physical, as we have the technology and materials. Increasing grid capacity is not just a matter of building more but of building better. Technologies like ultra-high-voltage (UHV) lines can double the capacity of existing infrastructure. In Europe and the United States, 380 kilovolts and 500 kilovolts, respectively, are the standard voltage for long-distance transmission.[49] UHV lines that are rated 800 kilovolts or higher are already being used. For instance, Brazil's Belo Monte UHV line carries electricity over an 800-kilovolt line from Belo Monte Hydropower plant in the Amazon River Basin more than 2,500 kilometers south to Rio de Janeiro. China and Japan have installed lines rated 1,000 kilovolts and above. Making grids smarter would also help. Dynamic line rating like that employed by the New York Independent System Operator and the UK National Grid uses real-time sensors and weather data to adjust transmission capacity, which boosts capacity by 10 to 30 percent without building new lines.

High-voltage electrical tower, Spain.

Having sufficient materials to manufacture all those solar panels and turbines is another issue, and we address that in the next chapter. But there is one more matter that we can talk about here: land. Solar panels and wind turbines could cover 550,000 square kilometers, roughly the size of France, though faster-than-expected improvements in panel efficiency and tracking technologies that increase panel capacity could reduce that amount. And, of course, the enormous grid that stitches it all together takes up more land. That land needs to be suitable for sun and wind, and not all of it is. Nevertheless, a lot of land can be dual use. Farmers can raise animals or grow crops on the same land that holds solar panels, for instance.[50]

Solar and wind have strong potential to supply 40 percent of the energy in our 2100 scenario, so long as we invest heavily in storage and grids. Advancing beyond 40 percent would require quicker advances in storage technologies and a more rapid scale-up of the grid. We also have other options to supply low-carbon electricity that are already at commercial scale. So now let's look at nuclear fission.

A nuclear power revolution?

Eyebrows may be raised by our energy scenario that would see nuclear fission providing 40 percent of the energy we will need, matching the share from renewables. But we have a long and surprisingly successful history of using it. And it delivers. It is a proven technology that produces a lot of reliable, low-emissions, and consistent energy. It is compact and uses only limited resources. And it is long-lived.

For these reasons, nuclear was once seen as the hope for an abundant and environmentally friendly energy future. In 1971, US President Richard Nixon declared, "We can have a cleaner America, a better America, through nuclear energy. It is essential to our future." The United States wasn't alone. Brazil, France, India, and Japan also turned to nuclear energy to get the power they needed, but after two high-profile accidents—Three Mile Island in 1979 and Chernobyl in 1986—growth in nuclear plateaued.

Now the tide is turning again. Nuclear is once again firmly in the frame as we look for more clean energy, particularly given that a new generation of technologies and practices has greatly reduced the dangers and impact of nuclear power. Confidence seems to be rising.

Germany has recently softened its opposition to new reactors within the EU, and Sweden has overturned its 1980 ban on new reactors. Developing economies have been particularly fast at building nuclear. China quadrupled capacity; Russia increased it by one-quarter. At the 2023 COP28 and 2024 COP29 climate summits, 31 nations, including China, Japan, Kenya, Türkiye, and the United States, signed a declaration committing to tripling nuclear capacity by 2050. It is notable that Microsoft, Google, and Meta are signing multigigawatt deals to power data centers with nuclear energy. Tech giants usually know which way the wind is blowing![51]

With nuclear gaining momentum, we wanted to test a scenario in which nuclear fission is a major contributor of our energy system. What would it take for nuclear to contribute 40 percent of our 2100 energy needs?

Assuming each reactor averages one gigawatt, we would need roughly 26,500 reactors generating about 215,000 terawatt hours of electricity. That would be a substantial increase from today, building an average of 350 new reactors each year.[52] Many of those could be small modular reactors (SMRs) of less than one gigawatt, so while the number could well

Doel nuclear station, Antwerp Port.

be much higher, SMRs are much easier to build, and more of them in the mix would make scaling up easier to achieve.

And, again, this significant ramp-up is in the context of a much larger economy and electricity system. We would need to add about 2 percent of our electricity capacity every year in the form of nuclear. In today's world, that would mean adding about 70 nuclear plants starting in 2026, and that number would increase as the electricity system expands (with an average of 350 from 2025 to 2100). That is a lot more than the ten per year we are planning to build in the next few years, but still not physically impossible.[53]

There have been nuclear booms before. After the 1973 oil crisis, under its Messmer Plan, France built about 50 reactors with a combined capacity of 55 gigawatts in 15 years. That is about four a year (Exhibit 30). This more than doubled France's electricity capacity. These same reactors humming along today are the prime reason France's carbon intensity per kilowatt hour is nearly half that of neighboring Germany's. At France's Messmer speed, scaled globally, the world today could add more than 100 reactors per year.[54] And that was in an electricity system that was 30 percent as large as today's.

We are already seeing ways of building nuclear that overcome some of the complexities involved. Some Asian countries have opted for standard plants and are building them back-to-back to streamline and accelerate their effort. South Korea built 12 reactors in quick succession between 1989 and 2005, and eight of these were an identical model. This was effective. Some plants were completed in 56 months, which is two-thirds of the time needed on average in our scenario, and at one-third of the cost of the latest US nuclear build.[55] Building even more standardized, smaller SMRs could further reduce the time and cost.

And the cost of nuclear has ample room to fall. The United States paid about $14 million per megawatt for its most recent reactor completed in

EXHIBIT 30

Electricity generation by fuel in France
TWh

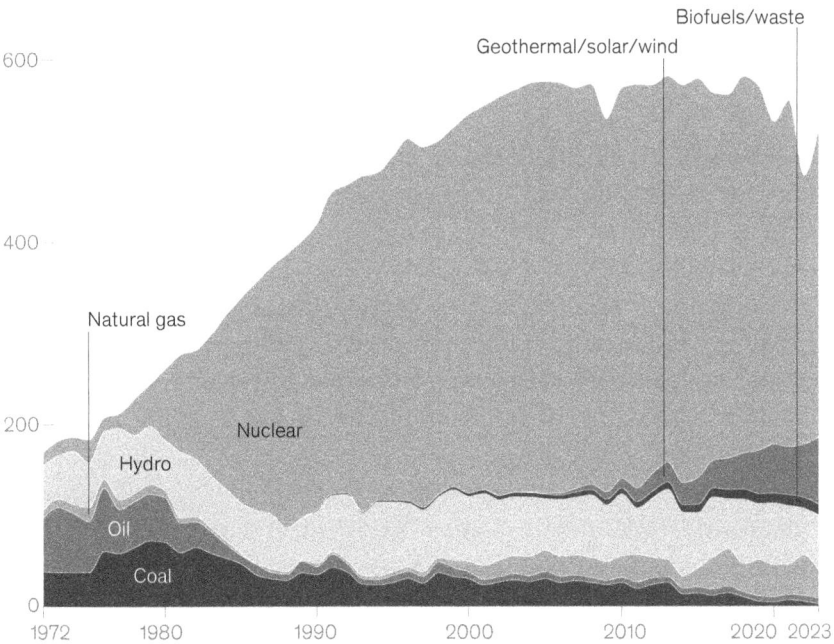

2024, but South Korea has built comparable units for roughly $3 million per megawatt. South Korea's plants meet international standards, including those for safety. US costs are higher because of cumbersome building codes, lengthy licensing and litigation, immature supply chains, and a workforce that hasn't built reactors in decades. If construction becomes routine, costs fall. In fact, in long-run electricity optimization models, even modest year-on-year improvements in the cost- and time-effectiveness of nuclear results in substantially more nuclear plants being built.[56]

In three energy scenarios created by McKinsey's Energy Practice, which are built on a bottom-up demand outlook across 68 sectors, nuclear fission power plants in 2050 cost $3 million to $5 million per megawatt to build, and nuclear power generates 10 to 15 percent of electricity.[57] We also modeled other example scenarios in which the cost of nuclear power falls further. In the scenario in which the cost of nuclear in India and the United States falls to less than $2 million and $3 million per megawatt, respectively, the optimal share of nuclear power in total electricity generation rises to exceed 50 percent (excluding any assumptions on whether supply chains can deliver).

There are other issues to consider. One is whether enough uranium will be available. Current uranium reserves could power existing reactors for about 25 more years at the industry's modest historical growth rate. At first glance, this seems to be woefully insufficient. But with nuclear coming back into fashion, the incentive to invest in uranium exploration and mining is stronger. The oceans are one potential avenue. They are thought to hold about 4.5 billion tonnes of uranium, enough to power nuclear plants for millennia. Extracting uranium from the sea is roughly two to four times more expensive than extracting it on land, but that premium would fall as technologies improve, and a premium would be worth paying if demand is strong. Meanwhile, alternative nuclear fuels like thorium are extremely abundant. The technology to use it is not quite there yet, but it is progressing.[58]

We cannot complete a discussion about the potential for nuclear power without considering safety and waste. Let's look at them now.

Nuclear accidents are real and dangerous, and safety is, and must be, a key component of nuclear plants. After Chernobyl, for instance, radioactive iodine largely dissipated within two months due to its fast decay, but its impact on the food chain, especially milk, lingered far longer. Cleanup took decades and required sweeping environmental remediation.[59]

Over time, stringent safeguards have been, and continue to be, developed. Today's nuclear plants are far less likely to have a Chernobyl or even a Fukushima-style meltdown. Modern reactors have a more robust containment structure, added redundancies, and passive safety systems, which means that if power or cooling is lost, natural processes like gravity and convection help cool the reactor without using electricity or indeed a human operator intervening. The Fukushima incident was primarily caused by the tsunami disabling cooling systems; new reactors are now designed or retrofitted to withstand such natural disasters.[60]

Despite past incidents, nuclear power remains one of the safest energy sources. When considering the entire life cycle, including mining, operation, and accidents, nuclear results in significantly fewer deaths than fossil fuels. Per terawatt hour, coal causes 25 deaths, oil 19, gas three, and nuclear just 0.03, even less than wind power.[61]

Nuclear waste, though long-lived and hazardous, is generated in small volumes. In over 70 years, we've produced only enough high-level waste to fill two Olympic pools while generating 31,000 terawatts of power. At the scale of energy we imagine, this equates to about 14 such pools a year, or roughly one beer can of waste per person over a lifetime. With reprocessing, even less waste is produced.

Still, for 50 years the waste remains radioactive enough to harm human health and thus needs to be stored carefully. Many fission plants have deep pools on-site that can store this high-level waste for 50 years until it is placed in deep geological repositories like Finland's Onkalo facility.[62] We would need more of these repositories, but that may be a small price to pay for a vast amount of reliable, low-carbon energy. And remember that other energy sources have costs, too. Fossil fuels emit carbon. Solar and wind require large amounts of space. Would we rather give up space on land or space deep underground? Nuclear plants also use lots of water for cooling. That is not an issue at the current scale, but with many more reactors, the industry would require more infrastructure and careful consideration about where to site plants.[63]

We acknowledge that nuclear raises political and social issues, not the least of which is that the same technology that enables nuclear power can also be used to make nuclear weapons. Preventing nuclear proliferation for the purposes of aggression requires political solutions. The 2009 nuclear

The cooling water system of a nuclear power plant.

cooperation agreement between the United States and the United Arab Emirates is widely held up as a benchmark for what can be achieved.[64] Another strictly nonphysical challenge is ensuring that we have enough skills to support a broad-based revival of nuclear.

But these are limits of the mind rather than physical restrictions. It would certainly take ambition and real commitment to get nuclear to 40 percent, but it is not physically impossible.

Yet more science and technology to come

Our energy scenario for 2100 is based on known and tested technologies. In reality, brainpower and money are pouring into energy, and transformative breakthroughs could make meeting our goal much easier than we have posited. Let's look at just four technologies that could be on the horizon.

Nuclear fusion has long been seen as energy's holy grail. It is clean, limitless, and safe. Grid-scale fusion would be a game changer, eliminating intermittency and fuel constraints. Progress is real and investment is rising, but substantial uncertainty remains about both feasibility and how long it will take for fusion to become commercially viable. In an exciting glimpse of the potential, in early 2025 France's CEA WEST fusion reactor maintained a fusion reaction for more than 20 minutes. That was promising, but many steps remain until full commercial viability.[65]

Advances in battery technology like new chemistries or breakthroughs in mechanical or thermal technologies could massively reduce the cost and difficulties of deploying wind and solar.

Carbon capture is expensive and a technological challenge, but some innovations such as oxyfuel and adsorption capture show promise. We do assume that CCUS paired with gas plants plays some part in our 2100 system, but a breakthrough that would make it significantly cheaper or easier would greatly expand the energy options available.

We also assume a small amount of low-emissions hydrogen, ammonia, and synthetic fuels used in sectors like aviation, shipping, and heavy industry that are hard to decarbonize. Today, these fuels are expensive and often less efficient than fossil fuels. But if there are breakthroughs that lower costs and raise efficiency, our energy scenario would become even more doable.

※　※　※

Having enough energy to power the plentiful world we want in 2100 is pivotal. An energy mix that is largely low emissions courtesy of solar, wind, and nuclear is physically possible so long as we are ambitious. The incentive of clean, abundant energy is strong. There is still a major question of whether a much larger global economy is compatible with the health of our planet, and we discuss this later. But before that, let's discuss whether we have the materials we need.

CHAPTER 17

THE MATERIALS TO BUILD THE FUTURE

"We are living in a material world."

MADONNA

—

There is enough stuff in the crust of the Earth to sustain progress in the coming century.

FOR MILLENNIA, HUMANS HAVE BUILT their world using Earth's natural materials. Minerals and metals are the physical backbone of industrialization and prosperity. Steel forms everything from kitchen forks and medical tools to cars and skyscrapers. Aluminum goes into window frames, airplane fuselages, laptop casings, power lines, and soda cans. The century of plenty hinges on a steady supply of diverse, high-quality materials for myriad uses, like infrastructure, technology, and clean energy. The crucial question is whether Earth holds enough materials to be refined and made available in an environmentally responsible and timely manner to support plenty in 2100. We believe the answer is yes.

One key to answering this question is that supply of materials is dynamic, not static. In many cases, the amount that we know is in the ground and we can extract today may not be enough to deliver on a century of plenty. But for many materials, history shows us that when we search more, we find more. And when we invest time, we also develop better ways to make the materials economically usable.

The Escondida mine in Chile, the world's largest copper mine, illustrates this. When operations began in 1990, it was already a major copper discovery. Over the decades, something striking happened. The mine's known resources—the total estimated copper in the ground—tripled. Even more importantly, the share of those resources that could be recovered profitably (its reserves) doubled. This partly reflected higher copper prices amid increasing global demand, which made more of the ore economically viable to extract. Higher prices also encouraged more investment in exploration and new technologies. As a result, Escondida now produces close to 900,000 tonnes of copper annually, which is about 5 percent of all copper mined globally.[66]

Keep these two concepts in mind. Known *resources* are the total known quantity of any given material in the ground. Recoverable *reserves* are a subset of known resources that are economically viable, or what some call "in the money."

Escondida's growth was attributable not only to new discoveries but also to technological innovation in mining and processing. Escondida introduced new concentrators, autonomous haul trucks, and advanced cable-powered shovels. These upgrades made it possible to access ore that had previously been too difficult or expensive to reach. Innovation transformed processing, too. The mine deployed air-injection systems, coarse particle flotation, and more efficient grinding systems. These advances boosted throughput and improved Escondida's overall recovery from low-quality ores.[67]

Escondida amply demonstrates how a well-run, innovative mine can expand its economically extractable reserves by accessing difficult-to-reach materials and improving processing of lower-quality ore. And it is by no means the only example.

Aerial image of the Escondida copper mine in the Atacama Desert, Chile.

Here's another interesting story. A client of one of our authors is a major iron ore producer in Australia. In the mid-2000s, the company had to adapt to China's booming demand for steel. But it hadn't expanded its operations since the 1980s, and no one on the management team had ever had to grow the output before. Like any good company, it explored all kinds of scenarios about how to meet demand. The result was straightforward. It made its mines bigger, built a few new ones near existing rail lines, and added to capacity at the port it used. Without any complicated rethink, Australia quintupled iron ore production since the 1970s and doubled it in the 2010s alone.[68]

In short, what we can use is not limited to what we already know but to what we can affordably extract in the future. Neither resources nor reserves are fixed. They can, and do, grow over time.

Enough materials in the ground

To ascertain whether we will have enough materials for a century of plenty, we estimated the theoretical limits on those that are most prevalent today in infrastructure, electrification, and industrial manufacturing. We assumed that everyone in our abundant world consumes at roughly the same levels as residents of wealthy countries with modern infrastructure and widespread access to advanced technologies, and we considered additional demand as the world electrifies. This is a conservative approach, because it is very likely that we will become much more efficient at using materials and even discover better and cheaper substitutes.

Let's start with steel. Each person in wealthy countries has about 9.8 (metric) tonnes of steel embedded in the things around them, including home appliances, cars, and infrastructure like bridges, highways, and skyscrapers. That is the total in-use stock per person, roughly equivalent to a full truckload of steel. By contrast, in India, each person has only about 1.2 tonnes. And in Sub-Saharan Africa, the figure is less than 0.4 tonne.[69]

If all eight billion people in the world today were to have the same amount of steel as people in an advanced economy, we would need 45 billion more tonnes of steel. Today, we produce about 1.9 billion tonnes of steel a year, so that would be 23 years of current production. That's a lot.[70]

But the amount of steel we would need for a plentiful century could be even greater, since there are more people who are more prosperous. In a century of plenty, everybody in the world doesn't just match the amount of steel in wealthy countries but exceeds it by 20 percent to account for potential new uses, such as deep-sea mining or even fusion energy. That is 11.7 tonnes for each person. Once we account for a population of 12 billion instead of eight billion and replacement of old steel that is not recycled, the global steel consumed between now and 2100 would total a whopping 134 billion tonnes. That's nearly double the amount we consumed in the previous 75 years.[71]

The question is whether we can produce that much.

Building enough steel production plants does not seem to be the issue. Even though steel plants are huge, sometimes the size of Central Park in Manhattan, we have shown that we can scale production rapidly.[72] In 2000, China produced roughly 130 million tonnes of steel, which was about 15 percent of global output at the time. In 2024, China produced more than one billion tonnes, more than half of the world total. In other words, China alone has nearly doubled the world's steel production capacity since 2000.[73] Constructing plants is not the sticking point. But there are challenges. To scale steelmaking will require sufficient energy (of the right kind) to be available. And it will need capital. But arguably the biggest question is whether there will be enough of the raw materials needed to make steel.

The key input for steelmaking is iron ore. There are about 230 billion tonnes of known resources of usable iron content today. That's about 70 percent more than the amount we would need in a plentiful 2100.

And it seems plausible to believe that we can turn much of these known resources into extractable reserves.[74] Extractable reserves today contain about 88 billion tonnes of usable iron content, which produces an equivalent amount of steel. That means we can already economically extract about 66 percent of the 134 billion tonnes of steel that we need.[75]

However, over the past 30 years, extractable reserves have grown by about 1 percent per year.[76] If we matched that pace, we would have more than enough iron ore to produce the amount of steel that we need. In fact, reserves would not even need to grow as fast as the historical rate. In sum, based on current known resources and historical growth in extractable reserves, it is likely that we can supply enough iron ore to meet demand in 2100.

Now let's look at a material that is more associated with our electrified future than with our industrial past: lithium.

The largest and fastest-growing use for lithium is in EVs. If global car ownership in 2100 reached Switzerland's current level of six cars for every ten people, and 90 percent of them were electric, there would be about 6.5 billion EVs on the road. Since EVs last about 15 years, maintaining that number would require manufacturing roughly 19.5 billion vehicles between now and 2100. Visualize it: 19.5 billion EVs would cover about 160,000 square kilometers, which is an area the size of Bangladesh or Tunisia. To power them all using today's technologies, we would need approximately 174 million tonnes of lithium. That's a huge number of cars that we may never reach: Growth in shared autonomous vehicles, better public transportation infrastructure, and other new transportation technologies could massively lower the number. We use the example of EVs with today's lithium need per vehicle to illustrate the maximum demand that we might expect between now and 2100.[77]

Lithium is also used in other cases, like electronics and grid storage. Taking all uses into account, cumulative demand between today and

2100 for lithium could reach 213 million tonnes. That is equivalent to the combined weight of 35 Great Pyramids of Giza. Since we are recycling more, in reality, we may need to mine only about 168 million tonnes. That is still more than known resources of approximately 115 million tonnes, of which 30 million are classified as economically recoverable reserves.[78]

That may seem like a big gap, but it is not one that we can put down to geology. The real challenge is ramping up discovery and extraction fast enough to meet surging demand. Until about a decade ago, there was little incentive to look for lithium. Now, exploration is booming. Since 2010, global known resources have more than tripled, growing at nearly 11 percent annually. Recoverable reserves more than doubled in the same period, at 6.6 percent annually. That's nearly three times faster than the 2.3 percent annual growth rate needed to meet demand by century's end.[79]

Another reason for confidence is that future batteries may require far less lithium per unit of capacity. Innovation has reduced materials demand before. Lithium iron phosphate batteries, for instance, reduced dependence on cobalt and nickel. Now, emerging chemistries like sodium-ion and next-generation lithium iron phosphate variants promise to lower lithium use, too.[80]

Overall, we will need a lot of lithium, but momentum is on our side. With continued exploration, innovation, and recycling, supply looks far from constrained. As with copper in Chile and iron ore in Australia, serious effort tends to uncover more than expected. Even if demand is at the high end, the challenge of securing sufficient supply of lithium is considerable, but our outlook remains promising.

Much as we enjoy discussing individual materials, we take a shortcut for the rest of the critical materials. Applying the same approach we used for steel and lithium, we categorize them based on long-term availability: plentiful and promising (Exhibit 31 and Table 5).[81]

Aluminum, copper, and steel are plentiful. These metals are foundational to energy systems, construction, transportation, and global industry. While the current recoverable reserves of their associated ores may not be sufficient, known resources are large enough to meet projected demand through 2100. The challenge is converting those known resources into extractable reserves, although the growth in reserves required for copper and steel is well within historical norms.

Although historical growth rates for reserves of bauxite, the primary ore

Advanced robotic machinery assembles an EV battery unit.

used to produce aluminum, do not meet our future needs, we believe it still remains plentiful. Forms of aluminum account for roughly 8 percent of Earth's crust, and history shows that when we actively search for more, we tend to find more. And even if bauxite supply were to plateau, alternative aluminum sources, such as extracting alumina from clay, offer viable options to meet future demand.[82]

Rare earth elements are not rare. Their name comes from the fact that they are present in rock in tiny concentrations, not because they are uncommon. Reported reserves are bigger than needed to meet expected long-term demand. But we need to be a little careful. Reported reserves are for all 17 rare earths. Only four of these are crucial for magnetic application—neodymium, praseodymium, dysprosium, and terbium, which are used in EV motors, wind turbines, and emerging technologies like portable MRI machines. Other rare earths, like cerium and lanthanum, are abundant but not as useful. There is another caveat. Because these magnetic rare earths appear in such low concentrations in ore, their processing is complex and expensive. Moreover, geopolitical

EXHIBIT 31

Potential key materials demand compared with historical consumption

Cumulative global consumption of key materials from 2026 to 2100 in a century of plenty, as a multiple of historical levels

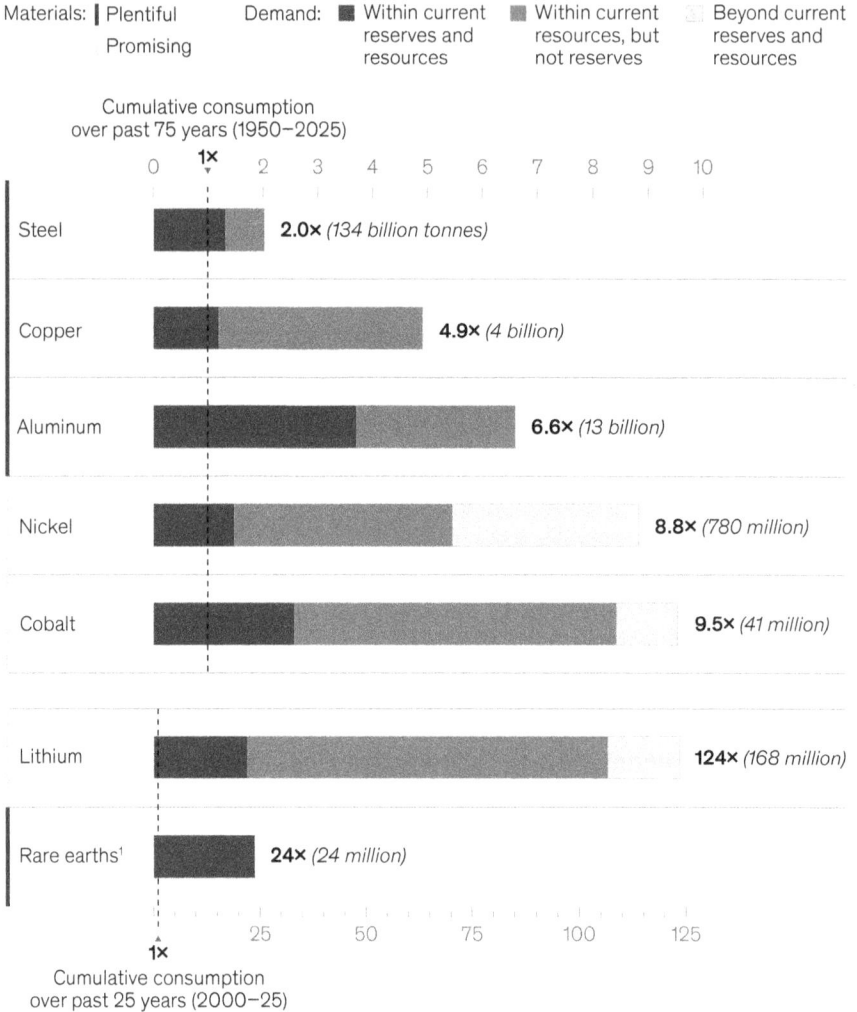

Materials: | Plentiful
Promising

Demand: ■ Within current reserves and resources   ■ Within current resources, but not reserves   Beyond current reserves and resources

Cumulative consumption over past 75 years (1950–2025)

| | 0 | 1× | 2 | 3 | 4 | 5 | 6 | 7 | 8 | 9 | 10 |

Steel 2.0× *(134 billion tonnes)*

Copper 4.9× *(4 billion)*

Aluminum 6.6× *(13 billion)*

Nickel 8.8× *(780 million)*

Cobalt 9.5× *(41 million)*

Lithium 124× *(168 million)*

Rare earths[1] 24× *(24 million)*

25   50   75   100   125

1×

Cumulative consumption over past 25 years (2000–25)

Note: All cumulative stock needs are calculated in material-equivalent terms. For most materials, resources and reserves are reported directly in metal or material content, as defined by USGS data. For steel and aluminum, USGS reports reserves and resources in terms of iron content and bauxite, respectively. To enable comparability, we converted these to metal-equivalent values using approximate yields: 1 tonne of steel per tonne of iron content and 0.25 tonne of aluminum per tonne of bauxite. These ratios reflect industry averages and may vary by ore quality and process efficiency.
[1]Rare earths reserves shown reflect all 17 elements, not just the 4 magnetic rare earth elements used in electrification. See main text for details.
Source: US Geological Survey, *Mineral commodity summaries;* IEA. *Global EV outlook;* IEA, *Global minerals outlook;* World Bank; McKinsey MineSpans; McKinsey Global Institute analysis

tensions already affect rare earth supply chains.[83] In short, sourcing rare earths is more complicated than the simple finding that reserves are more than enough for what we need. The hope is that some of those issues can

Growth rates of materials that would need to grow beyond current reserves and resources in a century of plenty

Historical growth rates compared to growth rates needed for cumulative consumption from 2026 to 2100

Materials Promising	Future cumulative consumption from 2026 to 2100, tonnes	Metal content in today's known resources, tonnes	Metal content in today's recoverable reserves, tonnes	Historical annual growth rate of reserves, 2010 to 2023, %	Annual growth rate of reserves needed for future consumption, %
Promising materials, whose current reserves and resources would have to grow					
Nickel	780 million	350 million	130 million	3.8%	2.4%
Cobalt	41 million	25 million	11 million	3.0%	1.7%
Lithium	168 million	115 million	30 million	6.6%	2.3%

Source: US Geological Survey, *Mineral commodity summaries;* IEA, *Global EV outlook;* IEA, *Global minerals outlook;* World Bank; McKinsey MineSpans; McKinsey Global Institute analysis

be solved through more innovation and investment, which are more likely to occur as demand rises. As Plato wrote, need is the true creator.[84]

The second group, promising materials, includes cobalt, lithium, and nickel. Today, both their reserves and resources fall short of long-term demand. But as with lithium, economically viable reserves have been growing well above the pace required. Demand for these materials has surged only recently, driven by batteries. These materials are essential for energy storage and electrification. Lithium is the core of the cathode active material, and nickel and cobalt boost energy density and thermal stability. Overall, these promising materials are still in the early stages of scaling. If the lithium story is any guide, exploration, investment, and technological innovation will all play a crucial role in meeting future demand.[85]

Here's the punch line: For each of these promising materials, extractable reserves have grown at the same rates required for abundance in 2100, or faster. None would need to exceed historical growth rates.

Even with conservative assumptions on efficiency, recycling, and substitution, it is reasonable to believe that we have enough resources to support another flourishing century. The few materials that demand attention are not likely to be geological bottlenecks. They pose scaling challenges. And with the right investment, innovation, and coordination, they are likely within our reach.

We would be remiss not to mention oil and natural gas. They differ from other materials in one crucial respect: They are consumed, not accumulated. Unlike metals or minerals that can be reused or recycled, oil and gas are mostly burned or transformed, leaving no lasting stock.

Both serve dual roles. As energy sources, they have long powered vehicles, heated homes, and generated electricity. As industrial feedstocks, they are essential for producing chemicals, fertilizers, and plastics that underpin modern economies.

In a century of plenty, oil is fully phased out as an energy source while natural gas supplies 10 percent of primary energy, as we have previously discussed. We assume modest efficiency gains, which moderate the rise in consumption even as global energy demand grows.

As feedstock, however, oil and gas remain important for producing plastics, fertilizers, and other chemicals. If every country matched the materials consumption of advanced economies, global feedstock demand could rise by 2.3 percent annually for oil and 1.4 percent annually for natural gas.[86]

The good news is that current extractable reserves are sufficient. We estimate that about 80 to 90 percent of today's oil and gas reserves would be needed to meet cumulative demand through 2100.[87]

The technology to keep digging deeper

So far, we have based our assessment on past growth of reserves and resources, but we have not accounted for breakthroughs that could boost efficiency or introduce alternative materials. Much more is around the corner. Past progress gives us confidence that there is enormous room to improve. Materials use is fundamentally an economic choice driven as much by affordability as availability. As markets evolve, alternative materials like bio-based plastics and recycled composites will become more cost-effective and attractive.

Substitution is nothing new. The first Boeing 747 in 1969 was 80 percent aluminum, but by 2009, half of the new Boeing 787 consisted of nonmetallic composites like carbon fiber, which is more durable, strong, and lightweight. Similarly, between 2010 and 2023, the energy density of lithium-ion batteries roughly doubled.[88] And even without substituting them, we also continuously learn to use materials more efficiently: The amounts of polysilicon and silver used in solar panels fell about 85 and 65

Airplanes under construction.

percent, respectively, over the past 20 years.[89]

We also have room to manage demand better. Advances in recycling are one way to achieve this. The IEA estimates that by 2050, recycling could meet about 20 to 30 percent of lithium demand, 30 to 40 percent of rare earths demand, and 20 to 40 percent of cobalt demand, with potential for more as recycling technology improves.[90]

Skeptics have long warned of looming shortages, finite geological deposits, geopolitical risks, and environmental constraints, as we discuss later. It is true that declining ore quality or slow discovery could raise costs and complicate scaling. But to date, many dire predictions haven't materialized. In the 1950s, scientists claimed that the United States would reach "peak oil" in the 1970s. Yet oil continued to grow. Peak oil did not happen due to technological advances like hydraulic fracturing and to new discoveries from the North Sea to shale basins. In fact, oil supply has expanded, and, despite volatility, prices have remained affordable for industry and consumers.[91]

No matter which material you are talking about, we have found more when we have looked for more. Deep-sea mining, for example, could lead to the discovery of vast new deposits of materials like copper and nickel on unexplored ocean floors. And who knows—one day we may even look to space mining for small-volume, high-value materials. We will continue to find deposits in places we haven't yet explored.[92]

We are not being glib when we say there is sufficient material to support a century of prosperity. These are the facts. But there is no room for complacency. We need to do everything in our power to become more efficient and to continue innovating.

Digging but without the damage

We have shown that we have enough materials to make our world of plenty in 2100 realistic and that scaling is likely within reach. Yet it is not just a matter of whether we can extract more, but of whether we can do so at the required scale without causing widespread environmental damage. As demand rises, so do concerns about the impact of large-scale mining on ecosystems and landscapes. The idea of vast open-pit mines gouging the land feels dystopian. The real question is whether a wealthier global

Open cast mine with wind turbines in North Rhine–Westphalia, Germany.

population will lead to irreparable harm.

It doesn't have to.

In 2022, global mining activities occupied less than 1 percent of the world's inhabitable land. And for many materials, it is often possible to extract significantly more without taking up a great deal more land.[93] The physical footprint of mining is far smaller than its reputation might suggest. The real challenge is not space but ensuring that mining is effective and responsible.

Poorly managed mining can be destructive. Examples like nickel in Indonesia, gold in the Amazon, and coal in Appalachia show how unregulated extraction can lead to deforestation, water contamination, and ecosystem collapse. These problems are real. But they occur when governance is weak and investment inadequate.[94]

Well-run and -capitalized mines, by contrast, can be both cost-competitive and environmentally sound. Consider BHP's Spence copper mine in Chile. Operating in the arid Atacama Desert, it uses desalinated water, draws power from wind and solar, and avoids more than 1 million tonnes of CO_2 emissions every year, all while producing 250,000 tonnes of copper annually.[95]

As countries grow richer, higher environmental standards and greater efficiency tend to go hand-in-hand. Dirty, inefficient mines are not the price of progress; they are something we grow out of.

Of course, critical questions about geopolitics, investment, labor, and equity for local communities remain to get these materials into the hands of the global population. But these are not questions of possibility. They are questions of will. The materials are there, and we are improving exploration, extraction, and processing, aided and abetted by impressive technological advances. From a purely resource standpoint, the message is clear. We have the materials we need.

Growing materials use without growing emissions

We have so far considered only the physical availability of materials and the pollution created when getting those materials. But what about the emissions that come from processing the ore once we have pulled it out of the earth? What do we do with the emissions related to the processing of the materials we need?

Let's dig a little deeper (pun intended).

Bauxite ore needs to be transformed before it can be used as aluminum for new window frames or new airplanes. Similarly, iron ore must be turned into steel before it can be used for new railways or construction beams. These processes emit greenhouse gases, so more materials mean, all other things being equal, more emissions.[96]

There are two aspects to this problem. The first is that the more materials we use, the more energy we use. That may not be a problem in our world of plenty, in which low-carbon energy is abundant. Furnaces and smelters that rely on fossil-based fuels can be exchanged for those that use either electricity or bio-based alternatives such as biogas. Logistics and transportation can similarly be net zero by 2100. Solving the energy issue will address a large share of the problem of emissions.

The second, and harder, problem is one of emissions that are unavoidably part of industrial processes. Consider steel. Of all the heavy industries, iron and steel create the most direct CO_2 emissions. Of total emissions, 12 percent come directly from the process. To produce primary steel (as opposed to recycled steel) from iron ore, refined coal (also known as coke) is used to generate the necessary heat as well as to extract oxygen from the iron ore. Then carbon is removed from the iron to make steel. Both processes are chemical reactions that release CO_2 as a byproduct.[97]

Steel is an important input for producing reinforced concrete, which, despite the use of new materials, inevitably will be in high demand when building the world of plenty. Another important input for making concrete is cement.

Cement is particularly tricky because close to 50 percent of the CO_2 that is released when producing cement comes from a chemical process called calcination, which turns limestone into lime. Calcination is required for the production of clinker, the key ingredient in cement.[98]

However, in many cases, the path toward reducing emissions from processes is already being explored. In cement, clinker can be exchanged for other cementitious materials or fillers.[99] In steel, coke can be exchanged for hydrogen such that water, not CO_2, will be the byproduct.[100] These technologies are still in early stages and face major challenges in widespread commercial implementation in the next decade. For example, today 70 percent of all primary steel is made via the highest-emitting production method. But these problems are solvable with time.[101]

This holds true for most materials. The emissions from making aluminum mainly come from electricity; we solve that problem by using low-emissions energy. And process-related emissions can be significantly reduced by using different types of anodes. For chemicals and plastics, bio-based feedstocks can sometimes substitute for oil, coal, and natural gas. The emissions that cannot be avoided through the implementation of known technologies might be able to be removed through new technologies or ultimately through sequestration. In some cases, it may be possible to store the carbon directly in the finished product. In the case of concrete, carbon can be injected into cured concrete. In the case of plastics, carbon from oil is stored in the plastic until the plastic is incinerated. In other cases, conventional carbon capture and storage will be necessary to reach net-zero emissions.[102]

While the road map for reducing process-related emissions exists for many of these materials, it relies on large-scale investments to update the existing asset base to low-carbon alternatives.[103]

We believe that this is more possible in a world of plenty. In addition, a prosperous world can enable a higher degree of innovation into new technologies toward abating process-related emissions.

＊ ＊ ＊

So, we can have enough energy and materials, two ingredients vital for growth and a continued rise in prosperity. Now let us turn to another of our five critical questions. Few of us have a personal experience in a nuclear plant or a mine, but all of us have an intimate relationship with food, the topic of our next chapter.

CHAPTER 18

THE FOOD TO NOURISH
A GROWING POPULATION

"One cannot think well, love well, sleep well,
if one has not dined well."

VIRGINIA WOOLF

———

We can produce enough food to feed 12 billion people while preserving biodiversity.

WHAT WILL BE ON YOUR grandchildren's plates? In a plentiful world of 2100, people will no longer simply eat what they can afford. They will eat what they prefer. That means not just more food but different food: more variety, more meat and dairy, more fresh produce. Think juicy burgers sizzling on a Fourth of July grill in the United States, fragrant curries in India, and fresh sushi in Japan, but now truly accessible globally.

As recent decades have shown, rising incomes, particularly in Asia, are already driving greater consumption of meat and fish.[104] By the end of the century, everyone will expect the kind of food choice and quality currently enjoyed in high-income countries.

To be clear, this chapter does not attempt to describe solutions for every challenge relating to feeding a prosperous world. Hunger today is a matter less of scarcity than of inequality. Nearly one in ten people worldwide remain undernourished, and one in five in Sub-Saharan Africa. This is not because the world fails to produce enough food, but because many people cannot afford or access it.[105] Overcoming barriers such as poor infrastructure, limited finance and technology, and conflict is essential—and a world of plenty arguably makes the job easier.

Here, we explore one essential question: whether we can produce enough food to feed 11.7 billion people eating a protein-rich diet using only the land we already cultivate. Our answer is yes. It is possible to feed everyone eating a diet as rich as Switzerland's diet today, adapted to local preferences, without expanding farmland.[106]

Feeding 12 billion people with our current footprint

Today, agriculture spans nearly 4.8 billion hectares, which is about one-third of all the land on Earth, and that footprint has grown by more than 85 percent since 1920.[107] Meeting tomorrow's needs should not mean pushing further into forests or grasslands, which is the leading cause of biodiversity loss, but transforming how we farm the land already under the plow. In a future shaped by shared prosperity and accessible innovation, the path to abundance lies not in more land but in more knowledge, ingenuity, and cooperation.

Here is the scale of the challenge. In 2022, 7.4 billion tonnes of agricultural produce were available for human consumption and livestock feed.[108] For a world of plenty in 2100, we would require this figure to almost double to 13.3 billion tonnes. The mix of food would look different, too: more red meat, dairy, and fruit, more feed for more livestock, and less rice and potatoes.

The key to achieving this is higher productivity. If yields improve each year by between 0.2 percent and 1.3 percent, depending on the crop or animal, we can meet global demand using existing farmland.[109]

We have pulled this off before. It has been said that compounding is one of the most powerful forces in the universe. A 2 percent annual increase in yields quadruples output in 72 years. Since 1961, global food production has increased fourfold, thanks to smarter tools, better seeds, and improved techniques.[110] Yield improvements over that period for key food categories ranged from 1.5 percent per year in the case of rice to 4.5 percent for chicken, far exceeding the more modest gains we need by 2100.

Despite these gains, global agricultural land use still grew from 4.4 billion to 4.8 billion hectares. This was largely driven by Sub-Saharan Africa, which needed to feed a population that quintupled.[111] Particular emphasis should therefore be put on improving yields in that region to prevent further growth in the amount of land we use.

Agriculture remains suboptimal in many parts of the world. Farming practices, adoption of technology, and the productivity that results vary enormously depending on where you are. Even after decades of effort, raising yields has remained a challenge in some places, especially where farms are small, resources are limited, and support systems are weak. The good news is that this is a tremendous opportunity to improve productivity simply by disseminating today's best practices and technologies, from cover cropping and irrigation to better seed varieties.

Let's look at rice, a staple for billions. Since 1961, rice yields have increased by 1.5 percent a year, slowing slightly to 1.3 percent after the 1970s as initial gains from the Green Revolution decelerated. That is far above the 0.3 percent annual improvement needed to meet future demand in 2100 without expanding the amount of land we use. Today, the world's average rice yield is 4.8 tonnes per hectare. However, Zimbabwe harvests less than half a tonne per hectare, while Australia produces nearly ten tonnes.[112] Of course, soils and climates vary, but in many cases, countries fall short of their potential because farmers lack access to improved seeds or knowledge of best practices.

For many crops, countries have vast areas of underperforming farmland that could deliver more with smarter practices and existing tools. If every rice-growing country reached just the top quartile of productivity—about 5.5 tonnes per hectare, a 16 percent improvement over the current global average—we could meet nearly 90 percent of the world's projected rice demand in 2100. Push just a bit further, to Vietnam's current level of 6.1

tonnes, and we would close the gap entirely. And this isn't a moonshot. Vietnam made a leap of 2.5 times, from 2.5 to 6.1 tonnes, in just under 50 years.[113] Countries have 75 years to get to its level, and small improvements over time add up (Exhibit 32).

Some of the driest places on Earth have defied the odds with the help of technology. Let's head to Australia, the world's driest inhabited continent. In the Murrumbidgee Irrigation Area, rice yields frequently average about ten tonnes per hectare, and there are records of yields as high as 15 tonnes, some two to three times the global average. Their edge comes from better seeds, smarter systems, and a culture of knowledge sharing. Since 1986, the Ricecheck program has pushed farmers to benchmark yields against the best paddocks, exchange insights at meetings and field days, and learn from one another. Semi-dwarf Japonica varieties bred for yield lifted harvests from 6.8 to 8.4 tonnes per hectare in a single decade. Irrigation has gone high-tech, with gravity-fed canals upgraded with automation, sensors, and real-time watering, so now Australia's rice growers use about 50 percent less water per hectare than the world average. Overall, this extremely dry continent has the most productive rice farms on the planet. In Asia, China now grows award-winning wine grapes in the Gobi Desert, which is arid all year round. Turning *no* water into wine. These cases are proof that abundance comes not from more land but from relentless innovation.[114]

Cultivating enough meat is a bigger challenge. In our world of plenty, global demand for beef more than doubles, from 70 million tonnes today to 170 million tonnes. A 1.1 percent annual improvement in productivity is needed to meet that demand without cutting down more trees. In fact, the opposite is needed: planting more trees on pastureland. This is the silvopastoral approach.

In Colombia, the adoption of silvopastoral systems has boosted beef output by as much as 12 times and doubled daily milk yields per cow by improving nutrition and reducing heat stress. Protein-rich forage from trees sustains cattle through dry seasons, while shade keeps them cooler, helping animals convert more feed into growth and milk instead of expending energy to stay cool. These systems also sequester carbon, reduce methane concentration, and restore biodiversity, increasing local populations of beetles, birds, and plants. Silvopastoral systems could be applied to about 40 percent of Earth's pasture and are most efficient in

Yield curve of rice productivity levels by country
Average yields in 2023, tonnes per hectare

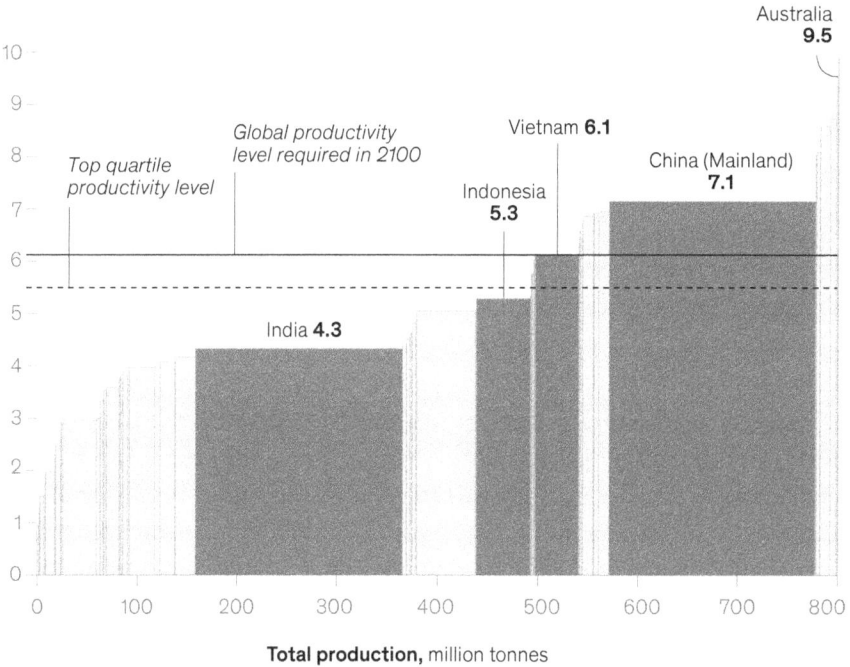

Source: FAOSTAT, *Crops and livestock products;* McKinsey Global Institute analysis

subtropical and tropical climates. For example, in Brazil, cattle stocking rates rose 125 percent between 1970 and 2017 because degraded pastures were restored so that more animals could feed on existing land.[115]

Boosting the amount of meat produced per animal is another way to reduce pressure on land. With better breeding and feeding techniques, chickens, pigs, and cows grow bigger, grow faster, and require less food to gain weight than they did in the past. In the United States, for instance, the average meat cow now produces nearly 40 percent more meat than it did in 1975, thanks to innovation in genetics, nutrition, and farm management. But there's a wide gap between high- and low-efficiency regions. In the United States today, an average meat cow needs six kilograms of feed to gain one kilogram of weight. In less productive regions, it takes 12 kilograms.[116] Sharing more widely the tools and techniques that make modern farms more productive would make beef production more sustainable with higher yields, greater animal welfare, and benefits to natural ecosystems.

That's farming the land. Farming the oceans is also important if we are to achieve a protein-rich diet for many more people. In 2022, oceans and aquaculture yielded about 120 million tonnes of fish. By 2100, we will need nearly 220 million tonnes in our world of plenty. That seems a big ask given that wild fisheries are already approaching their ecological limits. That is where cultivated fish—aquaculture—comes in. It accounts for more than half of the seafood we eat and is growing faster than any other kind of protein production.[117]

As they have in animal farming, smarter systems are helping aquaculture produce more with less. In fact, we are now producing fish on land. Indoor salmon farms, which rely on tightly controlled environments, like vertical farms for crops, are scaling up quickly. Other innovations changing the way we produce aquatic protein include biofloc, in which microbes convert fish waste into protein-rich feed, and multitrophic farming, in which seaweed and shellfish absorb excess nutrients from the water and help recycle waste into usable fish food. Improved genetics and alternative feeds, from algae to insects, are also pushing fish yields higher even while having a lower environmental impact.[118] Precision aquaculture brings together AI, sensors, and real-time monitoring to fine-tune feeding, track the health of fish, and optimize growing conditions.

As with meat, intensifying fish production is essential if we are to meet demand, but the onus is on us to be more efficient and produce responsibly to protect biodiversity. The way we grow food can either degrade or restore the natural world.

Plenty while respecting our planet

The intensification of agriculture has often harmed biodiversity through habitat loss, chemical runoff, and soil degradation, but today's technologies offer powerful alternatives. Take precision drip irrigation. It

A fish farm in Türkiye.

cuts water use by up to 60 percent, easing pressure on rivers and keeping wetland habitats thriving through dry seasons. AI-powered spraying systems can target exactly where fertilizer or herbicide is needed, slashing the use of chemicals and runoff into rivers and protecting aquatic life. And planting multiple crops together can help rebuild healthy soil ecosystems to bring back the insects, worms, and microbes that make farmland thrive for generations. These innovations don't just improve food security—they help heal ecosystems.[119]

Yet these tools are only as effective as their reach, and getting them to farmers remains a major hurdle. Smallholder farmers face a range of systemic barriers. Their plots are not only small but sometimes scattered. Modern equipment, high-quality seeds, and fertilizers are often unaffordable. Labor is scarce or expensive. Because farm work is often done by hand, labor productivity is low. Farmers find it hard to get credit, and this complicates the adoption of new technologies. The main way in which improved technologies and techniques reach the farmers who need them is through agricultural extension programs, which have proven to be remarkably effective. In Sub-Saharan Africa, for instance, extension programs like Sasakawa Global 2000 raised maize yields by 50 to 100 percent in the 1980s and 1990s by promoting modern varieties and fertilizers as well as training farmers.[120] Scaling these efforts is critical. Only when more farmers gain access to such innovations can the promise of sustainable agriculture be fully realized.

Even with our assumptions of high red meat intake and calorie demand, the food needs of generations can be met without further encroaching on forests and biodiversity. But that is actually a conservative view. We can do even better if we use three powerful levers to take even more pressure off the food system, shrink the amount of land we use, and enable us to do more to restore biodiversity.

The first lever is improving supply chains and storage to cut the amount of food we lose and waste, which is currently a shocking 30 to 40 percent of all we produce.[121] The second lever is shifting to healthier, lower-calorie diets, which can reduce demand for food, especially for resource-intensive animal products and crops. We are already seeing rising health awareness and a revolution in the fight against obesity with appetite-suppressing drugs nudging behaviors in this direction.[122] The third lever is advancing frontier innovations like vertical farming and lab-grown proteins, both of which are showing promise and developing rapidly. Both could reduce the immense footprint—or hoofprint—of grazing livestock at nearly two-thirds of all agricultural land as well as cropland. Vertical farms could dramatically increase productivity, yielding ten to 20 times more spinach or lettuce per hectare. Lab-grown meat could reduce the amount of land we use by up to 99 percent and cut CO_2 emissions by as much as 96 percent, especially if clean energy powers production. Meatly, a British pet-food startup, has developed technology that enables the company to cultivate chicken at prices comparable with chicken currently sold in the EU.[123]

These shifts are also connected to the climate challenge. Agriculture and the wider food system generate about a quarter of global emissions. Within this, livestock and fisheries contribute 31 percent (largely methane from cattle), crop production another 27 percent, land-use change another 24 percent, and supply chains the remaining 18 percent. Fortunately, a world of plenty, despite rising demand, is also better equipped to grow more food while cutting emissions. Halting the expansion of land use and stopping or reverting deforestation is one important step we have addressed.

Farm worker harvesting hydroponic kale in a vertical farm in Thailand.

Additionally, feed additives such as seaweed are already cutting cattle methane emissions by more than 80 percent, while selective breeding for animals that emit less methane and convert feed more efficiently offers an additional, permanent pathway to lower emissions. By 2100, these technologies can be refined and scaled globally. Alternative proteins that rival the taste of meat can further curb livestock demand, and as the global energy system decarbonizes, new machinery, desalination plants, and precision agriculture can be powered by clean energy.[124]

In a world of plenty, with the social will, the right investments, and global adoption of technology, doubling food production in a sustainable way is within reach.

* * *

The tools to grow more with less are already in our hands. From precision irrigation to gene-edited seeds, today's technologies can cut costs, raise yields, and ease the strain on nature and biodiversity. With a dose of human ingenuity and a shared commitment to spreading these and future advances, we can feed nearly 12 billion people by 2100 with a plethora of choice without further damage to our planet's biodiversity. But what about the broader issue of the climate? Can we protect that, too, even while reaching for broad-based prosperity? We look at that question in our next chapter.

CHAPTER 19

THE CLIMATE PROTECTED IN A WORLD OF PLENTY

"The Earth is what we all have in common."

WENDELL BERRY

———

We can continue to grow and decouple economic progress from greenhouse gas emissions.

SO FAR, WE HAVE SHOWN that humanity can secure enough energy to power a century of plenty, extract sufficient materials from the Earth to build it, and produce enough food to nourish 12 billion people. A fundamental question remains, without which this reflection would be incomplete. Can we do all of this without causing irreparable damage to the natural systems that sustain humanity? Unless we can answer in the affirmative, all bets are off. What is the point of growth and prosperity if, in its pursuit, we forever alter the climate that lets us enjoy it? If we ended up with a planet of extreme temperatures, prosperity for future generations would become impossible. To put it bluntly, we would be setting our home on fire to keep warm.

The world is already warming. The fossil-fuel-powered 20th and early 21st centuries lifted billions from poverty. But those fossil fuels also released large amounts of greenhouse gases, causing global warming: Average global temperatures are now more than 1.2°C above preindustrial levels.[125]

Each degree of warming increases the risk of physical consequences. If we follow the trajectory of McKinsey's continued momentum pathway, which we have extended from 2050 to 2100, global warming could reach 2.2°C to 2.6°C above preindustrial levels by 2100. At this temperature, climate hazards such as hot extremes, heavy precipitation, and droughts are expected to be more frequent and intense, risking increased damage to ecosystems and to other resources on which humans rely, such as freshwater supplies and agricultural systems.[126] At 2.0°C, the intensity of heat extremes could be double compared with 1.5°C. At 3.0°C, it could quadruple.

We hope that we have convinced you in this book that economic growth is good—good for incomes, education, health, and more. But it is also clear that past economic growth has been associated with increased greenhouse gas emissions. Therefore, the defining challenge of our age is to *decouple* economic growth from the emission of greenhouse gases. We have shown that this is already happening across many advanced economies. We have to break the link, decisively, everywhere.

We believe this is possible. We have described a viable 2100 energy scenario that achieves net zero in emissions and under which 80 percent of the energy the world uses comes from a combination of solar, wind, and nuclear power. The remaining energy comes from biofuels and from natural gas paired with carbon capture. We have also discussed how to reduce non-energy greenhouse gas emissions like those from agriculture and materials production. With that energy mix and new technologies to handle non-energy emissions, we can reduce the amount of greenhouse gases we emit without constraining economic growth.

We are confident that we can create a low-carbon future. But timing matters, and we have two questions: How long will it take to get to net zero, and how much do we emit on our way there? These questions are central for determining the cumulative emissions that have an impact on the concentration of greenhouse gases in the atmosphere and, ultimately, global warming.

EV car charging station using solar panels to generate electricity.

Net zero by when?

Many nations are trying to reduce emissions, and some have made impressive progress. But when we look at the world as a whole, our efforts have been uneven and too limited to counteract the continued increase in greenhouse gas emissions. Governments are trying to strike a balance between their sustainability goals and the need for affordable, reliable, and secure energy supplies and the economic welfare of citizens. We have myriad competing priorities.

The 2015 Paris Agreement sets an ambitious goal of pursuing efforts to limit global warming to 1.5°C above preindustrial levels in the second half of this century, which many countries have translated into achieving net-zero emissions by 2050. This is what the IPCC determined would help avoid the most severe risks of climate change. Countries that are today responsible for three-quarters of emissions have signed up to a net-zero target, and countries that generate about 30 percent of emissions have discussions or a policy commitment to do so by 2050.[127]

Yet since the Paris Agreement, global greenhouse gas emissions have risen by 8.5 percent.[128]

Since the 2050 deadline is fixed, each year of growth in emissions just steepens the targets for the remaining years. In 2009, the IEA's "450 scenario" required annual emissions reductions of about 400 million tonnes of CO_2 to stay under 2.0°C. By 2019, this almost doubled in its "sustainable development scenario" to 730 million tonnes of CO_2 a year.[129]

The world's top four greenhouse gas emitters (in order of emissions)— China, the United States, India, and Russia—account for the majority of the world's emissions. None have policies to hit net zero by 2050.[130]

In fact, between 2015 and 2023, China, India, and Russia increased greenhouse gas emissions by 22, 25, and 18 percent, respectively. The United States achieved a reduction of 6 percent, much of that improvement coming from replacing one fossil fuel (coal) with another (gas).[131]

In 2015, the six countries making up the rest of the top ten for emissions were Japan, Brazil, Germany, Indonesia, Iran, and Canada. Their emissions trajectories vary. Germany cut fastest (25 percent since 2015), followed by Japan (22 percent since 2015), and Canada declined a little (1 percent since 2015). But the increases by the other three erased all these gains.[132]

What is going on? Why, despite a very big policy push and huge waves of investment, are we not yet even at peak emissions, let alone on track for net zero by 2050? We point to three reasons.

First, in developing countries, the goal of resolving energy poverty is trumping climate concerns. While China and India are huge builders of renewables, accounting for 57 percent of global solar and wind additions between 2019 and 2024, they have kept growing their thermal power capacity as well. They continue to need, and use, fossil fuels for their growing industrial and transportation sectors. These countries have a lot of coal, and rising concern about energy security necessitates that they use it.[133]

Second, the physical challenges we have referred to a few times in this book are really starting to bite. Remember that to date 80 percent of the energy we use is not electrified. Here, we are seeing little progress. Green hydrogen, green steel, green cement, and other green materials remain at the concept stage. And despite incredible improvements in solar technologies, the difficulty of integrating them into the grid is starting to show. Witness the massive Spanish blackouts of 2025.[134]

Wind turbines on farmland, Austria.

Third, realpolitik has reasserted itself. The climate problem is a particularly tough coordination problem. Most countries are not big enough to influence the global climate, and many countries might find it optimal to free ride on the emissions reduction efforts of others. Effectively reducing emissions requires persistence. Even in countries that have robust emissions reduction trajectories, like Germany and the United Kingdom, net-zero policies are coming up against the challenges of rising costs, concerns about energy security, and deindustrialization. Especially when competing countries do not deliver emissions reductions, holding the political line may get tougher and tougher. Climate policy is relitigated every time the ballot box opens.

Now to the punch line. Hopefully by now you find our angle predictable. We are massive optimists about the possibilities for abundance and firmly believe that the future of humankind is net-zero emissions. You've already read about our world of plenty where we swim in clean energy.

But we cannot ignore the facts. Net zero by 2050 is in all likelihood out of reach.

The question now is whether we can make a better world than the one we seem to be heading toward. To reach a judgment on that, we need a realistic baseline to measure against. That baseline is the topic of the next section. Spoiler alert: While we put very low odds on net zero by 2050, we also put very low odds on emissions remaining high indefinitely. The latter simply defies the direction of technological improvement.

We show that on our current trajectory, the rise in temperature by 2100 is likely to land somewhere between 2.2°C and 2.6°C. Then we show why we think a high-growth world makes the emissions story not worse, but much better.

Accelerating growth without increasing emissions

Rising prosperity can put us on a better emissions trajectory than the one we are on, reducing cumulative greenhouse gases emitted.

In Exhibit 33, we show annual global carbon emissions for four different pathways to 2100, each with a line of its own. Of the four, only one shows global warming limited to 1.5°C. But as we have argued, the likelihood of achieving net zero by 2050 appears to be receding as the world tracks a pathway depicted as the uppermost line in the exhibit: the continued momentum with baseline economic growth (line 4).[135]

McKinsey's Energy & Materials Practice reckons that one available option is "sustainable transformation with baseline economic growth" (line 2), but as the title suggests, that would take a huge transformation that is beyond what is currently happening. It requires that nations intensify their sustainability commitments, increase global coordination to alleviate bottlenecks, and increase investment in low-carbon technologies.

Our question is: What conditions get us closer to this line? We would need a world with high economic capacity, rapid technological development, a radically improved ability to build stuff, and genuine energy security, which can happen only if there truly is energy abundance. Higher economic growth can make all of them easier.

How much would the resulting emissions be? The end point is not in question. We have already shown the possibility of a 2100 energy scenario where energy is abundant, electrified, and practically carbon-free. This

EXHIBIT 33

Emissions scenarios
Global annual net emissions, 2015–2100, $GtCO_2e$[1]

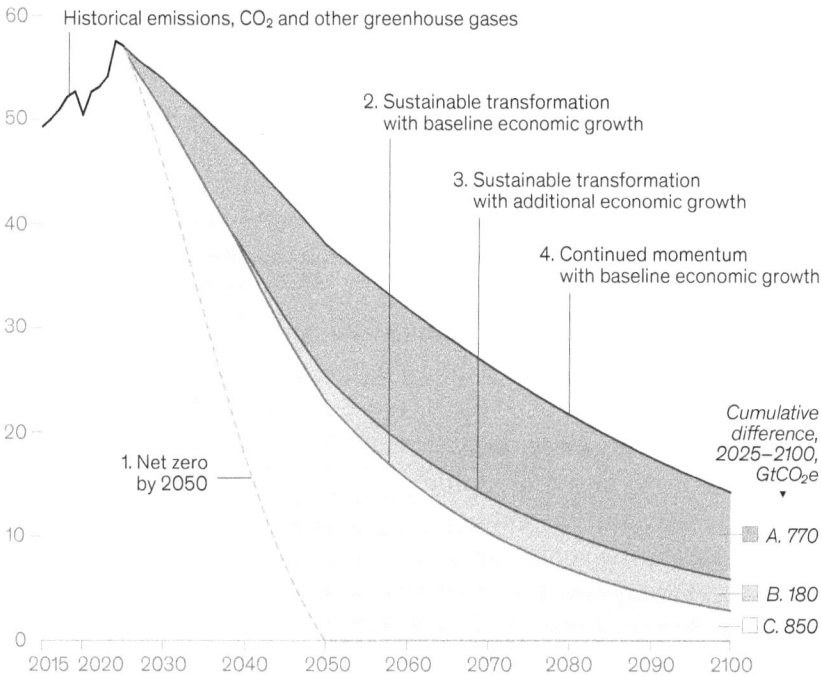

60 — Historical emissions, CO_2 and other greenhouse gases

50

2. Sustainable transformation
with baseline economic growth

3. Sustainable transformation
with additional economic growth

40

4. Continued momentum
with baseline economic growth

30

*Cumulative
difference,
2025–2100,
$GtCO_2e$*

20

1. Net zero
by 2050

10

A. 770

B. 180

C. 850

0

2015 2020 2030   2040   2050   2060   2070   2080   2090   2100

Scenario summary metrics	Net zero by 2050	Sustainable transformation with baseline economic growth	Sustainable transformation with additional economic growth	Continued momentum with baseline economic growth
Cumulative emissions 2025–2100, $GtCO_2e$	680[2]	1,530	1,710	2,480
Annual net emissions by 2100, $GtCO_2e$	0	3	6	14
Temperature rise, °C[3]	1.5	1.8–2.1	1.9–2.2	2.2–2.6
Atmospheric concentration, ppm CO_2[3]	380–410	440–470	450–480	500–540

[1]Uses the European Commission Joint Research Centre's EDGAR database estimates of historical emissions, McKinsey Global Energy Perspective projections of global greenhouse gases for 2023–50, and projections of emissions for 2050–2100 based on internal McKinsey Global Institute analysis; all outputs are measured in carbon dioxide equivalents using 100-year Global Warming Potentials (GWP100). [2]Cumulative emissions in line with net zero by 2050 and 67% likelihood of not exceeding 1.5°C by 2100. This allows for temporarily exceeding 1.5°C before returning to 1.5°C by 2100. [3]Temperature increases and atmospheric CO_2 concentrations are estimated using best fit regression (reporting 10th and 90th percentiles), based on the 67th percentile of projected global surface air temperature and atmospheric CO_2 concentrations from the MAGICCv7.5.3 climate model, across AR6 IPCC scenario ensembles.
Source: European Commission (EDGAR); *McKinsey Global energy perspective 2025*; Climate Resource (MAGICCv7.5.3); McKinsey Global Institute analysis

means we are already beating the continuous momentum line.

The question is the area under the curve to get there: cumulative emissions. We think our world of plenty contains many of the conditions required to get to the transformation line.

There is one catch, though. The global economy in our century of plenty is about double the size compared with the baseline scenario in which GDP grows at about 1.8 percent per year. And a larger economy takes more energy, as we have demonstrated.

We therefore draw another line, in which our ability to convert energy into GDP is as good as the sustainable transformation line with baseline growth, but GDP is much larger. This is "sustainable transformation with additional economic growth" (line 3).[136]

The remarkable thing is that because the marginal economic growth comes at lower and lower carbon intensity, the carbon added by the growth is just 180 gigatonnes of CO_2e ($GtCO_2$e), or about 10 percent more. This is because economic prosperity is used to finance green technologies and ensure that enough money is spent to decarbonize energy production.[137]

In reality, we think we will land somewhere in the boundary of the shaded areas. Our two points remain: With more abundance, we have a better shot of getting toward the bottom of this range, and with improving energy efficiency, growth does not need to be at the expense of our planet.

To get a sense of what this implies, let us think about the key ratio here: $GtCO_2$e per unit of GDP, also known as the emission intensity of GDP. Today, it is slightly greater than 0.3 $GtCO_2$e per trillion dollars of GDP. In the pathway of continued momentum with baseline economic growth, the intensity decreases by 3.7 percent per year toward 2050. But in the sustainable transformation scenarios, it decreases by 5.5 percent. In other words, we have to believe that an abundant world can increase the rate of improvement by 1.5 times, through things like a faster pace of electrification and more technological innovation. For reference, the net-zero 2050 line requires improvement of more than 15 percent every year.[138]

What does this mean for temperatures? Global warming is a function of the concentration of greenhouse gases in the atmosphere. The concentration of CO_2 went from about 310 parts per million (ppm) in 1925 to about 430 ppm today. The momentum case lands at 500 to 540 ppm, resulting in a temperature increase of 2.2°C to 2.6°C above the preindustrial baseline. Remember we are already at 1.2°C above that baseline, so this is an incremental 1.0°C to 1.4°C.[139]

In the case of sustainable transformation with baseline economic growth, atmospheric concentration of greenhouse gases reaches 440 to 470 ppm, yielding global warming of 1.8°C to 2.1°C. Now add the economic growth, and the atmospheric concentration is modeled to be 450 to 480 ppm by 2100, with a temperature increase of 1.9°C to 2.2°C.

The link between economic growth and emissions can become much more decoupled than is the case today. It is possible to accelerate growth without increasing emissions to the same degree.

Using growth to be greener

Greater prosperity can enable a safer climate future only if we commit to using that growing wealth to take action to reduce emissions or, indeed, to adapt ourselves for those emissions that remain.

Economic growth provides resources that can be used to develop and deploy low-emissions technology. A wealthier world has more capital to build smarter electric grids, expand solar and wind power, roll out EV charging networks, and create new factories to produce EVs and advanced batteries. Even if low-carbon solutions are not cheaper than the emitting alternative, wealthy economies can afford to choose them. Growing economies can also finance research and innovation to speed up progress on breakthrough technologies like next-generation nuclear reactors, solid-state batteries, and commercially viable nuclear fusion. This drives down costs of sustainable technologies, making them more attractive. What is more, an economy that is already in "build" mode can better execute on new projects, including renewable ones. And rich economies have more funds to put toward education, which helps alleviate the shortage of skilled labor.

A tight interdependence connects economic growth and a sustainable transformation. But the proceeds from growth must be deployed wisely to safeguard affordability, industrial competitiveness, and energy reliability. Done poorly, the transition risks undermining all three. If grids are not designed with the higher electricity needs of EVs and heat pumps in mind, or if innovation stalls and new technologies fail to become cost competitive, the result could be rising energy costs, a slower

Eastern Scheldt storm surge barrier in Zeeland, the Netherlands.

transformation, and lower economic growth. Done well, however, the transition can create a virtuous cycle: Investment and innovation lower costs, strengthen competitiveness, and accelerate the shift to a sustainable economy, ultimately reducing the overall cost of transformation.[140]

Indeed, in multiple examples, economic growth and progress on climate change go hand in hand. In China, LONGi has rapidly grown to become the global leader in solar photovoltaic products, responsible for one out of four solar modules in use. LONGi has invested heavily in innovation and attained world-record power conversion efficiency rates on its solar cells. Its rise illustrates how prosperity and climate ambition can reinforce each other: From 32.9 billion renminbi in 2020, its revenue surged to 129 billion renminbi in 2023, and the company now employs 60,000 people.[141]

A similar story is unfolding in the United States, where Microsoft cofounder Bill Gates is backing TerraPower in Wyoming. With public and private support, the company is developing SMRs that promise clean energy and economic renewal in former mining towns. TerraPower shows how targeted investment can turn cutting-edge innovation into real-world impact, driving both climate progress and prosperity.

Prosperity is not just relevant to climate mitigation efforts. Wealthier countries are also better equipped to invest in adapting to the climate change we cannot avoid through initiatives such as widespread access to air-conditioning, early warning systems that reduce vulnerability to a wide range of hazards, and building flood defenses. It is worth noting that as incomes rise, a smaller share of the workforce tends to be in sectors most exposed to heat, such as agriculture and construction. Moreover, there tends to be a shift toward larger, formal enterprises that can more easily adapt ways of working, like adjusting working hours.[142]

The Netherlands proved to be an adept adapter early on, using its wealth to protect itself. One-third of the country lies below sea level, and the Dutch have been investing in land reclamation, dikes, and windmill-driven pumps for centuries. Massive public investment sparked by the deadly 1953 floods funded the Delta Works, a vast system of dams, levees, and storm-surge barriers. Today, it protects two-thirds of Dutch GDP and millions of lives and livelihoods. Without these adaptations, the country's prosperity would not have been possible.[143]

Adaptation isn't the full answer, though. Flood protection may mitigate risk but cannot completely prevent the damage and disruptions that floods cause. Increased use of air-conditioning can help us feel comfortable inside but does not give us back the days we might have spent outdoors. Adaptation can soften the blow, but it cannot fully shield societies from the disruptions of a warming world.[144]

We need both mitigation and adaptation to address climate change. Both depend on high degrees of innovation and investment to be successful. We believe high economic growth and prosperity can make that possible.

❄ ❄ ❄

Over the past century, humans have had a direct impact on the natural planetary systems on which we rely. Greater prosperity has come at a cost. If we aspire now to spread that prosperity to all our citizens, we need to find a way to decouple the century of plenty from emissions, as some countries are already doing. The best way to combat global warming is not to arrest growth but to use growth to accelerate away from our dependence on fossil fuels. If we do that with vigor, we can limit global warming and achieve a century of plenty. The difference between success and failure comes down to our ability to innovate and invest.

CHAPTER 20

THE INNOVATION TO ACCELERATE PRODUCTIVITY

"The real voyage of discovery consists not in seeking new landscapes, but in having new eyes."

MARCEL PROUST

———

Science and technology can deliver a powerful new wave of productivity growth.

ENERGY, MATERIALS, AND FOOD are critical foundations of prosperity, and we have shown that we can have enough of them without irreparably harming the planet. But they are merely inputs. For the machine of progress to endure, productivity needs to grow and, in most countries, accelerate. As discussed, advanced economies need relentless innovation: scientific discoveries, breakthrough technologies, and novel processes. Only through creative destruction can we expand the frontiers of what is possible and ensure a prosperous future for all. For emerging economies, the main path lies in investing to catch up, adopting existing and proven technologies.

We are confident that we can achieve the innovation needed to unlock a fresh wave of productivity growth.

The need to accelerate productivity growth

To achieve a century of plenty, global productivity must grow by 2.7 percent a year on average—significantly faster than the 1.8 percent achieved over the past 25 years—to deliver the 2.6 percent income growth needed to lift every country to match or exceed Switzerland's level today. This comes against a backdrop of a slowdown in productivity growth in countries at all income levels since the global financial crisis of 2008.[145]

In our world of plenty in 2100, 132 countries, which account for about 60 percent of global economic output, would need to accelerate productivity growth from the trajectory of the past quarter century. The productivity picture varies enormously. Let's go back to our four income groups. Advanced economies in the top income group, like Australia, European countries, Japan, and the United States, need to increase productivity to 1.8 percent a year on average. That is considerably more than the 0.5 percent achieved from 1997 to 2023 (Table 6). Countries in the bottom income group, mostly from Sub-Saharan Africa, would require 4.2 percent, up from 3.1 percent. Thirty of the 48 bottom income group countries would need at least a two-percentage-point acceleration.[146]

Employment patterns could move the bar in either direction. In simple terms, there are two ways for countries to grow their economies. They can work more hours, or they can squeeze more output from each hour worked. For our productivity calculations, we assume hours worked do not change from today's. In reality, if people remain in the workforce longer thanks to healthier longevity, or more women join the workforce, for example, the productivity target will come down and be easier to achieve. Conversely, if working hours shrink, for example if workweeks of four days or shorter are widely adopted, the target will rise and become harder to hit. We cannot be certain of the likely direction of future hours, and therefore we have taken a neutral approach.[147]

While this may seem like a tall order, we should note that, in the past, the world has repeatedly achieved the productivity advances necessary to deliver the income growth needed to attain the 2100 world of plenty we describe. History shows that productivity growth comes in waves (Exhibit 34). For instance, Europe's productivity growth was low before World War II, then surged between 1945 and 1970 before settling into a downward trend that has been particularly marked since the global financial crisis in 2008.

For advanced economies, the United States can serve as an example. It has increased productivity by 1.5 percent a year over the past quarter century. This is very close to the 1.8 percent needed, despite a sharp slowdown after the financial crisis. Between 1995 and 2004, rapid

TABLE 6

Productivity growth, historical and needed, by income group

Country groups by income level[1]	Historical productivity growth, 1997–2023			Productivity growth required, 2023–2100, %[2]
	Average growth rate, %[2]	Top growth rate within group, %	Top performer within group	
All	1.8	n/a	n/a	2.7
Top	0.5	2.1	Czechia	1.8
Second	1.8	4.4	Romania	2.3
Third	2.3	6.7	Armenia	3.0
Bottom	3.1	8.0	China	4.2
China[3]	8.0	n/a	n/a	2.6

[1]Membership of the groups varies slightly between columns. For forward-looking productivity, membership is determined by income rankings in 2023. For historical productivity, membership depends on the income rankings in 1997.
[2]All averages are simple averages of the countries in the income group, not weighted by population. This is to more accurately reflect the historical performance of an average country without skewing by figures for countries with large populations. This can then serve as a benchmark for future requirements for an average country in a given income group.
[3]China was in the bottom income group in 1997, but has since moved into the second income group. It is shown separately here but is also included in the second and fourth income groups' averages where relevant.
Source: The Conference Board; McKinsey Global Institute analysis

Trendline of labor productivity growth, total economy
Year on year, 1925–2019, %

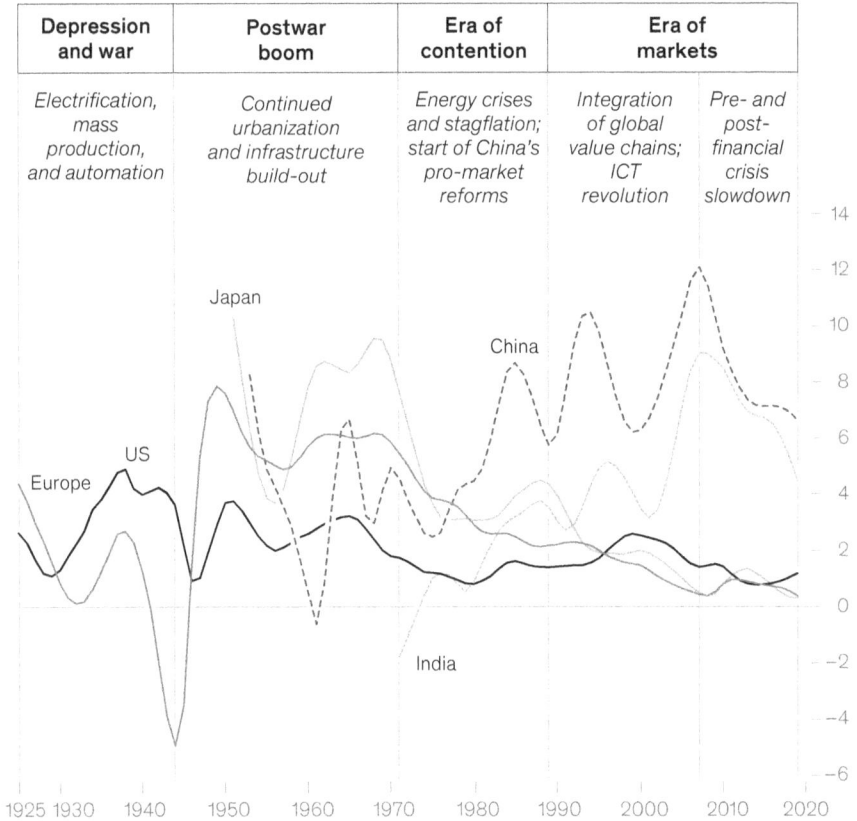

Depression and war	Postwar boom	Era of contention	Era of markets	
Electrification, mass production, and automation	Continued urbanization and infrastructure build-out	Energy crises and stagflation; start of China's pro-market reforms	Integration of global value chains; ICT revolution	Pre- and post-financial crisis slowdown

Japan

China

US

Europe

India

```
 14
 12
 10
  8
  6
  4
  2
  0
 -2
 -4
 -6
1925 1930    1940    1950    1960    1970    1980    1990    2000    2010    2020
```

Note: Productivity defined as GDP per hour worked, US 2010 PPP. Calculated using a Hodrick-Prescott filter (lambda=6.25). Europe is the simple average of France, Germany, Italy, Spain, Sweden, and the United Kingdom. Source: Bergeaud, Cette and Lecat, 2016 (for Europe and US data); The Conference Board Total Economy Database, 2023 (for China, India, Japan); McKinsey Global Institute analysis

advances in electronics manufacturing, an offshoring boom, and levels of investment delivered 2.4 percent productivity growth. After a decade-long lull after the global financial crisis when these trends ended and investment collapsed, it has come back strongly over recent years amid a renewed investment and technology boom, notably in AI.[148]

For emerging economies, China and India have set the example. China's productivity growth forged ahead after market-oriented reforms in the late 1970s, and India followed in the 1990s. Over the past 25 years, China's productivity has grown by 7.9 percent annually and India's by 5.1 percent annually.[149]

Several other emerging countries have also achieved sustained high productivity growth rates, well above those needed for a century of plenty, as we discussed in Part II. They include countries as diverse as Bangladesh, Poland, and Vietnam. They followed in the footsteps of countries like Japan, Singapore, South Korea, and Spain, all of which had similarly fast productivity growth rates as they graduated to being advanced economies.[150]

It has been possible to grow productivity at the rates needed in the future. But what could reverse the downward trend? The United States would need to sustain its recent growth rates, while Europe would need to engage in decisive competitiveness reform to unleash comparable rates of productive investment. Such reform is indeed possible. To take one example in the United States, Idaho has reduced its regulations by 95 percent since 2019 and has attracted an abundance of labor and capital, thereby growing its economy quicker than neighboring states have.[151]

Meanwhile, emerging economies would need to cultivate the type of institutions and reform that can shift them onto the fast lane. We look into that in depth at the end of this chapter. But the real ace up our sleeves might be innovation and notably AI, which we turn to next.

AI and next-gen robotics: The aces in our pack

AI and its embodied incarnation in next-generation robotics have the potential to be the star runners in the race to reignite innovation and productivity growth. AI isn't just a tool—it's a game changer, transforming work and turbocharging the very process of invention.

Like electricity or steam power, AI is a general-purpose technology, usually defined as a transformative innovation that has widespread, long-lasting impact on multiple sectors of the economy.[152] It tackles cognitive tasks, slashing diagnosis times in medicine by sifting through patient data or crafting tailored lesson plans for teachers in a flash. It can also

AI data center in Ashburn, Virginia, United States.

revolutionize marketing and sales by producing brand advertising and product descriptions and can help urban planners navigate complicated zoning laws and building regulations. In seconds, it can give us authors the most insightful, detailed, and structured critique of this book we have ever received, and early reviews were justifiably harsh!

Across the world economy, our research estimates, AI and automation technologies could boost productivity growth by 0.5 to 3.4 percentage points annually through 2040. This is a wide range, conveying the current uncertainty of AI's potential. Between 2040 and 2100, it could be much more, but that gets too far into the future to be able to estimate with any accuracy. In any case, compare that with other historical general-purpose technologies. The steam engine probably accelerated British productivity growth by 0.3 percentage point annually. Electrification added 0.4 percentage point to US productivity growth in the 1920s, and the IT revolution of the late 1990s and early 2000s 1.5 percent.[153] AI's potential is very likely larger.

At least three reasons account for this. First, AI spreads fast. While electricity took 40 years to achieve mass adoption and was mostly limited to Western nations and Japan initially, ChatGPT hit a million users in five days in 2022. By mid-2025, at the time of writing, this single AI tool has reached 800 million weekly users in 160 countries. That's one in ten people. Second, the cost of adopting AI is low. Unlike the $7,000 (in today's dollars) Macintosh of the 1980s that was inaccessible to all but the wealthiest, many of today's advanced AI tools, including large language models, are virtually free or available at minimal cost—at least some versions of them.[154] Beyond dollars, past technologies have found adoption barriers like coding skills. Users of generative AI can simply speak or write to it in natural language, making it easier to use. Third, AI's reach is much wider, potentially penetrating large service sectors like education and healthcare. By contrast, electrification was largely limited to manufacturing and ICT to the technology sector.[155]

But there is a fourth reason. AI's real magic may be its capacity to supercharge innovation itself. As we argued in chapter 13, this is particularly crucial at a time when many economists warn that innovation has grown increasingly costly. Those economists argue that we have been able to maintain the momentum of innovation only by throwing more resources, including researchers, at it. AI has the potential to flip the script. It can churn out thousands of design ideas, test them with lightning-fast simulations, and dig through data for breakthroughs. Take DeepMind's AlphaFold2. It unlocked a thousandfold increase in known protein structures overnight, slashing years off drug development.[156]

While precisely quantifying the impact of future innovations remains uncertain, our latest research, *The next innovation revolution—powered by AI*, indicates that the potential for acceleration across sectors is substantial. Industries centered on intellectual property or closely linked to fundamental scientific discoveries could experience a doubling in their rate of innovation, while, for example, complex manufacturing sectors could achieve a 50 percent acceleration in their R&D processes.[157]

Agentic AI, which is capable of pursuing goals autonomously and making decisions, could further amplify AI's contribution to productivity growth by orchestrating complex R&D workflows or optimizing entire supply chains with minimal human input.

At the end of the day, though, we exist in a physical world, beyond software. For instance, 75 percent of work hours in the United States require either physical or sensory capabilities.[158] The rise of robotics can carry AI's productivity promise into the physical world, building, moving, and caring with ever greater precision. From autonomous warehouses to, who knows, care companions for the elderly, AI-powered robots may become ubiquitous in the economy of 2100—or much earlier. The jury is still out on the physical form AI will take. Humanoid robots could revolutionize manufacturing and healthcare by executing intricate tasks at scale, slotting seamlessly into infrastructure designed around the human form. But it is equally likely that we could see a new generation of robots that look nothing like us and are instead tailored to the specific environments in which they operate. Either way, from research efforts to streamlined factories, AI is a force multiplier.

Such advances, enabled by AI's unique dual role as both invention and inventor, suggest a powerful new engine for productivity growth, exactly what is required to deliver a future of broad-based prosperity and empowerment.[159]

Will we still have jobs?

Some people wonder if they will still have jobs in a future defined by high productivity growth and AI. Will technology make us obsolete? Every leap in technology, from steam engines chugging through the Industrial Revolution to computers shaping the digital age, has raised similar fears.

But the evidence shows unequivocally that each wave of technology has resulted in more, not fewer, jobs.

When mechanized plows transformed farming, they didn't doom farmhands to unemployment and penury, but freed them to work better-paid jobs in factories. As assembly lines grew smarter with automation, workers pivoted to service and knowledge roles, from designing software to crafting marketing campaigns or, to use a favorite example of ours, becoming dog hairdressers. Technology boosted incomes, didn't destroy work, and birthed whole new industries, from app development to renewable energy generation to dog salons.

Could AI be the exception that breaks the rule? Nobody knows for sure. AI can be a big leap and has huge potential to change the way we work and live. What we can say is that similar mechanisms to those that prevented job losses in the past, namely higher incomes from growing productivity

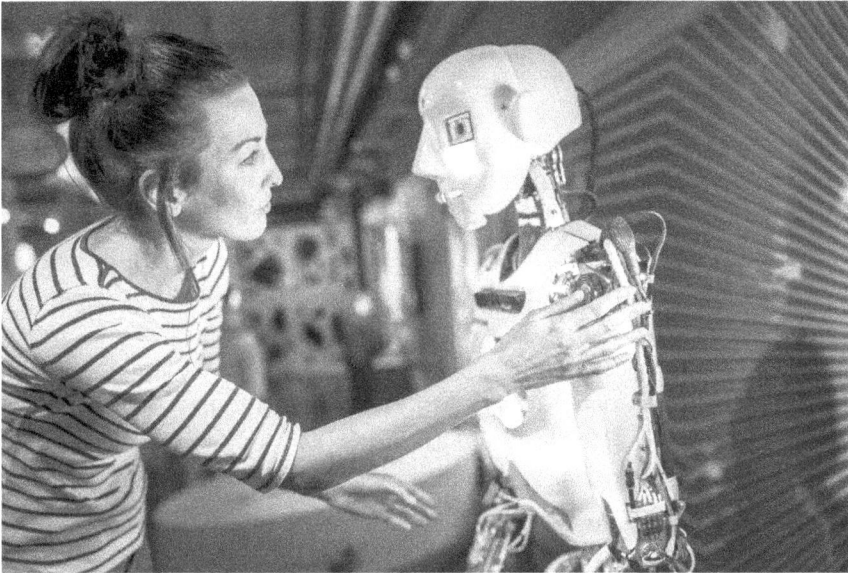

Technician and humanoid robot, Germany.

increasing demand, human work concentrating in bottlenecks, technology replacing some tasks but creating others, and the possibility of entirely new industries, may be with us for quite some time. Just as in 1925 we could not have imagined what humans would be doing in 2025, it is normal that we can't imagine what we will be doing in 2100. We may work many fewer hours but earn more. That is exactly what happened over the past 100 years.

Should other technologies outperform humans at every task, the spread of conceivable scenarios becomes wider. Perhaps many more people will produce art and entertainment instead of working behind a desk. Maybe income from work will be less relevant than today, and a much bigger portion will be capital income—from the robots and other technologies, now ubiquitous, that people have. Or maybe people will, on the other end of the spectrum, enhance themselves with AI, exoskeletons, and more, and work alongside machines. The possibilities are infinite.

The past makes us optimistic, and the future is promising. Just like in the past century, it will require adaptation in how we learn, work, interact, and live.

Beyond AI and robotics

AI and robotics may be the stars, but a whole constellation of emerging technologies is poised to reshape our world and drive the productivity needed for a century of plenty. From the space economy to modular construction, gene editing to advanced biomaterials, new technologies are already sparking change and have significant potential up to 2040. Beyond that, there could be much more, including breakthroughs we cannot yet imagine.

Take the rapidly expanding space economy. The cost of launching satellites has plummeted nearly 95 percent over the past four decades, democratizing access to space and paving the way for a wave of innovative commercial applications. The sector is set to grow 7 to 10 percent a year by 2040, opening new horizons for connectivity and industry. Satellites are game changers, guiding farmers to boost crop yields with pinpoint precision, streamlining global shipping with real-time tracking, and beaming high-speed internet to remote villages. This isn't just about space. It is about lifting education and jobs in places that have struggled in the past, fueling productivity worldwide.[160]

Other fields are just as thrilling. Modular construction promises faster, cheaper, more sustainable cities. Gene editing could unlock healthier lives and more resilient crops. Other breakthroughs in healthcare, from AI-enabled drug discovery to regenerative medicine, could herald a revolution in longevity. Advanced biomaterials might reinvent everything from medical implants to sustainable packaging. And nuclear fusion? If humanity cracks the code, it could deliver near-limitless clean energy, transforming economies.[161]

Here's the catch: Making all this happen takes investment. In advanced economies, investment, as we noted earlier, slumped after the 2008 global financial crisis. But there is good news. Titans like Amazon, Alphabet, Meta, Microsoft, Apple, and TSMC are stepping up. As mentioned in chapter 8, in 2024 alone, these six companies poured more than $500 billion into R&D and capital expenditure. Google has signed up for 200 megawatts of power from nuclear fusion produced by a plant that hasn't even been built yet. And it is not just about the tech giants. Many smaller innovative companies like India's Pixxel, which is building hyperspectral imaging satellites that offer much finer resolution than conventional systems, and Japan's Astroscale, which is helping ensure space sustainability through orbital debris removal, are boldly going where no startups have gone before.[162] These companies are making audacious bets that push boundaries and lift entire economies.

Emerging economies in the fast lane

Emerging economies can benefit from catch-up growth. As we discussed in chapter 7, they need to move into the fast lane of productivity growth, by investing in building cities and infrastructure, achieving higher service-sector productivity, and connecting their manufacturing sectors with the world to climb up the value chain toward higher-value-added activities.

For these economies, innovation doesn't necessarily mean inventing new technologies and production methods. Instead, they can adopt a vast stock of technologies that have already been invented, refined, and scaled. This makes productivity growth cheaper and less complicated than in advanced economies, which have had to invent these technologies.

They can even leapfrog old technologies. Kenya didn't bother with landlines, instead jumping straight to mobile phones, sparking a digital economy with M-Pesa. Bangladesh took advantage of plummeting solar costs to put in place the world's largest off-grid solar program by 2020.[163]

What's interesting is that, increasingly, it's not just old tech that's available to emerging economies, but frontier technology, too. Whereas 60 years ago, an entrepreneur from most emerging economies could never have hoped to access (or afford) advanced machinery to export manufactured goods, she can now access the best AI models at a relatively affordable price and use them to export a service, such as customer care operations or telemedicine, globally. The lower barriers to adoption mean that emerging economies have an opportunity to plug into the global economy by trading not only in manufacturing but also in services, as India has done.

Adding to that, knowledge and investment are flowing across borders faster than they did in the past century. Foreign direct investment has surged over the past decade and now stands at ten times what it was in the early 1990s.[164] Alongside those flows come flows of knowledge as multinational corporations help train workers in the countries in which they invest.

Just as standout firms have a role to play in pushing forward the frontier, they also drive catch-up growth by helping to foster investment, competition, urbanization, and international integration. In countries dominated by informal or subsistence-based activities, these large, highly productive companies elevate productivity by investing in physical assets, digital technologies, and essential infrastructure. This enables a shift from labor-intensive slow growth toward sustained, productivity-led expansion.[165]

Intense competition among these high-performing companies fosters rapid turnover. Over half lose their top positions within a decade. This generates a dynamic, innovation-focused business environment. On the global stage, these firms serve as gateways for international integration, positioning economies such as Brazil and Vietnam within global supply chains and driving export competitiveness. Their scale further benefits entire economic ecosystems. Large firms anchor supply chains, integrate small and medium-size enterprises into formal networks, provide training, and elevate productivity standards across industries. This translates into improved livelihoods through higher wages, formal employment, and skills development while indirectly supporting education, health, and infrastructure, filling crucial development gaps where governments alone fall short.[166]

Some of the poorest economies in the world, which are also the least politically stable, have the tallest order for achieving a century of plenty. They include Afghanistan, Haiti, and Yemen as well as several in Sub-Saharan Africa, like Burundi, Chad, and Zimbabwe. Is there a case for optimism? On the one hand, such countries need to overcome the "cold start" problem in which the pieces of the puzzle, such as poor infrastructure and institutions, and a lack of education, reinforce one another. On the other, they abound with potential. They are largely rural and can harness the dividends of urbanization. They have very little infrastructure, technology, energy, and human capital, so even small advances can yield very high returns. They also represent some of the last young labor pools in the world, which they can use to their advantage as the rest of the world ages.[167]

We don't think it's easy, but it is certainly possible. You don't have to take our word for it. Just look, once again, at history. China was as poor as all of these countries not just in 1925, but until the 1970s. Other success stories include Bangladesh, Malaysia, South Korea, and Vietnam. Think of Botswana, right next to Zimbabwe, which has managed to multiply its income per person by a factor of 33 since 1950. The Dominican Republic, on the same small island as Haiti, did it by a factor of 11.[168] Such progress is not easy, but it is possible.

✻ ✻ ✻

There is no substitute for productivity. Scientific and technological innovation has always played a big role in helping us to do more with less, boosting living standards. AI is the next big frontier, and if we harness its potential, it could be the most revolutionary technology that humanity has ever witnessed. It will be accompanied by an array of other exciting advances, while emerging economies have vast potential to catch up with the technological frontier, too. We have more tools and knowledge than ever before.

In the previous five chapters we have shown that a century of plenty is possible. Now we need to make it probable. And so to some brief final thoughts.

CHAPTER 21

CHOOSING PLENTY

"The only limit to our realization of tomorrow
is our doubts of today."

FRANKLIN D. ROOSEVELT

———

A century of plenty is possible; we need to make it probable.

THE PAST 100 YEARS were a century of unprecedented progress, but we have unfinished business. Progress is a winding ascent. In the past, we have reinvented our societies and economies when this was needed. We can do so again and can bring everyone to empowerment and beyond. Future generations around the world *can* enjoy a time of plenty.

We fully acknowledge that somebody picking up this book in 2100 may laugh at everything we have gotten wrong. But we wanted to dream positive and dream big. Several failure points could bring us far from the path we've laid out. High on our list are poor governance, difficulty in translating technological progress into productivity gains, and prolonged conflicts chilling global cooperation or worse. But the failure that we face today is one of imagination.

The times in which we write are uncertain. People, especially in mature economies, seem to be losing hope. The Edelman Trust Barometer Survey that we quoted in chapter 13 found that only 30 percent of Americans, 14 percent of Germans and Japanese, and a paltry 9 percent of the French say that "compared to today, the next generation will be better off." Increasingly, people appear to have stopped believing in our machine of progress. And for good reasons, which we have discussed. Many people feel left behind. We are at an inflection point, entering a new era, living through rapid changes. Not only is this scary and unsettling, but it affects people's livelihoods. Hopelessness can also become self-fulfilling, trapping us in a zero-sum sociopolitical stasis.

We set out armed with a sense of what might be possible. In that spirit, let us leave you with five propositions:

1.   The opportunity for a century of plenty is real.

2.   Growth is good.

3.   There is enough for all.

4.   It's time to build our future.

5.   It starts with a new story.

We can write a narrative of scarcity or a narrative of plenty. We know where our hearts lie.

The opportunity for a century of plenty is real

Today, we face economic, demographic, geopolitical, social, technological, and environmental challenges, which we have discussed at length in this book.

These challenges are real, but we remain optimistic. First, because it would be foolish to bet against human ingenuity. We are undoubtedly fallible, but we have proven, time and again, our capacity to solve the toughest problems. Second, because history shows the way to the future. Put yourself back in 1925, when the world was still recovering from a global war and unknowingly heading toward another one, with challenges much more serious than the ones we face today. Yet, 100 years later, we have experienced unprecedented progress in almost every place, across virtually every dimension.

There is good reason to believe that progress can continue. The progress machine needs upgrading to bring us into a new era. But many of the machine shortcomings are of our own making, and we have upgraded the machine in the past, adapting to new times. It is in our hands to do it again.

Innovation will be at the heart of this, as it has always been. When we have run into trouble, new science, technology, and fresh thinking have dug us out of it. Over the past century, countries that embraced innovation and invested in their future most enthusiastically have made the most dramatic progress. Think of America in the 1950s and 1960s, Japan in the 1970s and 1980s, South Korea in the 1990s and 2000s, and China in the 2000s and 2010s. Scientific and technological change can be complex, sometimes even painful, as we transition from one world to the next. But they enable many amazing things that improve our lives. They raise our productivity, improve our incomes, and offer us myriad possibilities that improve our well-being.

Progress has plenty of race left yet to run, and it's our job to make it happen. By 2100, our children and grandchildren from the poorest to the richest countries can be much more prosperous. They can be more empowered, able to tap into many more opportunities, and enabled by more science and technology, so long as we act today.

Growth is good

If there is one thing that the past 100 years has shown us, it is that growth isn't just about incomes. It means that people can live more secure, healthier, empowered lives. It broadens our life experience. We gain access to ideas, to other cultures, to other people, to choice. Growth expands our possibilities.

A world without growth is one in which we must make choices about who gets the benefits of progress and who is left behind. We cannot forge toward a century of plenty if one person's gain is another person's loss. A world of winners and losers.

Economic growth is not without hazards. Prosperity has required abundant energy, primarily from fossil fuels, leading to rising carbon emissions. Pollution, deforestation, and biodiversity loss are serious issues we still grapple with. The churn of markets and technology can unsettle communities and exacerbate inequalities. Sometimes these lead some to question growth's broader worth.

Yet growth itself remains the most powerful tool to address precisely these pitfalls. Rising incomes allow societies to fortify themselves against climate threats through investments in resilient infrastructure, advanced warning systems, and more effective disaster preparedness. Greater prosperity also increases our possibilities to innovate in and deploy at scale low-carbon technologies: Advanced economies have shown that it is possible to decouple economic expansion from emissions, charting paths toward sustainability without sacrificing affluence. It is often not economic progress, but the lack thereof, that leads to environmental degradation. Wealthier countries have cleaner cities and are polluting less and less, have better waste management systems that prevent plastic from reaching oceans, and are often reforesting.

Furthermore, growth is the cornerstone of greater empowerment. Economic growth generates the resources that are necessary to invest in the things, from skills to healthcare to infrastructure, that lift everyone. It also allows us to fund robust welfare systems and redistributive measures. Surely, it needs to be accompanied by affordable essentials such as housing or energy, which we attain by building more of them—that is, more growth. Over time, economic progress has raised living standards across the income spectrum, even if sometimes unevenly.

The essential task, therefore, is not to restrain growth but to channel it wisely, using prosperity itself as the lever for addressing both sustainability and inclusion challenges.

Nobody wakes up aspiring to grow GDP figures, but people everywhere wake up hoping their children can attend a better school, their families can quickly reach a hospital in an emergency, or a new bridge can reduce their commute and expand their job prospects. Economic growth, seen in this light, is not an abstract number but a concrete measure of progress. It is the road in Kenya linking isolated villages to vital markets, the hospital built in Rwanda that sharply reduces infant mortality, or the emergent electronics industry in Vietnam giving young people a path to prosperity. It is also the new medication curing Alzheimer's disease, the service robots helping nurses improve old-age care, the drones propelling packages and people through congested cities, or the autonomous low-emissions vehicles turning the daily commute from frustration to joy. And it is also a shiny new home appliance, the excellent new restaurant in your neighborhood, and a play you can enjoy at the theater this weekend.

Growth matters precisely because it translates into tangible improvements in daily life, delivering dignity, choice, and real opportunities to millions.

There is enough for all

We do not believe that there are physical limits to delivering this century of plenty. We can have the energy, materials, food, and innovation we need to make it reality. We have explored the physical boundaries of how much clean energy we can create, how many materials a plentiful world would need, and how to drive productivity to bring growth around the world.

We would need about two to three times today's energy to power a world of plenty, but with increasing electrification and an ambitious expansion of clean energy supply, we can make that possible. We need to build the nuclear, solar, wind, storage, and smarter grids that can deliver abundant power while reducing emissions.

Earth holds enough materials to sustain a century of growth. Reserves expand as exploration, technology, and investment unlock more, while recycling and substitution further ease constraints. Scaling is the challenge, but well-managed mining shows it can be done without devastating ecosystems. Materials need not be a barrier to prosperity.

It is possible to feed nearly 12 billion people by 2100 without expanding farmland and thereby further encroaching on biodiversity. Agricultural productivity gains, smarter farming, and innovations like aquaculture, vertical farming, and lab-grown proteins can deliver more with less.

Tackling waste and shifting diets could add further resilience.

Net zero by 2050 may be out of reach, and the emissions path we are on would likely result in long-term warming above 2.0°C. Far from worsening the climate, it is growth that can put us on a more sustainable pathway, helping us mitigate emissions and adapt to climate hazards so long as the fruits of growth are used for those purposes.

Finally, sustaining this progress requires faster productivity growth, driven by relentless innovation and investment. AI is the ace, a transformative technology that boosts efficiency and accelerates discovery. Other breakthroughs in space, biotech, energy, materials, and robotics, among many others, can also push the productivity frontier. Emerging economies have ample margin for catch-up growth through investing, urbanizing, and transforming their economies. Prosperity for all is within reach.

It's time to build our future

Then comes the hard work. We need to actually build the world that we want: the houses, advanced transportation systems, robust digital networks, clean energy systems, businesses, and political institutions that can drive us forward. A century of plenty is not virtual. It has to be real. If the farmer in Kenya doesn't get a water pump, she will not be able to improve the yield of her crop. If we don't build power plants and data centers from now on, at pace, we will not have the clean, electricity-based system we want nor the potential productivity boost that AI may bring. We will not have a century of plenty.

We have built the present, and we can build the future. Europe rebuilt after World War II. China built a modern economy in a few decades. Texas builds more renewable energy projects each month than the rest of the top ten US states combined.[169] When we decide to build, we do it.

Making what is physically possible actually happen will not be straightforward. There may be no physical limits on achieving a century of plenty, but we may still find ourselves stopped short by barriers of politics or economics, or even by the barriers of our social and cultural practices and behavior. Our book has been about economics, about nuts and bolts, about numbers. But economies don't work in a vacuum. They are influenced by politics, which are never easy or even predictable. Economies unfold in the context of vibrant, richly textured societies made up of very different people with hugely varied viewpoints and needs.

We cannot achieve all that we need to if we are stymied by political push and pull, polarization, and bureaucracy. Markets need to do what they do best: provide the capital that we need to power growth and innovation, allocating the world's resources to where they can be used most effectively. And governments and institutions need to regain the trust of citizens and do their job, ensuring fair play, limiting externalities, safeguarding competition, and investing in infrastructure and public goods like innovation. We also need effective international institutions that can foster coordination on the global challenges that countries and new technology alone cannot solve. In sum, markets, governments, and institutions need to each play their role in creating a world that offers people the prospect of a more plentiful future.

As individuals, we can make enormous strides, but to go far, we need to go together. We need collective discussion and wisdom to take the big steps.

It starts with a new story

It's not hard to find stories today that are about worry and even fear, of limits and boundaries, of reining in rather than letting loose. There is another story to tell, one that we share. An expansive story of potential yet to be tapped, guided by a sense of optimism, always based on facts.

It is precisely at these inflection points, like the one we are in today, when we adjust, refresh the progress machine, and write a new narrative of progress.

To do that most effectively, we need to over-index on what *is* possible. We need to stay open to new ideas and get comfortable with the risks associated with putting them into practice. If all we see is problems, it is much less likely that we will have the energy to think about solutions.

Times are confusing and contentious. But let's look beyond the microscope of today, through the telescope to the decades ahead, and think about the world we want to build for the precious generations to come. The many pages of detailed analysis that you have read are about the potential to bring a better world into existence. At the most fundamental level, we have a responsibility to make decisions for which our children and grandchildren will thank us.

At the same time, we need to be clear-eyed about the challenges we face and determined to tackle them. Each individual can make a difference. Now is the time to mobilize every ounce of human ingenuity we have, devoting energy, time, resources, and brain and muscle power to build a lasting legacy.

And we need inspirational leadership. Effective leaders can reframe the moment, name a future worth building, and inspire us to act together. Particularly at times of challenge, we need leaders to craft a story of progress, grounded in facts, charged with optimism, generous with hope. The hardships are real, but so is our capacity to make change.

Some narratives risk thwarting our chances of success. Growth is a good thing, not an enemy of a high quality of life but its guarantor. Our economy is not zero-sum; everyone can have more. The planet is not a limiting factor so long as we build a new, expanded, cleaner energy system, lifting our sights beyond mere replacement to building big.

The new narrative of progress should be ambitious, fearless, can-do. We need to write it. Let's pick up the pen, not with a dread of writer's block, but with excitement about the words that will flow onto the page.

"*In this world, the optimists have it,*
not because they are always right,
but because they are positive. Even when wrong,
they are positive, and that is the way of achievement,
correction, improvement, and success.
Educated, eyes-open optimism pays; pessimism can
only offer the empty consolation of being right.
The one lesson that emerges is the need to keep
trying. No miracles. No perfection. No millennium.
No apocalypse. We must cultivate a skeptical faith,
avoid dogma, listen and watch well,
try to clarify and define ends,
the better to choose means."

DAVID S. LANDES

—

The Wealth and Poverty of Nations:
Why Some Are So Rich and Some So Poor

NOTES

PART I
WHAT ON EARTH HAPPENED?

————

PREFACE

1   See, for instance, George Friedman, *The Next 100 Years: A Forecast for the 21st Century*, Allison & Busby, 2010; and Michio Kaku, *Physics of the Future: How Science Will Shape Human Destiny and Our Daily Lives by the Year 2100*, Penguin, 2011.

2   Nouriel Roubini, *Megathreats: Ten Dangerous Trends That Imperil Our Future and How to Survive Them*, Little Brown, 2022; Gordon Brown, Mohamed El-Erian, and Michael Spence, *Permacrisis: A Plan to Fix a Fractured World*, Simon & Schuster, 2023; and Toby Ord, *The Precipice: Existential Risk and the Future of Humanity*, Hachette Books, 2020.

3   For a few examples of positive narratives, see Tyler Cowen, *Stubborn Attachments: A Vision for a Society of Free, Prosperous, and Responsible Individuals*, Stripe Press, 2018; Johan Norberg, *Open: The Story of Human Progress*, Atlantic, 2020; Matt Ridley, *Rational Optimist: How Prosperity Evolves*, Fourth Estate, 2011; Steven Pinker, *Enlightenment Now: The Case for Reason, Science, Humanism, and Progress*, Penguin, 2019; Hans Rosling, *Factfulness: Ten Reasons We're Wrong about the World—and Why Things Are Better than You Think*, Sceptre, 2019; and Peter M. Diamandis and Steven Kotler, *Abundance: The Future Is Better than You Think*, Free Press, 2014.

4   Oswald Spengler, *The Decline of the West*, George Allen & Unwin, 1926; and T. S. Eliot, "The Hollow Men," poets.org.

CHAPTER 1 – A CENTURY OF PROGRESS

5   GDP per capita, purchasing-power parity (PPP), expressed in constant 2021 international dollars, *World development indicators, World Bank*, 2024.

6   GDP per capita, PPP, expressed in constant 2021 international dollars, *World development indicators*, World Bank, 2024.

7   For the income figure, see the Maddison Project Database 2023, in Jutta Bolt and Jan Luiten van Zanden, "Maddison-style estimates of the evolution of the world economy: A new 2023 update," *Journal of Economic Surveys*, volume 39, number 2, April 2025. For life

expectancy, see Riley, 2005; Zijdeman et al., 2015; HMD, 2024; UN WPP, 2024, processed by Our World in Data.

8   Other composite metrics are often used. One is the Human Development Index, which combines income, health, and education, and its augmented version, which adds freedom to the mix. These are highly correlated with GDP per capita, too. They have shorter time series, which complicates 500-year-long comparisons that GDP per capita allows. For more information on these indices, see, for example, Human Development Index (HDI), Human Development Reports, United Nations Development Programme, accessed June 2025; and for the Augmented Human Development Index, see Leandro Prados de la Escosura, *Human Development and the Path to Freedom: 1870 to the Present*, Cambridge University Press, 2022.

9   This only shows how outcomes such as, for example, happiness, correlate with a measurable, current variable such as income per person. Surely people take different perspectives for assessing progress, including based on perceptions. Perceptions of fairness or inequality, or perspectives about the future, among others, matter for assessing progress, too, and will have different weights for different people.

10   Maddison Project Database 2010 and 2023. All figures are adjusted for inflation and purchasing-power parity unless otherwise indicated.

11   Maddison Project Database 2010 and 2023. All figures are adjusted for inflation and purchasing-power parity unless otherwise indicated.

12   The term "the Great Divergence" first appeared in Kenneth Pomeranz, *The Great Divergence: China, Europe, and the Making of the Modern World Economy*, Princeton University Press, 2021. Also see Robert C. Allen, *The British Industrial Revolution in Global Perspective*, Cambridge University Press, 2009; Joel Mokyr, *A Culture of Growth: The Origins of the Modern Economy*, Princeton University Press, 2016; Mark Koyama and Jared Rubin, *How the World Became Rich: The Historical Origins of Economic Growth*, Polity, 2022; Gregory Clark, *A Farewell to Alms: A Brief Economic History of the World*, Princeton University Press, 2009; David S. Landes, *The Unbound Prometheus: Technological Change and Industrial Development in Western Europe from 1750 to the Present*, Cambridge University Press, 2003; and Deirdre Nansen McCloskey, *Bourgeois Dignity: Why Economics Can't Explain the Modern World*, University of Chicago Press, 2011.

13   Maddison Project Database 2010 and 2023. All figures are adjusted for inflation and purchasing-power parity unless otherwise indicated.

14   According to the World Bank, in nominal terms, the $20,000 figure is $14,000 (that is, in current US dollars). However, living costs vary across the world: $14,000 in Congo can buy more than it can in the United States. The $20,000 figure adjusts incomes to account for the buying power of incomes in each country (this is what is meant by purchasing-power parity, PPP), as well as inflation by fixing to a base year (constant dollars). The Rwanda figures are 2024 GDP per capita (constant 2021 international dollars), World Development Indicators, World Bank; and Maddison Project data converted from constant 2011 international dollars to constant 2021 international dollars for the 1920 estimate, accessed April 2025.

15   Maddison Project Database 2023: Jutta Bolt and Jan Luiten van Zanden, "Maddison style estimates of the evolution of the world economy: A new 2023 update," *Journal of*

Economic Surveys, 2024, accessed April 2025.

16   For a discussion of long-term extreme poverty, see Michail Moatsos, "Global extreme poverty: Present and past since 1820," in *How was life? Volume II: New perspectives on well-being and global inequality since 1820*, OECD, 2021. For other estimates with more recent data, see Poverty & Inequality Platform, World Bank.

17   See *Income levels*, Gapminder, accessed June 2025. Also see Hans Rosling, *Factfulness: Ten Reasons We're Wrong About the World—And Why Things Are Better than You Think*, Sceptre, April 3, 2018.

18   See *Income mountains*, Gapminder, accessed June 2025. Note that Rosling's $2 threshold is slightly below the World Bank's $2.15 described above, and he uses income instead of consumption data, but the implications are very similar. The essentials that households can purchase at each income level can differ from country to country, even after adjusting for overall price levels, but the income bands provide stable markers for showing progress.

19   *Pixels of Progress: A granular look at human development around the world*, McKinsey Global Institute, December 2022.

20   *From poverty to empowerment: Raising the bar for sustainable and inclusive growth*, McKinsey Global Institute, September 2023; and McKinsey Global Institute, "Economic empowerment made-to-measure: How companies can benefit more people," January 2025. The concept was not new; we first explored it in 2014. See *India's path from poverty to empowerment*, McKinsey Global Institute, February 2014.

21   The empowerment line is calculated in PPP terms. We built on an emerging consensus of academics and practitioners like Homi Karas, co-founder of World Data Lab and author of *The emerging middle class in developing countries*, OECD Development Centre, working paper number 285, January 2010. The global middle-class line was defined as $10 in 2005 PPP, which has since been raised to $12 in 2017 PPP.

22   *From poverty to empowerment: Raising the bar for sustainable and inclusive growth*, McKinsey Global Institute, September 2023. The report used 2020 population figures when the global total was about 7.8 billion people.

23   Analysis of 28 mostly high-income countries in the Human Mortality Database shows that, before the 1960s, most of the rise in life expectancy was driven by steep declines in mortality among children and young adults. Since the 1960s, however, more than 70 percent of the gains have come from people living longer into old age with the most common age of death shifting later. See Marie-Pier Bergeron-Boucher, Marcus Ebeling, and Vladimir Canudas-Romo, "Decomposing changes in life expectancy: Compression versus shifting mortality," *Demographic Research*, volume 33, article 14, September 1, 2015. For life expectancy, see Riley, 2005; Zijdeman et al., 2015; Human Mortality Database, 2024; UN Population Division, *World population prospects 2024*, processed by Our World in Data.

24   For child mortality, see Gapminder, 2015; UN Inter-agency Group for Child Mortality Estimation, 2025, processed by Our World in Data. For maternal mortality, see WHO, UNICEF, UNFPA, World Bank Group, and UNDESA, 2025, processed by Our World in Data. We note that the United States has higher maternal mortality rates than other high-

income nations at 18.6 deaths per 100,000 live births, almost twice the OECD average. For more, see *Closing the Black maternal-health gap: Healthier lives, stronger economies*, McKinsey Institute for Economic Mobility, August 2025. For infectious disease, see G. L. Armstrong, L. A. Conn, and R. W. Pinner, "Trends in infectious disease mortality in the United States during the 20th century," *JAMA*, January 1999; and Saloni Dattani et al., *Causes of death*, Our World in Data, accessed June 2025. For deaths from conflict, see *Deaths in state-based conflicts by region*, Our World in Data, accessed July 2025.

25   *Pixels of Progress: A granular look at human development around the world*, McKinsey Global Institute, December 2022.

26   For life expectancy, see Riley, 2005; Zijdeman et al., 2015; Human Mortality Database, 2024; UN Population Division, *World population prospects 2024*, processed by Our World in Data.

27   For literacy rates and primary school enrollment, see UNESCO Institute for Statistics and World Bank Gender Data Portal 2024. For average years of schooling, see Barro and Lee, 2015; Lee and Lee, 2016, processed by Our World in Data. For women's university enrollment, see World Bank, 2024; Lee and Lee, 2016; UNESCO Institute for Statistics, 2025, processed by Our World in Data.

28   For female labor force participation rates, see ILO Modelled Estimates database (ILOEST) – ILOSTAT, via World Bank, 2025, processed by Our World in Data. For 1925 figures, 25 percent is an estimate based on the few countries with available data: Canada, Germany, and the United States.

29   ILO Modelled Estimates database (ILOEST), International Labour Organization (ILO), accessed July 2025.

30   For annual working hours per worker, see Feenstra et al., Penn World Table, 2023; Huberman and Minns, 2005, processed by Our World in Data.

31   Data on airline passengers come from Civil Aviation Statistics of the World, International Civil Aviation Organization, accessed via World Bank, July 2025. International tourist arrivals data come from UNWTO World Tourism Barometer and Statistical Annex, January 2020; Travel & Tourism Economic Impact Research (EIR), World Travel & Tourism Council, accessed June 2025. For consumer wellness, see "The trends defining the $1.8 trillion global wellness market in 2024," McKinsey, January 2024.

32   *Liberal democracy index*, V-Dem, 2025, on a population-weighted basis.

33   Daniel Kahneman and Angus Deaton, "High income improves evaluation of life but not emotional well-being," *Proceedings of the National Academy of Sciences*, volume 107, number 38, September 2010; Matthew A. Killingsworth, "Experienced well-being rises with income, even above $75,000 per year," *Proceedings of the National Academy of Sciences*, volume 118, number 4, January 2021; and Betsey Stevenson and Justin Wolfers, "Subjective well-being and income: Is there any evidence of satiation?" *American Economic Review*, volume 103, number 3, May 2013.

34   Population distribution above $50 from *Income mountains*, Gapminder, accessed June 2025. For the global population, see UN Population Division, *World population prospects 2024*, processed by Our World in Data.

35   All income figures converted to constant 2021 international dollars; World Development
      Indicators, World Bank, accessed April 2025; and Maddison Project Database 2023. For
      life expectancy, see Riley, 2005; Zijdeman et al., 2015; Human Mortality Database, 2024;
      UN Population Division, *World population prospects 2024*, processed by Our World in Data.

36   For child mortality, see Gapminder, 2015; UN Inter-agency Group for Child Mortality
      Estimation, 2025, processed by Our World in Data. For the death of the Churchills'
      daughter, see *Marigold*, International Churchill Society, January 1970. For Coolidge
      history, see "Medicine: A president's grief," *Time*, July 18, 1955. For penicillin, see *How was
      penicillin developed?*, Science Museum, February 23, 2021.

37   Agriculture share of labor force from Steven Mintz, *Statistics: Trends in American farming*,
      The Gilder Lehrman Institute of American History, accessed July 2025. The services share
      of employment comes from ILOEST, ILO, July 29, 2025. For annual hours per capita, see
      Feenstra et al., Penn World Table, 2023; Huberman and Minns, 2005, processed by Our
      World in Data.

38   For high school graduation rates, see *Statistics of state school systems, 1923–1924*, ERIC,
      Bulletin, number 42, 1925; for car ownership, see Shari Eli, Joshua K. Hausman, and Paul
      W. Rhode, "Transportation revolution: The car in the 1920s," *AEA Papers and Proceedings*,
      volume 112, May 2022; for indoor plumbing, see *Historical census of housing tables:
      Plumbing*, United States Census Bureau, accessed July 2025; for electricity, see Arthur
      G. Woolf, "The residential adoption of electricity in early twentieth-century America," *The
      Energy Journal*, volume 8, number 2, April 1987; and for women's right to vote, see *19th
      amendment to the U.S. Constitution: Women's right to vote (1920)*, National Archives,
      accessed July 2025.

CHAPTER 2 – THE WINDING ASCENT

39   For the microprocessor, see Stanford Engineering, *Ted Hoff: The birth of the
      microprocessor and beyond*, accessed June 2025; for the gold standard and oil shocks,
      see David Hammes and Douglas Wills, "Black gold: The end of Bretton Woods and the
      oil-price shocks of the 1970s," *The Independent Review*, volume IX, number 4, Spring
      2005; and for Japan's national income growth, see William McCubbin, *A history of Japan's
      economy*, JM Finn, December 2024.

40   *On the cusp of a new era?* McKinsey Global Institute, October 2022. This paper covered
      the period starting in 1944 and looked at the latter three eras.

41   James Harvey Rogers, "Foreign markets and foreign credits," in *Recent Economic Changes
      in the United States*, volumes 1 and 2, National Bureau of Economic Research, January
      1929; and *Great Depression and the collapse of global trade—an overview*, Explaining
      History podcast, June 9, 2025.

42   *Fact #841: October 6, 2014 Vehicles per thousand people: U.S. vs. other world regions*, US
      Department of Energy, accessed August 2025.

43   The US child mortality rate was about 100 per 1,000 live births in 1915 and less than 30
      by 1950. See Amiya Bhatia, Nancy Krieger, and SV Subramanian, "Learning from history

about reducing infant mortality: Contrasting the centrality of structural interventions to early 20th-century successes in the United States to their neglect in current global initiatives," *The Milbank Quarterly*, volume 97, number 1, March 2019.

44 *World population prospects*, UN Population Division, 2022.

45 For oil consumption and prices, see "World oil reserves 1948–2001: Annual statistics and analysis," *Energy Exploration and Exploitation*, volume 19, number 2/3, April 2001; and BP, *Statistical review of world energy*, 71st edition, 2022. For global fossil fuel consumption, see Energy Institute, *Statistical review of world energy*, 2025; Smil, 2017, processed by Our World in Data. US oil consumption figures include transportation, heating, cooking, and electricity. For US energy consumption data, see US Energy Information Administration, 2025; Energy Institute, *Statistical review of world energy*, 2025; population based on various sources, 2024, processed by Our World in Data. Energy consumption for low-income countries has been approximated with energy used in lower-middle-income countries. For the Green Revolution, see "Nitrogen—historical statistics (data series 140)," US Geological Survey, National Minerals Information Center, February 26, 2024.

46 Maddison Project Database 2020; Jutta Bolt and Jan Luiten van Zanden, *Maddison style estimates of the evolution of the world economy: A new 2020 update*, Maddison Project working paper WP-15, October 2020. "Emerging world" countries are those later defined as "least developed countries" by the United Nations Department of Economic and Social Affairs.

47 For technology adoption in US households, see Horace Dediu; Comin and Hobijn, 2004; other sources collated by Our World in Data, processed by Our World in Data. Also see "Timeline: Historical nodes on the Net," *Computer World*, March 20, 2006.

48 Lucas Chancel et al., eds., *World inequality report 2022*, Harvard University Press, 2022.

49 Vaclav Smil, "Energy in the twentieth century: Resources, conversions, costs, uses, and consequences," *Annual Review of Energy and the Environment*, Volume 25, 2000.

50 Donella H. Meadows et al., *The Limits to Growth: A Report for The Club of Rome's Project on the Predicament of Mankind,* A Potomac Associates Book, 1972. For daily supply of calories per person, see Food and Agriculture Organization of the United Nations, 2024; other sources, processed by Our World in Data.

51 Penn World Table (v10.0, 2021), in Robert C. Feenstra, Robert Inklaar, and Marcel P. Timmer, "The next generation of the Penn World Table," *American Economic Review*, volume 105, number 10, October 2015.

52 Francis Fukuyama, *The End of History and the Last Man*, Penguin Books Ltd., 2012.

53 For a discussion of the drivers of globalization from 1970 to 2000, see, for example, Geoffrey Garrett, "The causes of globalization," *Comparative Political Studies*, volume 33, number 6/7, 2000.

54 For mobile phone ownership, see *The mobile economy*, GSM Association, 2020;

for internet penetration, see "Individuals using the internet as a percentage of the population," *World development indicators*, World Bank, 2022; for landlines, see "Fixed telephone subscriptions (per 100 people)," *World development indicators*, World Bank, 2022. Also for recent technology trends, see *McKinsey Technology Trends Outlook 2022*, McKinsey, August 2022; *Addressing Europe's corporate and performance gap*, McKinsey Global Institute, September 2022; and *Notes from the AI frontier: Applications and value of deep learning*, McKinsey Global Institute, April 2018. Moore's law observes that the number of transistors on computer chips doubles approximately every two years. See Gordon E. Moore, "Cramming more components onto integrated circuits," *Electronics*, volume 38, number 8, April 1965.

55 An estimated 20 percent of two billion people were urban in 1920 or about 400 million, compared with 4.7 billion today. For shares of urban population in 1920, see United Nations, Department of Economic and Social Affairs, Population Division, 2018; HYDE, 2023, processed by Our World in Data. For urban population today, see *World urbanization prospects*, United Nations, 2018.

56 *Poorer than their parents? Flat or falling incomes in advanced economies*, McKinsey Global Institute, July 2016.

57 For energy use per person, see US Energy Information Administration, 2025; Energy Institute, *Statistical review of world energy*, 2025; population based on various sources, 2024, processed by Our World in Data.. This figure represents primary energy consumption including electricity, transportation, heating, and cooking.

58 For meat production, see Food and Agriculture Organization of the United Nations, 2025, processed by Our World in Data. For steel production, see *Steel statistical yearbook*, World Steel Association (formerly International Iron and Steel Institute), 1993 and 2020; for cement production, see *Cement—historical statistics (data series 140)*, US Geological Survey, National Minerals Information Center, July 2022; for man-made materials, see Vaclav Smil, *Making the modern world: Materials and dematerialization*, Wiley, 2013; and Emily Elhacham et al., "Global human-made mass exceeds all living biomass," *Nature*, volume 588, issue 7838, 2020.

59 Yang Yao, "The Chinese growth miracle," in Philippe Aghion and Steven N. Durlauf, eds., *Handbook of economic growth, volume 2*, North Holland, 2014.

60 For productivity growth, see *Investing in productivity*, McKinsey Global Institute, March 2024. On low- and middle-income countries generating the majority of global growth for the first time, GDP is measured in constant 2015 US dollars. See *World development indicators*, World Bank, 2022. Also see *How IT enables productivity growth*, McKinsey Global Institute, November 2002; and *The productivity puzzle*, McKinsey Global Institute, March 2017. For debt as a share of GDP, see *2021 update of the IMF Global Debt Database*, IMF, December 15. 2021; for global trade, see *Global flows: The ties that bind in an interconnected world*, McKinsey Global Institute, November 2022.

CHAPTER 3 – ON THE CUSP OF A NEW ERA

61   The five domains are world order, technology platforms, demographic forces, resource and energy systems, and capitalization. See *On the cusp of a new era?* McKinsey Global Institute, October 2022.

62   Economy rankings are in nominal terms unless otherwise specified. GDP data come from the World Bank. For tariffs and semiconductor export controls, see Barath Harithas et al., *"Liberation Day" tariffs explained*, Center for Strategic and International Studies, April 2025; and Sujai Shivakumar, Charles Wessner, and Thomas Howell, *The limits of chip export controls in meeting the China challenge,* Center for Strategic and International Studies, April 2025. For the CHIPS Act, see Jeff Brown, *The effects of the CHIPS Act*, Brownstone Research, August 2024. MGI developed a new measure of "geopolitical distance" constructed by looking at UN General Assembly votes as a proxy for alignment on global issues. For more on this, see *Geopolitics and the geometry of global trade: 2025 update*, McKinsey Global Institute, January 2025.

63   For a comparison of the Chinese and United States naval fleets, see David Ganezer, "The Chinese navy already has more ships than the US. How will Trump address this, when China's shipbuilding capacity is 100 times greater than the US?" *Santa Monica Observer*, June 9, 2025; and Alexander Palmer, Henry H. Carroll, and Nicholas Velasquez, *Unpacking China's naval buildup*, Center for Strategic and International Studies, June 2024. For solar panels and EVs, see Yujie Xue, "China to dominate global markets for solar panels, EVs, despite EU, US hurdles: IEA," *South China Morning Post*, November 1, 2024. For drones, see Farah Stockman, "Drones are key to winning wars now. The U.S. makes hardly any," *New York Times*, July 21, 2025.

64   In 2025, NATO members committed to investing 5 percent of GDP annually in core defense requirements and defense- and security-related spending by 2035. See *Defence expenditures and NATO's 5% commitment*, NATO, June 27, 2025.

65   Martine Paris, "ChatGPT hits 1 billion users? 'Doubled in just weeks' says OpenAI CEO," *Forbes*, April 12, 2025.

66   Microsoft CTO Kevin Scott has said he expects 95 percent of code to be AI-generated in the next five years; see Sarah Perkel, "Microsoft CTO breaks down how he sees software developer jobs evolving in the next 5 years," Business Insider, April 3, 2025. For the pace of AI development, see Anson Ho et al., *Algorithmic progress in language models*, Cornell University, March 2024; Rachel Gordon, *From recurrent networks to GPT-4: Measuring algorithmic progress in language models*, MIT CSAIL, March 2024; and *The next big arenas of competition*, McKinsey Global Institute, October 2024. For the cost of a teraflop per second, see Epoch, 2024, processed by Our World in Data.

67   On funding of AI, in 2024, the United States attracted $109.1 billion in private AI funding, almost 12 times China's $9.3 billion, and 24 times more than the United Kingdom's $4.5 billion. On foundation models, US-based institutions developed 40 notable AI models, compared with China's 15 and Europe's three. See *2025 AI Index Report*, Human-Centered Artificial Intelligence, Stanford University, April 2025. For shares of patents and robots, see *China leads in global AI patents with 60% share*, TechinAsia, April 26, 2025; and *IFR World Robotics report says 4M robots are operating in factories globally*, The

Robot Report, September 24, 2024.

68   Our estimate of 15 to 30 percent is detailed in *Jobs lost, jobs gained: What the future of work will mean for jobs, skills, and wages*, McKinsey Global Institute, November 2017. On AI replacing coders, see Matt O'Brien, "Is AI causing tech worker layoffs? That's what CEOs suggest, but the reality is complicated," Associated Press, July 30, 2025; and Alexandra Tremayne-Pengelly, "A.I. drives job cuts across Silicon Valley giants: By the numbers," Observer, July 8, 2025. On GitHub Copilot, see Sida Peng et al., *The impact of AI on developer productivity: Evidence from GitHub Copilot*, Cornell University, February 2023. The experiment showed that programmers with access to GitHub Copilot were able to implement an HTTP server in JavaScript 55 percent quicker than the control group. However, for more general applications of AI, most companies were achieving a 10 to 15 percent productivity boost as of 2025.

69   There is some anecdotal evidence of AI replacing jobs. For example, in large logistics companies, one-quarter of dispatching roles have been replaced using AI route optimization. Fast-food chains using AI-based kitchen systems say entry-level kitchen staff positions are down 30 percent. Freelance writer contracts offered by publishing companies have almost halved in a year. See Michael Baumgartner, *AI replacing jobs: 100+ statistics that will surprise you (2025 research)*, Zebracat, May 2025. Some early research appears to show declines in employment in occupations most exposed to AI. See, for instance, Erik Brynjolfsson, Bharat Chandar, and Ruyu Chen, *Canaries in the coal mine? Six facts about the recent employment effects of artificial intelligence*, Stanford Digital Economy Lab working paper, August 2025. Others express doubt about AI replacing human labor more broadly. See, for instance, Noah Smith, *AI and jobs, again*, Noahpinion, August 30, 2025; Noah Smith, *Stop pretending you know what AI does to the economy*, Noahpinion, July 20, 2025; and John Burn-Murdoch, "Rising graduate joblessness is mainly affecting men. Will that last?" *Financial Times*, July 18, 2025. Of course, this is all very recent; only time will tell.

70   For births per year, see United Nations Population Division, *World population prospects*, 2024, processed by Our World in Data.

71   On Japan, see Daiji Kawaguchi and Hiroaki Mori, *The labor market in Japan, 2000–2018*, IZA, July 2019; and *Japan: 2025, looking ahead*, L&E Global, January 13, 2025. On retirement ages rising, see *Retirement age by country 2025*, World Population Review, accessed August 2025. Also see *Dependency and depopulation? Confronting the consequences of a new demographic reality*, McKinsey Global Institute, January 2025.

72   On EU opinion on migration, see *EU challenges and priorities*, Eurobarometer Report, June–July 2024. On advances in medicine and public health, see, for instance, Darren Orf, "A revolutionary new drug could stop your cells from self-destructing—and hit the pause button on aging," *Popular Mechanics*, July 22, 2025. On Japan and Singapore, see, for instance, Yoshiko Someya and Cullen T. Hayashida, "The past, present and future direction of government-supported active aging initiatives in Japan: A work in progress," *Social Sciences*, volume 11, number 2, February 2022; and Y-Jean Mun-Delsalle, "Singapore's great urban experiment: Using design to bolster well-being and longevity," *Forbes*, November 1, 2024. On women working for longer, see Estaban Ortiz-Ospina, Sandra Tzvetkoca, and Max Rose, *Women's employment*, Our World in Data, March 2024.

73 *Global warming of 1.5°C*, Intergovernmental Panel on Climate Change, 2018; and John Lang, *Net zero: A short history*, Energy & Climate Intelligence Unit, January 2021.

74 On investment in oil and gas exploration and liquefied natural gas terminals, see, for instance, Eleanor Butler, "BP scraps renewables target, returns to oil and gas in strategy reset," Euronews, February 2, 2025; and Bob Shively, *National gas consumption: Global outlook 2023–2034*, Energy Currents blog, Enerdynamics, accessed August 2025. On China being the world's largest crude importer, see *China imported record amounts of crude oil in 2023*, Today in Energy, Energy Information Administration, April 2024. On carbon emissions, see Zeke Hausfather and Pierre Friedlingstein, *Analysis: Global CO_2 emissions will reach new high in 2024 despite slower growth*, Carbon Brief, November 2024; and Laura Myllyvirta, *Analysis: Clean energy just put China's CO_2 emissions into reverse for the first time*, Carbon Brief, May 2025.

75 On energy storage, see Nelson Nsitem, "Global energy storage market records biggest jump yet," BloombergNEF, April 25, 2024. On nuclear reactors, see *China and Russia drive surge in global nuclear energy plant development*, Institute of Energy for South-East Europe, April 2025. On nuclear in Japan, see Harry Dempsey, "Japan switches back to nuclear, 14 years after Fukushima," *Financial Times*, July 7, 2025. On EV sales, see *Global EV outlook 2025*, IEA, May 2025. On environmental, social, and governance, see, for instance, *Report: 80% of corporations recalibrate ESG strategies in response to policy shifts*, ESG News, June 2025. On data centers, see *AI is set to drive surging electricity demand from data centres while offering the potential to transform how the energy sector works*, IEA, April 2025.

76 McKinsey Global Institute Global Balance Sheet database.

77 On inflation trends, see Olaf Storbeck and Ian Smith, "Eurozone inflation stayed at ECB's 2% target in July," *Financial Times*, August 1, 2025; and Sonal Varma and Si Ying Toh, "Asia: Low inflation is here to stay," Nomura, March 2025. On the United States, see Lucia Mutikani, "US inflation warms up in June as tariffs boost some goods prices," Reuters, July 31, 2025.

78 On China's growth rate, see Rachel Farmer, "China's economy rallies to reach growth target, 2025 outlook remains uncertain," China Market Intelligence, The US–China Business Council, January 24, 2025. On India, see *IMF Executive Board concludes 2024 Article IV consultation with India*, IMF, February 27, 2025. On global growth, see *Global economy: Tenuous resilience amid persistent uncertainty*, World Economic Outlook Update, IMF, July 2025.

79 *General government gross debt, percent of GDP*, IMF, accessed August 2025.

PART II
HOW WAS PROGRESS ACHIEVED?

CHAPTER 4 – THE MACHINE OF PROGRESS

1   Jutta Bolt and Jan Luiten van Zanden, "Maddison-style estimates of the evolution of the world economy: A new 2023 update," *Journal of Economic Surveys*, volume 39, number 2, April 2025.

2   Tertiary education attainment increased from about 5 percent in 1940 to some 40 percent in 2022. See *Highest educational levels reached by adults in the U.S. since 1940*, US Census Bureau, March 2017; and *Census Bureau releases new educational attainment data*, US Census Bureau, February 16, 2023.

3   *Our history*, Sir William Dunn School of Pathology, University of Oxford, accessed June 2025.

4   Matt Ridley, *The Rational Optimist: How Prosperity Evolves*, Harper Perennial, 2011.

CHAPTER 5 – WORKERS: FROM FARM TO FUTURE

5   *Asia on the cusp of a new era*, McKinsey Global Institute, September 2023.

6   *Employment (persons) by sector (as at year end)*, Department of Statistics Singapore, April 2, 2025.

7   Robust global data for 1925 are not available, so we made estimations using historical records from countries including the United Kingdom and the United States. Applying a conservative 45 percent employment rate to a global population of two billion yields a labor force of roughly 900 million, of which one-third, or about 300 million, were in nonfarm work. By the 2020s, the global labor force is roughly 3.5 billion. With only 26 percent in agriculture, the nonfarm workforce has grown to about 2.7 billion. See *Long-term trends in UK employment: 1861 to 2018*, Office for National Statistics, April, 2019; *Statistical abstract of the United States: 1925*, Bureau of the Census Library, 1926; D. B. Grigg, "The world's agricultural labor force 1800–1970," *Geography*, volume 60, issue 3, 1975, cited in Donald F. Larson and Kevin L. Bloodworth II, "Mechanization and the intersectoral migration of agricultural labor," in *Agricultural Development in Asia and*

Africa, Jonna P. Estudillo, Yoko Kijima, and Tetsushi Sonobe, eds., Springer Singapore, 2022; and Max Roser and Hannah Ritchie, *How has world population changed over time?* Our World in Data, June 2023. For employment in agriculture, see International Labour Organization (via the World Bank) and historical sources, processed by Our World in Data, accessed September 2025.

8   Building on the same sources cited above, we estimate that about two-thirds of workers globally were engaged in agriculture and one-third in nonfarm employment. Of these, about 83 percent were men and 17 percent were women. Had male labor force participation remained at 1925 levels, the global nonfarm labor force would have increased by three billion workers. Of this, we estimate that about 0.9 billion (30 percent) is due to a quadrupling in the working-age population, about 1.4 billion (45 percent) reflects workers moving out of agriculture into industry and services, and women's rising participation accounts for the remaining 0.7 billion (25 percent). However, given the decline in male labor force participation, the net increase was 2.4 billion nonfarm workers. For female labor force participation rates, see ILO Modelled Estimates and Projections database (ILOEST), ILOSTAT via World Bank, 2025, processed by Our World in Data. For the women's share in the United States in 1920, see *An overview 1920–2021*, Women's Bureau, US Department of Labor, accessed August 2025.

9   Maddison Project Database 2023, in Jutta Bolt and Jan Luiten van Zanden, "Maddison-style estimates of the evolution of the world economy: A new 2023 update," *Journal of Economic Surveys*, volume 39, number 2, April 2025.

10 Max Roser, *The global decline of the fertility rate*, Our World in Data, 2014; and *Dependency and depopulation: Confronting the consequences of a new demographic reality*, McKinsey Global Institute, January 2025.

11 For penicillin, see Robert Gaynes, "The discovery of penicillin—new insights after more than 75 years of clinical use," *Emerging Infectious Diseases*, volume 23, number 5, May 2017. For maternal mortality, see WHO, UNICEF, UNFPA, World Bank Group, and UNDESA, 2025, processed by Our World in Data. For life expectancy, see Riley, 2005; Zijdeman et al., 2015; Human Mortality Database, 2024; UN Population Division, *World population prospects 2024*, processed by Our World in Data.

12 Thomas Malthus, *An Essay on the Principle of Population*, J. Johnson, in St Paul's Church-yard, 1798; and Paul R. Ehrlich, *The Population Bomb*, Sierra Club, 1969.

13 For the fertility rate, see UN Population Division, *World population prospects 2024*; Human Fertility Database, 2024, processed by Our World in Data. For average family size, see *Family size by country 2025*, World Population Review, accessed July 2025.

14 *Dependency and depopulation? Confronting the consequences of a new demographic reality*, McKinsey Global Institute, January 2025.

15 In the United Kingdom, it may have been as low as 7 percent, while the United States and Germany trailed at 25 and 30 percent of their total labor forces, respectively. See D. B. Grigg, "The world's agricultural labour force 1800–1970," *Geography*, volume 6, number 3, July 1975.

16 *Employment in agriculture (% of total employment) (modeled ILO estimate)*, World Bank, accessed June 2025.

17   *2020 Census urban area by the numbers*, US Census Bureau, updated June 2023; and
      History of urban and rural areas, US Census Bureau, accessed July 2025.

18   Development economists emphasize that this surge in farm productivity is not incidental
      but the necessary first push of modernization without which industrialization rarely
      succeeds. In one account, East Asian success stories, such as those of Japan, South
      Korea, and Taiwan, began with sweeping land reform that raised farm productivity and rural
      incomes, laying the groundwork for industrialization. See Joe Studwell, *How Asia Works:
      Success and Failure in the World's Most Dynamic Region*, Profile Books, 2014. Another,
      using a dual-sector model, emphasized the transfer of surplus labor from low-productivity
      farming to higher-productivity industry. See W. Arthur Lewis, "Economic development with
      unlimited supplies of labor," *The Manchester School*, volume 22, issue 2, May 1954.

19   *Farming and farm income*, US Department of Agriculture (USDA), March 12, 2025; Eric
      Njuki et al., *U.S. agricultural output, inputs, and total factor productivity, 1948–2021*,
      USDA, September 10, 2024; and Katherine Lacy, *The number of U.S. farms continues slow
      decline*, USDA, March 12, 2025.

20   *Asia on the cusp of a new era*, McKinsey Global Institute, September 2023.

21   International Labour Organization, World Bank, and historical estimates, 1925 to 2024.
      One study finds that the average wage in nonagricultural sectors was approximately 1.8
      times higher than in agriculture across 13 developing countries, with the ratio ranging
      from 1.5 to 2.7. See Berthold Herrendorf and Todd Schoellman, "Why is measured
      productivity so low in agriculture?" *Review of Economic Dynamics*, volume 18, number 4,
      2015.

22   For the supply shock and its impact on manufacturing elsewhere, see David H. Autor,
      David Dorn, and Gordon H. Hanson, "The China shock: Learning from labor-market
      adjustment to large changes in trade," *Annual Review of Economics*, volume 8, 2016;
      and *Sustaining employment growth: The role of manufacturing and structural change,
      Industrial development report 2013*, United Nations Industrial Development Organization,
      2013. For long-term prices of electronics see *Long-term price trends for computers, TVs,
      and related items*, The Economics Daily, US Bureau of Labor Statistics, US Department of
      Labor, October 13, 2015.

23   *Asia on the cusp of a new era*, McKinsey Global Institute, September 2023; and
      *Employment in agriculture (% of total employment) (modeled ILO estimate) – Sub-Saharan
      Africa*, World Bank, accessed July 2025.

24   *Labor force participation rate, female (% of female population ages 15+) (modeled ILO
      estimate)*, World Bank, accessed June 2025.

25   *Women in the labor force: A databook*, US Bureau of Labor Statistics, accessed April
      2025; and Claudia Goldin, "The quiet revolution that transformed women's employment,
      education, and family," *American Economic Review*, volume 96, number 2, May 2006.

26   *Labor force participation rate, female (% of female population aged 15+) (modeled ILO
      estimate) – OECD members*, World Bank, accessed July 2025.

27   Daiji Kawaguchi and Hiroaki Mori, *The labor market in Japan, 2000–2018*, IZA World of
      Labor, 2019; *Infra-annual labor statistics: Labor force participation female: From 25 to*

54 years for Japan, Federal Reserve Bank of St. Louis, updated August 15, 2015. Labor force by age group and labor force status data are available from chapter 19 of the *Japan Statistical Yearbook 2025*, Statistics Bureau of Japan, accessed August 2025. Data on population by age group and indices of age structure for 2000 to 2023 are available from chapter 2 of the same edition of the *Japan Statistical Yearbook* for 2025. Also see Takehiko Sawaji, "Labor force at record high, more elderly and women working," *Asahi Shimbun*, January 31, 2025.

CHAPTER 6 – SKILLS: MOBILIZING MINDS

28   *An overview of Singapore's education system from 1819 to the 1970s*, National Library Singapore, July 2009.

29   For years of schooling in Singapore, see Barro and Lee, 2015; Lee and Lee, 2016, processed by Our World in Data. For share with a university degree, see *Education profile and key educational indicators*, Department of Statistics Singapore, accessed August 2025; for university rankings, see *World University Rankings 2025*, Times Higher Education, accessed August 2025. PISA is a study of 15-year-old students' performance on mathematics, science, and reading, administered every three years. For more on the SkillsFuture program, see the SkillsFuture Singapore website; and "Singapore" in "Education GPS," OECD, accessed August 2025.

30   *GDP per capita (constant 2021 international dollars)*, World Bank, accessed June 2025. Data for years prior to 1960 converted from 2015 US dollars to constant 2021 international dollars. See *Employment in services (% of total employment) (modeled ILO estimate)*, World Bank, accessed August 2025.

31   Max Roser and Esteban Ortiz-Ospina, *Literacy*, Our World in Data, revised March 2024; *Average years of schooling*, Our World in Data, accessed August 2025; and *Human capital: The value of experience*, McKinsey Global Institute, June 2022.

32   *Employment in services (% of total employment) (modeled ILO estimate)*, World Bank, accessed July 2025; and David H. Autor, Frank Levy, and Richard J. Murnane, "The skill content of recent technological change: An empirical exploration," *The Quarterly Journal of Economics*, volume 118, issue 4, November 2003.

33   Andy Moose, Kana Enomoto, and Harris Eyre, *Brain gain: How improving brain health benefits the economy*, World Economic Forum, September 9, 2024.

34   *Reskilling China: Transforming the world's largest workforce into lifelong learners*, McKinsey Global Institute, January 2021.

35   *Skills transformation for the 2021 workplace*, IBM, December 2020; and *The enterprise guide to closing the skills gap: Strategies for building and maintaining a skilled workforce*, IBM, September 2019.

36   *Human capital: The value of experience*, McKinsey Global Institute, June 2022.

37   For literacy, see Robert J. Barro and Jong-Wha Lee, *Education matters: Global schooling gains from the 19th to the 21st century*, Oxford University Press, 2015; and UNESCO, 1957; UNESCO, 1953; Buringh and van Zanden, 2009; van Zanden, J. et al.; UNESCO Institute

for Statistics, 2025, processed by Our World in Data. For creative thinking and problem-solving skills, see *Creative thinking*, OECD, accessed August 2025.

38   Gary S. Becker, *Human Capital: A Theoretical and Empirical Analysis, with Special Reference to Education*, University of Chicago Press, 1994; and Tyler Cowen, *The Great Stagnation: How America Ate All the Low-Hanging Fruit of Modern History, Got Sick, and Will (Eventually) Feel Better*, Dutton, 2011.

39   For government spending on education as a share of GDP, see UNESCO Institute for Statistics, 2025; Tanzi & Schuknecht, 2000, processed by Our World in Data. For average years of schooling, see Barro and Lee, 2015; Lee and Lee, 2016, processed by Our World in Data.

40   *43% of EU's 25-34-year-olds have tertiary education*, Eurostat, May 27, 2024; and *Educational attainment,* Spain, EDU2Oc.org, accessed September 2025.

41   International benchmarks include PISA, Trends in International Mathematics and Science Study and The Southern and Eastern Africa Consortium for Monitoring Educational Quality. For spreading effective educational solutions globally, see S*park & Sustain: How all the world's school systems can improve learning at scale*, McKinsey, February 2024; and Jake Bryant, Emma Dorn, Stephen Hall, and Frédéric Panier, *Reimagining a more equitable and resilient K–12 education system*, McKinsey, September 2020.

42   *PISA 2022 results (Volume I): The state of learning and equity in education*, OECD, 2023; and *Spark & Sustain: How all the world's school systems can improve learning at scale*, McKinsey, February 2024.

43   Notably, the workers who do go the furthest, who are the most upwardly mobile, tend to do so by making frequent, bold moves between roles. Most often these moves are between companies, and because new roles generally require additional skills and responsibilities that were not part of the previous job, they serve as major learning opportunities. This catalyzes a growth in an individual's skills that compounds with each move, resulting in a far bigger shift in capabilities and responsibilities over the entirety of a working life. See *Human capital at work: The value of experience*, McKinsey Global Institute, June 2022.

44   *Trends in adult learning: New data from the 2023 Survey of Adult Skills*, OECD, July 2025; Philip Oltermann, "Importing Germany's dual education system is easier said than done," *Guardian*, July 9, 2020; and *Human capital at work: The value of experience*, McKinsey Global Institute, June 2022.

CHAPTER 7 – INVESTMENT: BUILDING CAPITAL

45   For productivity and capital per worker, see Antonin Bergeaud, Gilbert Cette, and Rémy Lecat, "Productivity trends in advanced countries between 1890 and 2012," *The Review of Income and Wealth*, volume 62, issue 3, September 2016.

46   Antonin Bergeaud, Gilbert Cette, and Rémy Lecat, "Productivity trends in advanced countries between 1890 and 2012," T*he Review of Income and Wealth*, volume 62, issue 3, September 2016.

47   For capital per hour, see Bergeaud, A., Cette, G. and Lecat, R., 2016, processed by Our

World in Data. Total capital stock is from McKinsey Global Institute's Global Balance Sheet database.

48   The global figure is an average of the 23 countries for which long-term data are available. For capital intensity 1925 to 2015, see Bergeaud, A., Cette, G. and Lecat, R., 2016, processed by Our World in Data.

49   *Investing in productivity growth*, McKinsey Global Institute, March 2024. The Solow growth model explains how economies grow over time. It posits that growth comes from three main sources: labor (chapters 5 and 6), capital (this chapter), and technology (chapter 8).

50   China produced its first car in 1956. See *13 July 1956: China's first automobile successfully produced*, Fun Facts, July 2024; and *Global and EU auto industry: Full year 2024, Economic and Market Report*, ACEA, March 2025.

51   For more on the automation in Shanghai's ports, see *The world's largest automated container port*, Huawei, accessed July 2025; and Katherine Si, "Shanghai port handles 50 million teu in 2024," Seatrade Maritime News, January 2, 2025.

52   For more on how automation boosts productivity growth, see *Investing in productivity growth*, McKinsey Global Institute, March 2024. For the impact of the moving assembly line, see Dennis Abrams, *The Inventions of the Moving Assembly Line: A Revolution in Manufacturing*, Chelsea House, 2011. One example of a highly automated EV production line is Tesla, whose Gigafactory in Shanghai produces a vehicle approximately every 40 seconds. See Suvat Kothari, "Tesla rolls out one EV every second at Gigafactory Shanghai," Inside EVs, July 28, 2023. BYD figures come from the BYD Group website.

53   Under broader definitions of intangibles, the shares are even higher. The ten European economies and the United States achieved 63 percent growth in the value they created. The top companies for growth invest 2.6 times more in intangibles than those with the slowest growth. See *Unlocking investment in intangible assets in Europe*, European Commission, CompNet Annual Conference, Leopoldina, Halle (Saale), Germany, June 6, 2018; *Getting tangible about intangibles: The future of growth and productivity?* McKinsey Global Institute, June 2021. Also see *Forward Thinking on the transformative role of intangible assets in companies and economies with Jonathan Haskel and Stian Westlake*, McKinsey podcast, January 12, 2022; and *Profile: Professor Jonathan Haskel on demystifying the intangible economy*, Imperial Business School, September 3, 2024.

54   Note that revenue is a "flow" value that occurs on a recurring basis—every year—compared with the $2.5 million capital "stock" figure that reflects an accumulation of assets. See *TSMC valuation multiples*, Multiples, accessed July 2025.

55   For investments and productivity, see *Investing in productivity growth,* McKinsey Global Institute, March 2024; on roads, see Luo Wangshu, "Domestic road network grew by over 1 million kilometers in past decade," *China Daily*, November 24, 2023; on railway tracks, see *Factbox: Highlights of China's comprehensive transport network*, The State Council of the People's Republic of China, December 2020; and on cement, see Vaclav Smil, *How the World Really Works: A Scientist's Guide to Our Past, Present and Future*, Viking, 2022.

56   *Investing in productivity growth*, McKinsey Global Institute, March 2024.

57   This is, of course, a simplified view. For instance, significant liabilities are also created for

consumption or the public sector, which are not backed by assets, and some of the equity of wholly owned private firms is more a matter of accounting than a liability to someone else. See *The future of wealth and growth hangs in the balance*, McKinsey Global Institute, May 2023.

58   See, for instance, *The rise and rise of the global balance sheet: How productively are we using our wealth?* McKinsey Global Institute, November 2021; and *The future of wealth and growth hangs in the balance*, McKinsey Global Institute, May 2023.

59   For bank account ownership, see *Global Findex Database 2021 survey headline findings on account ownership*, World Bank, accessed July 2025; and *OECD members – account ownership*, Index Mundi, accessed July 2025; for loans, see *Global Banking Annual Review 2024: Attaining escape velocity*, McKinsey, October 2024.

60   *The enterprising archipelago: Propelling Indonesia's productivity*, McKinsey Global Institute, April 2025.

61   Felix Richter, *U.S. stock ownership is high but unequally distributed*, Statista, August 13, 2024; *The Economics of the Great Depression*, NCPedia, State Library of NC, Anchor, 2009. For Disney, see *Disney Magic comes to NYSE in IPO*, Goldman Sachs, accessed June 2025. The stock market multiples are calculated in real terms. China figures include Hong Kong. Also see *Market statistics – March 2025*, WFE Statistics, February 2025.

62   *Capital markets fact book*, Sifma, July 28, 2025; and Pallavi Rao, *Visualizing the $105 trillion world economy in one chart*, Visual Capitalist, August 2023.

63   MGI Global Balance Sheet database. For the United States, see *Total investment and transportation investment in fixed assets: 2014–2023*, Bureau of Transportation Statistics, accessed June 2025. For the EU, see *National accounts and GDP*, Statistics Explained, Eurostat, June 2025. For China, see *Investment in fixed assets in 2024*, National Bureau of Statistics of China, January 2025.

64   *Accelerating Europe: Competitiveness for a new era*, McKinsey Global Institute, January 2024.

65   For global R&D investment, see *Trends at the frontier in corporate R&D in the digital era: Facts, prospects and policies*, European Commission, discussion paper number 120, October 2019; for the effect of enterprise size on productivity, see *A microscope on small businesses: Spotting opportunities to boost productivity*, McKinsey Global Institute, May 2024; and Andrea Cani et al., *Making it big: Why developing countries need more large firms*, World Bank, 2020.

66   *Business dynamics and productivity*, OECD, March 2017.

67   *The power of one: How standout firms grow national productivity*, McKinsey Global Institute, May 2025.

68   *The power of one: How standout firms grow national productivity*, McKinsey Global Institute, May 2025.

CHAPTER 8 – INVENTION: IDEAS THAT MATTER

69   Tim Harford, *Fifty Things that Made the Modern Economy*, Little, Brown, 2017.

70   The cost of phone calls and computer memory and storage are adjusted for inflation. See "Rates on overseas phone calls decline," *New York Times*, May 19, 1982; and John C. McCallum, 2023; US Bureau of Labor Statistics, 2024, processed by Our World in Data. For the 1990s estimate of computer power costs, see *University of Kentucky supercomputer breaks the $1,000 per GFLOPS barrier*, May 2000. For a current estimate, see *Current flops prices*, AI Impacts, accessed August 2025. For the decline in the cost of TVs, see Ed Gresser, *PPI's trade fact of the week: The price of a 40-inch TV set has fallen by 99% in 25 years*, Our Work, January 3, 2024. See also Brian Santo, *The consumer electronics hall of fame: Fujitsu Plasma TV*, IEEE Spectrum, October 17, 2019.

71   *Harmonized Index of Consumer Prices: Hairdressing salons and personal grooming establishments for European Union*, Federal Reserve Economic Data (FRED), updated June 18, 2025; and US Census Bureau price index of new single-family homes under construction (inflation-adjusted) from the US Census, accessed August 2025. Crude oil prices are inflation-adjusted. For crude oil prices (1861 to 2024), see Energy Institute based on S&P Global Platts, *Statistical review of world energy*, 2025, processed by Our World in Data.

72   General-purpose technologies are transformative innovations with widespread applications across multiple industries, which drive significant economic and social change. They are pervasive, they evolve over time, becoming more efficient and cost-effective, and they catalyze complementary innovations, an example being the internet enabling e-commerce and cloud computing. General-purpose technologies often lead to surges in productivity. See Matt Ridley, *When ideas have sex*, TedGlobal, July 2010; and Deirdre N. McCloskey, "How the West (and the rest) got rich," *Wall Street Journal*, May 20, 2016.

73   *The first step: Langley's contributions to Apollo*, NASA, March 2019.

74   J. Bradford DeLong, *Slouching Towards Utopia: An Economic History of the Twentieth Century*, Basic Books, 2022; and "How Bell Labs invented the world we live in today," *Time*, March 21, 2012.

75   *Thomas Edison and Menlo Park*, Thomas Edison Center, accessed August 2025; and Paul B. Israel, "Inventing industrial research: Thomas Edison and the Menlo Park Laboratory," *Endeavour*, volume 26, issue 2, June 2002.

76   Jon Gertner, *The Idea Factory: Bell Labs and the Great Age of American Innovation*, Penguin, 2013.

77   For a discussion, see Joel Mokyr, *The Lever of Riches: Technological Creativity and Economic Progress*, Oxford University Press, 1990.

78   John Uri, *55 years ago: The first test flight of the Apollo Lunar Module*, NASA, January 23, 2023; *Boeing marks 30th anniversary of Apollo 11; built major components for lunar mission*, Boeing, July 14, 1999; and *Apollo*, IBM Heritage, accessed August 2025.

79   Chris Beyrer, *The long history of mRNA vaccines*, Johns Hopkins Bloomberg School of Public Health, October 2021; and *Shot of a lifetime: How Pfizer and BioNTech developed*

and manufactured a COVID-19 vaccine in record time, Pfizer, accessed August 2025.

80   The 2023 US R&D funding figures come from *Survey of federal funds for research and development 2023 – 2024*, US National Science Foundation and National Center for Science and Engineering Statistics, accessed August 2025. For funding of the Apollo program, see Nicolo Pastrone, *Space race and the cost of industrial policy*, Tax Foundation, July 2024.

81   *The next big arenas of competition*, McKinsey Global Institute, October 2024.

82   *National patterns of R&D resources: 2018–19 data update*, US National Science Foundation and National Center for Science and Engineering Statistics, April 2021; and "What is the current state of innovation? How rapidly is technology progressing and being embraced? What are the resulting societal impacts?" *Global Innovation Tracker 2024*, World Intellectual Property Organization, 2024.

83   This is Michael Kremer's O-ring theory, which sees tasks becoming more valuable economically as they become the bottleneck in the value chain, explained in David Autor, *Will automation take away all our jobs?* Ideas.Ted.com, March 2017. For IKEA, see Helen Reid, "IKEA bets on remote interior design as AI changes sales strategy," Reuters, June 13, 2023.

84   *Labour-saving technologies and employment levels: Are robots really making workers redundant?* OECD Science, Technology and Industry Policy Papers, January 2022; and Myrto Oikonomou, Nicola Pierri, and Yannick Timmer, *IT shields: Technology adoption and economic resilience during the COVID-19 pandemic*, Federal Reserve Board Finance and Economics Discussion Series, 2023.

CHAPTER 9 – ENERGY: POWERING PROGRESS

85   Jutta Bolt and Jan Luiten van Zanden, "Maddison style estimates of the evolution of the world economy: A new 2023 update," *Journal of Economic Surveys*, volume 39, issue 2, April 3, 2024.

86   For phosphate reserves, see *What is phosphate?* OCP, accessed September 2025; for Africa's first battery gigafactory, see "China's Gotion High-Tech to set up $1.3 billion EV battery gigafactory in Morocco," Reuters, June 6, 2024; and for mining in the Atlas Mountains, see *Morocco (advance release), 2020–2021 minerals yearbook*, US Geological Survey, 2025.

87   For share of electricity production from renewables, see Ember, 2025; Energy Institute, *Statistical review of world energy*, 2025, processed by Our World in Data. Also see *Universal electrification in Morocco*, International Energy Agency (IEA), August 2, 2023; and Magnus Johanson, *World's largest solar power plan delivers 24-hour energy*, World Steel Association, 2021.

88   For energy consumption, see US Energy Information Administration, 2025; Energy Institute, *Statistical review of world energy*, 2025; population based on various sources, 2024, processed by Our World in Data. Crude oil has an energy content of roughly 42 megajoules per kilogram. See J. T. Houghton et al., eds, *Revised 1996 IPCC guidelines for national greenhouse gas inventories, reference manual (volume 3), table 1–2*, accessed

September 2025. A person can generate about 100 watts—the power of steady cycling. This is roughly 660 megajoules over the course of a working year. That makes the 77,000 megajoules in 1,800 kilograms of oil equal to the annual labor of about 115 workers.

89   Fridolin Krausmann et al., "Growth in global materials use, GDP and population during the 20th century," *Ecological Economics*, volume 68, issue 10, August 15, 2009.

90   Keith O. Fuglie, Stephen Morgan, and Jeremy Jeliffe, *World agricultural production, resource use, and productivity 1961–2020*, US Department of Agriculture, February 2024; for statistics on sufficient production to meet global demand, see *Keynote address by CFS chair to the Community of Portuguese Speaking Countries*, Committee on World Food Security, October 19, 2022; for undernourishment statistics, see *Hunger numbers stubbornly high for three consecutive years as global crises deepen: UN report*, World Health Organization, July 24, 2024.

91   For the number of vehicles on the road, see Kersten Heineke, Nicholas Laverty, Timo Möller, and Felix Ziegler, "The future of mobility," *McKinsey Quarterly*, April 2023. For global statistics on large power plants, see *The world's nine largest operating power plants are hydroelectric facilities*, Today in Energy, US Energy Information Administration, October 2016. For the global electrification rate, see *Number of people lacking access to reliable electricity services*, United Nations Development Programme, 2022. See *Global energy perspective 2023*, McKinsey, October 2023; and *Pipeline network*, Pakistan Credit Rating Agency, 2022.

92   Global CO_2 emissions from energy combustion and industrial processes total about 37 gigatonnes, with about five gigatonnes in agriculture, forestry, and other land use. In the case of methane, more than approximately 35 percent of global emissions arise from the energy system, from combustion and industrial processes, with the remaining 65 percent divided between agriculture, at about 40 percent, and waste and other sectors, at about 25 percent; McKinsey EMIT database, 2023.

93   *Liquefied natural gas: Understanding the basic facts*, US Department of Energy, 2005; and *Flexibility in thermal power plants: With a focus on existing coal-fired power plants*, Agora Energiewende, June 2017. In the case of fertilizer, natural gas is a feedstock for most of today's production of ammonia, which is in turn used in nitrogen-based fertilizers. In the case of steel, while coking coal is the most commonly used fossil fuel, natural gas can also be used as a reductant in direct iron reduction processes. In the case of plastics, natural gas is used as feedstock in many regions, as a source of ethane.

94   For a discussion on the different commonly measured forms of energy, see Hannah Ritchie, *Primary, secondary, final, and useful energy: Why are there different ways of measuring energy?* Our World in Data, April 4, 2022.

95   Efficiency values here and in Exhibit 13 for fossil fuel vehicles represent the ratio of fuel burned to useful mechanical work performed; values for EVs represent battery-to-wheel efficiency. For turbines, efficiency represents the amount of primary energy converted into final energy in the form of electricity.

96   Adjusted for today's dollars.

97   Fossil fuel price index 1976 to 2024 draws on data from Energy Institute based on S&P Global Platts, *Statistical review of world energy*, 2025, processed by Our World in Data.

Also see *U.S. energy spending increased by more than 20% in 2022*, Today in Energy, US Energy Information Administration, August 28, 2024.

98   Global average energy use is in primary energy using the substitution method. See US Energy Information Administration, 2025; Energy Institute, *Statistical review of world energy*, 2025; population based on various sources, 2024, processed by Our World in Data. For people who do not yet have access to energy, see *Number of people lacking access to reliable electricity services*, United Nations Development Programme, 2022; and Laura Cozzi et al., *Access to electricity improves slightly in 2023, but still far from the pace needed to meet SDG7*, IEA, September 2023. Note that animal and human power are excluded.

99   For the increases in income per person, see Jutta Bolt and Jan Luiten van Zanden, "Maddison style estimates of the evolution of the world economy: A new 2023 update," *Journal of Economic Surveys*, volume 39, issue 2, April 3, 2024. For energy use per person, see US Energy Information Administration, 2025; Energy Institute, *Statistical review of world energy*, 2025; population based on various sources, 2024, processed by Our World in Data.

100   For data on dams, see Kimberly Nicole Lyon, Marcus J. Wishart, and Antonia Sohns, *What's the deal with dam data?* World Bank blog, September 23, 2024. For data on roads, see Nicolas de Loisy, *Transportation and the Belt and Road Initiative: A paradigm shift*, Transportation and the Belt and Road Initiative, Supply Chain Management Outsource Ltd., June 15, 2019.

101   *The problem with our dwindling sand reserves*, UN Environment Programme, February 6, 2023; and *Lime*, Mineral Commodity Summaries from 2005 to 2025, US Geological Survey.

102   Ed Conway, *Material World: A Substantial Story of Our Past and Future*, WH Allen, 2023; *Global materials perspective*, McKinsey, September 2024; and *Minerals products*, The Observatory of Economic Complexity, accessed April 2025.

103   Donella H. Meadows et al., *The Limits to Growth: A Report for The Club of Rome's Project on the Predicament of Mankind*, A Potomac Associates Book, 1972; Paul Alain-Hunt, "BHP partner says Filo copper discovery is largest in 30 years," Bloomberg, May 5, 2025; and *Russia begins production at largest untapped copper deposit*, Mining Technology, September 13, 2023. For copper reserves today, see *Copper*, Mineral Commodity Summary 2025, US Geological Survey. For copper reserves in 1950, see Dennis P. Cox, Nancy A. Wright, and George J. Oakley, *The nature and use of copper reserve and resource data*, Geological Survey professional paper 907-F, US Geological Survey, 1981.

104   *Lithium*, Mineral Commodity Summaries, US Geological Survey, in both 1996 and 2025.

105   See *Keynote address by CFS chair to the Community of Portuguese Speaking Countries*, Committee on World Food Security, October 12, 2022; and Figure 5.5, FAOSTAT: Suite of Food Security Indicators, Food and Agriculture Organization, October 2022.

106   *Norman E. Borlaug, 1914–2019*, Biographical Memoirs, National Academy of Sciences, accessed July 2025. Between 1970 and 1990, fertilizer use in developing countries soared by 360 percent, while pesticide application grew by 7 to 8 percent annually. Irrigation infrastructure expanded rapidly, bringing one-third more land under managed water

supply. See *Keynote address by CFS chair to the Community of Portuguese Speaking Countries,* Committee on World Food Security, October 12, 2022; and *Lessons from the green revolution: Towards a new green revolution*, technical background document, World Food Summit, November 13–17, 1996, Rome, Italy, Food and Agriculture Organization, 1996. For the proportion supported by fertilizer, see Hannah Ritchie, *How many people does synthetic fertilizer feed?* Our World in Data, November 7, 2017.

107   For instance, globally, wheat yields rose from 1.1 tonnes per hectare in 1961 to 2.2 tonnes per hectare by 1985, and rice yields from 1.9 tonnes per hectare to 3.3 tonnes per hectare over the same period, according to FAOSTAT data. See "Crops and livestock products," UN Food and Agriculture Organization (FAO), accessed July 2025; *Number of persons fed per farmer in the United States from 1940 to 2016*, Statista, accessed July 2025; for undernourishment statistics, see Food and Agriculture Organization of the United Nations, 2025, processed by Our World in Data.

108   Through multigenerational selection, broiler chickens now reach market weight in just six weeks—down from 16 weeks in the 1950s—using Cornish Cross lines bred for rapid growth and increased breast size. Dairy breeds like Holstein–Friesians yield about eight times more milk than their early-20th-century counterparts. Crop improvements include the popular UK potato variety Maris Piper (released in 1966), which was bred using wild potato genes to resist cyst nematodes, combining high yield with effective pest defense. See *How has selective breeding impacted agricultural species?* Tutor Chase, accessed July 2025; *Holstein–Friesian*, Britannica, accessed July 2025; and *Pyramiding resistances to potato cyst nematodes to produce potato cultivars with durable and broad-spectrum resistance*, AHDB, accessed July 2025. For the impact of novel gene-editing tools like CRISPR on agriculture, see Raj Kumar Joshi, Suhas Sutar Bharat, and Rukmini Mishra, "Engineering drought tolerance in plants through CRISPR/Cas genome editing," *3Biotech*, volume 10, article 400, August 2020; Dileep Kumar et al., "CRISPR-based genome editing for nutrient enrichment in crops: A promising approach toward global food security," *Frontiers in Genetics*, volume 13, 2022; and Suryapratap Ray, Sneha K, and Chitra Jangid, "CRISPR-Cas9 for sustainable food production: Impacts, recent advancements and future perspectives," *Food and Humanity*, volume 1, December 2023. For precision agriculture and the use of AI, see Abdellatif Soussi et al., "Smart sensors and smart data for precision agriculture: A review," *Sensors*, volume 24, issue 8, April 21, 2024; and Garima Gupta and Sudhir Kumar Pal, "Applications of AI in precision agriculture," *Discover Agriculture*, volume 3, number 51, April 25, 2025.

109   Interestingly, as incomes rise across Asia, Latin America, and Africa, diets are increasingly converging. Today, global diets are about 36 percent more similar than they were 50 years ago, reflecting a shift away from early-20th-century staples like cassava and sorghum toward homogenized plates centered on wheat, maize, and soy. Over the same period, global meat production has increased fivefold. Meat now accounts for 21 percent of total protein supply. In parallel, a growing interest in longevity is drawing people worldwide toward Japanese, Mediterranean, and plant-based diets that are valued for helping people live longer, healthier lives. For global meat production, see Food and Agriculture Organization of the United Nations, 2025, processed by Our World in Data. Also see *Food balance sheets 2010–2024. Global, regional, and country trends*, FAO, July 2024; Bryan Walsh, "Our global diet is becoming increasingly homogenized—and that's risky," *Time*, March 14, 2014; Marco Fiore et al., "Increasing life expectancy with plant

polyphenols: Lessons from the Mediterranean and Japanese diets," *Molecules*, volume 30, number 13, 2025; Max Roser, Hannah Ritchie, and Pablo Rosado, *Food supply*, Our World in Data, March 2013; and *World squanders over 1 billion meals a day – UN report*, UN Environmental Programme, March 27, 2024. Roughly 2.1 billion adults worldwide are overweight or obese today, up sharply from the past decade. The health toll is severe. In 2019, five million deaths and 160 million lost years of healthy life (disability-adjusted life years or DALYs) were directly linked to excess body weight, with rates of diet-related disability rising by 18 percent since 1990. As the World Health Organization warns, obesity now drives a wide range of noncommunicable diseases: diabetes, heart disease, hypertension, stroke, and even cancer. See "Global, regional, and national prevalence of adult overweight and obesity, 1990–2021, with forecasts to 2050: A forecasting study for the Global Burden of Disease Study 2021," *The Lancet*, March 2025; Saeid Safiri et al., "Burden of disease attributable to excess body weight in 204 countries and territories, 1990–2019," *Nutrition Journal*, volume 24, number 23, 2025; and *Controlling the global obesity epidemic*, World Health Organization, accessed July 2025.

CHAPTER 10 – CITIES: BETTER TOGETHER

110   For megacities in the 1950s, see *Urbanization and the megacity*, World Population History, accessed September 2025. For megacities in 2025, see *The largest cities worldwide in 2025*, Statistisches Bundesamt, accessed September 2025. For the discussion of Shanghai, see Lila Tj, *Shanghai Port City: The gateway of global maritime commerce*, Top China Freight, August 5, 2025; Christian Henriot, Shi Lu, and Charlotte Aubrun, *The Population of Shanghai (1865–1953)*, Brill, 2018; and *Resident population of the administrative area of Shanghai municipality, China from 1980 to 2024*, Statista, accessed September 2025.

111   Sarah Moser and Laurence Côté-Roy, "New cities: Power, profit, and prestige," *Geography Compass*, volume 15, issue 1, October 14, 2020.

112   For urban areas in India, see *Reforms in urban planning capacity in India*, NITI Aayog, September 2021. For the impact of urbanization on productivity, see *Investing in productivity growth*, McKinsey Global Institute, March 2024. For lifting 800 million out of poverty in China, see *Lifting 800 million people out of poverty – new report looks at lessons from China's experience*, World Bank, April 1, 2022. For urban vs rural income in China, see *Households' income and consumption expenditure in the first quarter of 2025*, National Bureau of Statistics of China, April 17, 2025.

113   *Canopy UK rental affordability index: Q1 2025*, Canopy, May 15, 2025.

114   *Urban world: Mapping the economic power of cities*, McKinsey Global Institute, March 2011; and Ed Glaeser, *Triumph of the City: How Our Greatest Invention Makes Us Richer, Smarter, Greener, Healthier, and Happier*, Penguin Books, 2002. The World Bank refers to dense cities as "pyramids" and sprawling ones as "pancakes"; development thrives on pyramids. See *Pancakes to pyramids: City form to promote sustainable growth*, World Bank, June 2021.

115   For a case study on Bangalore, see Ed Glaeser, *Triumph of the City: How Our Greatest Invention Makes Us Richer, Smarter, Greener, Healthier, and Happier*, Penguin Books,

2002. For its contribution to India's economy, see *IT ministers of Telangana, Karnataka on AIM list of top Indian policymakers*, South First, August 12, 2025.

116   Scottish Water annual accounts 2023/24; and *Keeping Singapore's potable water pipe network in good order*, PUB (Singapore's National Water Agency), February 5, 2025.

117   *Pixels of Progress: A granular look at human development around the world*, McKinsey Global Institute, December 2022; and *Global cities index 2024*, Oxford Economics, accessed June 2025.

118   For the urban-rural wage gap, see Sévane Ananian and Giulia Dellaferrera, *Employment and wage disparities between rural and urban areas*, International Labour Organization working paper, February 2024. For the disparity in Thailand and Mexico specifically, see "GDP per capita and population data for the provinces of Thailand," ThaiWebsites.com, updated November 2023; and *Distribution of gross domestic product (GDP) of Mexico in 2023, by federal entity*, Statista, accessed June 2025; and *GDP per capita (current US$) – Mexico*, World Bank, accessed June 2025.

119   Catherine Jewell, "The geography of innovation: Local hotspots, global networks," *WIPO Magazine*, World Intellectual Property Organization, December 2019.

120   Niall McCarthy, "Bollywood: India's film industry by the numbers (infographic)," *Forbes*, September 3, 2014.

121   *Company and employee statistics*, Region Stuttgart, IHK, accessed September 2025.

122   *Automotive industry in Baden-Württemberg*, Baden-Württemberg, accessed September 2025.

123   For the Huaqiangbei district area, see *Huaqiangbei Subdistrict*, The People's Government of Futian District, accessed September 2025. For the number of businesses, see Han Xin, "China's largest electronics commercial area Huaqiangbei propels entrepreneurship," *People's Daily*, August 16, 2024. Since 1997, prices of computer software and accessories and of televisions have decreased by more than 75 percent, according to the US Bureau of Labor Statistics, 2024.

CHAPTER 11 – TRADE: SHARED PROSPERITY

124   No precise share of employment can be determined, but agriculture represented 70 percent of GDP and had lower-than-average productivity, hence the 80 percent estimate. See Myung Soo Cha and Nak Nyeon Kim, "Korea's first industrial, 1911–1940," *Explorations in Economic History*, November 2010.

125   Assuming an eight-hour workday. See *Minimum wage system*, Minimum Wage Commission, Republic of Korea, accessed July 2025. Export-import figures come from the WTO and exclude intra-EU trade. See *Statistical tables*, World Trade Statistical Review, 2022.

126   Song Jung-a, "South Korea's academic race pushes half of under-6s into 'cram' schools," *Financial Times*, March 16, 2025.

127 For South Korean travel, see Moon Joon-hyun, "South Korea tourism surges in 2024 with record spending and arrivals," *Korea Herald*, February 5, 2025. For Netflix shows, see Govind Bhutada, *Ranked: The most-watched Netflix shows of all time*, Visual Capitalist, May 18, 2025.

128 World Bank Open Data, 2024.

129 See, for instance, Jeffrey A. Frankel and David Romer, "Does trade cause growth?" *American Economic Review*, volume 89, number 3, June 1999; *World Development Report 2020: Trading for development in the age of global value chains*, World Trade Organization, 2020; Elhanan Helpman and Paul Krugman, *Market Structure and Foreign Trade*, MIT Press, 1985; Philippe Aghion et al., "Competition and innovation: An inverted-U relationship," *Quarterly Journal of Economics*, volume 120, number 2, 2005; Wilfred Ethier, "National and international returns to scale in the modern theory of international trade," *American Economic Review*, volume 72, number 3, 1982; Gene Grossman and Elhanan Helpman, "Quality ladders in the theory of growth," *Review of Economic Studies*, volume 58, number 1, 1991; and James Markusen, "Trade in producer services and in other specialized, intermediate inputs," *American Economic Review*, volume 79, number 1, 1989.

130 Sharat Ganapati and Woan Foong Wong, "How far goods travel: Global transport and supply chains from 1965–2020," *Journal of Economic Perspectives*, volume 37, number 3, Summer 2023.

131 Marc Levinson, *The Box: How the Shipping Container Made the World Smaller and the World Economy Bigger*, Princeton University Press, 2010.

132 For the increase in container ship capacity, see Jitendra Bhonsle, *Evolution and upsizing of container vessels*, Margin Insight, February 2022; and Peter Nilson, *The top 10 largest container ships in the world*, Ship Technology, April 2024. For share of containerized trade, see *Value of containerized trade, 2020*, Port Economics, Management and Policy, accessed July 2025.

133 Katrina Kay, "Liquefied natural gas: The driving force behind global energy trade," *Oil & Gas Research*, volume 10, number 6, November 2024; *50 years of LNG carriers*, LNG Industry, June 2014; and *Global LNG market in 2023 and outlook for 2024*, Global LNG Hub, accessed August 2025. Oil tankers are typically sized in deadweight tons (DWT), which can then be converted to barrels of oil equivalent at about 7.33 barrels per ton. For example, the *Petrokure* in 1952 had a capacity of 38,000 DWT, while modern-day very large crude carriers and ultra-large crude carriers have capacities closer to 320,000 DWT to 550,000 DWT. See *Oil tanker sizes range from general purpose to ultra-large crude carriers on the AFRA scale*, Today in Energy, Energy Information Administration, September 16, 2014.

134 David Hummels, "Transportation costs and international trade over time," *Journal of Economic Perspectives*, volume 21, number 3, Summer 2007.

135 "The busiest flight routes of 2024," OAG, 2025.

136 *WTO annual report 2024*, World Trade Organization, 2024; and US International Trade Commission DataWeb, 2024.

137 Mario Larch, Erdal Yalcin, and Yoto V. Yotov, *Valuing the impact of the World Trade*

Organization (WTO), UK Department for International Trade, August 2022.

138 *Globally digitally delivered services trade surges to $4.3 trillion in 2023*, Econovis, January 2025; and *Digital trade for development*, IMF, OECD, United Nations, World Bank, and World Trade Organization, 2023.

139 Alan Mauldin, "International bandwidth demand surpasses 6.4 Pbps," TeleGeography, May 12, 2025.

140 Bastian Herre, Lucas Rodés-Guirao, and Max Roser, *War and peace*, Our World in Data, 2024.

141 Regional Trade Agreements Database, WTO OMC, accessed August 2025; and *Regional trade agreements*, World Trade Organization, accessed August 2025.

142 *What are the main criticisms of the World Bank and the IMF?* FAQ, Bretton Woods Project, June 4, 2019.

143 David Ricardo, *On the Principles of Political Economy and Taxation*, 1817.

144 For unbundling, see Richard Baldwin, T*rade and industrialization after globalisation's 2nd unbundling: How building and joining a supply chain are different and why it matters*, NBER working paper 17716, revised January 2013; on YKK, see Molly Liebergall, "The business empires you've never heard of behind 3 things you use every day," Morning Brew, March 28, 2024.

145 Samsung started out trading noodles in 1938, but entered electronics in 1969 before evolving into the corporation it is today. See Peter Bondarenko, *Samsung*, Britannica Money, August 24, 2025.

146 Jack Daly et al., *Trade flows in the age of automation*, Atlantic Council Geoeconomics Center, September 2020.

147 Leonard E. Read, *I, Pencil*, Foundation for Economic Education, 2015.

148 *Risk, resilience, and rebalancing in global value chains*, McKinsey Global Institute, August 2020.

149 *Geopolitics and the geometry of global trade*, McKinsey Global Institute, January 2024.

CHAPTER 12 – MARKETS: SCALING COOPERATION

150 "Walmart releases Q4 and FY24 earnings," Walmart, February 20, 2024.

151 *The power of one: How standout firms grow national productivity*, McKinsey Global Institute, May 2025; and *A microscope on small businesses: Spotting opportunities to boost productivity*, McKinsey Global Institute, May 2024.

152 *The enterprising archipelago: Propelling Indonesia's productivity*, McKinsey Global Institute, April 2025.

153 *Gross fixed capital formation, private sector (% of GDP)*, World Bank, accessed September 2025; and *Gross fixed capital formation (% of GDP)*, World Bank, accessed September 2025.

154   *The next big arenas of competition*, McKinsey Global Institute, October 2024. Sixty
      percent is not a precise average, but all large, R&D-intensive economies (China, Japan,
      and the United States) hover between 55 and 65 percent. Smaller, R&D-intensive
      economies (Israel, Sweden, and Switzerland) are closer to 70 percent. Most other
      countries fall below 50 percent. See *Global investments in R&D*, UNESCO Institute for
      Statistics, fact sheet number 59, June 2020.

155   For the difference between large and small firms, see Norman Loayza, *Achieving growth
      and resilience: Governments can't do it alone*, World Bank blog, August 1, 2023. Pay varies
      significantly in different countries and industries. Because wages are tightly linked to
      productivity per worker, industries and countries where the productivity gap between
      small and large firms is big will have higher pay gaps. See Andrea Ciani et al., *Making it
      big: Why developing countries need more large firms*, World Bank 2020; and *Updated
      and expanded small business statistics 2022*, Survey of Current Business, US Bureau of
      Economic Analysis, 2023. For the contribution of work experience to lifetime earnings,
      see *Human capital at work: The value of experience*, McKinsey Global Institute, June 2022.

156   *Responsible supply chain: Environmental and social responsibility embedded in the supply
      chain*, Airbus, accessed July 2025.

157   Caroline Freund and Martha Denisse Pierola, "Export superstars," *The Review of
      Economics and Statistics*, volume 97, number 5, December 2015; *Global flows: The ties
      that bind in an interconnected world*, McKinsey Global Institute, November 2022; *Global
      value chains and development: Investment and value added trade in the global economy*,
      UNCTAD, 2013; and Patrick McGee, *Apple in China: The Capture of the World's Greatest
      Company*, Simon & Schuster UK, 2025.

158   Spencer Y. Kwon, Yueran Ma, and Kaspar Zimmermann, "100 years of rising corporate
      concentration," *American Economic Review*, volume 114, number 7, July 2024. Large firms
      as defined by each of the 16 countries studied; definitions vary; see *A microscope on
      small businesses: Spotting opportunities to boost productivity*, McKinsey Global Institute,
      May 2024; Zhang Chen, *Economic growth and the rise of large firms*, STEG working
      paper, August 2023; *The "New American" Fortune 500*, Partnership for a New American
      Economy, June 2011; and *Fortune 500*, accessed August 2025.

159   McKinsey Value Intelligence Platform.

160   *The next big arenas of competition*, McKinsey Global Institute, October 2024.

161   *Annual Report 2025*, Walmart, 2025.

162   Mary Meeker et al., *Trends – artificial intelligence (AI)*, Bond, May 2025.

163   *The power of one: How standout firms grow national productivity*, McKinsey Global
      Institute, May 2025.

164   For poverty in China, see "Lifting 800 million people out of poverty – new report looks
      at lessons from China's experience," World Bank, April 1, 2022. Alibaba's revenue
      figures from *Alibaba Group Holding Limited*, Form 20-F, US Securities and Exchange
      Commission, accessed July 2025.

165   *The Richard C. Adkerson Gallery on the SEC role in accounting standards setting*,

Securities and Exchange Commission Historical Society, accessed July 2025.

166 Daron Acemoglu and James A. Robinson, *Why Nations Fail: The Origins of Power, Prosperity, and Poverty*, Profile Books, 2013; and Daron Acemoglu and James A. Robinson, *The Narrow Corridor: States, Societies, and the Fate of Liberty*, Penguin, 2019.

167 Antoine Dechezleprêtre, Daniel Nachtigall, and Frank Venmans, "The joint impact of the European Union emissions trading system on carbon emissions and economic performance," *Journal of Environmental Economics and Management*, volume 118, March 2023.

168 *Education at a glance 2024 – country notes: Switzerland*, OECD, September 10, 2024; *Swiss teachers: Well-paid but stressed*, Expatica News, accessed August 2025; and *World University Rankings 2025*, Times Higher Education, accessed July 2025.

169 Robert D. Putnam, "Bowling alone: America's declining social capital," *Journal of Democracy*, volume 6, issue 1, January 1995; Jonathan Muringani, Rune D. Fitjar, and Andrés Rodríguez-Pose, "Social capital and economic growth in the regions of Europe," *Environment and Planning A: Economy and Space*, volume 53, issue 6, March 2021; and Luigi Guiso, Paola Sapienza, and Luigi Zingales, *The role of social capital in financial development*, NBER working paper number 7563, February 2000.

PART III
PROGRESS AT THE CROSSROADS

————

CHAPTER 13 – CAN THE PROGRESS MACHINE KEEP HUMMING?

1   *Dependency and depopulation: Confronting the consequences of a new demographic reality*, McKinsey Global Institute, January 2025.

2   The concept of Medicine 3.0, introduced by Peter Attia, is now popularly used to describe a proactive form of healthcare that focuses on preventing chronic illnesses, such as heart disease, diabetes, and Alzheimer's, through personalized tests, technology, lifestyle changes, and early screenings. Instead of waiting to treat people after they get sick (as in Medicine 2.0), it aims to keep people healthier for longer. See Peter Attia, MD, *Outlive: The Science and Art of Longevity*, Harmony, 2023.

3   These older adults most often cite a lack of attractive opportunities and difficulty in landing jobs as their primary barriers to work. See Hemant Ahlawat, Anthony Darcovich, Martin Dewhurst, Ellen Feehan, Viktor Hediger, and Madeline Maud, "Age is just a number: How older adults view healthy aging," McKinsey Health Institute, May 22, 2023.

4   Andrew J. Scott, *The 100-Year Life: Living and Working in an Age of Longevity*, Bloomsbury Information, 2016; and Andrew J. Scott, *The Longevity Imperative: How to Build a Healthier and More Productive Society to Support Our Longer Lives*, Basic Books, 2024.

5   *Dependency and depopulation: Confronting the consequences of a new demographic reality*, McKinsey Global Institute, January 2025.

6   A 2025 United Nations report found that 39 percent of people in 14 countries said they were having fewer children than they wanted, mostly because of financial pressure. An additional 21 percent cited job insecurity, and 19 percent pointed to unaffordable housing. One in six globally face infertility at some point in their lives. See "The real fertility crisis: The pursuit of reproductive agency in a changing world," *State of world population 2025*, UNFPA, 2025; and "Infertility prevalence estimates, 1990–2021," World Health Organization, 2023. For a discussion on extending reproductive lives, see Ruxandra Teslo, *Fertility on demand*, Works in Progress, March 2025. For a discussion on how new home appliances and antibiotics drove the 20th-century baby boom, see Derek Thompson, *What caused the "baby boom"? What would it take to have another?*, Derek Thompson Substack, July 15, 2025.

7   *On the cusp of a new era?* McKinsey Global Institute, October 2022.

8   *Investing in productivity growth,* McKinsey Global Institute, March 2024.

9   MGI has published extensively on the global balance sheet. See *The rise and rise of the global balance sheet: How productively are we using our wealth?* November 2021; *Global balance sheet 2022: Enter volatility,* December 2022; *The future of wealth and growth hangs in the balance,* May 2023; and research published in 2025 on scenarios for the next decade.

10   The situation is somewhat different for emerging economies, where more financial market development is needed to support a catch-up in financial balance sheets relative to GDP and to productive assets toward ratios seen in advanced economies. However, even in these cases, rapid growth in assets such as infrastructure relative to GDP can be a sign of low capital productivity, and debt and financial deepening growth can become excessive.

11   For global debt, see *Fiscal consolidation: An optimal control approach,* Conseil D'analyse Economique (CAE), July 2024. The debt numbers include debt across governments, nonfinancial corporations, and households. For debt in Japan and China, see *Japan general government gross debt to GDP,* Trading Economics, accessed August 2025; and *Assessing vulnerabilities of China's corporate sector,* International Monetary Fund, August 2024.

12   For transmission lines in the United States, see Nathan Shreve, Zachary Zimmerman, and Rob Gramlich, *Fewer new miles: The US transmission grid in the 2020s,* Grid Strategies, July 2024; on housing shortages, see *Spain: Reasons behind the scarce supply of housing,* BBVA Research, July 2024.

13   Ezra Klein and Derek Thompson, *Abundance: How We Build a Better Future,* Profile Books, 2025.

14   Jonathan Jones, *U.S. cities building the most homes,* Construction Coverage, July 2025.

15   This impact was driven by specific interventions. For instance, Aadhaar eKYC and DigiLocker enabled banks, telecom providers, and governments to verify identities and documents in minutes instead of weeks. The Jan Dhan–Aadhaar–Mobile trinity connected more than 400 million people, such as farmers receiving crop subsidies, women accessing maternity benefits, and rural households receiving wages from employment programs to no-frills bank accounts, while UPI eliminated the need for cards and ATMs by enabling instant, zero-cost digital payments, even on basic phones, helping street vendors, gig workers, and small businesses transact seamlessly. See *Digital public infra added 0.9% to India's GDP in 2022; contribution to triple by 2030: report,* ETGovernment.com, February 22, 2024.

16   *IP facts and figures,* World Intellectual Property Organization, accessed August 2024.

17   See Nicholas Bloom et al., *Are ideas getting harder to find?* NBER working paper number 23782, September 2017. In 1971, "improvement" meant Moore's law—doubling transistors and computing power every two years through relatively simple advances in silicon and lithography. Today, by contrast, progress requires nanometer-scale fabrication, EUV lithography, 3D architectures, and highly specialized processes that demand cutting-edge equipment, precision engineering, and expertise across multiple scientific disciplines.

18 Some new research questions the thesis that ideas are getting harder to find, claiming that ideas are plentiful and that the bottleneck is translation into economic impact. See, for instance, Teresa C. Fort et al., *Growth is getting harder to find, not ideas*, Center for Economic Studies, April 2025. For new inventions like the internet being less transformative than past ones, see Robert Gordon, *The Rise and Fall of American Growth: The U.S. Standard of Living since the Civil War*, Princeton University Press, 2016; the topic is also discussed in Tyler Cowen, *The Great Stagnation: How America Ate All the Low-Hanging Fruit of Modern History, Got Sick, and Will (Eventually) Feel Better,* Dutton, 2011.

19 For opportunities beyond AI, see *The next big arenas of competition*, McKinsey Global Institute, October 2024; and *The bio revolution: Innovations transforming economies, societies, and our lives*, McKinsey Global Institute, May 2020. For CRISPR technology, see Heidi Ledford, "World's first personalized CRISPR therapy given to baby with genetic disease," *Nature*, May 2025; on novel materials, see *Caliche: A startup harnessing microbes to capture industrial carbon emissions*, Your Story, June 9, 2025; and *Super Bamboo – eco-friendly "super bamboo" outperforms steel, providing a low-cost green material solution,* CityU, October 2024.

20 *Investing in productivity growth*, McKinsey Global Institute, March 2024; Erik Brynjolfsson, Daniel Rock, and Chad Syverson, "The productivity J-curve: How intangibles complement general purpose technologies," *American Economic Journal: Macroeconomics,* volume 13, number 1, January 2021; and *Erik Brynjolfsson: The key to growth? Race with the machines. Summary and Q&A*, TED Videos, August 2025.

21 Energy Institute, *Statistical review of world energy*, 2025; Smil, 2017, processed by Our World in Data. Electricity accounts for roughly 20 percent of final energy consumption. See *Global energy perspective 2025,* McKinsey, September 2025.

22 Hannah Ritchie and Pablo Rosado, *Energy mix*, Our World in Data, July 2020 (updated January 2024); *Global electricity review 2025*, Ember, April 2025; and Alex Lawson, "Google to buy nuclear power for AI datacentres in 'world first' deal," *Guardian,* October 15, 2024.

23 *Renewable energy statistics 2024,* International Renewable Energy Agency, July 2024; Lauren Holtmeier, "Global renewables capacity increased by new record in 2024, IRENA boss says," S&P Global, January 12, 2025; *Global EV outlook 2024*, International Energy Agency, April 2024; and EV Volumes (2024). Note that all passenger BEV sales from 2010 to 2024 (including only cars) are accounted for in the calculation of the share of passenger BEV sales that occurred in the past five years.

24 *The hard stuff: Navigating the physical realities of the energy transition,* McKinsey Global Institute, August 2024.

25 *The hard stuff: Navigating the physical realities of the energy transition*, McKinsey Global Institute, August 2024.

26 "The energy transition: Where are we really?" McKinsey, August 27, 2024.

27 Global Trade Alert; and *Geopolitics and the geometry of global trade*, McKinsey Global Institute, January 2024.

28 *Geopolitics and the geometry of global trade*, McKinsey Global Institute, January 2024;

Global flows: The ties that bind in an interconnected world, McKinsey Global Institute, November 2022; and "The complication of concentration in global trade," McKinsey Global Institute, January 12, 2023.

29   For rare earths, see Gracelin Baskaran, "What China's ban on rare earths processing technology exports means," Center for Strategic & International Studies, January 2024; on pharmaceutical ingredients, see Chandana D, "Overview of the active pharmaceutical ingredient market," IQVIA Chemical Intelligence, February 2024; and on semiconductors, see "Taiwan's dominance of the chip industry makes it more important," *Economist*, March 6, 2023.

30   As introduced in Part I, geopolitical distance is defined as the difference between countries' political positions based on their UN General Assembly votes between 2005 and 2022. See *Geopolitics and the geometry of global trade*, McKinsey Global Institute, January 2024.

31   "The great trade rearrangement," McKinsey Global Institute, June 25, 2025.

32   For Asia trade, see *Asia on the cusp of a new era*, McKinsey Global Institute, September 2023. For cross-border flows, see "The great trade rearrangement," McKinsey Global Institute, June 25, 2025; and *Digital globalization: The new era of global flows*, McKinsey Global Institute, March 2016. The OECD found that a "localized regime" in which trade was 18 percent lower would result in the level of global GDP being 6 percent lower. See *Global value chains: Efficiency and risks in the context of COVID-19, OECD Policy Responses to Coronavirus (COVID-19)*, OECD, February 2021. The Peterson Institute for International Economics estimated that 11 percent of US GDP was a direct result of increased trade since the 1960s. See Gary Clyde Hufbauer and Zhiyao (Lucy) Lu, *The payoff to America from globalization: A fresh look with a focus on costs to workers*, policy brief number 17-16, Peterson Institute for International Economics, May 2017. Also see Arnaud Costinot and Andrés Rodríguez-Clare, "Trade theory with numbers: Quantifying the consequences of globalization," in *Handbook of International Economics*, volume 4, Gita Gopinath, Elhanan Helpman, and Kenneth Rogoff, eds., Elsevier, 2014; and Richard Baldwin, *Globalization's three unbundlings*, Harvard University Press, 2016.

33   Bob Sternfels, Oliver Bevan, Daniel Pacthod, and Olivia White, "Strengthening fraying ties: The Global Cooperation Monitor 2024," McKinsey, February 27, 2024.

34   Peter Van den Bossche, *Can the WTO dispute settlement system be revived? Options for addressing a major governance failure of the World Trade Organization*, WTI working paper number 03, World Trade Institute, 2023.

35   *Geopolitics and the geometry of global trade*, McKinsey Global Institute, January 2024.

36   Andrew Daniller, *Americans take a dim view of the nation's future, look more positively at the past*, Pew Research Center, April 2023; and Jacob Poushter, *Worldwide, people are divided on whether life today is better than in the past,* Pew Research Center, December 2017.

37   Young adults in the Anglosphere are losing faith in the idea that hard work is rewarded with success. See John Burn-Murdoch, "Why are young adults in the English-speaking world so unhappy?" *Financial Times*, July 25, 2025. For zero-sum thinking, see Sahil Chinoy et al., *Zero-sum thinking and the roots of US political differences*, NBER working

paper number 31688, April 2025.

38   *Public trust in government: 1958–2024*, Pew Research Center, June 2024; and Edelman Trust Barometers for 2021 and 2025, Edelman, accessed September 2025.

39   *2025 Edelman Trust Barometer reveals high level of grievance towards government, business, and the rich*, Edelman, January 2025.

40   *Public trust in government: 1958–2024*, Pew Research Center, June 2024; Edelman Trust Barometers for 2021, 2023, and 2025; and *Is trust in crisis?* Ipsos Global Trustworthiness Monitor, accessed August 2025.

41   Rachel Minkin et al., *The experiences of U.S. adults who don't have children*, Pew Research Center, July 2024.

42   Joel Mokyr, *A Culture of Growth: The Origins of the Modern Economy*, Princeton University Press, 2016.

CHAPTER 14 – THE BALANCE OF PROGRESS

43   David H. Autor, David Dorn, and Gordon H. Hanson, "The China Syndrome: Local labor market effects of import competition in the United States," *American Economic Review*, volume 103, number 6, October 2013; and Daron Acemoglu and Pascual Restrepo, "Robots and jobs: Evidence from US labor markets," *Journal of Political Economy*, volume 128, number 6, April 2020.

44   In the United States, many prominent people have made this argument. Here are just a few examples. In 2015, Elizabeth Warren said, "Well, since 1980, guess how much of the growth in income over the last 32 years—how much of the growth in income did the 90 percent get? Zero. None. Nothing. In fact, it is worse than that. The average family not in the top 10 percent makes less money today than they were making a generation ago." See Lauren Carroll, *Warren: The average family in the bottom 90 percent made more money 30 years ago*, Politifact, The Poynter Institute, January 2015. In 2016, Bernie Sanders said that real wages had been falling for 40 years. See "Bernie Sanders, On how to hold Donald Trump accountable," *PBS News Hour*, November 21, 2016. *Time* magazine reported Donald Trump saying during the 2016 presidential campaign that the real wages of workers had not been raised for 18 years. See Haley Sweetland Edwards, "Why Donald Trump might be wrong about the economy," *Time*, June 22, 2016. Nobel laureate Joseph Stiglitz has observed that since the late 1970s, the productivity of workers has doubled, but wages have stagnated. See Jon Healey, *Joseph E. Stiglitz: A Nobel laureate reflects*, Table Talk, UCLA Blue Print, Fall 2015. In a documentary, economist Robert Reich said that, since 1980, productivity had continued to rise, but inflation-adjusted wages had dropped. See *Inequality for all*, 2013. Finally, and most recently, an opinion piece in the *New York Times* said, "Blue-collar private-sector workers were actually earning more, on average, in 1972, after adjusting for inflation, than they are now." See Nicolas Kristoff, "Maybe now Democrats will address working-class pain," *New York Times*, November 9, 2024.

45   See Adam Ozimek, John Lettieri, and Benjamin Glasner, *The American worker: Toward*

a new consensus, Economic Innovation Group, June 2024. This study evaluates several metrics: hourly wage, weekly wage, hourly compensation, weekly compensation, and workers' annual family income. All of them show a 35 to 45 percent increase.

46   For the United States, see *Trends in the distribution of household income from 1979 to 2021,* Congressional Budget Office, September 2024. For the bottom quintile, we use 1980 to 2019 because the latest data point, 2021, is highly distorted by the impact of the COVID-19 pandemic, making income gains even higher due to temporary pandemic-related transfers. For reference, the income of the top 20 percent grew by 122 percent pretax and 131 percent posttax. For France, the numbers are after taxes and transfers, from 1979 to 2018. See *Household income and wealth 2021 edition*, INSEE, May 2021. For China, see Sonali Jain-Chandra et al., *Inequality in China: Trends, drivers and policy remedies*, IMF working paper number 18/127, 2018. Another popular, and in this case global, way to look at this is using Milanovic's "Elephant Chart," which shows the evolution of global incomes by percentile between 1988 and 2008. See Christoph Lakner and Branko Milanovic, *Global income distribution: From the fall of the Berlin Wall to the Great Recession*, Policy Research working paper number 6719, World Bank, December 2013. This chart has been widely interpreted as proof that the working class in advanced economies has been stagnant for decades. The reality is that what the trough of the chart reflected was Japan's lost decade and the collapse of the Soviet Union, not stagnant middle classes in the United States and Europe; see Homi Kharas and Brina Seidel, *What's happening to the world income distribution? The elephant chart revisited*, Global Economy & Development working paper number 114, Brookings Institution, April 2018. Additionally, the updated chart until 2018 has lost the original shape and no longer supports the thesis of working-class stagnation. See Chris Giles, "The globalization elephant has left the room," *Financial Times*, November 24, 2022.

47   The debate on wages decoupling from productivity has a long history. An Economic Policy Institute report initiated it. See Josh Bivens and Lawrence Mishel, *Understanding the historic divergence between productivity and a typical worker's pay: Why it matters and why it's real,* Economic Policy Institute briefing paper number 406, September 2015. Later research has established that the link between wages and productivity remains strong, and decoupling can be explained. See, for example, Scott Winship, *Understanding trends in worker pay over the past 50 years*, American Enterprise Institute, May 2024; Anna Stansbury and Lawrence H. Summers, *Productivity and pay: Is the link broken?* Peterson Institute for International Economics, June 2018; and *A new look at the declining labor share of income in the United States,* McKinsey Global Institute, May 2019. For the United Kingdom, see Andreas Teichgräber and John Van Reenen, *Have productivity and pay decoupled in the UK?* Centre for Economic Performance, November 2021.

48   For empowerment, see *From poverty to empowerment: Raising the bar for sustainable and inclusive growth,* McKinsey Global Institute, September 2023. For the rising costs of basic necessities, see Mark J. Perry, *Chart of the day ... or century?* AEI, July 2022. For Germany, see *Inflation rate at +7.9% in 2022*, Statistisches Bundesamt, January 2023.

49   We focus on income inequality and generally use the ratio of the top 10 percent to the bottom 50 percent, or the Gini coefficient. In any case, the broad patterns over a century are similar across inequality metrics.

50   The Great Divergence started earlier, in the 19th century, and the pattern we capture here is its continuation. See Kenneth Pomeranz, *The Great Divergence: China, Europe, and the Making of the Modern World Economy,* Princeton University Press, 2000; Angus Maddison, *The world economy: A millennial perspective*, OECD, 2001; Mark Koyama and Jared Rubin, *How the World Became Rich: The Historical Origins of Economic Growth*, Polity, 2022; and Joel Mokyr, *The Enlightened Economy: An Economic History of Britain, 1700-1850*, Yale University Press, 2010. For more on the Great Convergence, see Richard Baldwin, *The Great Convergence: Information Technology and the New Globalization*, Harvard University Press, 2019; Branko Milanovic, *Global Inequality: A New Approach for the Age of Globalization*, Harvard University Press, 2016; and Xavier Sala-i-Martin, "The world distribution of income: Falling poverty and … convergence, period," *The Quarterly Journal of Economics*, volume 121, number 2, May 2006.

51   The Gini coefficient is a statistical measure of inequality, usually applied to income or wealth distribution. It uses a scale from zero, which means total equality, to one, which is total inequality. Inequality sparks vivid debates in the economics community. Some argue that US inequality has increased less than is often claimed, and practically not at all after accounting for taxes and transfers. But the majority of studies find growing inequality in the United States since the 1980s. See Gerald Auten and David Splinter, "Income inequality in the United States: Using tax data to measure long-term trends," *Journal of Political Economy,* volume 132, number 7, July 2024; Thomas Piketty, Emmanuel Saez, and Gabriel Zucman, "Distributional national accounts: Methods and estimates for the United States," *The Quarterly Journal of Economics*, volume 133, number 2, May 2018; and *Trends in the distribution of household income from 1979 to 2021*, Congressional Budget Office, September 2024.

52   For the Kuznets curve, see Simon Kuznets, "Economic growth and income inequality," *The American Economic Review*, volume XLV, number one, March 1955. For China's Gini coefficient, see World Bank Poverty and Inequality Platform, 2025, processed by Our World in Data.

53   For inequality, see *Rising inequality? A stocktake of the evidence*, Australian Government Productivity Commission, August 2018; and *Fairly equal? Economic mobility in Australia*, Australian Government Productivity Commission, 2024. For social spending, see OECD, 2023; OECD, 1985; Lindert, 2004, processed by Our World in Data; and *Social expenditure database (SOCX)*, OECD, accessed June 2025.

54   MGI has published a series on the future of work, including *Jobs lost, jobs gained: What the future of work will mean for jobs, skills, and wages,* November 2017; *Skill shift: Automation and the future of the workforce*, May 2018; and *The future of work after COVID-19*, February 2021.

55   David H. Autor, David Dorn, and Gordon H. Hanson, *On the persistence of the China shock,* National Bureau of Economic Research working paper number 29041, October 2021; and David H. Autor, David Dorn, and Gordon H. Hanson, *The China syndrome: Local labor market effects of import competition in the United States,* National Bureau of Economic Research working paper number 18054, May 2012.

56   For Flint auto job decline, see Employees: Manufacturing: Durable Goods: Motor Vehicle Manufacturing in Michigan, FRED, accessed September 2025. For population declines,

see "Flint census reflects dwindling GM presence," ABC7 Chicago, March 23, 2011; and US Census data. For a broader history of Flint, Detroit, Michigan, and the auto industry, see Eric Scorsone and Nicolette Bateson, "Case study: City of Flint, Michigan," in *Long-Term Crisis and Systemic Failure: Taking the Fiscal Stress of America's Older Cities Seriously*, Michigan State University, 2011; Andrew Highsmith, *Demolition Means Progress: Flint, Michigan, and the Fate of the American Metropolis*, University of Chicago Press, 2015; and Edward McClelland, *Midnight in Vehicle City: General Motors, Flint, and the Strike that Created the Middle Class*, Beacon Press, 2021. For more recent investment news, see Melissa Burden and Michael Wayland, "GM to invest $877M in Flint truck plant," *Detroit News*, April 8, 2015.

57   For the "Bilbao effect," see Marc Wouters, "Reinventing Bilbao, the story of the Bilbao Effect," in *Innovating Strategies and Solutions for Urban Performance and Regeneration*, Cristina Piselli et al., eds., Springer, 2022; for foreign investment, see "fDi European cities and regions of the future 2024," *fDi Intelligence*, 2024.

58   Noah Smith, *Globalization did not hollow out the American middle class,* Noahpinion, May 8, 2025; Noah Smith, *So why *did* U.S. wages stagnate for 20 years?* Noahpinion, May 18, 2025; *Current Employment Statistics and Current Population Survey (CPS) – Merged Outgoing Rotation Group Earnings Data.* Data treated by the Economic Innovation Group. The two surveys are conducted by the US Bureau of Labor Statistics.

59   *Global energy perspective 2025,* McKinsey, September 2025.

60   The ten-year average global temperature (2013 to 2023) relative to the average from 1850 to 1900. See *State of the global climate 2023*, World Meteorological Organization, March 2024.

61   Hannah Ritchie, *Who has contributed most to global CO_2 emissions?* Our World in Data, October 1, 2019.

62   For China's emissions, see Global Carbon Budget, 2024, processed by Our World in Data. For poverty reduction, see *Four decades of poverty reduction in China: Drivers, insights for the world, and the way ahead (English)*, World Bank, July 2022. Over the past 40 years, the number of people in China with incomes below $1.90 per day—the international poverty line as defined by the World Bank to track global extreme poverty—has fallen by close to 800 million. Income per person went from $1,600 to $22,100 between 1990 and 2023, and energy consumption per capita from 6,881 kilowatts per hour to 33,267. See Hannah Ritchie, Max Roser, and Pablo Rosado, *Energy*, Our World in Data, 2022.

63   *Climate change 2021: The physical science basis*, IPCC Sixth Assessment Report, IPCC, August 2021.

64   RCP8.5 is a high-emissions scenario that was referred to as "baseline," suggesting that it was a likely outcome if society did not make concerted efforts to cut greenhouse gas emissions. See, for example, "Summary for policymakers," in *AR5 synthesis report: Climate change 2014*, IPCC, 2014. Today the equivalent scenario is SSP5-8.5, according to which temperatures would rise between 3.3°C and 5.7°C. SSP2-4.5 is a middle-of-the-road scenario with intermediate greenhouse gas emissions. For these two pathways, see "Summary for policymakers," in *Climate change 2021: The physical science basis, Contribution of Working Group I to the Sixth Assessment Report of the Intergovernmental*

Panel on Climate Change, IPPC, 2021.

65   About one-third of greening between 2000 and 2017 came from China and India thanks to land-use management. Overall, one-third of Earth's vegetated lands are greening, while 5 percent are growing browner. See *China and India lead the way in greening*, Earth Observatory, accessed July 2025; Chi Chen et al., "China and India lead in greening of the world through land-use management," *Nature*, February 2019; Xin Chen et al., "The global greening continues despite increased drought stress since 2000," *Global Ecology and Conservation*, volume 9, January 2024; and Karl B. Hille, "Carbon dioxide fertilization greening Earth, study finds," NASA, April 26, 2016. For mortality from heat and cold, see David García-León et al., "Temperature-related mortality burden and projected change in 1368 European regions: A modelling study," *The Lancet,* volume 9, number 9, September 2024; and Bjorn Lomborg, *The heresy of heat and cold deaths,* accessed July 2025.

66   Eurostat, OECD, and World Bank, 2025; Global Carbon Budget, 2024, processed by Our World in Data. A common argument is that advanced countries simply offshore their production, but the argument rests on consumption-based data, so already accounts for offshored emissions. The only data point that does not account for offshored emissions is the UK one, because such a long time series does not exist on a trade-adjusted basis. If we factor in offshored emissions, the United Kingdom has not had rising emissions at least since 1990 and has experienced sharply falling emissions since 2005. For a full treatment of not only emissions but also most materials use decoupling from economic growth, see Andrew McAfee, *More From Less: The Surprising Story of How We Learned to Prosper Using Fewer Resources—and What Happens Next*, Scribner, 2019.

67   China's share of emissions comes from EDGAR, accessed June 2025. GDP data come from the World Bank. For China's electricity, see *Where does China get its electricity?* IEA, accessed June 2025; and *Why is solar PV important?* IEA, accessed June 2025. For China's nuclear energy, see *World energy investment 2024*, IEA, June 2024. For whether China's emissions have peaked, see Lauri Myllyvirta, *Analysis: Clean energy just put China's CO_2 emissions into reverse for first time*, Carbon Brief, May 2025.

68   Max Roser, *Why did renewables become so cheap so fast?* Our World in Data, December 2020 (updated April 2025); and *Nuclear power plants generated 68% of France's electricity in 2021*, Today in Energy, EIA, January 23, 2023.

69   For deaths from natural disasters, see Our World in Data based on EM-DAT, CRED/ UCLouvain, Brussels, Belgium (D. Guha-Sapir), processed by Our World in Data, accessed June 2025. The list of natural disasters in this data set includes droughts, floods, earthquakes, storms, extreme temperatures, volcanoes, wildfires, glacial lake outbursts, mass movements (dry and wet), and fogs. For Bangladesh, see Ubydul Haque et al., "Reduced death rates from cyclones in Bangladesh: What more needs to be done?" *Bulletin of the World Health Organization*, volume 90, number 2, October 2011. For other natural disasters, see Hannah Ritchie, Pablo Rosado, and Max Roser, *Natural disasters: How many people die from disasters, and how are these impacts changing over time?* Our World in Data, accessed July 2025.

70   See, for instance, Alex Epstein, *Fossil Future: Why Global Human Flourishing Requires More Oil, Coal, and Natural Gas—Not Less,* Portfolio, 2022; Bjorn Lomborg, *False Alarm: How Climate Change Panic Costs Us Trillions, Hurts the Poor, and Fails to Fix the Planet,*

Basic Books, 2020; and Michael Shellenberger, *Apocalypse Never: Why Environmental Alarmism Hurts Us All,* Harper, 2020.

71   Matt Brannon, *Home insurance rates to rise 8% in 2025, after a 20% increase in the last two years,* Insurify, accessed August 2025.

72   Simon Dietz and Bruno Lanz, "Growth and adaptation to climate change in the long run," *European Economic Review*, volume 173, April 2025.

73   Jonathan Haidt, *The Righteous Mind: Why Good People Are Divided by Politics and Religion,* Vintage Books, 2013.

74   *Global burden of disease*, Institute for Health Metrics and Evaluation, 2024.

75   Hannah Ritchie, *The world has probably passed "peak air pollution,"* Our World in Data, January 2025.

76   For the United Kingdom, see *Emissions of air pollutants in the UK – sulphur dioxide (SO₂),* Department for Environment, Food & Rural Affairs, United Kingdom, March 2025; for the United States, see *U.S. sulfur dioxide emissions 1970–2016,* StatInvestor, accessed August 2025; and for London, see Hannah Ritchie, *What the history of London's air pollution can tell us about the future of today's growing megacities,* Our World in Data, June 20, 2017.

77   For Germany, see *How has air quality in Germany changed in the last 40 years?* Breeze Technologies, accessed August 2025. For China, see Hannah Ritchie, *China has reduced sulphur dioxide emissions by more than two-thirds in the last 15 years*, Our World in Data, January 3, 2025; and Lili Pike, *From "Airpocalypse" to Olympic blue: China's air quality transformation,* University of Chicago Energy Policy Institute, February 2022.

78   Wealthy countries historically exported their plastic waste to poorer economies, but the recipients of this unwanted trade have fought back with bans on such imports. In 2016, China imported more than half the world's plastic waste, a figure that plunged to less than 1 percent after a 2017 ban. Cambodia, Indonesia, Malaysia, Thailand, and Türkiye have also imposed bans. Estimates suggest that trade of plastics could explain between 1.6 and 10 percent of the problem at most, not the bulk of it. See Hannah Ritchie, *Ocean plastics: How much do rich countries contribute by shipping their waste overseas?* Our World In Data, October 2022. For plastics production, see Geyer et al., 2017; OECD, 2022, processed by Our World in Data. For plastic waste in the ocean, see Hannah Ritchie, *How much plastic waste ends up in the ocean?* Our World in Data, October 5, 2023; and Hannah Ritchie, *Not the End of the World: How We Can Be the First Generation to Build a Sustainable Planet,* Chatto & Windus, 2024.

79   See, for instance, Hannah Ritchie, *The world has lost one-third of its forest, but an end to deforestation is possible*, Our World in Data, February 2021; Hannah Ritchie, *Deforestation and forest loss*, Our World in Data, February 2021 (updated November 2024); Diana Roy, *Deforestation of Brazil's Amazon has reached a record high. What's being done?* Council on Foreign Relations, August 2022; Adam Vaughan, "Deforestation in Brazil has rocketed since Bolsonaro became president," *New Scientist*, July 22, 2019; and *Livestock's long shadow: Environmental issues and options*, UN Food and Agriculture Organization, 2006. For cocoa plantations, see Nikolai Kalischek et al., "Cocoa plantations are associated with

deforestation in Cote d'Ivoire and Ghana," *Nature Food*, 2023.

80   Hannah Ritchie, *Global deforestation peaked in the 1980s. Can we bring it to an end?* Our
        World in Data, September 2023; Hannah Ritchie, "Deforestation in the Amazon peaked
        decades ago. Can we get it to zero?" Sustainability by Numbers Substack, January 1,
        2023; Annette Wiedenbach, *Since 2010 forest cover in China has doubled, although
        losses in primary forests have also occurred*, Climate Scorecard, November 2024; *China –
        forest area (% of land area)*, Trading Economics, accessed August 2025; Claus Andersen,
        Climate performance: France versus Spain, Climate Positions, accessed August 2025;
        France: Forest area, percent, theglobaleconomy.com, accessed August 2025; *Thailand
        & Vietnam: Mycorrhizal afforestation and reforestation project,* Earthcare Foundation,
        accessed August 2025; and Katie Reytar et al., "These countries have gained more trees
        than they have lost," World Economic Forum, July 11, 2022.

81   See, for instance, A. S. Mather and C. L. Needle, "Development, democracy and forest
        trends," *Global Environmental Change,* volume 9, number 2, July 1999; and Edward B.
        Barbier, Joanne C. Burgess, and Alan Grainger, "The forest transition: Towards a more
        comprehensive theoretical framework," *Land Use Policy*, volume 27, number 2, April 2010.

82   Hannah Ritchie, Fiona Spooner, and Max Roser, *Biodiversity. Explore the diversity of
        wildlife across the planet. What are species threatened with? What can we do to prevent
        biodiversity loss?* Our World in Data, accessed June 2025; Fred Pearce, *Global extinction
        rates: Why do estimates vary so wildly?* Yale Environment, August 2015; Sean L. Maxwell et
        al., "Biodiversity: The ravages of guns, nets and bulldozers," *Nature*, 2016; and Christoph
        Schwitzer et al., eds., *Lemurs of Madagascar: Strategy for their conservation 2013–2016*,
        Conservation International and Bristol Conservation & Science Foundation, 2013.

83   James Ashworth, "Over half of coral reef cover across the world has been lost since 1950,"
        Natural History Museum, September 26, 2021. The claim of record-high coral cover on
        the Great Barrier Reef in 2022 originates from the Australian Institute of Marine Science.
        See *Annual summary report of coral reef condition 2021/22*, Australian Institute of Marine
        Science, August 2022. This report details surveys of 87 reefs conducted between August
        2021 and May 2022 and shows that the northern and central regions of the Great Barrier
        Reef reached their highest hard coral cover in 36 years of monitoring, with averages of
        36 percent (up from 27 percent in 2021) in the northern region and 33 percent (up from
        26 percent in 2021) in the central region. The southern region, however, experienced a
        decline from 38 percent to 34 percent due to crown-of-thorns starfish outbreaks. The
        recovery was driven by fast-growing Acropora corals, although these are vulnerable to
        bleaching and other stressors.

84   Hans Bauer et al., "Lion *(Panthera leo)* populations are declining rapidly across Africa,
        except in intensively managed areas," *Proceedings of the National Academy of Sciences*,
        December 2015; and Andrew J. Loveridge et al., "Where have all the lions gone?
        Establishing realistic baselines to assess decline and recovery of African lions,"
        Diversity and Distributions, volume 28, number 11, November 2022.

85   Kunming–Montreal Global Biodiversity Framework, UN Environment Programme,
        December 2022; for wild mammal populations, see Hannah Ritchie, *Wild mammals are
        making a comeback in Europe thanks to conservation efforts*, Our World in Data, 2022;
        for lion conservation, see Hans Bauer et al., "Lion (Panthera leo) populations are declining

rapidly across Africa, except in intensively managed areas," *Proceedings of the National Academy of Sciences*, December 2015.

86   For Costa Rica, see *National Parks in Costa Rica*, Global Alliance of National Parks, accessed June 2025. For protected areas, see *World met target for protected area coverage on land, but quality must improve*, International Union for Conservation of Nature, May 2021. For conservation financing, see *Financing nature: Closing the global biodiversity funding gap*, The Paulson Institute, The Nature Conservancy, and the Cornell Atkinson Center for Sustainability, 2020.

87   For depression in the United States, see Debra J. Brody and Jeffery P. Hughes, *Depression prevalence in adolescents and adults: United States, August 2021–August 2023*, NCHS Data Brief number 527, April 2025; on loneliness in Canada, see *Research shows 50% of Canadians are lonely*, GenWell, accessed August 2025; on consumerism, see Tori DeAngelis, "Consumerism and its discontents," *Monitor on Psychology*, volume 35, number 6, June 2004; for the impact of social media, see Sakshi Prasad et al., "Anxiety and depression amongst youth as adverse effects of using social media: A review," *Annals of Medicine & Surgery*, volume 85, number 8, July 2023. The crude mortality rate from "deaths of despair," defined as suicide-, drug-, and alcohol-related deaths, rose from 21.5 per 100,000 in 1970 to 45.8 in 2017, driven mainly by drug overdoses. Suicides and alcohol-related deaths were flat. See *Long-term trends in deaths of despair*, United States Congress Joint Economic Committee, September 2019.

88   Matthew Ridley et al., "Poverty, depression, and anxiety: Causal evidence and mechanisms," *Science*, volume 370, number 6522, December 2020.

89   Sahil Chinoy et al., *Zero-sum thinking and the roots of US political differences*, working paper number 31688, National Bureau of Economic Research, September 2023 (revised April 2025); and Benjamin M. Friedman, *The Moral Consequences of Economic Growth*, Knopf Doubleday, reprint 2006.

90   *Liberal democracy index*, V-Dem, 2025, on a population-weighted basis.

91   For more on development as the expansion of freedoms, or "removal of various types of unfreedoms" which constrain the agency of individuals, see Amartya Sen, *Development as Freedom*, OUP Oxford, January 18, 2001.

PART IV
THE POSSIBILITY OF PLENTY

<hr>

CHAPTER 15 – THE AMBITION OF PLENTY

1   Switzerland has consistently ranked in the top five countries according to the World Competitiveness Ranking published every year by the International Institute for Management Development in Lausanne. See World Competitiveness Ranking, International Institute for Management Development, accessed May 2025. For wealth management in Switzerland, see, for example, Ricardo Fernandes, *Largest wealth management firms by AUM in 2025*, Investing in the Web, August 6, 2025. For innovation, Switzerland has ranked at the top of the Global Innovation Index published by the World Intellectual Property Organization every year since 2011. See Global Innovation Index, World Intellectual Property Organization, accessed May 2025.

2   Employment figures from the Swiss Federal Statistical Office, accessed August 2025. For years at school, see Barro and Lee, 2015; Lee and Lee, 2016, processed by Our World in Data. For other measures, see the OECD Better Life Index, accessed May 2025. Regarding COVID-19, Switzerland's pandemic response was both generous and fiscally responsible. It rolled out a major support package worth about 10 percent of its economy to support workers and businesses without piling on debt. Praised by the OECD and IMF for its balanced approach to COVID response, Switzerland maintained a strong economy, thanks in part to its focus on industries less affected by lockdowns, like finance and pharmaceuticals. Meanwhile, communities supported one another, and public trust remained high, showing the kind of unity and resilience that helped Switzerland weather the storm better than many of its peers. See *Economic policy during the pandemic: The OECD praises Switzerland*, Swiss Federal Authorities, January 2022; and Mijie Li et al., "Changes in social capital during the COVID-19 pandemic: Empirical evidence from Singapore and Switzerland," *Natural Hazards Review*, volume 25, number 4, 2024.

3   Most air pollutants like nitrogen oxides, sulfur dioxide, and carbon monoxide have not only peaked but are nearing zero emissions. See Hoesly et al., 2024; Community Emissions Data System, processed by Our World in Data, accessed July 2025; and Global Carbon Budget, 2024; population based on various sources, 2024, processed by Our World in Data.

4   Of course, other countries have achieved similar outcomes and levels of prosperity, but for
        the purposes of having a point target for our scenario, we have picked Switzerland as one
        example of a successful country on multiple dimensions.

5   As with income and growth rates cited earlier in the book, these figures are stated in real
        terms, adjusted for purchasing-power parity, and in constant 2021 international dollars.
        That means that they have adjusted for inflation between years and different price levels
        across countries, to allow a better comparison across time and countries.

6   Historical growth rates in this section are from the World Bank unless otherwise specified.
        GDP per capita (constant 2021 international dollars), World Bank, accessed June 2025.

7   The World Bank defines "high income" as income per person greater than $14,000
        (in nominal terms). See World Bank income database; *Informal employment by sex
        (thousands)—annual*, ILOSTAT Data Explorer, accessed July 2025; and *The enterprising
        archipelago: Propelling Indonesia's productivity*, McKinsey Global Institute, April 2025.

8   Maddison Project Database 2023; World Development Indicators, World Bank, accessed
        June 2025; and using Maddison and IMF GDP estimates for Venezuela as it is unavailable
        in the World Bank data set, see *A critical juncture amid policy shifts*, *World Economic
        Outlook*, IMF, April 2025.

9   *Investing in productivity*, McKinsey Global Institute, March 2024. We discussed the fast
        and slow lanes of productivity growth in Part II, and will return to them later in this part.

10   Our scenario blends the UN's medium scenario with its instant replacement and high-
        fertility scenarios. In our hybrid scenario, most countries converge as closely as possible
        to 2.1 by 2100. Data for all UN scenarios from *World population prospects 2024*, United
        Nations, 2024. Also see Madeleine North, *With life expectancy increasing, here's how 4
        countries are addressing their ageing populations*, World Economic Forum, September 21,
        2023.

11   For world population, see *Total population by country 2025*, World Population Review,
        2025, accessed September 2025; for more on the impact of depopulation, see
        *Dependency and depopulation: Confronting the consequences of a new demographic
        reality*, McKinsey Global Institute, January 2025.

12   Saloni Dattani, Lucas Rodés-Guirao, and Max Roser, UN Population Division, *World
        population prospects*, 2024, processed by Our World in Data.

13   Dean Spears and Michael Geruso, *After the Spike: Population, Progress, and the Case for
        People*, Simon & Schuster, 2025.

14   *World population prospects 2024*, United Nations, 2024.

15   For a discussion on how new home appliances among other factors drove the 20th-
        century baby boom, see Derek Thompson, *What caused the 'baby boom'? What would
        it take to have another?* Derek Thompson Substack, July 15, 2025; for the research on
        what makes people likely to have children, see *Society at a glance 2024: OECD Social
        Indicators*, OECD, June 20, 2024.

16   To calculate global momentum of GDP, we take each country's current income per person
        and apply the historical growth rate since 1960 of the income group in which the country

sits and then multiply by our population projection in 2100 for that country. We then sum up GDP for all the countries. For China's GDP, for example, we take its current income per person, apply the historical growth rate of the second income group (in which it sits today), and multiply by our population projection for China in 2100. The high proportion of total growth coming from advanced economies might seem counterintuitive given their lower growth in percentage-point terms. But even though they grow slower in percentage terms, they are growing from a much larger base, which translates to high growth in absolute terms.

17   Australian philosopher Toby Ord estimates the cumulative existential risk in this century at roughly one in six. Ord apportions the risk to AI misalignment (10 percent), engineered pandemics (3 percent), and smaller but real risks from nuclear conflict and climate disaster, warning that our destructive capabilities have outpaced our wisdom, a gap we must close through responsible governance. William MacAskill echoes this call for long-term thinking and resilient institutions to protect humanity's potential in thousands more generations to come. See Toby Ord, *The Precipice: Existential Risk and the Future of Humanity*, Hatchette Books, 2020; and William MacAskill, *What We Owe the Future*, Oneworld Publications, 2022.

CHAPTER 16 – THE ENERGY TO MAKE THE WORLD GO ROUND

18   In this section, unless specified otherwise, we use the term "energy" to refer to primary energy. Primary energy refers to the initial energy inputs, such as crude oil, coal, or natural gas, that power our activities. Final energy is the energy that reaches the end user in a consumable form, such as electricity, gasoline, or district heating. After final energy is used, what remains to perform actual work, like a motor turning, heating a home, or powering a device, is called useful energy. Useful energy is the portion that effectively contributes to the desired task after losses in conversion and transmission. Energy efficiency could refer to the efficiency of any steps along this chain; here we use it specifically to reference the overall ratio of primary energy to useful energy. There are different ways to account for primary energy. In this chapter, for fossil fuels we account for primary energy as the total energy content in the coal, oil, and gas input. For low-carbon sources (solar, wind, and nuclear), we account for primary energy as the electrical output generated by a power plant; we count the electricity generated by these sources, but not the full amount of potential energy in a ray of sunshine or a brick of uranium.

19   Electrification share comes from the IEA, accessed July 2025. The 30 times expansion figure is calculated relative to today's share of low-emissions electricity, which is about 40 percent of the electricity generated today. See *Low-emissions sources of electricity*, IEA, September 2023. Electricity and low-emissions electricity multiples refer to the higher end of the range of estimates.

20   By 2100, nuclear provides 40 percent of global energy (about 215,000 terawatt hours), solar 25 percent (some 134,000 terawatt hours), wind 15 percent (roughly 80,000 terawatt hours), and the remaining 20 percent from a mix of from hydro, geothermal, and gas backed by CCUS. Some 90 to 140 terawatt hours of storage would be needed to manage intraday fluctuations.

21   Using constant 2021 international dollars (PPP).

22   For steam and diesel engine efficiencies, see Exhibit 13. Electric power-train efficiency here refers to battery-to-wheel efficiency, a measure of how much energy in the battery is converted into forward motion in the wheels. See, for instance, Hussein Togun et al., "Development and comparative analysis between battery electric vehicles (BEV) and fuel cell electric vehicles (FCEV)," *Applied Energy*, volume 388, June 2025; and Conor Molloy, *Under the bonnet*, Sustainable Energy Authority of Ireland, February 2023. To determine a range for how much more energy efficient we might get, we did not just maintain the historical trajectory. Instead, we analyzed a scenario where road transportation, industry, and building heat all increase substantially their electrification rates, which enables a global increase in the ratio of primary to useful energy slightly lower than 50 percent in 2025 to between 70 and 90 percent in 2100. This represents a range from slightly quicker to slightly slower than the historical rate at which the ratio has changed.

23   For a discussion of the energy intensity of different sectors, see Namit Sharma, Bram Smeets, and Christer Tryggestad, "The decoupling of GDP and energy growth: A CEO guide," *McKinsey Quarterly*, April 24, 2019. Analysis comparing aluminum and digital services is based on an assumption of an average $2,500 price per tonne of aluminum and 15 megawatt hours of electricity consumed per tonne. Google's data centers used about 24 terawatt hours of electricity in 2023. See Sebastian Moss, *Global emissions jump 48% in five years due to AI data center boom*, DCD, July 5, 2024. Alphabet earned $307 billion in revenue, of which about 77 percent or $238 billion came from advertising. See *Alphabet announces fourth quarter and fiscal year 2023 results*, Alphabet, January 30, 2024; and Florian Zandt, *Google's ad revenue dwarfs competitors*, Statista, September 10, 2024. Using these figures, 15 megawatt hours of electricity can generate roughly $150,000 of advertising revenue, about 60 times the value of a tonne of aluminum. Also see *Reconciling growth and decarbonization amidst the energy crisis: European Aluminium reaction to the RePowerEU Plan*, European Aluminium, May 2022.

24   For data center energy consumption growth, see "Scaling bigger, faster, cheaper data centers with smarter designs," McKinsey, August 1, 2025; and for historical US power generation growth, see Table 7.2a, *Electricity net generation: total (all sectors)*, US Energy Information Administration, accessed August 2025.

25   Data center electricity demand could increase by more than 200 times over today and still account for less than 20 percent of our estimate for 2100 global electricity.

26   *Global energy perspective 2025*, McKinsey, September 2025.

27   Energy in Exhibit 28 refers to final energy rather than primary energy as elsewhere in this chapter.

28   For some transportation segments, battery weight-to-energy ratios are a physical challenge for increasing electrification. Batteries are too heavy for long-haul trucks to carry heavy loads over long distances and for electric-powered long-haul flights. We think that batteries will develop sufficiently to power most trucks but imagine that, even in the longer term, some combination of biofuels and hydrogen would probably supply most energy for aviation and maritime use rather than electricity, because these fuels have high energy density. We assume 50 to 60 percent electrification of transportation, with more than 90 percent of passenger cars and rail electrified, 60 to 70 percent of trucking electrified, and almost no electrification of aviation or maritime use. Unlike the up to 90 percent figure for EV battery-to-wheel efficiency cited earlier in this chapter, this analysis

includes the embodied energy of both ICE vehicles and EVs in their manufacturing and the energy infrastructure required to fuel or power them. We assume a world in which the grid improves from 40 percent to 70 percent efficiency, roughly from today's US average to today's average for Brazil, which has a much higher percentage of renewable generation sources. We also assume that ICE power trains improve from 25 percent to 40 percent efficiency.

29 An average natural gas heater has 95 percent efficiency, and a standard air-source heat pump generates three units of heat per unit of electricity. A gas boiler will take 100 units of gas and generate 95 units of heat. A heat pump powered by natural gas at 55 percent power plant efficiency would take 100 units of natural gas, generate 55 units of electricity, and then turn that into 165 units of heat, about 40 percent less gas per unit of heat. See *Building value by decarbonizing the built environment*, McKinsey, June 2023; and *The hard stuff: Navigating the physical realities of the energy transition*, McKinsey Global Institute, August 2024. For gas boiler efficiency, see *High-efficiency gas furnaces*, Watkins Heating, May 23, 2025; for air-source heat pump performance, see *In-depth Guide to Heat Pumps*, Energy Saving Trust, 2024; for natural gas power plant efficiency, see *Energy efficiency indicators for public electricity production from fossil fuels*, IEA, 2022, and *Gas power plants are efficiency giants*, ASME, 2021.

30 *The hard stuff: Navigating the physical realities of the energy transition*, McKinsey Global Institute, August 2024; and *Global energy perspective 2025*, McKinsey, September 2025.

31 Paolo Malanima, *WEC world energy consumption, a database 1820-2020* (2022 revision), Guangxi Normal University, 2022.

32 Daan Walter, Kingsmill Bond, and Sam Butler-Sloss, *The electrification imperative*, Ember, June 25, 2025.

33 *Top five transmission line projects in China*, Power Technology, July 19, 2023, updated September 10, 2024.

34 This would require significant investment. Construction costs could run to about $190 trillion over 75 years, or roughly $2.5 trillion a year. That is five times current annual spending. Substantial, but not unreasonable. By 2100, the annual cost of building energy infrastructure could be 16 times higher than it is now. But the world's economy would be eight times larger. As a share of GDP, the outlay would only need to double. Today, energy infrastructure accounts for 0.6 percent of global GDP. In 2100, that would rise to 1.0 to 1.5 percent. That is a relatively cheap mortgage payment for energy abundance.

35 To eliminate energy-related emissions completely, the 10 percent from natural gas would have to be paired with carbon capture, created from waste or another carbon-neutral process, or offset through net carbon removals. Because of the 40 percent share coming from variable renewables that are, by their nature, intermittent sources of energy, we think we would need 90 to 140 terawatt hours of storage capacity to manage intraday and inter-day intermittency.

36 "U.S. shale gas is the fastest-growing source of energy in history," X, @RichardMeyerDC, June 30, 2025.

37 For US shale production and comparison with Saudi Arabia's oil output, see Bohyun Hwang, Joonghyeok Heo, and Joon Kyu Park, "Environmental implications of shale gas

hydraulic fracturing: A comprehensive review on water contaminations and seismic activities in the United States," *Water*, volume 15, number 19, September 2023; *The shale revolution: Reshaping the U.S. oil and gas industry*, Voronoi, September 2024; *Natural gas gross withdrawals from shale gas wells (million cubic feet)*, US Energy Information Administration, accessed September 2025; and *Saudi Arabia: Primary energy production*, The Global Economy, accessed July 2025. For the decline in coal's share of US energy, see Energy Institute, *Statistical review of world energy*, 2025, processed by Our World in Data.

38   Current solar photovoltaics generally can convert up to 20 percent of sunlight's energy into electricity, a number that is likely to improve with advancing technology. See *What is the typical efficiency range for commercial solar panels?* Go Solar Wolf River Electric, May 2025. But some panels have hit the 30 percent efficiency mark. See "LONGi announces the new world record efficiency of 30.1% for the commercial M6 size wafer-level silicon-perovskite tandem solar cells," LONGi, June 19, 2024.

39   The energy efficiency of renewables raises concerns. Studies have shown that the energy return on investment (EROI) of fossil fuels at a primary level ranges between 25 and 30 to one. This is much higher than solar energy's EROI of between three and ten to one. But the picture is different when we look at "useful" energy, where the EROI of solar and fossil fuels has been shown to be roughly the same. See Paul Brockway et al., "Estimation of global final-stage energy-return-on-investment for fossil fuels with comparison to renewable energy sources," *Nature Energy*, volume 4, number 7, July 2019; Charles A. S. Hall, Jessica G. Lambert, and Stephen B. Balogh, "EROI of different fuels and the implications for society," *Energy Policy*, volume 64, January 2014; and David J. Murphy et al., "Energy return on investment of major energy carriers: Review and harmonization," *Sustainability*, volume 14, number 12, June 2022.

40   For recent solar energy additions and annual targets, see *Global Solar Council announces 2 terawatt milestone achieved for solar*, Global Solar Council, November 8, 2024; and for wind installations, see *Renewables 2024: Analysis and forecast to 2030*, IEA, October 2024.

41   "Those electric school buses are on their way to save the grid," Wired, May 15, 2024; and *SA creates Australia's largest virtual power plant*, CEFC, accessed July 2025.

42   This assumes Tesla batteries in a model S of about 100 kilowatt hours, and current battery technology and weights. This figure in terawatt hours gives only a scale of the battery energy capacity needed and not the power, meaning that we also have to test the speed at which the system can deliver such energy, and that is between ten and 15 terawatts. Today, we have just 0.14 terawatt installed, meaning that a 70- to 110-fold leap will be needed. That's a big jump, but estimates have capacity increasing by ninefold in the next ten years, an additional 1.1 terawatts.

43   Prices in China are already 50 percent lower than the global average, hinting at further price reductions to come. For lithium-ion battery growth, see Teo Lombardo et al., *The battery industry has entered a new phase*, IEA, March 5, 2025. For the trend of battery prices, see Michael Cembalest, *The Alchemists: Eye on the Market: Outlook* 2025, J. P. Morgan, January 2025.

44   *Pumped storage hydropower: The world's oldest battery*, International Hydropower Association, accessed July 2025.

45   "Finland activates world's largest sand battery to store renewable heat," *Helsinki Times*, June 19, 2025.

46   Marija Maisch, "Eneco, Corre Energy partner on compressed air energy storage project," *PV Magazine*, May 16, 2024; and Marija Maisch, "320MW/640MWh battery to complement compressed air storage in the Netherlands," *PV Magazine*, July 8, 2024.

47   *The hard stuff: Navigating the physical realities of the energy transition*, McKinsey Global Institute, August 2024.

48   *The hard stuff: Navigating the physical realities of the energy transition*, McKinsey Global Institute, August 2024; and Energy technology perspectives 2023, IEA, January 2023.

49   For Europe's transmissions, see *Grids and infrastructure*, Federal Ministry for Economic Affairs and Energy, Germany, accessed August 2025; and for the United States, see "How it works: Electric transmission & distribution and protective measures," in *Learning series: Energy security & resilience*, Office of Cybersecurity, Energy Security, and Emergency Response, US Department of Energy, November 2023.

50   For the land used by solar panels and wind turbines, if we take account of the space between them, the amount of land they need could be ten times greater than the projected 550,000 square kilometers at five million square kilometers. Our analysis considers that solar panels require 19 square meters for every megawatt hour, improving to ten square meters by 2100, and wind turbines improve from 99 square meters to 70 square meters. See Hannah Ritchie, *How does the land use of different electricity sources compare?* Our World in Data, June 2022. We assume that technologies start at today's median land use and over time reach their minimum. Land use is measured by total life cycle, including material extraction, construction, fuel inputs, decommissioning, and waste. We further assume that 40 percent of solar is installed on roofs and 80 percent of wind will be onshore. This aligns with IEA estimates. Helping to address the land issue, solar panels are sprouting up everywhere in places that you might not expect. There is a floating solar farm on a reservoir in Singapore. India has installed solar panels between train tracks. In the United States, solar arrays have been installed in otherwise unusable land in closed landfills. And now researchers are experimenting with solar panels submerged just underwater, combining photovoltaics with aquaculture. This last example builds on an established tradition of agrivoltaics where solar panels are placed on agricultural land. France already has about 300 megawatts of agrivoltaic capacity live and aims to install two gigawatts more a year by 2026. Wind turbines also work on farmland.

51   Recent nuclear developments in China and Russia, including China quadrupling capacity and Russia increasing it by one-quarter, are reported by *Nuclear power in China*, World Nuclear Association, June 2025; *Nuclear power in Russia*, World Nuclear Association, May 2025; and *Six more countries endorse the Declaration to Triple Nuclear Energy by 2050 at COP29*, World Nuclear Association, November 2024. Also see Karen Hanson, *Why are Microsoft, Google and Meta investing in nuclear energy?* EE Power, December 2024.

52   Nuclear power uses a negligible amount of land. This amount of capacity would occupy 65,000 square kilometers, or roughly the size of Sri Lanka. That is about one-tenth the land that would be needed if solar and wind were supplying a similar amount of energy.

53   Roughly ten per year are planned between 2025 and 2030. See *Plans for new reactors*

worldwide, World Nuclear Association, June 2025.

54   *Nuclear power plants generated 68% of France's electricity in 2021*, US Energy
     Information Administration, January 2023; *France energy issues*, IEA Energy Statistics,
     accessed July 2025; and US Energy Information Administration, 2025; Energy Institute,
     Statistical review of world energy, 2025; population based on various sources, 2024,
     processed by Our World in Data. For more on adding reactors at Messmer speed, see
     Global electricity: By source, by use, by region? Thunder Said Energy, accessed July 2025.

55   *Nuclear power in South Korea*, World Nuclear Association, June 2025; and for typical
     construction times of reactors, see Hannah Ritchie, *How long does it take to build a
     nuclear reactor?* Our World in Data, April 3, 2023.

56   The cost is indexed to 2023 US dollars. See *The next big arenas of competition*, McKinsey
     Global Institute, October 2024.

57   *Global energy perspective 2025*, McKinsey, September 2025.

58   Recent experiments have demonstrated the possibility of extracting uranium from
     seawater at half the cost, although it is not yet proven on a commercial scale. See Jeremy
     Tsu, "New way to pull uranium from water can help China's nuclear power push," *New
     Scientist*, May 12, 2025. Promising pilots of alternative nuclear fuels have focused on
     developing better absorbents to extract the uranium from gallons and gallons of water
     where it is present in tiny concentrations. Thorium is abundant but is still an experimental
     fuel. In 2024, China successfully refueled a commercial thorium reactor without having
     to shut it down. This is a significant milestone in the development of a high-potential
     alternative fuel to uranium to power nuclear energy. "China refuels thorium reactor without
     shutdown," *Nuclear Engineering International*, April 22, 2025.

59   *Chernobyl's legacy: Health, environmental and socio-economic impacts and
     recommendations to the governments of Belarus, the Russian Federation and Ukraine*,
     The Chernobyl Forum: 2003–2005, International Atomic Energy Agency, April 2006.

60   *Modern nuclear power plant design and safety measures*, Biology Insights, April 2025.
     Additional safety measures include negative void coefficient of reactivity, which makes
     meltdowns physically impossible; an out-of-control reaction will cool the core. Other
     modern generators include core catchers, which contain molten fuel during a meltdown,
     reducing the risk of a containment breach. See *Current and future generation,* World
     Nuclear Association, accessed July 2025; and *RBMK reactors – appendix to nuclear power
     reactors*, World Nuclear Association, February 2022.

61   Hannah Ritchie and Pablo Rosado, *Nuclear energy: Explore global data on nuclear energy
     production and the safety of nuclear technologies*, Our World in Data, revised April 2024;
     and Hannah Ritchie, *What are the safest and cleanest sources of energy?* Our World in
     Data, February 10, 2020.

62   More fanciful ideas have included ejecting radioactive spent nuclear fuel into space.

63   Today, about 30 percent of nuclear plants use pass-through cooling from rivers and
     lakes, where cold water passes through the reactor before returning to the water source;
     45 percent use seawater for pass-through cooling; and 25 percent use recirculating
     cooling towers, which have a lower water need. Pass-through cooling from rivers and

lakes can face shortages when hot or dry weather causes high water temperatures or low water levels. Historically, this has lowered annual capacity factors by less than 1 percent. Nevertheless, if nuclear scales up significantly, it makes sense to reduce this risk by building more plants with coastal access to seawater or with cooling towers. Other options being explored include air-cooling reactors and using treated wastewater for cooling as Arizona's Palo Verde plant does. See *Cooling power plants*, World Nuclear Association, October 2020; and *Power trip*, Arizona Department of Water Resources, December 2016.

64   Under the agreement, the United Arab Emirates agreed to renounce uranium enrichment and the reprocessing of spent fuel and to put in place extra safeguards.

65   Miklós Dietz, Bill Lacivita, Amélie Lefebvre, and Geoff Olynyk, "Will fusion energy help decarbonize the power system?" McKinsey, October 12, 2022; and David Szondy, *France runs fusion reactor for record 22 minutes*, New Atlas, February 2025.

CHAPTER 17 – THE MATERIALS TO BUILD THE FUTURE

66   John Zadeh, *The world's ten largest copper mines: Global giants revealed*, Discovery Alert, March 30, 2025; T. Mike Porter, *The Escondida Porphyry Copper Deposit, Northern Chile: Discovery, Setting, Geology, Hypogene Mineralisation and Supergene Ore – A Review*, PGB Publishing, 2005; and *2024 Chilean copper site tour: Escondida, Presentation & Speech*, BHP, November 19, 2024. For the copper price, see *Global price of copper*, FRED, July 18, 2025. For more on global copper production, see US Geological Survey, *Mineral Commodity Summaries 2025*, 2025.

67   *Escondida Mine*, Chile, NS Energy, May 2023; "BHP on Escondida's pathways for growth— from leaching to Hydrofloat to AHS," International Mining, November 20, 2024; and Ed Conway, *Material World: A Substantial Story of Our Past and Future*, W. H. Allen, 2023.

68   John Zadeh, *Australia's iron ore industry: Global leadership and innovation*, Discovery Alert, March 28, 2025; *Iron ore mining in Australia: An outlook to 2030*, Mine, November 2024.

69   Rather than use one country as benchmark, like Switzerland, we use a group of countries to ensure that we do not anchor on country-specific idiosyncrasies. Here we define wealthy as those in the top 25 percent measured by income per person. In-use stocks of steel and other metals come from McKinsey's MineSpans.

70   Here we are talking about in-use stock, not annual consumption. For example, if a building is constructed in the previous year, the steel used is counted in the current year's in-use stock but not in the current year's consumption. If all eight billion people in the world had 9.8 tonnes of in-use steel, that would mean a total of about 78 billion tonnes. That is 45 billion tonnes more than the 33 billion tonnes of steel in use globally today. For annual steel production, see *World steel in figures 2024*, World Steel Association, 2024.

71   Darren Orf, "Scientists developed 'super steel' that could take fusion to the next level," *Popular Mechanics*, August 6, 2025. For the amount of steel that would be used, including nonrecyclable replacements, our numbers assumed an 85 percent recycling rate and a 35-year average lifespan for the steel. For more on US minerals and materials, see Thomas D. Kelly and Grecia R. Matos, *Historical statistics for mineral and material commodities in the United States*, National Minerals Information Center, US Geological

Survey, accessed September 2025. Also see MineSpans data.

72   Rowan Hawthorne, *Biggest steel plant in the world: Where is it?* Sydler Electro
        Manufacturing India, May 17, 2025.

73   *Steel statistical yearbook 2001*, International Iron and Steel Institute, December 2001; and
        Total production of crude steel, world total 2024, World Steel Association, March 25, 2024.

74   *Mineral commodity summaries 2025*, US Geological Survey.

75   This assumes that one tonne of iron content produces one tonne of steel. See *Mineral
        commodity summaries 2025*, US Geological Survey.

76   *Mineral commodity summaries 2025*, US Geological Survey.

77   For use of lithium in EVs, see *Executive summary, Batteries and secure energy, World
        energy outlook special report*, IEA, April 2024. For Swiss car ownership, see *Road vehicles
        – stock, level of motorisation*, Federal Statistical Office, Switzerland, accessed September
        2025. For EV manufacturing, see Geraldine Herbert, "How long will an EV battery last
        before it has to be replaced? A guide to electric car battery life," Euronews, May 12, 2024.
        For the country comparison, see *List of the world's largest countries and dependencies
        by area*, Britannica, accessed September 2025. For our assumption of lithium demand,
        we assume 90 percent electrification of the global vehicle fleet, which is a considerable
        transition but not a full one. We recognize that some specialized or remote-use vehicles
        may still rely on combustion fuels, though those fuels may also be carbon neutral.
        This aligns with our broader energy scenario, which targets about 70 to 80 percent
        electrification of final energy. This is a generous assumption, but one that does not involve
        a fully gas-free world. For additional context, today, EVs account for 3.2 percent of the
        global light-duty vehicle fleet, and the IEA net-zero scenario projects that this will be 34
        percent by 2035. We assume that each EV uses about 8.9 kilograms of lithium to reach
        the total 168 million tonnes of lithium that we need. We keep this constant, but it will likely
        reduce over time given new technologies that will use lithium more efficiently or find new
        substitutions; 5.323 tonnes of lithium carbonate equivalent contains one tonne of lithium.

78   For the comparison with the pyramids, see Sayed Hemeda and Alghreeb Sonbol,
        "Sustainability problems of the Giza pyramids," *Heritage Science*, volume 8, number 8,
        2020. For calculating how much lithium we might need, we scale demand for lithium from
        EVs using the IEA's net-zero emissions scenario for the lithium demand mix in 2050. In
        this scenario, EVs account for 84 percent of total lithium demand globally. However, this
        scenario accounts for only 7 percent of total lithium for grid storage, which is 15 million
        tonnes of the total of 213 million. Our scenario, which has faster electrification and a larger
        population, adds about 18 million tonnes for energy storage to support 490 terawatt hours
        of cumulative storage capacity, including replacements for a 15-year battery lifespan. The
        IEA predicts that lithium recycling rates will increase from 3 to 33 percent by 2050, and
        we hold that constant from 2050 to 2100. Historical lithium data from the US Geological
        Survey.

79   Lithium historical known resource and extractable reserves figures are from the US
        Geological Survey.

80   Solomon Evro et al., *Navigating battery choices: A comparative study of lithium iron
        phosphate and nickel manganese cobalt battery technologies*, University of North Dakota,

October 2024; Monica Sawicki and Leon L. Shaw, "Advances and challenges of sodium iron batteries as post lithium iron batteries," *RSC Advances*, volume 5, 2015; and Sam Abuelsamid, "Lithium ion phosphate set to be the next big thing in EV batteries," *Forbes*, August 16. 2023.

81   We did not prioritize graphite, chromium, silicon, or zinc, because they have fewer physical long-term supply risks. Synthetic graphite can replace natural graphite. The production of the synthetic version may cost more in some cases, but the technology is already mature, and the material is likely to become more economical and sustainable as that technology advances further. Chromium and silicon have stable trajectories with steady growth in reserves, natural abundance, and continued innovation. Demand for zinc may exceed current reserves, but strong recyclability and large identified resources suggest that it remains manageable. Bulk materials like limestone and potash are effectively unlimited, especially in a future with abundant clean energy. Clean, cheap energy also enables effective desalination, increasing available freshwater resources.

82   For aluminum in the Earth's crust, see *Aluminum (Al)*, EBSCO, accessed September 2025. For alternative sources for aluminum, see Aileen I. Pogue and Walter J. Lukiw, "The mobilization of aluminum into the biosphere," *Frontiers in Neurology*, December 2014.

83   Dolf Gielen and Martina Lyons, *Critical materials for the energy transition: Rare earth elements*, technical paper 2/2022, International Renewable Energy Agency, 2022.

84   Plato, *The Republic*, Penguin Classics, 2007.

85   "Trends in batteries," in *Global EV outlook 2023*, IEA, April 2023.

86   Based on oil and natural gas consumption for non-energy purposes in the United States and Germany in 2022 from the IEA, accessed July 2025.

87   Related to changing demand for gas and oil is whether sufficient sulfuric acid will be available. This acid is used to extract cobalt and nickel, for instance, and is a crucial chemical in the production of phosphorous fertilizers. More than 80 percent of world supply currently comes from waste sulfur from refining of gas and oil for energy. As the global population expands and the energy transition progresses, demand for sulfur is estimated to grow substantially, and this could necessitate finding alternative sources as gas and oil refining eventually ramp down.

88   Daan Walter, Sam Butler-Sloss, and Kingsmill Bond, *The rise of batteries in six charts and not too many numbers*, RMI, January 25, 2024.

89   Jörg Woidasky, Christian Klinke, and Sebastian Jeanvré, "Materials stock of the civilian aircraft fleet," *Recycling*, volume 2, November 5, 2017; John Fitzgerald Weaver, "Silicon cost per watt down 98% over last two decades," *PV Magazine*, January 10, 2023; and *Silver's important role in solar power: Market trend report*, The Silver Institute, June 2020.

90   *Recycling of critical minerals: Strategies to scale up recycling and urban mining*, IEA, November 2024.

91   For peak oil, see David Deming, "M. King Hubbert and the rise and fall of peak oil theory," *AAPG Bulletin*, volume 107, number 6, June 1, 2023. For prices, see Tevjan Pettinger, *The relationship between oil prices and inflation*, Economics Help, June 2022.

92 Further examination of the environmental impact of these alternative mining methods would be needed. Currently, that impact is not known.

93 Victor Maus et al., *The global economy used more than 100,000 km² of land for mining*, FINEPRINT brief number 16, November 2022; and Gauthier Canart, Lukasz Kowalik, Mukani Moyo, and Raj Kumar Ray, "Has global mining productivity reversed course?" McKinsey, April 27, 2020.

94 *Ecological impacts of mountaintop removal*, Appalachian Voices, accessed September 2025; Michaela G. Y. Lo et al., "Nickel mining reduced forest cover in Indonesia but had mixed outcomes for well-being," *One Earth*, volume 7, issue 1, November 15, 2024; and *MAAP #178: Gold mining deforestation across the Amazon*, Monitoring of the Andes Amazon Program, March 2, 2023.

95 *BHP targets 100 percent renewable energy at Escondida and Spence operations and elimination of water usage from aquifers in Chile*, BHP, October 20, 2019; and *BHP's Spence copper mine in Chile now fully autonomous*, Mining.com, July 29, 2024.

96 *Aluminium sector greenhouse gas emissions*, International Aluminium, 2024; and *Iron and steel technology roadmap*, IEA, accessed August 2025.

97 *Iron and steel technology roadmap*, IEA, accessed August 2025. Of the 2.6 gigatonnes of CO_2 emitted by the steel industry, 2.3 gigatonnes are energy emissions and 0.3 gigatonne are process emissions. In the first process, coke produces carbon monoxide (CO), which binds with the oxygen (O) in the iron ore and generates CO_2. In the second process, oxygen is blasted through the molten iron, which binds with the carbon in the molten iron, creating CO_2. Exchanging oxygen for hydrogen (H) in the second step creates water (H_2O) instead.

98 Michael Purton, *Cement is a big problem for the environment. Here's how to make it more sustainable*, World Economic Forum, September 13, 2024.

99 *Clinker substitution in the cement industry*, Cembureau position paper, The European Cement Association, March 5, 2024.

100 McKinsey Global Energy and Materials Practice; and *The hard stuff: Navigating the physical realities of the energy transition*, McKinsey Global Institute, August 2024.

101 In 2024, global production of steel totaled 1.9 billion tonnes. Of this, 72 percent was produced via the blast furnace (BF–BOF) route, which emits 2.3 tonnes of CO_2 per tonne of steel. Five percent was produced using the electric arc furnace route (DRI–EAF), emitting on average 1.4 tonnes of CO_2 per tonne of steel. An additional 23 percent was made from recycled steel (EAF–scrap). See *World steel in figures 2025*, World Steel Association, 2025; and Kali Benavides et al., "Mitigating emissions in the global steel industry: Representing CCS and hydrogen technologies in integrated assessment modeling," *International Journal of Greenhouse Gas Control*, volume 31, January 2024.

102 For reducing emissions, see Archy de Berker, *Understand your aluminum emissions*, Carbon Chain, June 27, 2022. For bio-based inputs, see *Bioproduct basics*, US Department of Energy, accessed September 2025. For storing carbon in concrete, see Dan Meng et al., "Carbon sequestration and utilization in cement-based materials and potential impacts on durability of structural concrete," *Construction and Building Materials*, volume 361, December 26, 2022. For CCUS, see *CCUS in clean energy transitions*, IEA, September 2020.

103   For example, 1,400 blast furnaces are in operation across the world. They account for
      70 percent of steel emissions. See *The hard stuff: Navigating the physical realities of the
      energy transition*, McKinsey Global Institute, August 2024.

CHAPTER 18 – THE FOOD TO NOURISH A GROWING POPULATION

104   Hannah Ritchie, *People in richer countries tend to eat more meat*, Our World in Data,
      August 2024; and Christophe Béné et al., "Feeding 9 billion people by 2050: Putting fish
      back on the menu," *Food Security*, volume 7, number 2, April 10, 2015.

105   Food and Agriculture Organization of the United Nations, 2025, processed by Our World in
      Data.

106   We identified five distinct dietary archetypes (all high-income, high calorie consumption)
      based on the proportion of animal-source foods (that is, beef, pork, chicken, and dairy)
      consumed, and mapped all countries to those archetypes to project future food demand.

107   *Land statistics 2011–2022. Global, regional and country trends*, FAOSTAT, July 4, 2024;
      and Taylor & Rising, 2021; *World population prospects*, UN, 2021, processed by Our World
      in Data.

108   The 7.4 billion tonnes differs from total agricultural production as reported by the FAO,
      which cites 9.6 billion tonnes of primary crops in 2022. That figure reflects gross output
      measured before losses from storage, processing, and transport, and includes both food
      and nonfood products, such as cotton, rubber, silk, and wool. In contrast, our analysis
      includes only the portion of agricultural output that is ultimately available for human
      consumption and livestock feed. This encompasses edible crop and animal products, such
      as grains, vegetables, milk, and meat, but excludes nonfood outputs and post-harvest
      losses. This refined baseline forms the foundation for our comparison and projection
      of food demand in 2100. See *Agricultural production statistics 2010–2023*, FAOSTAT,
      accessed April 2025.

109   Yields, or agricultural productivity, are defined as the amount of agricultural output per
      hectare of farmland or pastureland. For meat, yield is the amount of meat produced on
      the land where the animals are raised, like barns or pens for chicken and pork, or pasture
      and feedlots for beef, and does not account for the land needed to grow their feed. The
      amount of improvement needed varies across major food types like beef, chicken, pork,
      maize, wheat, and rice.

110   Keith O. Fuglie, Stephen Morgan, and Jeremy Jelliffe, *World agricultural production,
      resource use, and productivity, 1961–2020*, Economic Information Bulletin, number 268,
      US Department of Agriculture, February 2024.

111   HYDE, 2023, processed by Our World in Data, accessed September 2025; and *Sub-
      Saharan Africa population (1950–2025)*, Macro Trends, accessed September 2025.

112   *Crops and livestock products*, Food and Agriculture Organization of the United Nations,
      accessed September 2025.

113   More than doubling rice yields in Vietnam between 1960 and 2023 came down to a few

practical changes. Alongside adopting high-yielding rice varieties developed through selective breeding during the Green Revolution, Vietnam embraced smarter farming methods. The System of Rice Intensification focused on planting fewer, younger seedlings with more space, loosening soil, and reducing use of water, producing stronger plants and more rice. Farmers also adopted alternate wetting and drying, a technique that lets fields partially dry before reflooding, which saves water, cuts emissions, and sustains high yields. See Prabhu L. Pingali, "Green Revolution: Impacts, limits, and the path ahead," *PNAS*, July 2012; *Vietnam*, SRI International Network and Resources Center, College of Agriculture and Life Sciences, Cornell University, accessed July 2025; and Krishna et al., "Rice production in water-scarce environments: A review of conservation agriculture techniques," *Journal of Advances in Biology & Biotechnology*, volume 27, number 11, 2024.

114   For rice yields in Australia, see Rajinder Pal Singh et all., *An assessment of the economic, environmental and social impacts of the Ricecheck program*, Economic Research Report number 28, NSW Department of Primary Industries, December 2005; *Rice in the Riverina*, prepared for the Independent Murray-Darling Basin Social and Economic Assessment Panel, Marsden Jacob Associates, March 2020; and J. Lacy et al., *Bridging the rice yield gap in Australia*, Achieving Sustainable Rice Cultivation, FAO Rice Conference, Rome, 1998. For Gobi Desert wine, see "World-class wine-producing zone emerges in northwest China's Gobi Desert," Xinhua, August 22, 2024.

115   For the silvopastoral approach in Colombia, see Daniel Suarez, *Silvopastoral dairy farming in Southern Colombia*, CIPAV, June 2019; Isabel Molina-Botero et al., "Effect of a silvopastoral system with *Leucaena diversifolia* on enteric methane emissions, animal performance, and meat fatty acid profile of beef steers," *Agroforestry Systems*, volume 98, July 2024; Pablo L. Peri et al., "Current trends in silvopastoral systems," *Agroforestry Systems*, volume 98, October 2024; Ricardo Gonzalez Quintero et al., "A case study on enhancing dairy cattle sustainability: The impact of silvopastoral systems and improved pastures on milk carbon footprint and farm economics in Cauca Department, Colombia," *Agroforestry Systems*, volume 98, 2024; Ermas Aynekulu et al., "Carbon storage potential of silvopastoral systems of Colombia," *Land*, volume 9, number 9, September 2020; and *Not the COW, the HOW: Increasing livestock productivity, improving natural resource management, and enhancing environmental services in Colombia*, World Bank, March 2021. For cattle stocking in Brazil, see Tiago Santos Telles et al., "Livestock changes in Brazil and sustainable intensification challenges," *Agronomy 2024*, volume 14, number 10, October 2024.

116   Between 1960 and 2005, selective breeding increased the size of pig litters by 50 percent, boosted the lean pork yield by 37 percent, and doubled feed efficiency; for chickens, it cut the time to market weight (two kilograms) from 100 to 40 days, doubled breast meat yield, halved feed conversion ratios, and improved egg yield per feed by 80 percent. While these genetic gains have improved productivity, they also highlight the importance of addressing animal welfare concerns, like injuries from aggressive behavior in crowded spaces, lameness, vulnerability to disease, and poor tolerance to heat or scarce forage. Added to this are wider worries about antibiotic overuse and, in some systems, growth hormones. Together, these issues highlight the need for new breeding approaches that improve efficiency without compromising animal welfare, public health, or the environment. See Christine Tait-Burkard et al., "Livestock 2.0 – genome editing for fitter, healthier, and more productive farmed animals," *Genome Biology*, volume 19, number 204, November 2018;

and Olivia Hodges, "Advancing livestock welfare through genetic improvement: A path towards sustainable production," *Research & Reviews: Journal of Zoological Sciences*, volume 12, number 2, June 2024. For beef in the United States, see Steve Boyles, *Cow size*, Ohio BEEF cattle Letter, The Ohio State University College of Food, Agricultural, and Environmental Sciences, July 2017; *Optimizing feed efficiency*, C-Lock blog, December 15, 2020; and Dan Buskirk and Tasia Kendrick, *Beef cattle breeding selection for improved feed efficiency*, Department of Animal Science, Michigan State University, accessed July 2025.

117 Henrik Österbloma and Jean-Baptiste Jouffray, *The status and future of aquaculture*, The Soneva Dialogue, 2022; and Mark Handy, "Aquaculture as a key pillar for sustainable global seafood production and development," *Fisheries and Aquaculture Journal*, volume 15, number 2, June 2024.

118 *Sustainable fish farming technology: 7 eco innovations*, Farmonaut, accessed July 2025; and *7 top digital farming innovations impacting agriculture*, Pearse Lyons Cultivator, 2020.

119 For precision irrigation, see Anne Wilson, "Smart irrigation technology covers 'more crop per drop,'" MIT Sustainability Initiative, October 2023; Dan Li et al., "Importance of stopping groundwater irrigation for balancing agricultural water use and wetland conservation," *Ecological Indicators*, volume 127, number 107747, August 2021; and *Precision agriculture and the future of farming in Europe*, European Commission, 2021. For targeted chemical use, see Pauline Anne et al., "The reduction of chemical inputs by ultra-precise smart spot sprayer technology maximizes crop potential by lowering phytotoxicity," *Frontiers in Environmental Economics*, volume 3, 2024. For multiple crops together, see Wilhelm Klümper and Matin Qaim, "A meta-analysis of the impacts of genetically modified crops," *PLOS One*, volume 9, number 11, October 2014.

120 See E. T. Seyoum, G. E. Battese, and E. M. Fleming, "Technical efficiency and productivity of maize produced in eastern Ethiopia: A study of farmers within and outside the Sasakawa–Global 2000 project," *Agricultural Economics*, volume 19, number 3, December 1998; Kassa Belay, *The contribution of Sasakawa Global 2000 (SG 2000) to the Ethiopian agricultural extension system: A review of literature*, September 2008; and Mohammed D. Toungos, "Sasakawa technology a panacea to maize yield improvement and meeting the vagaries of climate challenge in Mubi," *International Journal of Research–GRANTHAALAYAH*, volume 6, number 10, October 2018.

121 Liz Goodwin and Brian Lipinski, *How much food does the world really waste? What we know — and what we don't*, World Resources Institute, November 25, 2024.

122 *The path toward a metabolic health revolution*, McKinsey Health Institute, May 2025.

123 For the land footprint of livestock grazing, see *Land statistics 2001–2022: Global, regional and country trends*, Food and Agriculture Organization of the United Nations, April 2024. For frontier tech, see *Vertical farming—no longer a futuristic concept*, Agricultural Research Service, US Department of Agriculture, January 2025; and Hanna Tuomisto and Joost Teixeira de Mattos, "Environmental impacts of cultured meat production," *Environmental Science & Technology*, volume 45, number 14, July 15, 2011. For Meatly, see Anay Mridul, *Meatly "proves critics wrong" with dramatic cost reductions for cultivated pet food*, Green Queen, May 29, 2025.

124   For emissions from agriculture, see J. Poore and T. Nemecek, "Reducing food's environmental impacts through producers and consumers," *Science*, volume 360, issue 6392, June 1, 2018. For cattle methane emissions, see Breanna M. Roque et al., "Red seaweed *(Asparagopsis taxiformis)* supplementation reduces enteric methane by over 80 percent in beef steers," *PLOS One*, March 2021; M. Angellotti et al., "*Asparagopsis taxiformis* supplementation to mitigate enteric methane emissions in dairy cows—Effects on performance and metabolism," *Journal of Dairy Science*, volume 108, number 3, March 2025; and N. K. Pickering et al., "Animal board invited review: Genetic possibilities to reduce enteric methane emissions from ruminants," *Animal*, volume 9, number 9, 2015.

CHAPTER 19 – THE CLIMATE PROTECTED IN A WORLD OF PLENTY

125   Greenhouse gases are gases that trap heat in the atmosphere, causing a greenhouse effect. They include CO_2, methane, nitrous oxide, and fluorinated gases. Ten-year average global temperature (2013 to 2023) relative to the average from 1850 to 1900. See *State of the global climate 2023*, World Meteorological Organization, March 2024. We measure greenhouse gases in CO_2e, or the CO_2 equivalent of their warming potential, to standardize measurements across multiple greenhouse gases.

126   McKinsey's continued momentum scenario is a middle-of-the-road scenario, which mirrors current trends and assumes that they will continue, balancing sustainability with priorities related to affordability and energy security. This scenario projects technology uptake in line with today's trend and does not achieve Paris Agreement targets. For this book, we extend the pathway beyond 2050 using UN population projections and assuming constant growth rates in GDP per capita and emission intensities from 2050 to 2100. This method deviates slightly from that used in previous McKinsey research, which estimates that global warming will reach 2.3°C along the continued momentum trajectory, in line with the estimates presented here. See *Global energy perspective 2025*, McKinsey, September 2025.

127   The Paris Agreement (Article 4.1) reads, "Parties aim to [...] achieve a balance between anthropogenic emissions by sources and removals by sinks of greenhouse gases in the second half of this century," which has been interpreted as saying that nations should seek global net-zero emissions by 2050. For net-zero commitments, this includes countries that have set a target of one of the following: net zero, climate neutral, net negative, greenhouse gas neutrality, carbon negative, carbon neutral, or carbon neutrality. This includes targets either proposed or pledged, or implemented in law or policy document. It excludes countries that have self-declared (without external validation) that they have achieved the target. See *Data explorer*, Net Zero Tracker, accessed August 2025.

128   Emissions Database for Global Atmospheric Research (EDGAR), version 8.0 (2023), European Commission and the IEA, 2023. Greenhouse gas emissions expressed in CO_2e.

129   The IEA's 450 scenario (450S) describes a pathway consistent with (50 percent likelihood of) maximum 2.0°C global warming, limiting concentration of greenhouse gases to 450 parts per million of CO_2e. The IEA has changed its use of scenarios. The sustainable development scenario (SDS) maps out a way of meeting the Paris Agreement goal of keeping global temperatures well below 2.0°C and pursuing efforts to limit global warming

to 1.5°C. Part of the higher requirement in annual emissions reductions in the SDS versus the 450S is that the SDS aims for net-zero emissions in 2070 rather than 2100. See *World energy outlook 2019*, IEA, November 2019.

130   EDGAR, version 8.0 (2023), European Commission and the IEA, 2023. China and Russia have ambitions to be carbon neutral by 2060, while India aims for net zero by 2070; see *Data explorer*, Net Zero Tracker, accessed August 2025.

131   *Electric power sector CO_2 emissions drop as generation mix shifts from coal to natural gas*, US Energy Information Administration, June 2021.

132   Canada, Germany, and Japan decreased greenhouse gas emissions by 526 $MtCO_2e$ between 2015 and 2023, while Brazil, Indonesia, and Iran increased emissions by 536 $MtCO_2e$ during the same period. See *EDGAR*, version 8.0 (2023), European Commission and the IEA, 2023.

133   A total of 1,884 gigawatts of solar and wind capacity were added globally between 2019 and 2024. China and India added 995 gigawatts and 73 gigawatts, respectively, in that period. The amount of capacity added yearly is increasing. In 2024 alone, China and India added 358 gigawatts and 25 gigawatts, respectively. China added 300 gigawatts of thermal capacity between 2019 and 2025. India added 13.7 gigawatts. This includes coal, gas, lignite, and oil-based sources (including diesel in the case of India). For renewable capacity installations, see *Renewable capacity statistics 2025*, International Renewable Energy Agency, accessed August 2025. For thermal capacity installations, see power industry statistics from the National Energy Administration (China), and a summary of all installed capacity (by region) from National Power Portal (India). For coal reserves by 2020, see Energy Institute, *Statistical review of world energy*, 2025, processed by Our World in Data.

134   For cause of Spanish blackouts in 2024, see Ian Johnston and Alice Hancock, "Spain and Portugal blackout blamed by critics on solar power dependency," *Financial Times*, May 1, 2025.

135   This scenario builds on McKinsey's continued momentum scenario, extending it from 2050 to 2100. The extension assumes that country GDP per capita and emission intensities grow at the same rate in 2050 to 2100 as they do in 2023 to 2050. Global population growth is based on UN projections. See *World population prospects 2024*, United Nations, 2024. GDP growth from 2023 to 2050 is based on forecasts from Oxford Economics and *Global energy perspective 2025*, McKinsey, September 2025. The applied method deviates slightly from that of *Global energy perspective 2025*, a scenario in which global warming reaches 2.3°C along the continued momentum trajectory and 1.9°C along the sustainable transformation trajectory (not including additional economic growth), in line with the estimates presented here.

136   The pathway of sustainable transformation with additional economic growth takes the same emissions intensities as the pathway of sustainable transformation with baseline economic growth but accounts for increased GDP. Emission intensities in both scenarios decrease rapidly.

137   Calculated as the difference in cumulative emissions in the pathways of sustainable transformation with baseline economic growth (1,530 $GtCO_2e$) and sustainable transformation with additional economic growth (1,710 $GtCO_2e$).

138 Carbon intensities are indicated per international PPP dollar. Different pathways of carbon emissions may imply the same temperature increase. Temperature increases and atmospheric CO_2 concentrations are estimated using best fit regression (reporting tenth and 90th percentiles), based on the 67th percentile of projected global surface air temperature and atmospheric CO_2 concentrations from the MAGICCv7.5.3 climate model, across AR6 IPCC scenario ensembles.

139 *Trends in atmospheric concentrations of CO_2 (ppm), CH_4 (ppb) and N_2O (ppb) between 1880 and 2017*, European Environment Agency, modified September 20, 2024. The latest measurement in July 2025 from the Mauna Loa Observatory was 428 parts per million. See *Trends in atmospheric carbon dioxide (CO_2), Global Monitoring Laboratory, accessed September 2025.*

140 *An affordable, reliable, competitive path to net zero*, McKinsey, November 2023.

141 McKinsey Value Intelligence Platform.

142 Luc Christiaensen, Zachariah Rutledge, and J. Edward Taylor, *"What is the future of work in agri-food?"* Brookings Institution, December 2020; and Daniele Girardi and Antonio Mura, "The construction-development curve: Evidence from a new international dataset," *The IUP Journal of Applied Economics*, volume 13, number 3, July 2014.

143 See Mark Wiering, "Understanding Dutch flood-risk management: Principles and pitfalls," in *Facing Hydrometeorological Extreme Events: A Governance Issue*, Isabelle La Jeunesse and Corinne Larrue, eds., John Wiley & Sons, 2019.

144 Limits to adaptation have also led to the exploration of geoengineering: experimental methods such as marine cloud brightening, which uses seawater mist to increase cloud reflectivity, and stratospheric aerosol injection, which mimics volcanic cooling by spreading reflective particles above the weather layer. While not a substitute for emissions cuts, they may become part of a broader climate risk mitigation tool kit, despite risks and governance challenges to their implementation.

CHAPTER 20 – THE INNOVATION TO ACCELERATE PRODUCTIVITY

145 Productivity defined as GDP, or output, per employee, based on data from The Conference Board and McKinsey analysis. See *Output, labor and labor productivity*, Total Economy Database, The Conference Board, accessed May 2025.

146 *Output, labor and labor productivity*, Total Economy Database, The Conference Board, accessed May 2025.

147 Note that we also take demographic change into account. When the number of working-age people grows, countries enjoy a demographic dividend, so they can grow their economy with less productivity growth. When it falls, they suffer a demographic drag, requiring more productivity growth. We do not discuss this at length because it has a minimal effect. In our plentiful 2100, as birth rates recover, demographic change reduces growth of income per person by only 0.1 to 0.2 percentage point annually, so only 0.1 to 0.2 percentage point of the productivity requirements come from making up for demographic drag.

148 *Output, labor and labor productivity*, Total Economy Database, The Conference Board,

accessed May 2025; and *Labor productivity by major sectors: nonfarm business, business, nonfinancial corporate, and manufacturing*, US Bureau of Labor Statistics, accessed August 2025.

149 *Investing in productivity growth*, McKinsey Global Institute, March 2024; and updated productivity growth figures from *Output, labor and labor productivity*, Total Economy Database, The Conference Board, accessed May 2025.

150 *Investing in productivity growth*, McKinsey Global Institute, March 2024.

151 For the Idaho case example, see *Gov. Little cuts more red tape, celebrates historic milestone in regulation reform*, Idaho Office of the Governor, August 9, 2024; Robert McQuade and Justin Ruen, "Idaho's rapid growth brings challenges and opportunities," *Idaho Law Review*, volume 58, number 3, January 2022; and state employment data from the US Bureau of Labor Statistics, accessed September 2025.

152 Nicholas Crafts, "Artificial intelligence as a general-purpose technology: An historical perspective," *Oxford Review of Economic Policy*, volume 37, number 3, Autumn 2021.

153 Several thinkers and institutions have taken this task-based approach to estimate productivity gains from AI. Their estimates vary, but all fall within our range. Aghion and Bunel arrive at a range of 0.8 to 1.3 percent per year over the next decade. The Federal Reserve Bank of St. Louis finds that 1.4 percent of work hours can be automated with no fall in output. Brynjolfsson and Baily, factoring in both task-level automation and increased innovation, argue that AI will roughly double or triple productivity growth over 20 years versus the Congressional Budget Office's baseline, but they stress that the acceleration will not be linear because productivity gains materialize only after a period of investment in complementary intangible goods, such as business processes and new skills. Daron Acemoglu argues that AI's limited ability to transform entire workflow verticals will limit its productivity impact to 0.7 percent a year. See Philippe Aghion and Simon Bunel, *AI and growth: Where do we stand?* June 2024; Alexander Bick, Adam Blandin, and David Deming, *The impact of generative AI on work productivity*, Federal Reserve Bank of St. Louis, February 2025; Martin Neil Baily, Erik Brynjolfsson, and Anton Korinek, *Machines of mind: The case for an AI-powered productivity boom*, Brookings Institution, May 2023; and Daron Acemoglu, "The simple macroeconomics of AI," *Economic Policy*, volume 40, issue 121, January 2025. For general purpose technologies, see, for instance, Nicholas Crafts, "Artificial intelligence as a general-purpose technology: An historical perspective," *Oxford Review of Economic Policy*, volume 37, number 3, Autumn 2021.

154 For ChatGPT's adoption, see Martine Paris, "ChatGPT hits 1 billion users? 'Doubled in just weeks' says OpenAI CEO," *Forbes*, April 12, 2025; on the historical price of Macintosh computers, see Gale L. Pooley, *Macintosh computer prices at the age of 40*, Human Progress, February 15, 2024.

155 Nicholas Crafts, "Artificial intelligence as a general-purpose technology: An historical perspective," *Oxford Review of Economic Policy*, volume 37, number 3, Autumn 2021; and Kevin Curran et al., "The role of generative AI in cyber security," *Metaverse*, volume 5, number 2, November 2024.

156 For innovation getting more costly, see Nicholas Bloom et al., "Are ideas getting harder

to find?" *American Economic Review*, volume 110, number 4, April 2020; on AI's potential impact on innovation, see "The next innovation revolution—powered by AI," QuantumBlack AI by McKinsey, June 2025; and on AlphaFold2, see Zhenyu Yang et al., "AlphaFold2 and its applications in the fields of biology and medicine," *Signal Transduction and Targeted Therapy*, volume 8, number 115, 2023.

157   "The next innovation revolution—powered by AI," QuantumBlack AI by McKinsey, June 2025.

158   Based on McKinsey Global Institute's automation model.

159   Skeptics may point to the paradox of high adoption of AI not translating into bottom-line impact yet. However, we see this as a very natural and familiar phase of early adoption of nascent technologies and are confident that in 75 years, productivity gains will be realized.

160   *The next big arenas of competition*, McKinsey Global Institute, October 2024.

161   *The next big arenas of competition*, McKinsey Global Institute, October 2024.

162   For the post-financial crisis fall in investment, see *Investing in productivity growth*, McKinsey Global Institute, March 2024; on the six companies' R&D spend, see *The next big arenas of competition*, McKinsey Global Institute, October 2024; "Google signs up for power from future fusion plant," *World Nuclear News*, July 1, 2025; "Google-backed Pixxel successfully launches India's first private satellite constellation," Reuters, January 15, 2025; and *Astroscale*, International Astronautical Federation, accessed July 2025.

163   For M-Pesa, see Njuguna S. Ndung'u, *A digital financial services revolution in Kenya: The M-Pesa case study*, African Economic Research Consortium, 2021. For Bangladesh's solar power program, see *Bangladesh solar home systems provide clean energy for 20 million people*, World Bank, April 8, 2021; and Anil Cabraal et al., *Living in the light: The Bangladesh solar home systems story*, World Bank, 2021.

164   *Global foreign direct investment flows over the last 30 years*, UNCTAD, May 2023.

165   *Outperformers: High-growth emerging economies and the companies that propel them*, McKinsey Global Institute, September 2018.

166   *Outperformers: High-growth emerging economies and the companies that propel them*, McKinsey Global Institute, September 2018.

167   *Political stability and absence of violence/terrorism: Percentile rank*, World Bank, accessed July 2025; and David Lam, *The demography of youth in developing countries and its economic implications*, Policy Research working paper number 4022, World Bank, November 2006.

168   Maddison Project Database 2023, in Jutta Bolt and Jan Luiten van Zanden, "Maddison-style estimates of the evolution of the world economy: A new 2023 update," *Journal of Economic Surveys*, volume 39, number 2, April 2025.

CHAPTER 21 – CHOOSING PLENTY

169   Dan McCarthy, "Chart: Texas plans to build the most clean energy of any state," Canary Media, September 13, 2024.

ACKNOWLEDGMENTS

—

THE IDEA OF THIS BOOK was seeded during a conversation with Sir Ian Davis, former Global Managing Partner of McKinsey & Company. His view was that McKinsey Global Institute reports are such goldmines of information and often so long (!) that many readers would not appreciate the breadth and depth of what we have researched over the past 35 years since our institute was founded. That it was worth bringing it all together. The timing was propitious. In 2026, McKinsey celebrates its 100th birthday. And so the idea of looking back at the past 100 years and forward to the next century germinated.

This book draws on many years of MGI research. The project was led by Sven Smit, senior partner and MGI's chairman, in Amsterdam, Chris Bradley, senior partner in Sydney, and Nick Leung, senior partner in Hong Kong; Marc Canal Noguer, MGI senior fellow in Barcelona, Suhayl Chettih, MGI fellow in New York, and Sherlyn Chen, engagement manager in London. Janet Bush, an MGI executive editor, helped write, and edited, the book. Closely involved were MGI colleagues Jan Mischke, MGI partner in Zurich, and Jeongmin Seong, MGI partner in Tokyo. For the energy and emissions sections, we especially appreciate the advice and input from Mekala Krishnan, MGI partner in Boston. We thank our team: Luca Bandello, Stanley Sifan Bi (alum), Kenza Bouhaj, Anna Grebenchtchikova (alum), Schuyler Karr, Elinor Martinez (alum), Sebastian Erik Mayor, Mariia Molodyk, Shreyangi Prasad, and Shreyvardhan Sharma (alum). We also thank MGI's other leaders: Kweilin Ellingrud, Sylvain Johansson, Anu Madgavkar, Olivia White, and Lareina Yee, along with MGI colleagues Rebecca J. Anderson, Kanmani Chockalingam, Tiago Devesa, Annabel Farr, Camillo Lamanna, Michael Neary, TJ Radigan, María Jesús Ramírez Larraín, and Kevin Russell.

We are grateful to Chuck Burke, Laura Mandujano, and Juan Velasco for their data visualization expertise. Many thanks go to Rachel Robinson for planning and overseeing production of the book with help from Rishabh Chaturvedi. For communications, we express our appreciation for Suzanne Albert, May Alkhaldi, David Batcheck, Nienke Beuwer, Cathy Gui, Aydan Olcer, and Rebeca Robboy. We also thank Raju Narisetti, leader of McKinsey Global Publishing, for his advice, and Michele Brenner and Diane Rice for their help on photographs. For the cover and book design, we are grateful to freelance creative director Patty Alvarez. We acknowledge Getty Images and Alamy Limited from whom we licensed the photographs for the book.

For generously sharing their insights, we thank MGI advisors Martin N. Baily, senior fellow emeritus in economic studies at the Brookings Institution; Andrés Rodríguez-Pose, Princesa de Asturias Chair and Professor of Economic Geography and Director of the Cañada Blanch Centre at the London School of Economics; Matthew J. Slaughter, dean of the Tuck School of Business, Dartmouth College; and Wim Thiery, Associate Professor at Vrije Universiteit Brussel. We are also grateful for the insights shared with us by Simon Dietz, Professor of Environmental Policy at the Grantham Research Institute on Climate Change and the Environment at the London School of Economics.

Many McKinsey colleagues helped. We thank Ashwin Adarkar, Ankit Agarwal, Hemant Ahlawat, Sanjana Are (alum), Marcelo Azevedo, Magdalena Baczynska, Harald Bauer, Patricia Bingoto, Tom Brennan, Greg Callaway, Hugo del Campo, Kevin Chan, Patrick Chen, Michael Chui, Michael Conway, Klaus Dallerup, Dumitru Dediu, Harald Deubener, Carolyn Dewar, Anusha Dhasarathy, Diego Hernandez Diaz, Cherry Ding, Emma Dorn, Alexander Edlich, Michael Ellis, Dianne Esber,

Philipp Espel, Fernando Figueiredo, Michel Foucart, Søren Fritzen, Steffen Fuchs, Arne Gast, Anders Milde Gjendemsjø, Mariella Goebl, Reinout Goedvolk, Nicolas Goffaux, Stephan Görner, Brian Gregg, Bryce Hall, Holger Harreis, Brian Henstorf, Klemens Hjartar, Elaine Huang, Lari Hämäläinen, Mohsin Imtiaz, Dieuwert Inia, Kartik Jayaram, Sanjay Kalavar, Axel Karlsson, Gregory Kelly, Thomas Kilroy, Kristian Kinscher, Julian Kirchherr, Ilana Kochetkova, Sajal Kohli, Aleksandra Krauze, Vik Krishnan, Eric Kutcher, Bill Lacivita, Philipp Landauer, Olivier Leclerc, Richard Lee, Frédéric Lefort, Mateusz A. Lesniak, Audrey Lucas, Jukka Maksimainen, Rahul Mangla, Varun Marya, Chris Mulligan, Senthil Muthiah, Mihir Mysore, Marie-Claude Nadeau, Fritz Nauck, Michiel Nivard, Jesse Noffsinger, Daisuke Nozaki, Matteo Pacca, Daniel Pacthod, Asutosh Padhi, Alex Panas, Mike Parkins, Mark Patel, Allison Phua, Nina Probst, David Quigley, Emily Reasor, Diane Rice, Paul Roche, Erik Roth, Adam Sabow, Naveen Sastry, Jeremy Schneider, Ishaan Seth, Jonathan Shulman, Shubham Singhal, Jon Steitz, Bob Sternfels, Shelley Stewart, Alex Sukharevsky, Humayun Tai, Yael Taqqu, Jane Thomson, Andreas Tschiesner, Bryan Vadheim, Bart Van de Vyver, Steven Vercammen, Geert Vergoossen, Matt Watters, Brooke Weddle, Holger Wilms, Bill Wiseman, Tianwen Yu, and Martyna Zielinska.

As with all MGI research, this work is independent and has not been commissioned or sponsored in any way by any business, government, or other institution. While we gathered a variety of perspectives, our views have been independently formed and articulated in this book. Any errors are our own.

McKinsey Global Institute

The McKinsey Global Institute was established in 1990. Our mission is to provide
a fact base to aid decision making on the economic and business issues most critical
to the world's companies and policy leaders. We benefit from the full range of McKinsey's
regional, sectoral, and functional knowledge, skills, and expertise, but editorial direction and
decisions are solely the responsibility of MGI directors and partners. For further information
about MGI and to download all reports for free, please visit: **www.mckinsey.com/mgi**.

McKinsey & Company

McKinsey is a global management consulting firm committed to helping organizations
accelerate sustainable and inclusive growth. We work with clients across the private,
public, and social sectors to solve complex problems and create positive change for
all their stakeholders. We combine bold strategies and transformative technologies to
help organizations innovate more sustainably, achieve lasting gains in performance,
and build workforces that will thrive for this generation and the next.

About the authors

From left to right: Nick Leung, Marc Canal, Chris Bradley, and Sven Smit.

Sven Smit is a McKinsey senior partner and the former chair of the McKinsey Global Institute (MGI). During his 35-year McKinsey career he also led the firm's European region and the Strategy and Corporate Finance Practice. He is based in Amsterdam.

Chris Bradley is a McKinsey senior partner and director of MGI. Along with Sven, he was a coauthor of the best-selling book *Strategy Beyond the Hockey Stick*. He is based in Sydney.

Nick Leung is a McKinsey senior partner and director of MGI. In his 33 years at the firm, he was chairman of McKinsey's Greater China region for over a decade, and leader of the Corporate Finance Practice in Asia. He is based in Hong Kong.

Marc Canal is an MGI senior fellow and leads research on global progress, with a focus on productivity, demographics, human capital, and technology. He is based in Barcelona.

The McKinsey Global Institute is McKinsey's independent research arm, established in 1990. This book draws on that long research heritage, and on the specific contributions of our coauthor team: Janet Bush, MGI executive editor; Sherlyn Chen, engagement manager; Suhayl Chettih, MGI fellow; and MGI partners Jan Mischke and Jeongmin Seong.